The Complete Guide
to Walt Disney World ®

Julie and Mike Neal

coconut
press

COCONUT PRESS
Sanibel Florida

The Complete Guide to Walt Disney World®

ISBN 978-0-9709-5964-5
ISSN 1547-8491
Library of Congress Control Number: 2004094917

PUBLISHED BY COCONUT PRESS
Media Enterprises Inc.
Sanibel Island, Florida

Find us online at www.coconutpress.com

WRITING AND RESEARCH: Julie Neal
PHOTOGRAPHY AND DESIGN: Mike Neal
ADDITIONAL RESEARCH: Micaela Neal

This book is not endorsed or sponsored by the Walt Disney Co. or Disney Destinations LLC, or connected in any way to those companies. Neither Coconut Press nor Media Enterprises is associated with any product or vendor mentioned in this book.

PHOTOGRAPHS
Unless indicated all images © 2007 Media Enterprises Inc. Disney photos © Disney. La Nouba performance photos used under rights granted by Cirque du Soleil.

MAPS
Maps © 2007 Media Enterprises Inc. Illustrations by Vince Burkhead.

ACKNOWLEDGMENTS
WALT DISNEY WORLD PUBLIC RELATIONS: Our thanks to Jonathan Frontado, Jason Lasecki, Dave Herbst, Juliana Cadiz, Liz Benz, Darrell Fry and David Hillstrom, who helped arrange interviews, backstage access, photo rights, photo shoots and much more. OTHER ACKNOWLEDGMENTS: We also thank the others who supplied information, materials and resources, including: Ross Adams, Craig Albert, Ngonba Anadou, Odalys Aponte, Karen Aulino, Jasmine Barczyk, David Brady, William Burke, Shawn Cannon, Shelly Carter, John Chenciner, Steve Christ, the Cleary family and their beautiful princesses, Lee Cockerell, the Connells (Matthew, Sherri and Anna), Brian Cotten, Elise Cottle, Amy and Mitch Crews, Karen Derose, the Dixes (Daniel, Monica, Bella and GiGi), Catherine Ewer, Aiden Feeback, Andrea Finger, Susan Germer, Michelle Ginesin, Aurélie Grand, Jeff Green, Barbara Gross, Dana Hall, Liz Hall, Robert Hargrove, Trina Hofreiter, Roger Isako, Rob Iske, Jennifer Jacobsen, Eric Jacobson, Kristine Jones, Traci Kennedy, Mary Kenny, Tommy King, Kelly Knowlen, Daniel Lahr, Josh Little, Kathy Mangum, Amanda Maure, Roberto Martinez, Jennifer McKay, Bo Morris, Nenette Mputu, Kim and Diane Nelson, Sanja Novakovich, Sunni Petty, Thabo Pheto, Ernie Porterfield, Honor Rasch-Gush, Mark Renfro, Kevin Renzi, Alfonso Ribeiro, Laura Richeson, Charles Ridgway, Joe Rindler, Wally Robinson, Todd Roby, Kathy Rogers, Catherine Roth, Hanns-Claudius and Monika Scharff, Shannon Shelton, Brandon Sims, Theron Skees, Jennifer Smith, Lynne Smith, Courtney and Jerry Soares, Brian Spitler, Jason Surrell, Rheo Tan, Gary Terry, Dikeledi Tlhako, the Turners (Jeff, Anna, Laura, Michael and Andrew), Michelle Valle, Kim Veon, Jon Wagner-Holtz, Jenn Wakelin, Robin Walker, Andy Warren, Christopher White, Dave Williams, George Willis and all the various Disney resort managers and park duty managers.

Previous page: Orlando's Sunny Christiansen, 6, learns an African dance at Disney's Animal Kingdom

ABOUT THE AUTHORS

After writing a guidebook about their hometown islands of Sanibel and Captiva, Julie and Mike Neal — that's us below — decided to spend a year and write a book about Walt Disney World. Five years later, we're done! (Shows what we knew!) As a result, we've ended up visiting Disney World more often than nearly anyone — more than 700 times in just five years. All of it was fun, some of it surreal. For example, Julie spent a full day just riding the Twilight Zone Tower of Terror, finding details and dictating the drop sequences into a voice recorder ("Up! Down! Down! Up!"). We live with our daughter Micaela, dog Bear, and — now — a home full of Disney stuff.

Authors Julie and Mike Neal

Dedicated to the forgotten people of Mississippi and the hardworking crew of the American Red Cross Katrina Operations Center in Gulfport.

Printed in Canada

About this book

One thing you'll notice right away: there's so much stuff. And no wonder — this book has the most detailed information ever published about Walt Disney World. A thorough description of everything the resort has to offer as well as a cornucopia of advice to help you enjoy it, **this guide is a handbook on how to have fun.**

In addition, more than 400 color photos show you every aspect of Walt Disney World, from backstage dressing rooms to fireworks.

A comprehensive overview (starting on page 12) kicks off the book. It includes background articles about the life of Walt Disney, his classic cartoon characters, Imagineers, even the history of monorails.

A step-by-step planning chapter (page 26) makes organizing your Disney trip easy. It features practical information on subjects like what to pack and how to meet characters, and straightforward explanations of such key Disney concepts as the Fastpass system and Extra Magic Hours.

Most of the book — in fact, 75 percent of it — is devoted to Disney's theme parks, water parks and recreational activities. Comprehensive chapters (starting on page 38) are devoted to the Magic Kingdom, Epcot, Disney-MGM Studios and Disney's Animal Kingdom, as well as water parks (page 236) and Downtown Disney (page 254).

The attraction coverage is unprecedented, with exclusive tips, story lines, back stories, fun finds and fun facts unlike those in any other Disney guide book. You'll get a clear understanding of every attraction, so you can enjoy each one to the fullest.

Every park chapter also has at least one Magical Day plan — an hour-by-hour itinerary designed to give you a relaxed, enjoyable experience. Each schedule requires you to start your day bright and early, but follow it and you'll have a terrific time.

Like variety in your vacation? Check out our Diversions chapter (page 266) for options such as golf, water sports and backstage tours.

The back of the book has descriptions of special events and festivals (page 280); listings and specifications for almost 100 hotels and resorts both on and off the property (page 292); and a list of Walt Disney World's Hidden Mickeys, those secretly placed three-circle shapes that hide in the architecture, art and landscape (page 308).

Extras include a 10-page animal guide for Animal Kingdom (page 226) and bonus articles that tell the surprising histories of the Cinderella and Beauty and the Beast fairy tales (pages 55 and 178).

Want to have a *great* time on your Disney trip? This is the book for you.

✓ This checkmark identifies an attraction as one of Disney's best

✔ This checkmark identifies a top restaurant or live-entertainment option

Contents

61 It's a Small World
Magic Kingdom

122 Soarin'
Epcot

180 The Twilight Zone
Tower of Terror
Disney-MGM Studios

SMALL WORLD, SOARIN' PHOTOS © DISNEY

Expedition Everest
Disney's Animal Kingdom **214**

271 **Surfing lessons**
Typhoon Lagoon

Water Parks

Downtown Disney

Disney's Animal Kingdom

How to use Fastpass **34**

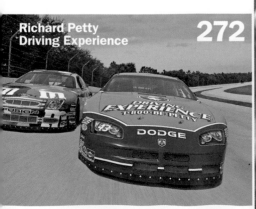

Richard Petty Driving Experience **272**

Lowland gorilla
Disney's Animal Kingdom **227**

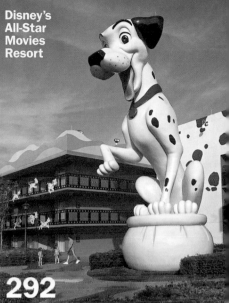

Disney's
All-Star
Movies
Resort

292

258

La Nouba
Downtown Disney

143 Princess storybook dining
Norway pavilion, Epcot

Walt Disney World Resort®

1 mi
1 km

TO TAMPA →

TO CELEBRATION →

Reedy Creek

■ — MICKEY WATER TOWER

GRIFFEN RD

WORLD DR

EXIT 62

4

192

SHERBERTH RD

DISNEY'S ANIMAL KINGDOM

WINTER SUMMERLAND MINIATURE GOLF

BUENA VISTA

BLIZZARD BEACH

DISNEY-MGM STUDIOS

DISNEY'S WIDE WORLD OF SPORTS

Florida Hospital Celebration Health

EXIT 64

VICTORY WAY

OSCEOLA PKWY

TYPHOON LAGOON

Bonnet Creek

EXIT 65

← TO CELEBRATION

INTERNATIONAL DRIVE SOUTH

IRLO BRONSON MEMORIAL HWY

OSCEOLA PKWY

417

192

535

536

TO AIRPORT →

LODGING KEY

1. Disney's All-Star Resorts
2. Disney's Animal Kingdom Lodge
3. Disney's Beach Club Resort
4. Disney's BoardWalk Inn and Villas
5. Disney's Caribbean Beach Resort
6. Disney's Contemporary Resort
7. Disney's Coronado Springs Resort
8. Disney's Fort Wilderness Resort & Campground
9. Disney's Grand Floridian Resort & Spa
10. Disney's Old Key West Resort
11. Disney's Polynesian Resort
12. Disney's Pop Century Resort
13. Disney's Port Orleans French Quarter
14. Disney's Port Orleans Riverside
15. Disney's Saratoga Springs Resort & Spa
16. Disney's Wilderness Lodge
17. Disney's Yacht Club Resort
18. Shades of Green
19. Walt Disney World Dolphin
20. Walt Disney World Swan
21. Best Western Lake Buena Vista
22. Buena Vista Palace Hotel & Spa
23. DoubleTree Guest Suites
24. Grosvenor
25. Hilton
26. Holiday Inn
27. Royal Plaza

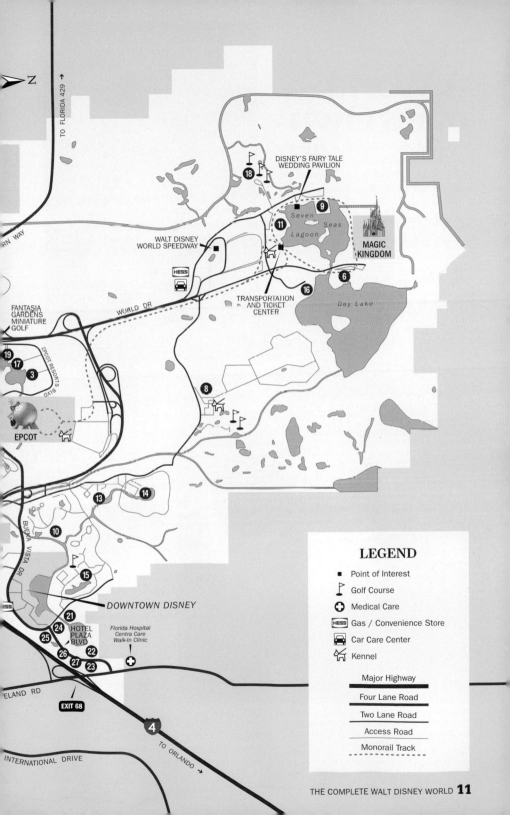

N

TO FLORIDA 429 →

RN WAY

DISNEY'S FAIRY TALE
WEDDING PAVILION

18

9

11 *Seven Seas Lagoon*

MAGIC
KINGDOM

WALT DISNEY
WORLD SPEEDWAY

HESS

6

16

Bay Lake

FANTASIA
GARDENS
MINIATURE
GOLF

WORLD DR

TRANSPORTATION
AND TICKET
CENTER

19
17
3

EPCOT RESORTS BLVD

8

EPCOT

13

14

BUENA VISTA DR

10

15

DOWNTOWN DISNEY

21

24

ESS

25

HOTEL
PLAZA
BLVD

*Florida Hospital
Centra Care
Walk-In Clinic*

26

22

27 23

ELAND RD

EXIT 68

4

TO ORLANDO →

INTERNATIONAL DRIVE

LEGEND

■ Point of Interest

⚑ Golf Course

✚ Medical Care

HESS Gas / Convenience Store

🚗 Car Care Center

🐕 Kennel

Major Highway

Four Lane Road

Two Lane Road

Access Road

‑ ‑ ‑ Monorail Track

A World of its Own

There's no place else like it. Twice the size of Manhattan — 47 square miles — Walt Disney World is unlike any other spot in the world. The world's largest collection of theme parks, water parks and resorts, this family-friendly vacation kingdom is also so, well, *inspiring*. A trip here is not just a way to spend time with your kids, not just an escape from day-to-day doldrums. It's a reawakening of that free-spirited, good-natured soul

who lives deep inside you — the one your spouse married, the one you want your kids to emulate. Yes it can be crowded, yes it can be expensive, yes it takes a good plan to see it all, but what other man-made vacationland so deliberately embraces creativity, optimism and a sense of wonder about the world? Populated daily by more than 100,000 visitors as well as 54,000 "cast members," it truly is a world of its own — and the No. 1 vacation destination on the planet.

Clockwise from top right: The namesake of the movie that funded much of Walt Disney World, Mary Poppins poses at Epcot; lifeguards take a break at Disney's All-Star Music Resort; the Dapper Dans perform on Magic Kingdom's Main Street U.S.A.; one of the resort's five main entrances

Clockwise from right: Swaying dancers at Beauty and the Beast Live on Stage; nighttime fun at Pleasure Island; a helpful Blizzard Beach lifeguard; a young Chinese acrobat poses for the camera crowd at Epcot

It's only 122 acres — 0.5 percent of the property — but to many folks the **Magic Kingdom** *is* Walt Disney World. A spacious version of California's Disneyland, it re-imagines that park's Main Street U.S.A., Adventureland, Fantasyland, Frontierland and Tomorrowland. The most popular theme park in the world, this young-family favorite has more than 40 attractions, including classics such as It's a Small World and Space Mountain.

A permanent World's Fair, the 300-acre **Epcot** park is divided into the science-themed Future World and the international pavilions of the World Showcase. Top Future World attractions include realistic simulators that give you the sensations of hang gliding (Soarin') and astronaut training (Mission Space). A globe-hopping tour of 11 countries, the World Showcase is highlighted by its architecture, entertainment, dining and shopping.

Also divided in half is the show-business-themed **Disney-MGM Studios.** The front is a tribute to Old Hollywood, with re-created 1940s-era icons such as Hollywood Boulevard and Grauman's Chinese Theatre. The rear was originally a working studio, and still carries that theme. This 135-acre park includes two of Disney's best thrill rides — the Twilight Zone Tower of Terror and the Rock 'n' Roller Coaster Starring Aerosmith.

The 500-acre **Disney's Animal Kingdom** combines exotic animals with quality attractions such as Expedition Everest, a roller coaster that travels backward into a mountain; Kilimanjaro Safaris, an exploration into a replicated African preserve aboard an open-sided truck; and Festival of the Lion King, a show

with energetic acrobats, dancers, singers and stilt walkers. The centerpiece of the park is the Tree of Life, a 145-foot man-made sculpture that includes 325 animal images.

Beyond the theme parks, Walt Disney World offers a wide array of entertainment, recreation and shopping options. It's hard to beat the family fun at the two themed water parks, **Blizzard Beach** and **Typhoon Lagoon.** Disney has five championship golf courses as well as a 9-hole, two miniature golf courses and many tennis courts, and also offers organized fishing, horseback riding, parasailing, stock-car driving, surfing, wake boarding and water-skiing.

Downtown Disney is a commercial center at the eastern edge of the property. The 120-acre site is made up of the Marketplace outdoor mall, Pleasure Island nightclub complex and West Side dining, entertainment and shopping district.

Disney's Wide World of Sports complex is 220 acres of sports facilities that host amateur — and some pro — competitions. It includes a baseball stadium, fieldhouse and many outdoor fields.

Distant lands and forgotten eras are among the themes at Disney's 19 **themed resorts.** Accommodations range from campsites to luxurious rooms and suites.

PROJECT X

Rumors of a mystery land buyer began swirling around Orlando in 1964. A company was buying up parcels 20 miles southwest of the town, but it was being done in secret, using false names and dummy corporations. Who could it be? Many folks had it figured out from the start. It was Boeing. Lockheed. Something NASA.

But it wasn't. In October, 1965, the Orlando Sentinel-Star reported the buyer was Walt Disney, who was planning a huge secret development internally called Project X. Then, a month later, Walt and his brother, Roy, confirmed the project at an Orlando press conference. Walt's vision was an Experimental Prototype Community of Tomor-

GINGERBREAD MEN PHOTO © DISNEY

Clockwise from top left: A window of Minnie's house, Animal Kingdom's DiVine, a touching moment at Frontierland, dancing gingerbread men at Christmas

row, a futuristic city where solutions to America's urban problems could be explored. There would be a theme park, too, an East Coast Disneyland at the back. After Walt's sudden death in 1966, his successors began work on the park.

Construction started in 1969. The largest private construction project in America's history, it was led by two military men — former Army General Joe Potter, who had overseen operations at the Panama Canal and the 1964 World's Fair, and former Navy Admiral Joe Vallor, who had supervised the building of California's Disneyland.

Charged with taming what was, for the most part, swampland, Potter, Vallor and 9,000 workers moved 8 million cubic yards of dirt and built 47 miles of canals and 22 miles of levees. They drained and cleaned the 406-acre Bay Lake, and created the adjacent 172-acre Seven Seas

Walt Disney World opened to the public on Oct. 1, 1971. It consisted of the Magic Kingdom, the Contemporary and Polynesian Resorts and the Fort Wilderness Resort & Campground. Disney's Golf Resort (today's Shades of Green military center) was built in 1973. Lake Buena Vista Village (today's Downtown Disney Marketplace) opened in 1975.

What about Epcot? Disney wrestled with the idea through the early '70s, but the vision just wasn't clear without its visionary. In 1976 Disney announced plans for Epcot Center, a theme park with "demonstration concepts" as well as an "international people-to-people exchange." It opened in 1982.

Lagoon. They built roads, maintenance shops, a food distribution center, a phone company, power plant, sewage plant, even a tree farm.

BUILDING BOOM

For everything Disney built on its property during the space-race and disco eras, it has created far more since. It opened Disney-MGM Studios, Pleasure Island and Typhoon Lagoon in 1989. The Osprey Ridge and Eagle Pines golf complex debuted in 1992. Blizzard Beach arrived in 1995. Downtown Disney's West Side and Disney's Wide World of Sports opened in 1999.

That same period saw a huge expansion of the property's hotel space — growing from 2,000 to 31,000 rooms.

The Caribbean Beach and Grand Floridian resorts opened in 1988.

The 1990s saw 13 new lodging facilities. These include the Yacht and Beach Club and Walt Disney World Swan and Dolphin (1990), Port Orleans French Quarter and Old Key West (1991), Dixie Landings (now Port Orleans Riverside, 1992), All-Star Sports Resort and Wilderness Lodge (1994), All-Star Music and BoardWalk (1995), Coronado Springs (1997) and finally All-Star Movies (1999). Disney's newest hotel properties are Animal Kingdom Lodge (2001), Pop Century (2003) and Saratoga Springs (2004).

Clockwise from top left:
A U.K. barmaid in Epcot, a trick-or-treating Tweedledum, the Lights Motors Action stunt show, scary sights on the Jungle Cruise

FUN FACTS ›› Disney buses log more than 15 million miles a year. **››** Walt Disney World is the world's largest consumer of fireworks, burning through a million shells a year. **››** Disney's employee wardrobe consists of 1.8 million pieces, and cast members wear 2,500 different costumes. **››** Walt Disney World sells enough Mouse Ear caps each year to cover the head of every man, woman and child in Portland, Oregon, and enough character T-shirts to clothe everyone in Chicago.

Making the Magic

How space-race ingenuity and cutting-edge technology combine to create a whole new World

When you think of Walt Disney World, do you think of rides that tell stories, high-tech experiences, or themed architecture? If so, you're thinking about the work of "Imagineers," a word coined by Walt Disney to describe his team of imaginative engineers, architects, artists, programmers, sculptors, special-effects designers and script writers that created California's Disneyland. Today numbering 1,400 people, Walt Disney Imagineering (WDI) has created every Disney park, attraction and resort.

Disney's best attractions often feature innovative high-tech concepts. Space Mountain was the world's first computer-controlled thrill ride. Mickey's PhilharMagic features the world's largest wraparound projection screen. The group's best known creation, however, is its collection of Audio Animatronic characters — the robotic people and animals that populate such attractions as the Carousel of Progress and Pirates of the Caribbean.

Basically, Disney's version of a robot is simply an electrical machine that has the appearance of a living creature. It doesn't really do much, but often seems to have a personality.

The concept began in the 1950s, when Walt's friend Wernher von Braun gave him some magnetic computer tape the famed scientist was using to synchronize the steps of rocket launches at Florida's Cape Canaveral. In 1961, Disney's engineers used similar tape to synchronize the sounds and movements of mechanical birds, flowers and Tiki carvings in the Disneyland attraction The Enchanted Tiki Room. And just like von Braun secured his computer in a nearby bunkhouse, Disney hid his backstage.

Humanistic characters debuted a few years later. The most famous Audio Animatronic figure — Abraham Lincoln at the Magic Kingdom's Hall of Presidents — is a copy of a figure that stunned audiences at the Illinois pavilion at the 1964 New York World's Fair.

Altogether Walt Disney World has more than 1,600 Audio Animatronic characters. The most complex include a spitting Stitch at Stitch's Great Escape, a walking Ben Franklin at The American Adventure and a Wicked Witch at The Great Movie Ride who looks amazingly real. Fanciest of all is Hopper, an 8-foot grasshopper with 68 functions at It's Tough to be a Bug and the gigantic Yeti at Expedition Everest that has 19 axes of motion.

John, the father at the Carousel of Progress, is among the Audio Animatronic characters that move through the manipulation of pressurized air, gas or fluid, which triggers actuators that move eyes, pinch lips or twist torsos. Electrical cables run from each figure to a backstage operations center, where a computer system uses flash memory cards to store the character's program. Each movement is timed to coincide with prerecorded dialogue, music or sound effects. In more recent characters, compliance circuits control the force that pushes or pulls each movement, and add a natural-style inertia that makes the motions more realistic.

Back to the Future

It's the future of transportation — as originally imagined in the 1870s. It's the elevated monorail.

The concept of a small train straddling an elevated beam debuted in 1876, at Pennsylvania's American Centennial Exposition. Inventor LeRoy Stone argued that a single beam was cheaper than a two-rail system, and that elevating it made it fit into America's growing cities. Two years later his idea became the world's first commercial monorail, a 4-mile system that ran between Bradford and Gilmore, Penn. The train was a hit — until it blew off of its tracks.

The idea reemerged after World War II. As traffic jams began to clog rebuilt German cities, industrialist Dr. Axel Wenner-Gren introduced a train with additional horizontal wheels that hugged its beam, making it stable even in strong winds. Working at a test track near Cologne, he built a full-scale test train in 1957.

A few months later, who should come driving through the Cologne countryside but the vacationing Walt and Lillian Disney. Glancing out his side window, Walt noticed a "a huge loaf of bread" gliding above the treetops. He followed it to a service yard, where he found the office of Dr. Wenner-Gren and his company, Alweg Research.

Wenner-Gren had his first sale. Making just one change — the bodies would be designed to look like Buck Rogers spaceships — Walt purchased an Alweg system to use at his theme park in California. Debuting as a Tomorrowland ride in 1959, the 4,200-foot Disneyland monorail was a serious demonstration of a future transportation system. It had overpasses, steep grades and tight turns.

Alweg built two other demonstrators. The 1961 Expo Italia fair in Turin, Italy, used one to connect its pavilions, and Seattle featured one at its 1962 Century 21 Exposition. The company made proposals to Cologne, Hamburg, Los Angeles and Mexico City, but was al-

Disney's monorails are powered by a 600-volt electrical system, which feeds current through a metal bar mounted along a 26-inch-wide concrete beam. Motors turn tires that roll along the top of the beam; horizontal stabilizing wheels hug its sides.

ways turned down. Wenner-Gren died in 1961; his track was demolished in 1967 to make room for a subdivision.

One Alweg-inspired system, however, fulfilled the doctor's dreams. The Walt Disney World monorail is a real transportation system, used by an average of 200,000 passengers a day. The two-track, 14-mile "highway in the sky" has six public stations as well as a backstage service hangar. Today's trains are built by Bombardier, whose Learjets share a similar style. Each is 203 feet long, has six cars and eight 113 hp motors and can carry 360 passengers. Top speed is 45 mph. The trains can be controlled from either end. Sometimes, after the parks close, drivers run the trains backward. Without equipment each fiberglass body weighs only 800 pounds.

Walt Disney

A tycoon with the mind of a farm boy. A storyteller who didn't finish high school. An artist who thought like an engineer. A visionary who loved the past. A mix of contradictory characters, Walt Disney was an American icon and the personification of the American dream. He introduced sound and color cartoons, perfected animated movies and invented theme parks. He received hundreds of accolades, including 32 personal Academy Awards and honorary degrees from Harvard and Yale. But just as he started his grandest dream... he died.

COWS AND CIGARS The namesake of Walt Disney World was born in Chicago on Dec. 5, 1901. He had three older brothers and a younger sister.

Walt lived on a farm during his most impressionable years. Between the ages of 4 and 10, from 1905 to 1911, his family lived on 45 acres near Marceline, Mo., an isolated town in the middle of the state. Often clad in overalls, the young boy spent much of his time playing with the farm animals, swimming in a pond, picking apples and often just daydreaming under a tall cottonwood tree. He often doodled pictures of animals instead of doing homework, and once talked his sister into helping him tar — he called it "paint" — the side of the family barn.

When still in grade school, Walt sold cigars, gum and soda pop to passengers at the town's railroad depot. His uncle was a train engineer. Free to roam, the boy came to know an old Civil War veteran who told him dramatic old stories.

CHAPLIN AND CHICAGO Walt impersonated Charlie Chaplin in skits he performed with neighborhood kids, after his father moved his family to Kansas City. Moving with his family back to Chicago, Walt went to high school for just one year, contributing cartoons and photos to the school paper. He took night courses at Chicago's Academy of Fine Arts.

OUT ON HIS OWN At 16 Walt left home. Germany had just signed an armistice ending World War I, but he still tried to enlist in the Army. Rejected because of his age, Walt instead snuck into the Red Cross, which sent him to France to drive an ambulance. He took up smoking.

Afterward Walt returned to Kansas City, and, at age 20, formed his own business. Using a borrowed camera and working in a shed, Walt made "Laugh-O-Gram" cartoons of a live girl in an animated world. When his distributor went bankrupt, he brought in some cash with a dental-health film ("Tommy Tucker's Tooth"), but soon went under, too.

ALICE AND THE RABBIT Raising train fare by going door-to-door photographing babies, Walt left Missouri and headed for Hollywood. "There was just one thing I wanted to do," Walt later recalled. "I wanted to be a director." His brother Roy was already there.

Carrying a print of his last Kansas City cartoon, an unfinished extravaganza called "Alice's Wonderland," Walt applied at every major studio. Finally, New York cartoon distributor Margaret Winkler agreed to market his work.

Forming the Disney Brothers Studio, Walt and Roy set up shop in the rear of a real estate office. Running the business side of the operation, Roy soon insisted its name should be the Walt Disney Studio, today's Walt Disney Company.

As the business prospered, Walt bought a fancy Moon roadster, grew a mustache and in 1925 got married to a young woman he had hired to ink and paint celluloids, Lillian Bounds. They were later blessed with two daughters, Diane and the adopted Sharon.

In 1927, Walt created a new character: Oswald the Lucky Rabbit. He produced 26 Oswald cartoons, which were distributed by Universal and popular enough to spawn an Oswald candy bar and some merchandise. But a year later, on a trip to New York to renew his contract, Walt learned of a clause in his deal that gave Universal ownership of his character.

On the train ride home, he realized he needed a star he owned outright.

Remembering a friendly mouse that used to climb up on his desk in Kansas

City, Walt turned to his wife and said "I think it will be a mouse, and I think I'll call him Mortimer."

"Mortimer?" Lillian asked. "I don't like it. What about Mickey?"

OF MOUSE AND MAN Using many of the visual cues of Oswald, Walt and partner Ub Iwerks designed their new character and cranked out two cartoons. Inspired by the fame of Charles Lindbergh, the first was a gag-filled short called "Plane Crazy." The second, "The Gallopin' Gaucho," cast Mickey as an Argentine outlaw.

Neither sold.

Walt's solution? Make one with sound. To raise the money, Walt sold his beloved Moon. He figured that, with the recent success of films like "The Jazz Singer," distributors would love an animated talkie, too.

He was wrong. Again and again, distributors still said no. When a promoter offered to run the cartoon for free, Walt, with no other options, agreed.

The first synchronized sound cartoon, "Steamboat Willie" premiered at New York's Colony Theatre on Nov. 18, 1928. The public loved it, but only one distribution company showed interest: Universal. Walt said no.

Finally, Walt did strike a distribution deal — with a sound-machine salesman.

COLOR, DEPTH AND 'WALT'S FOLLY' As his Mickey cartoons took the country by storm, Walt put his profits back into his company. To ensure his artists were highly skilled, he paid for them to attend art school and later set up an in-house training center. Walt introduced Technicolor to animation with the 1932 Silly Symphonies cartoon "Flowers and Trees." In 1937 he released "The Old Mill," which used a "multiplane" camera to add realistic depth to animation.

All of that, however, was simply a warm-up for Walt's next idea. He wanted to create an animated feature film — an idea that had been tried in Europe (with the box-office bomb "Lotte Reiniger's Adventures of Prince Achmed") but never in the United

NASA

Disney (left) with Dr. Wernher von Braun in 1954

States. Walt knew he had the story — a dramatic, romantic, sympathetic fairy tale he had seen as a kid as a silent film: "Snow White." Hollywood scoffed at the idea, dubbing it "Walt's Folly," but Walt believed. When money ran tight, he mortgaged his home for more.

The gamble paid off. Premiering December 21, 1937, "Snow White and the Seven Dwarfs" was such a smash that within six months the Disney company had millions in the bank. The film went on to gross $8 million — at a time when a child's movie ticket was just 10 cents.

HARD TIMES Refusing to make a sequel, Walt instead produced 1940's "Fantasia" and "Pinocchio," 1941's "Dumbo" and 1942's "Bambi." All lost money. They couldn't break even without a European market, which had disappeared with the outbreak of World War II.

And there was more trouble. As the films struggled, rumors spread throughout the studio that major salary cuts and layoffs were coming. Soon, union organizers appeared at the studio, and on May 29, 1941, many Disney animators went on strike. It ended in just a few weeks, but afterward Walt firmly believed the strike was inspired by communists. In 1947 he testified before the House Un-American Activities Committee that there was a threat of Communism in the motion-picture industry, though he added "I don't think they have gotten very far, and I think the industry is made up of good Americans, just like in my plant — good, solid Americans."

For awhile it seemed Walt couldn't catch a break. "Dumbo" was scheduled to appear on the cover of Time magazine the first week of December, 1941 — until Japan bombed Pearl Harbor. During the war the U.S. military took over the studio in an effort to protect a nearby Lockheed aircraft plant, which essentially shut down the company's commercial business for years.

By now Walt was a chain smoker. Studio workers could tell if he was coming down the hall by listening for his cough.

A DECADE ON TOP Walt's fortunes returned after the war. Animated films included 1950's "Cinderella," 1951's "Alice in Wonderland" and 1953's "Peter Pan." The 1954 movie "20,000 Leagues Under the Sea" was the first Disney live-action film made and the first to feature major stars, in this case Kirk Douglas, James Mason and Peter Lorre. Unlike many studio chiefs, Walt embraced television and found success with shows such as "The Mickey Mouse Club" and "Zorro."

During the '50s Walt also created a series of films on science and technology. Broadcasts of the "Disneyland" television show included three films produced with rocket designer Dr. Wernher von Braun. A 1957 episode featured "Our Friend the Atom," a collaboration with the government designed to enhance the image of nuclear energy.

Back during the war, Walt would take his daughters to Griffith Park, 10 miles from his home. As the girls rode the carousel he would sit on a dirty bench, eating peanuts. "As I'd sit there," he later recalled, "I felt there should be something built, some kind of an amusement enterprise, where the parents and the children could have fun together."

In 1951 he visited Copenhagen's Tivoli Gardens, a lushly landscaped park with fireworks, parades, a railroad and exotic buildings, many with little white lights. "Now this is what an amusement place should be!" Walt told his wife.

Two years later Walt purchased 160 acres near Anaheim. Gathering some of his best motion-picture talent, he set about building the world's first "theme" park. Walt decided its central attraction would be a castle, and that its entrance would be an elaborate re-creation of a turn-of-the-century small town. As budgets increased Walt hocked his life insurance to get more cash. Disneyland construction began in July of 1954, and the park opened just one year later.

It was an enormous hit.

IT ALL COMES TOGETHER Success continued in the 1960s. In 1961 Walt's "Wonderful World of Color" was among the first color television shows, "One Hundred and One Dalmatians" was the year's No. 1 movie and Walt and Roy even entered the field of education. They provided the funds to merge two professional schools, the Los Angeles Conservatory of Music and the Chouinard Art Institute (where Walt had earlier sent his animators) to create the California Institute of the Arts, the nation's first art institute to grant undergraduate and graduate degrees.

Everything came together in 1964. The New York World's Fair opened in April, and Disney's contributions, including the Audio Animatronic showcases Carousel of Progress, Great Moments with Mr. Lincoln and It's a Small World, became its most popular attractions. In August "Mary Poppins" premiered at Grauman's Chinese Theatre and soon became the studio's biggest hit ever.

In September President Johnson invited Walt to the White House to receive the Presidential Medal of Freedom, the nation's highest civilian honor. The man who 40 years earlier was bankrupt was now not only rich, but a national hero.

Now 62 years old, Walt had one dream left — to fix America's cities.

'I LIKE TO CREATE NEW THINGS' In 1965, Walt turned his attention toward the problem of improving urban life in America. His idea: Combine the money he made from "Mary Poppins" with corporate sponsorships, and then — using 43 square miles of land he had just secretly purchased in Florida — build an experimental city. Filled with technological advancements, it would demonstrate how communities could solve their problems of housing, pollution and transportation. Walt called it the Experimental Prototype Community of Tomorrow — EPCOT for short.

"I don't believe there is a challenge anywhere in the world that is more important than finding the solution to the problems of our cities," he said. "We think the need is for starting from scratch on virgin land and building a community that will become a prototype for the future. Epcot will be a community of tomorrow that will never be completed, but will always be introducing and testing and demonstrating new materials and new systems."

The design called for a 50-acre town center enclosed in a dome, an internationally themed shopping area, a 30-story hotel and convention complex, office space, apartments, single-family homes, monorail and PeopleMover systems, an airport and underground roads for cars and trucks. Walt even got approval for a nuclear power plant. To make money he'd have a theme park, too, a larger version of Disneyland.

Wanting to get started immediately, Walt planned to finish the project by 1985. On November 15, 1965, Walt and Roy held a press conference in Orlando to announce the project. "I'm very excited about it," Walt said, "because I've been storing these things up over the years. I like to create new things."

Less than a year later, he got sick. The smoking had caught up with him.

In November, 1966, doctors found a tumor the size of a walnut in Walt's left lung. But when they operated, they discovered the cancer had spread through the lung, and the entire organ had to be removed. Afterward Walt checked out of the hospital and went back to work, but he had to check back in just two weeks later. His body wasn't recovering.

On the night of December 14th, Walt lay in his hospital bed and discussed his Florida project with Roy, who sat at his side. Using the acoustical tiles on the ceiling above, Walt showed Roy his detailed, if imaginary, vision of the undertaking — the roads, airport, everything. The next morning, Walt died.

Some called Walt Disney too naive, a boy who never really became an adult. But to him that was just the point. "The American child is sensitive, humorous, open-minded, eager to learn, and has a strong sense of excitement, energy, and healthy curiosity about the world in which he lives," he wrote in 1963. "Lucky indeed is the grown-up who manages to carry these same characteristics into adult life. That's the real trouble with the world. Too many people grow up."

FUN FACTS 》 Married in 1888 in Acron, Florida, 40 miles north of today's Walt Disney World, Walt Disney's parents later grew oranges and ran a hotel in nearby Kissimmee. 》 In school, when one art assignment called for drawing a still life of flowers, Walt drew his with faces and arms. His teacher didn't approve. 》 The Disney company eventually regained the rights to Oswald. In 2006 Universal traded the bunny back to Disney for sportscaster Al Michaels. Really. 》 In 1949 Walt built a scale-model live-steam railway in his backyard. The half-mile layout included a 46-foot-long trestle, overpasses and a 90-foot tunnel underneath his wife's flower beds. 》 Walt's favorite meal was chili and beans with tomato juice. 》 Walt was unable to pronounce the word "aluminum." When he hosted his television show, writers made a point not to include it. 》 According to legend, Walt's last words came as he looked out of his hospital window and said how shabby the Disney water tower looked. Since then, Disney execs have made sure the tower is regularly repainted, as is its replica at Disney-MGM Studios. 》 Had he not smoked, Walt may have lived at least until the 1990s. One of his brothers lived until 98; his sister died at 92. Walt was born exactly one year earlier than U.S. Sen. Strom Thurmond, who died in 2003.

SOURCES FOR THIS ARTICLE INCLUDE "WALT DISNEY: AN AMERICAN ORIGINAL" BY BOB THOMAS AND "WALT DISNEY AND THE QUEST FOR COMMUNITY" BY STEVE MANNHEIM

The Fab Five

MICKEY MOUSE

Since his debut in 1928's "Steamboat Willie," Disney's cartoon titan has been a pop-culture icon. Modeled in part on silent-film star Charlie Chaplin, Mickey was an underdog who dreamed big — a character everyone could root for. In the 1930s, his optimistic attitude was an antidote to the Great Depression. During World War II Mickey become symbolic of the can-do attitude of the United States. During the 1960s he was embraced by the counterculture. Today he's still enormously popular — the most recognized and celebrated cartoon character in history. Sure he's a corporate symbol, but Mickey's also an honest, pure piece of Americana.

When Mickey Mouse cartoons debuted in the late 1920s, an opening cartoon had been a common feature at motion-picture theaters for more than a decade. Mickey, however, was different. First, his cartoons had sound, an incredible novelty at the time. And second, he had a personality — a happy-go-lucky approach to life that was said to be the alter ego of Walt Disney. At many theaters, a 7-minute Mickey short would draw more of a crowd than the main feature, and the name "Mickey Mouse" would be the largest on the marquee. "Mickey Mouse is an international hero," Fortune magazine wrote in 1934, "better known than Roosevelt."

After World War II Mickey's evolution into a Disney icon had made it difficult for artists to give him interesting behaviors — if he lost his temper or misbehaved, fans would complain. In 1955 Mickey became the walk-around host of California's Disneyland. In 1971 he took on the same role at Walt Disney World.

MINNIE MOUSE

Minnie is Mickey's girlfriend. She's always around to flatter, giggle at and swoon over her main squeeze. Still, she does have her own life. Quick-witted and energetic, she loves animals, cooking and gardening, and can play the harmonica, guitar and piano.

She also gets mad. After Mickey forces her to kiss him in 1928's "Plane Crazy," Minnie slaps him, then jumps out of their open-cockpit airplane, forcing it to crash. She smashes a lamp on Mickey's head when he pulls her nose in 1930's "The Cactus Kid." And when she mistakenly thinks Mickey has given her a bone for a present in 1933's "Puppy Love," she kicks Mickey out of her house and sobs "I hate him! I hate all men!"

They always make up. Mickey, in fact, rules Minnie's world. In 1995's "Runaway Brain," she goes shopping for a swimsuit. "Oh my!" she says, looking in a mirror as she eyes a skimpy two-piece number. "What would Mickey think?"

As portrayed in the 1928 cartoon "The Gallopin' Gaucho," the couple first lay eyes on each other when Minnie — a flirty saloon dancer — bats her eyes at Mickey, a cigarette-smoking outlaw. After Mickey chugs a beer, they tango.

Minnie has kids in 1933's "Mickey's Steam Roller" and an old flame (smooth talking, tap-dancing Mortimer) in the 1936 cartoon "Mickey's Rival."

DONALD DUCK

He's rude, he's crude, he doesn't wear pants. He shouts, he pouts and loses his temper at the drop of a pin. He has an eye for the ladies and often just likes to be mean. Yet who doesn't love Donald Duck? He responds to life the way we are tempted to, but never dare.

Created in 1934 as a foil for the then-gentlemanly Mickey, Donald soon emerged as Disney's most popular star. Besides his bombastic personality, Donald is known for his nearly unintelligible voice, originally done by bird impressionist Clarence "Ducky" Nash.

The "duck with all the bad luck" is also famous for his "hopping mad" boxing stance, a leaning, jumping posture with one arm straight and the other twirling like a windmill. (Watch closely during "The Lion King" segment of Mickey's PhilharMagic and you'll see it.)

GOOFY

A good-hearted simpleton, Goofy appeals to your inner idiot. He's clumsy and gullible, has a hard time concentrating and seldom finishes what he starts. He has lousy posture, his clothes don't fit, his stomach is too big — yet he mugs for a camera. Originally known as Dippy Dog, Goofy made his debut in 1930. He later became the host of a series of "How To" sports parodies. As for the eternal Goofy question — man or dog? — the answer is... both! Unlike Pluto, Goofy is an upright talking character. But he has the physical characteristics of a dog, including floppy ears and a long snout.

PLUTO

One of the greatest dogs in Hollywood history, Pluto brings the unique personality of Man's Best Friend to life. The only Five Fab character with no human traits, Mickey's pet doesn't speak or (ex-

Mickey Mouse and Donald Duck star in Mickey's PhilharMagic, a 3-D movie at the Magic Kingdom

cept at the theme parks) walk upright. Instead, the gangly yellow hound licks, sniffs, romps and runs in a fashion instantly recognizable to dog lovers everywhere. In Disney cartoons Pluto is known for his vivid facial expressions, as he is always thinking.

Pluto once spoke. In the 1931 short "The Moose Hunt," he looked into Mickey's eyes and whispered "Kiss me!"

FUN FACTS 》》 President Roosevelt showed Mickey cartoons at the White House in the 1930s. 》》 In 1933 Mickey received 800,000 fan letters, the most of any Hollywood star. 》》 During World War II, the password of the Allied forces on D-Day was "Mickey Mouse." 》》 Walt Disney originally did the voices for both Mickey and Minnie. 》》 Mickey was banned in Nazi Germany in 1933, in the Soviet Union in 1936, in Yugoslavia in 1937, in Italy in 1938 and in East Germany in 1954. 》》 In the 1950s Disney transformed Goofy into George Geef, a suburban everyman often drawn without ears.

PLANNING

YOUR TRIP

Before you leave home

Planning your Disney trip takes some thought, but it isn't brain surgery. All it takes is this book, access to the Internet, a cell phone and a couple of hours of your time. You can do it at Starbucks. Ideally you should put your plan together six months before your trip. Here's a step-by-step guide on how to do it:

1 DECIDE WHEN TO GO

The first two weeks of December is the **best time to go.** It's not crowded, and you get all the Christmas extras. Crowds are also light, and hotels often cheaper, from the middle of January to Valentine's Day, late April to late May and the weeks between Labor Day and mid-November. But it's not all good — some attractions shut down during these periods and the Magic Kingdom often closes at 6 p.m. The least crowded week is the one right after Labor Day. The **worst times to go:** the week between Christmas and New Year's, and the 4th of July, when crowds are incredible. In general, the parks can be packed any time kids are out of school — holidays, spring break and during the summer, when gazillions of Brazilians also visit in large tour groups. These

A van at the Typhoon Lagoon parking lot

busy times are so crowded that many families visit when school is in session (and yes, have their children miss class). On the positive side, during these times the Magic Kingdom is typically open until at least 10 p.m. For **yearly weather data** go to weather.com, type in the ZIP code 32830 and click on "Averages."

Beauties and the Buzz. Everyone — even teenagers — loves to pose with Disney characters.

DECIDE HOW LONG TO STAY

Want to relax on your vacation? Then **you'll need a week** to see the best of each theme park, go to a water park and still have time to have a couple of nice dinners, shop or relax at your pool. Each park takes at least a day to fully enjoy. Downtown Disney entertainment and diversions such as golf or fishing require time, too, but are usually worthwhile and add variety. Longer stays also cost less per day, as there's not much difference in price between a 3-day and a 7-day park ticket. A basic 3-day Walt Disney World theme-park ticket costs about $195. A fourth day adds only $10, and each day after that adds even less (there's more ticket info on the next page). Because of this, a typical family of four spends about $500 a day on their hotel room, food and tickets during a three-day Disney vacation, but only $400 a day if they stay a week. If you can't spend a week, **three days is long enough** to get a good dose of Disney, especially if you know just what to do. The column at right lists all the theme parks, water parks and other activities Disney offers.

DECIDE WHERE TO STAY

As for accommodations, you again have plenty of choices. Disney itself owns and operates 19 resorts. There are ten other resorts on Disney property, and most major chains have hotels within 15 miles. **What's the difference?** The Disney resorts have elaborate theming and offer benefits such as more time in the parks, convenient free transportation options and packaged dining and recreation plans. Rates range from $80 to $2,000 a night, though most rooms go for $100 to $300. Run by Starwood Hotels, the Swan and Dolphin offer first-class amenities and many Disney benefits in a pair of stunning buildings within walking distance of both Epcot and Disney-MGM Studios. Shades of Green is an Armed Forces Recreation

What there is to do

THEME PARKS
Magic Kingdom. The signature Disney park has Cinderella Castle, Main Street U.S.A. and the most characters and attractions. *Page 38.*
Epcot. A permanent World's Fair, Epcot showcases nature, science and technology in Future World and highlights 11 countries in its World Showcase pavilions. *Page 106.*
Disney-MGM Studios. This intimate park celebrates show biz with stage musicals, stunt performances and thrill rides. *Page 144.*
Disney's Animal Kingdom. This lush park includes live animals, elaborate attractions and African and Asian villages. *Page 188.*
WATER PARKS
Blizzard Beach. Big, thrilling slides highlight this "melting" ski resort. *Page 239.*
Typhoon Lagoon. Includes a surf pool, a water coaster and snorkeling with fish. *Page 246.*
DOWNTOWN DISNEY
AMC Theater. *Page 257.*
DisneyQuest. A high-tech arcade. *Page 257.*
House of Blues. Live concerts. *Page 257.*
La Nouba. A European circus. *Page 258.*
Pleasure Island. Nightclubs. *Page 261.*
DIVERSIONS
Bicycle and surrey rentals. *Page 274.*
Boat charters. *Page 276.*
Boat rentals. *Page 274.*
Campfire. *Page 276.*
Carriage and wagon rides. *Page 276.*
Disney Cruise Line. *Page 276.*
Disney's Wide World of Sports. *Page 279.*
Diving and snorkeling. *Page 277.*
Dolphin encounter. *Page 277.*
Fishing. *Page 274.*
Golf. *Page 268.*
Horseback riding. *Page 275.*
Jogging. *Page 275.*
Miniature golf. *Page 270.*
Spas. *Page 277.*
Stock car driving. *Page 272.*
Surfing lessons. *Page 271.*
Tennis. *Page 275.*
Tours. *Page 278.*
Water sports. *Page 273.*
DINING
Character meals. Disney stars visit your table as you eat. *Pages 81, 142, 159, 205, 300.*
Dinner shows. A Polynesian luau, western revue and outdoor-BBQ line dance. *Page 301.*
Downtown Disney restaurants. *Page 262.*
Resort restaurants. *Page 300.*
SHOPPING
Theme parks. *Pages 57, 140, 169, 209.*
Downtown Disney. *Page 264.*

Let your heart decide. Couples find romance easily.

Center near the Magic Kingdom. The Downtown Disney resorts are a collection of moderately priced brand-name hotels with inside halls, large rooms and often more availability. Dozens of hotels outside Walt Disney World offer good rates, inside halls, spacious rooms, availability and sometimes free breakfast. *For complete listings see page 292.*

4 CHOOSE YOUR TICKETS

With park tickets, besides the number of days you want (see previous page), you need to consider three options. The **Park Hopper** ($45 as of Feb. 2007) lets you visit more than one park a day. **Water Park**

Epcot's World Showcase Players crack up guest Christine Esposito outside the U.K. pavilion

Fun & More ($50) adds visits to Blizzard Beach, Typhoon Lagoon, DisneyQuest, Pleasure Island or Disney's Wide World of Sports Complex. **No Expiration** ($10–$155) means unused days never expire. The easiest way to go: buy the Park Hopper and, if you're going to be here awhile, the Water Park Fun & More. You can add the No Expiration choice anytime within 14 days of your first use. *You can always upgrade your tickets (at theme parks, Downtown Disney and Disney resorts), but can't downgrade them. AAA members, convention attendees, Florida residents and military personnel get deals. Details at 407-W-DISNEY (934-7639) or at disneyworld.com.*

5 WANT A PACKAGE DEAL?

If you're going to stay at a Disney resort, consider one of Disney's Magic Your Way vacation packages. Combining lodging with theme-park tickets, prepaid meals and even recreation options, these plans can help control costs and save you money if you use them wisely. The **Magic Your Way Plus Dining** package (about $40 per day per adult, $11 per child) gives you one table-service meal, one counter-service meal and one snack per day. You can choose from over 100 restaurants, including some with character meals. Is it a good deal? Yes, if you order the fancy stuff at the table-service restaurants. If you want an active vacation but don't want to spend much time in the parks, the **Magic Your Way Premium** package (about $150 per day per adult, $100 per child) can be a great deal. It gives you unlimited use of many recre-

GRAND GATHERINGS is a collection of events for groups of eight or more. These include a unique breakfast at Magic Kingdom, special dinners at Epcot and Disney's Animal Kingdom and a Wishes fireworks cruise, all with character appearances and entertainment. For details call 407-939-7526.

Not everyone jumps for joy when it rains, but the parks are usually less crowded and most attractions are indoors anyway. Most gift shops sell ponchos. The best thing to bring? A happy go lucky attitude.

ation options, including golf and water sports. You get three meals a day and all can be in table-service restaurants. The package even includes vouchers to La Nouba, unlimited use of child-care facilities and unlimited theme-park tours. You do need to buy at least a one-day park ticket. Book this plan six months early to get the most out of it — you'll be able to cherry-pick your restaurant times, tee times, etc. The **Magic Your Way Platinum** package (about $200 per day per adult, $130 per child, available only to guests of Disney Deluxe and Vacation Club Resorts) includes everything in the Premium Package and adds such extras as an itinerary planning service, a spa treatment, fireworks cruise and reserved seating for Fantasmic. Each package has some complications and restrictions (e.g., everyone staying in a room must be on the same plan). For details call 407-W-DISNEY (934-7639) or log on to disneyworld.com.

BOOK IT!

To book tickets, a Disney resort room or a package go to disneyworld.com or call 407-W-DISNEY (934-7639) from 7 a.m. to 10 p.m. Eastern time. Other resort numbers are in our Where to Stay chapter, which starts on page 292.

PLAN YOUR DAYS

First, determine what days to go to what theme parks. **Log on to disneyworld.com** and click "Calendar" to find the hours, Extra Magic Hours, special events and parade and fireworks times of the parks during your stay (available six months in advance). Then **make your restaurant and recreation reservations** around that schedule. Dinner shows take reservations a year in advance, restaurants six months early. For recreation, you can book fishing and surfing a year out, tours and stock car driving six months in advance, boat cruises and golf tee times 90 days early* and water sports 30 days early. Other reservations to consider: Birthday parties, florist services, special events, even stroller and ECV rentals (first-come first-served from Disney, but offered with reservations from outside vendors). Online, check pages.prodigy.net/stevesoares for Disney's live entertainment schedules and weather.com (ZIP Code 32830) for the Disney forecast. *For phone numbers, see the directory on the last page of this book.*

* 30 days for guests not staying at a Disney resort

Dog owners must return to walk their pets at Disney kennels

then west again 2 miles to Disney. Guests staying at a Disney-owned resort can take Disney's free Magical Express bus (see The Disney Difference, page 298). In Florida it's legal to turn right after stopping at a red light.

Practical Information

WHAT TO PACK

Clothes. Dress for comfort. Swimsuits, hats, loose-fitting cotton tops and shorts with large pockets are fundamental, as are comfortable, broken-in walking shoes. Pack two pair per person, so if it rains you have a dry pair. During the winter you'll need clothes you can layer, such as jackets, sweaters and sweatshirts, as days start off cool but warm quickly. January days can be 30 degrees at 9 a.m. but 60 by noon. Temperatures at 7 p.m. will be in the 50s through March.

Other essentials. Pack an umbrella, sunglasses and sunscreen (sweat-proof, SPF rating at least 30). Instead of a purse try a waist pack to keep hands free. Don't forget tickets and confirmations.

Packing for kids. Dress your kids like you dress yourself

They're popular, but thong-style sandals leave feet sore. The average guest walks 7 miles a day.

— casually, comfortably — but protect them more from the sun (wide-brimmed hats help). Bring snacks (granola bars, raisin boxes) and a Sharpie pen for autographs.

➡ **The most important item to pack? Broken-in shoes. You can't buy them here.**

GETTING HERE

By automobile. Disney World is southwest of Orlando along Interstate 4, 18 miles from downtown and 12 miles past the Florida Turnpike.

By plane. The resort is 19 miles southwest of the Orlando International Airport. You can travel to Disney by taxi *($40–$60, Yellow Cab: 407-699-9999)*, town car *($60–$90, Mears: 407-423-5566)*, shuttle van or bus *($18 per person, Mears: 407-423-5566)* or by renting a car *(Hertz: 800-654-3131. Avis: 800-331-1212. National: 800-227-7368.)* The simplest route (25 min.) is to take the airport's South Exit road 4 miles to Florida 417 ($2 toll), go west on 417 13 miles to Osceola Parkway (Exit 3),

EXTRA MAGIC HOURS

Each day one of the theme parks or water parks opens an hour early or stays open up to three hours later for guests staying at Disney-owned-and-operated resorts, the Walt Disney World Swan and Dolphin, Shades of Green and the Hilton on Hotel Plaza Blvd. To get in early you'll need a resort ID (and a park ticket); to stay late you stop by a table at the park to get a wristband. Not every attraction, restaurant and shop is open during the extra hours, but most of the major ones are.

➡ **If you're not going to take advantage of a park's early-open benefit, don't go to it at all that day. It will be extra crowded all day long.**

MONEY MATTERS

ATMs. There's at least one ATM at every theme park and resort. *Most debit and credit cards are accepted. $2–$2.50 fee per transaction.*

Banking. Across from the Downtown Disney Marketplace, **SunTrust Bank** handles cash advances (Discover, MasterCard or Visa) and wire transfers. *Open 9 a.m.–4 p.m. weekdays, until 5:30 p.m. Thursdays. 407-828-6103.* In the nearby CrossRoads shopping center, Gooding's **Supermarket** handles Western Union transfers. *8 a.m.–10 p.m. daily. 407-827-1200.*

Credit cards. All Disney charge locations accept American Express, Diner's Club, Discover, JCB,

MasterCard and Visa.
Disney Dollars. These character-faced bills are accepted as currency at the theme parks and Disney-owned resorts and gift shops. They're sold at Guest Relations centers, Disney concierge desks and the World of Disney store at Downtown Disney.
Traveler's checks. Nearly any purchase can be made with a traveler's check. The SunTrust Bank *(see left page)* handles the AmEx brand.
Currency exchange. Guest Relations centers will exchange up to $100 in foreign currency.

PETS
Five small Disney kennels offer daytime and overnight caged boarding for dogs, cats, rabbits and other small creatures. The animals are not exercised; dog owners must stop by at least twice a day to walk their pet (three times for puppies). You get 24-hour access to your animal. The kennels are at the Magic Kingdom *(407-824-6568)*, Epcot *(407-560-6229)*, Disney-MGM Studios *(407-560-4282)*, Disney's Animal Kingdom *(407-938-2100)* and Disney's Fort Wilderness Resort & Campground *(407-824-2735)*. Day boarding: $10 per day. Overnight: $15 ($13 for Disney resort guests). No reservations. Vaccinations req. Cats and dogs must be 8 weeks. Fort Wilderness campers may keep their pet with them for $5 per day.
➡ **Except for Fort Wilderness, only service animals are allowed in Disney resorts, theme parks, water parks or Downtown Disney.**

MEETING CHARACTERS
Though some fantasy-free parents may not appreciate it, the Disney characters *are* real. That's not a sweaty young woman in a fur suit,

it's Pluto (just ask your kids). Meeting one can make a lifelong memory. There are three ways to do it: at meet-and-greet lines, parades and character meals. Sometimes you find one alone.

Face or fur? Disney has two types of characters. **Face characters,** such as Cinderella, show a real head. **Fur characters,** such as Winnie the Pooh, are fully costumed. Though face characters rarely intimidate, the odd, huge heads of the fur family sometimes do.

To help your child feel comfortable, talk with her beforehand so she knows what to expect. For meet-and-greet lines, buy her an autograph book to give her something to focus on besides the face-to-fur encounter. Don't push her — the characters are super patient. Watch your time: each park has so many autograph lines (Disney-MGM has 20) that stopping at them all could take all day.

Wide-eyed wonder.
Though they love meeting characters, many children still back away.

Getting around. A free bus system connects all Disney resorts, theme and water parks and Downtown Disney. Monorails serve the Magic Kingdom, the Seven Seas Lagoon resorts and Epcot. Free water taxis serve resorts on connecting waterways. You can rent a car at the Car Care Center (Alamo, 407-824-3470) and at many resorts.

Where to find them.
Though Mickey, Minnie, Donald, Goofy and Pluto are everywhere, many characters are far less common. It's easy, however, to find the one you want. Each park's Times

MISSION SPACE

Enter Any
Time Between
10:15am
AND
11:15am
Another FASTPASS
ticket will be
available after
10:18am
03/18/06 3   9:31a

| | Your Fastpass reservation time | The time you can get another Fastpass | The time you got this one |

of all visitors use it. Those that do see 25 to 75 percent more attractions and shows, depending on crowds. Here's how to get the most from it: **1.** Designate someone in your party as your Fastpass supervisor. This person will hold all your park tickets, go off to get Fastpasses for your entire party throughout the day and watch the time. Hello, Dad? **2.** Always hold at least one Fastpass, so you're always "on the clock" for at least one attraction. Get one when you get in the park, then others as often as possible throughout the day. **3.** Don't sweat it if you miss the return time. Disney rarely enforces it. **4.** Use the service for every Fastpass attraction except those you'll be riding before 10 a.m. or very late at night.

➡ **Fastpasses can run out by lunchtime at hot rides such as Expedition Everest or Soarin'.**

Guide has an overview of character locations, and most cast members can track down the schedule of any character. If those ideas don't work try a park's Guest Relations office.

USING FASTPASS

You'll skip the line at the most popular attractions with this free service, an automated reservation system that saves you a place in line at a time later in the day. Here's how it works: When you place your park ticket into a Fastpass machine (located at attraction entrances), you get back a slip of paper that shows your reservation time, which is a one-hour window. When you return at that time, you enter the attraction through a separate, Fastpass-only entrance that has little or no

wait. You can't pick your time, but a display sign shows you what it will be before you get your pass. Each ticket-holder can get only one Fastpass at a time, but can accumulate many throughout a day. The service is free but not well promoted, so only about half

PHOTOS AND VIDEO

Keep a camera with you to capture spontaneous moments like dripping ice-cream cones and impromptu encounters with street characters, swimming pool silliness, or staged photos such

Disney's PhotoPass lets you build a collection of photos, but pay only for those you buy

Ask the concierge

Actual questions asked at Walt Disney World resorts:

How can I learn if a park is filled to capacity without going there? Call Disney at 407-939-4636.

Can I nurse my baby? Yes, you can nurse your baby anywhere; Disney cast members respect your privacy. Each park also has a Baby Care Center with rocking chairs and private nursing areas.

Can I get from Downtown Disney to a theme park? Yes. Disney's free buses run from the complex to all Disney parks.

Where can I find out about disability access? At each park's Guest Relations office, which has a printed guide with details on attraction access; hearing, visual and mobility services; service animals; companion restrooms; and parking issues.

I lost my digital camera two days ago. What should I do? Call the main Disney lost and found office (407-824-4245). Hours are 9 a.m.–7 p.m.

Where are XXXL Disney shirts? Typically World of Disney (Downtown Disney), the Emporium (Magic Kingdom) and MouseGear (Epcot).

What restaurant has the best view of fireworks? The California Grill, atop Disney's Contemporary Resort, has a birds-eye view of the Magic Kingdom Wishes display. It dims the lights and pipes in the soundtrack, and has an outdoor balcony.

Which are the toughest restaurants to get into?
❶ Cinderella's Royal Table at Magic Kingdom (breakfast and lunch). ❷ California Grill at the Contemporary Resort. ❸ Canada's Le Cellier in Epcot. ❹ Chef Mickey's at the Contemporary Resort. ❺ Victoria and Albert's at

the Grand Floridian Resort and Spa.

We're running late for a dinner reservation. How long will they hold our table? 15 minutes. If you are running late, call Disney Dining (407-WDW-DINE) and let them know. (Your "reservation" is really for "priority seating" — the restaurant will seat you at the first available table for your party size when you arrive.)

When is the hardest time to get a dinner reservation? Between 7 p.m. and 8 p.m. If you want to eat during this hour, call at least a few days early to book a reservation, especially if you have a party of six or more.

What's the easiest way to have a meal with Mickey? Eat lunch or dinner at Epcot's Garden Grill. Mickey is dressed as a farmer.

Where can I dine with Cinderella? Breakfast and lunch: Cinderella's Royal Table (Cinderella Castle, Magic Kingdom). Dinner: 1900 Park Fare (Disney's Grand Floridian Resort).

Can Cinderella hand my child her birthday present? No.

Where's the best fast food? Starring Rolls in Disney-MGM Studios has gourmet sandwiches made in the Hollywood Brown Derby kitchens.

What are the most common mistakes guests make when they visit Disney?
❶ They don't make meal reservations before they leave home. ❷ They don't get to a theme park right when it opens. ❸ They don't take advantage of the Fastpass system. ❹ They underestimate how long it takes to travel on Disney transportation. ❺ They try to go to too many parks in one

day. ❻ They wear themselves and their children out.

If I don't have a car, how do I travel from one Disney resort to another? There is no direct free service. Cabs and town cars are always available. After (usually) 8 a.m. you can take a Disney bus to a theme park or Downtown Disney, then transfer to a bus that runs to your destination. Downtown Disney buses often aren't as crowded, and run until after 1 a.m.

I'm allergic to peanuts. Where can I eat? Any table service restaurant. Just tell the reservation agent, or at least your server, your needs ahead of time.

Where can I get a long-sleeved white men's dress shirt? Ralph Lauren styles are at Commander's Porter at the Grand Floridian Resort. Hours are 9 a.m.–10 p.m.

Where can I buy non-Disney apparel on Disney property? In Epcot's World Showcase, at the water parks, in the gift shops of the Deluxe resorts and at Downtown Disney.

Can I return an item bought at a Disney park to a Disney Store in a mall? No.

Where's a good outlet mall? Orlando Premium Outlet Mall (8200 Vineland Ave., Orlando; 407-238-7787) is 15 minutes away just off I-4. Hours are Mon.–Sat. 10 a.m.–10 p.m. (11 p.m. in summer), Sun. 10 a.m.–9 p.m.

Where can I get diesel fuel? At the Hess station by the Car Care Center, near the Magic Kingdom parking lot.

What's the closest Catholic Church? Mary Queen of the Universe Shrine (8300 Vineland Ave. at I-4 Exit 68, 407-239-6600).

What is the easiest way to get an answer to a Disney question? Call the Walt Disney World information line (407-824-2222).

as posing while trying on Disney's character hats. Whatever shots you snap, take turns being the photographer. If dad takes all of the pictures, none of them will include dad. Another idea: buy each of your kids a disposable camera. The results are almost sure to add to your memories. Water parks sell waterproof versions.

Camera supplies. Every theme park has a Camera Center which sells still and video cameras, batteries, memory cards and other supplies. Each is easy to find: at each park the camera center is inside the first building on your right. At Magic Kingdom it's in Exposition Hall on Main Street U.S.A.; at Epcot it's the Gateway Gifts Camera Center under Spaceship Earth; at Disney-MGM Studios it's the Darkroom on Hollywood Blvd.; at Animal Kingdom it's inside Garden Gate Gifts. At water parks camera supplies are sold at the main gift shops.

Disney's PhotoPass. With this service Disney photographers take shots of you, but you pay for only those you choose. Here's how it works: The photographers are sta-

It melts quickly, but a Blizzard Beach Snow Ball is a nonfat, refreshing snack

tioned in front of each theme-park icon, most character locations and other park spots, as well as Downtown Disney and some hotels. Whenever you like, you hand one your credit-card-like PhotoPass (free from any photographer) and have him or her take your picture. Later, you review your shots and buy as many, or as few, as you like. You can see the images at Camera Centers and at a web site. Disney applies no sales pressure. You can view your images for up to three days at any Camera Center or up to 30 days online. (Once Disney snaps a photo, it takes about 90 minutes for it to appear at a Camera Center; about a day to show up online). The service has many buying options — single photos, photo packages, greeting cards, even DVD slideshows. Though it has its benefits, PhotoPass is not a replacement for your own camera. The photographers shoot only posed photos on walkways at particular locations, so never get spontaneous shots. If you do use it, write down the ID number of your PhotoPass on a separate sheet of paper. That way if you lose your card you won't lose access to your images.

Attraction photos. At some rides an automated camera takes your picture at a climactic moment, then a gift shop offers you the results. This happens at Splash Mountain and Buzz Lightyear's Space Ranger Spin at the Magic Kingdom, Test Track at Epcot, Rock 'n' Roller Coaster Starring Aerosmith and The Twilight Zone Tower of Terror at Disney-MGM Studios, and Dinosaur and Expedition Everest at Animal Kingdom. This system is being updated to let you add the photo onto your PhotoPass account.

FOOD CHOICES

Healthy meals. Disney's kids meals come with either unsweetened applesauce, baby carrots or fresh fruit, and a beverage of low-fat milk, 100-percent fruit juice or water (fries and soda are available on request). Many restaurants offer low-fat, no-transfat or vegetarian options. No restaurant serves food with added trans fats or partially hydrogenated oils.*

Smart choices. Disney's smoked turkey legs have zero grams of carbs. At the Magic Kingdom, the Crystal Palace offers a character buffet with a big salad bar, peel-and-eat shrimp and grilled meats and vegetables. Adventureland's Sunshine Tree Terrace has a guilt-free snack — its Citrus Swirl is frozen orange juice mixed with nonfat vanilla yogurt. The counter-service Columbia Harbour House has vegetarian chili. In Epcot, the nothing-fried menu at The Land's Sunshine Seasons food court offers everything from grilled salmon to packaged sushi. At the World Showcase, the Morocco pavilion has vegetable couscous, Japan's Tempura Kiku has

*Effective Jan. 2008

A morning wedding at Epcot

sushi and sashimi. The Brown Derby at Disney-MGM Studios offers the delicious original Cobb salad. At Disney's Animal Kingdom, the counter-service Tusker House has grilled salmon and rotisserie chicken. Healthy options at **resort restaurants** include the roasted salmon at Artist Point at Disney's Wilderness Lodge, the tuna tartare at the BoardWalk's Flying Fish Cafe and the seared scallops with golden-brown pap at Jiko at Disney's Animal Kingdom Lodge.

Kosher meals. Glatt kosher meals are available at most full-service restaurants with 24 hours notice at 407-WDW-DINE (939-3463). The food is prepared in Miami and flown in to Walt Disney World. Kosher meals are always available at the following quick-service locations: Cosmic Ray's Starlight Cafe in Magic Kingdom, Liberty Inn at Epcot, ABC Commissary at Disney-MGM Studios, Pizzafari at Disney's Animal Kingdom, and the food courts at Disney's All-Star, Caribbean Beach, Pop Century and Port Orleans Riverside resorts.

Other policies. Priority Seating reservations can be made 180 days in advance at 407-WDW-DINE (939-3463). Certain restaurants (California Grill, Chef Mickey's, Cinderella's Royal Table, Victoria & Albert's, Restaurant Akershus and the dinner shows) require a credit card and have strict cancellation policies. Parties of 13 or more always require a credit card. Some (Artist Point, California Grill, Citricos, Flying Fish Cafe, Jiko, Narcoosee's and Yachtsman Steakhouse) have a business-casual **dress code.** Men need to wear a

jacket, and women a dress or dressy pants suit, at Victoria & Albert's. **Lifestyle diets** (no-sugar, low fat, low sodium, vegetarian or vegan) can be met by telling the reservation clerk, host or server, though dinner shows need 24 hours notice. With a call three days in advance, full-service restaurants can accommodate **special dietary needs** such as allergies to gluten or wheat, shellfish, soy, lactose or milk, peanuts, tree nuts, fish or eggs. At buffet restaurants, guests who have had **gastric-bypass surgery** are charged the kids-buffet price for the adult buffet. *All Disney restaurants are nonsmoking and add an automatic 18-percent gratuity to the bill of parties of 8 or more.*

BIRTHDAYS
Free "It's My Birthday Today" **buttons** available at Guest Relations offices will cue cast members to recognize your birthday boy or girl — of any age. Goofy will call your Disney hotel room with a free birthday greeting; to arrange it call 407-824-2222. Many table-service restaurants will bring out a "surprise" 6-inch **birthday cake** ($12.50) with advance notice. The cakes can be personalized with 48 hours notice at 407-824-7091. You can arrange a **birthday party**

at the Winter Summerland miniature golf course, Blizzard Beach water park or Wide World of Sports Complex ($16–$20 per person, includes cake and either hot dogs or pizza) or a special **fireworks cruise** at Epcot. Details: 407 WDW BDAY (939-2329).

WEDDINGS AND HONEYMOONS
Up to a dozen couples tie the knot at Walt Disney World every day. From a practical standpoint, it has unrivaled facilities for a family gathering, great year-round weather and the one-stop shopping of Disney's Fairy Tale Weddings division. But it's also a home of romance — most of it fictional and childish to be sure, but meaningful nonetheless. Though prices start at $2,450, the average Disney wedding costs $26,000 and includes 100 people. There are honeymoon packages, too. For information call 877-566-0969 or log on to disneyweddings.com or disneyhoneymoons.com.

FUN FACT » Walt Disney World's 300 food locations serve 6,000 different items. Each year they sell 1.6 million turkey drumsticks, 2.6 million Mickey Mouse ice cream bars and 5 million bags of popcorn.

Princess pretty, three sisters are all dressed up for Fantasyland

Magic Kingdom

Crowds typically mob Fantasyland after 11 a.m., but are often light early in the morning

t's a world that, if real, you'd love to escape to. A land straight out of your imagination, filled with barbershop quartets and hoop skirts, small towns and clean streets, charming pirates and cute little dolls. A kingdom where everyone, peasant and princess, is always glad to see you. The definitive theme park experience, the Magic Kingdom has a universal appeal. For newcomers it's a postcard come to life; for veterans it's like seeing an old friend. "It's easy to be snippy about it," says film star Alan Cumming, "but once you're here you have to open your mind to it."

LAY OF THE LAND The park is laid out like a spoked wheel. You enter Main Street U.S.A., which leads to a central hub in front of Cinderella Castle. From there five paths lead to Adventureland; Liberty Square and Frontierland; Fantasyland; Mickey's Toontown Fair; and Tomorrowland.

Walt Disney's childhood home of Marceline, Mo., helped inspire **Main Street U.S.A.,** a bustling thoroughfare from a hundred years ago that's complete with horse-drawn trolleys, period entertainers, even a vintage barbershop.

The sound of beating drums welcomes you to **Adventureland,** an eclectic mix of African jungles, Arabian nights, Caribbean architecture and South Seas land-

"Partners," a statue of Walt Disney and Mickey Mouse, anchors the hub in front of the castle

▶ Consider using the resort monorail instead of the express. There's often no line.

With many modern attractions, Tomorrowland appeals to older children and young adults

scaping. Major attractions include the tongue-in-cheek Jungle Cruise and the newly updated Pirates of the Caribbean.

Liberty Square honors our country's Colonial heritage. Federal and Georgian architecture brings back the time of the Revolutionary War. The main attractions: the Haunted Mansion and the Hall of Presidents.

Frontierland looks to be a 19th-century rural American village. Theatrical touches include raised wooden sidewalks, rocking chairs, checkerboard tables and lots of banjo and fiddle music twangin' from the trees. Attractions here include Big Thunder Mountain Railroad and Splash Mountain.

Set within the stone walls of Cinderella's castle estate, **Fantasyland** resembles a royal courtyard during a Renaissance fair. Some buildings are designed as tournament tents; others blend in styles from Great Britain and Germany. Ideal for preschoolers, it has nine attractions, including Dumbo the Flying Elephant, It's a Small World, the Many Adventures of Winnie the Pooh and Mickey's PhilharMagic.

Themed to be a rural town that's holding a county agricultural exhibition, the two-acre **Mickey's Toontown Fair** also has the country homes of Mickey and Minnie Mouse. Built with cartoonish "Squash and Stretch" architecture, it has the park's only indoor, air-conditioned spots to get character autographs.

The theme of **Tomorrowland?** An intergalactic spaceport, a nostalgic trip back to the future as envisioned by 1930s comic books and sci-fi films. The concept applies mostly to the architecture, not the attractions. It's best appreciated at night, when the brushed-metal curves of the buildings are lit by colorful beacons, lasers and neon. Calling cards include the classic Space Mountain and the cutting-edge Laugh Floor Comedy Club.

TOURING TIPS There are three secrets to having fun at the Magic Kingdom. First, **get to the gate 30 minutes before the park**

GO WEST, YOUNG VISITOR You move both literally and figuratively from east to west as you travel from the start of Liberty Square to the end of Frontierland. You start off in New York, in the Hudson Valley of the Haunted Mansion. The Columbia Harbour House is Boston; the Hall of Presidents Philadelphia. The Diamond Horseshoe represents St. Louis, Grizzly Hall is Colorado, the Pecos Bill Tall Tale Inn is Texas and Big Thunder Mountain is Utah. (Splash Mountain is Georgia, apparently washed away from the South.)

▶ Be prepared for rain. A short thunderstorm is common on summer afternoons.

N

MICKEY'S TOONTOWN FAIR

FANTASYLAND

Pinocchio Village Haus

Columbia Harbour House

LIBERTY SQ.

Cinderella's Royal Table

FRONTIERLAND

Liberty Tree Tavern

Pecos Bill Cafe

Cosmic Ray's Starlight Cafe

TOMORROWLAND

ADVENTURELAND

The Crystal Palace

Casey's Corner

The Plaza Restaurant

Main St. Bakery

MAIN STREET U.S.A.

Tony's Town Square Restaurant

ENTRANCE

i Information
✚ First Aid
$ ATM Locations
(Pay Phones

- - - Parade Route

ATTRACTIONS

1. Walt Disney World Railroad
2. Cinderella's Golden Carrousel
3. Mickey's PhilharMagic
4. Peter Pan's Flight
5. It's a Small World
6. Dumbo the Flying Elephant
7. Snow White's Scary Adventures
8. Ariel's Grotto
9. The Many Adventures of Winnie the Pooh
10. Mad Tea Party
11. Swiss Family Treehouse
12. The Magic Carpets of Aladdin
13. Jungle Cruise
14. The Enchanted Tiki Room — Under New Management
15. Pirates of the Caribbean
16. The Hall of Presidents
17. Liberty Square Riverboat
18. The Haunted Mansion
19. Country Bear Jamboree
20. Frontierland Shootin' Arcade
21. Splash Mountain
22. Big Thunder Mountain Railroad
23. Tom Sawyer Island
24. Minnie's Country House
25. Mickey's Country House
26. The Barnstormer
27. Donald's Boat
28. Stitch's Great Escape
29. The Laugh Floor Comedy Club
30. Astro Orbiter
31. Buzz Lightyear's Space Ranger Spin
32. Walt Disney's Carousel of Progress
33. Space Mountain
34. Tomorrowland Indy Speedway
35. Tomorrowland Transit Authority

opens. You'll avoid the crush of people going through the security check, get to see the "Singin' in the Rain"/"Dumbo" inspired opening ceremony and then find no line at any attraction. The Magic Kingdom has dozens of attractions, but most take only a few minutes to experience. Get here first thing in the morning and you'll be able to zip through many of them during the first hour.

Second, **use the Fastpass system.** Take advantage of it and you'll rarely, if ever, wait in a line. See page 34 for details.

Third, **consider leaving after lunch.** Go back to your hotel for a swim or a nap, and come back after dinner. The Magic Kingdom can be hell during a hot, crowded afternoon, but your hotel bed, pool and shower will seem heavenly. Come back at dusk for the nighttime parade and fireworks.

THE UNDERWORLD When you stroll through the Magic Kingdom you're actually walking on its second floor. Underneath you — beneath the trees, flowers, grass, dirt and yes, waterways — are nine acres of warehouse-sized rooms, hallways and office space. Called the park's "utilidor," this network of interconnected service areas forms a unique support basement. Completely hidden from guests, it serves two roles.

First, it helps keep the kingdom magical, as its one-and-a-half miles of color coded tunnels give cast members and characters a way to travel from spot to spot without being seen by guests.

Second, the utilidor is the park's nerve center. Rooms off to the sides (all windowless, of course) include an employee lounge (with lockers, ping-pong tables and video games), barber shop, cafeteria, paycheck center and wardrobe headquarters; merchandise storage areas; utility hubs; and a huge computer center that controls virtually everything in the park, from the hundreds of audio recordings and projection systems in each attraction, to the water pressure needed to push various boats through each ride track, to all the fireworks and parade operations.

Whooshing above on the ceiling is the Magic Kingdom's Automated Vacuum Assisted Collection system. Every 15 minutes — after above-ground maintenance workers empty the park's trash cans into several backstage collection sites — the garbage is drawn through the tubes at speeds up to 60 miles per hour, on its way to a giant central trash terminal behind Splash Mountain.

Guests over 12 go into the utilidor on the park's Keys to the Kingdom Tour (see page 278).

Park resources

The Magic Kingdom has five **ATMs:** at the lockers, City Hall, in the Frontierland/Adventureland breezeway, near the Pinocchio Village Haus restrooms and inside the Space Mountain arcade. All restaurants, stands and stores accept credit cards and traveler's checks... The **Baby Care Center** *(next to The Crystal Palace)* has changing rooms, nursing areas and a microwave; and sells diapers, formula, pacifiers and over-the-counter medications... Exposition Hall *(Main Street U.S.A.)* sells **cameras and accessories** and burns photo CDs... The **First Aid Center** *(next to The Crystal Palace)* handles minor emergencies and has registered nurses on hand... The **Guest Relations** center *(outside the gate to the right; inside at City Hall on Main Street U.S.A.)* has cast members ready to answer any question or help with any problem. It has maps and Times Guides for all theme parks, exchanges foreign currency and stores items found in the park that day... One thousand **lockers** *(just inside the gate, on the right)* each go for $5 per day plus a $2 deposit.... Report **lost children** to Guest Relations or any cast member. Children who lose their parents should tell a cast member... Anything you buy can be sent to **Package Pick-Up** *(left of City Hall)* for you to pick up as you leave. Purchases can also be delivered to your Disney hotel or shipped to your home.... For day guests **parking** is $10 a day. Those staying at a Disney resort (and annual passholders) get free parking... The **Pet Care Kennel** *(107 824-6568, at the TTC)* has clean cages in air-conditioned rooms. See the chapter "Practical Information" for details... **Security guards** inspect all bags and purses outside the park entrance... Single **strollers and wheelchairs** ($10 per day), double-passenger strollers ($18) and Electric Convenience Vehicles ($35) rent from under the train station, inside the right tunnel. The ECVs are booked quickly; many are used by overweight guests... The park **tip board** *(Main Street U.S.A., past Casey's Corner)* displays waiting times for popular attractions... As for **transportation,** monorails and ferry boats arrive from the Transportation and Ticket Center (TTC). Contemporary, Grand Floridian and Polynesian resort guests take a monorail or boat to the park; those at Fort Wilderness and Wilderness Lodge can take a boat or bus. Buses also run from Animal Kingdom, Blizzard Beach, Disney-MGM Studios and every other Disney hotel. The park has no direct service to Downtown Disney or Typhoon Lagoon.

A Magical Day

How can you see all the top-rated attractions in one day and hardly ever wait in a long line? Just follow this plan. The key? *Get to the front gate no later than 8:30 a.m.; when it opens at 8:55 go straight to Fantasyland.* You want to be on one of the first two Dumbos of the day.

8:30 Arrive at the park

9:00 Fantasyland Do, in order, Dumbo, Peter Pan, Small World, PhilharMagic.

9:55 Get Fastpasses for the Many Adventures of Winnie the Pooh.

10:00 Toontown Fair Meet Mickey, then more characters at Toontown Tent.

11:30 Pooh's Adventures

11:45 Fastpasses for Space Mtn.

12:00 Lunch at Tony's Town Square.

1:00 Tomorrowland First, get Fastpasses for Buzz Lightyear's Space Ranger Spin. Then use your earlier Fastpasses to ride Space Mountain. Third, get in line for the Laugh Floor Comedy Club, but while you wait have a member of your party hike over to Splash Mountain for more Fastpasses. When you're done with Laugh Floor, your Buzz Lightyear Fastpasses should be valid.

3:30 Pirates of the Caribbean

4:30 Haunted Mansion

5:15 Fastpasses for Big Thunder Mtn.

5:30 Splash Mountain

6:15 Dinner with Cinderella at the Grand Floridian Resort. Reservations are a must!

8:00 SpectroMagic

9:00 Wishes

9:30 Big Thunder Mountain
Assumes operating hours of 9 a.m. to 10 p.m.

Freaky Tiki. An Adventureland statue squirts water at passersby near the Magic Carpets of Aladdin.

FUN FINDS ❶ A topiary of Elliot, the dragon star of 1977's "Pete's Dragon," swims through the grass of the plaza in front of Tomorrowland. ❷ In front of the Jungle Cruise, six Tiki statues sync water squirts to African rhythms. ❸ Crates stacked alongside the Liberty Square entrance recall the 1773 Boston Tea Party, when colonists boarded the ships of Britain's East India Tea Co. and threw the cargo into Boston Harbor. ❹ Streams of brownish pavement on the Liberty Square walkways symbolize sewage that often flowed along 18th-century building fronts and down streets. ❺ Across from the Hall of Presidents is a cast of the actual Liberty Bell. It was created in 1987 in recognition of the U.S. Bicentennial. ❻ Adjacent is Disney's Liberty Tree, a 160-year-old live oak that recalls a historic Boston elm. ❼ Stocks for adults and children stand in front of the Riverboat dock. ❽ The exterior surrounding the Hall of Presidents has three references to Colonial times and the American Revo-

BY THE NUMBERS » **100** Number of sunglasses turned in to Lost and Found daily. **» 122** Size of the park, in acres. **» 11,000** Spaces in the parking lot.

lution: Two lanterns in a second-story window facing the Haunted Mansion represent the famous line from the 1860 Longfellow poem "Paul Revere's Ride" ("One, if by land, and two, if by sea") that described how villagers signaled the patriot about invading British troops. ❾ A rifle sits in a window to the right, sending a message that the owner is home and ready to fight. ❿ Closer to the Hall's front door, a marble step beneath a blue townhouse door (No. 26) symbolizes Jefferson entering the hall to write the Constitution. ⓫ Showing four interlocking hands, a firemen's fund plaque is mounted on a set of green stable doors to the left of the Hall of Presidents. As some Colonial fire departments were, in essence, insurance companies, policyholders were given plaques that would tell arriving firefighters their fees had been paid. ⓬ The hanging sign for the Columbia Harbour House Restaurant features a U.S. shield with its eagle crying and holding arrows in its right claw, signs the country is at war on its own soil. ⓭ An invisible Tinker Bell flies around Tinker Bell's Treasures, spreading pixie dust on the gift shop's walls. Peek through the keyhole of a vanity on the left to see a flash of light. ⓮ Jousting lances form the canopy supports of the Small World building. ⓯ Donald Duck's great-great-grandfather is honored by a statue at Mickey's Toontown Fair. According to tales told in a series of 1989 comic books, Cornelius Coot founded the frontier outpost of Duckburg by popping some sweet corn to frighten away Spanish invaders. His deed was commemorated with this sculpture. ⓰ The key to the restroom at Pete's Garage is floating inside the gas pump. ⓱ A robot newsboy will speak to you in Tomorrowland. Standing between the entrances of the Tomorrowland Transit Authority and Astro Orbiter, a Galaxy Gazette hawker talks ("Extra Extra! Read all about it! Ringleader caught on Saturn!") when you stand directly in front of him. He may insult you, with a line such as "Would you get a load of you! It's times like this I wish I didn't have X-ray vision!"

ATTRACTION TIMELINE

1971 Original attractions: *Adventureland:* Jungle Cruise, Swiss Family Treehouse, Tropical Serenade. *Fantasyland:* Cinderella's Golden Carrousel, Dumbo the Flying Elephant, Peter Pan's Flight, Mad Tea Party, The Mickey Mouse Revue, Mr. Toad's Wild Ride, It's a Small World, Snow White's Adventures, Skyway, 20,000 Leagues Under the Sea Submarine Voyage. *Liberty Square:* Mike Fink Keel Boats, The Hall of Presidents, The Haunted Mansion, Liberty Square Riverboats. *Frontierland:* Frontierland Shootin' Gallery, Country Bear Jamboree. *Tomorrowland:* America the Beautiful, Flight to the Moon, Grand Prix Raceway. *Main Street U.S.A.:* Main St. Vehicles, Main St. Cinema, Plaza Swan Boats, Walt Disney World Railroad.
1972 If You Had Wings.
1973 Pirates of the Caribbean, Tom Sawyer Island.
1974 StarJets, Magic Carpet 'Round the World replaces America the Beautiful.
1975 Space Mountain, Carousel of Progress, WEDway PeopleMover, Mission to Mars replaces Flight to the Moon, America the Beautiful replaces Magic Carpet 'Round the World.
1979 Magic Carpet 'Round the World replaces America the Beautiful.
1980 Big Thunder Mountain Railroad.
1984 American Journeys replaces Magic Carpet 'Round the World.
1986 Magic Journeys replaces Mickey Mouse Revue.
1987 If You Had Wings renamed If You Could Fly.
1988 Mickey's Birthdayland.
1989 Delta Dreamflight replaces If You Could Fly.
1990 Mickey's Birthdayland becomes Mickey's Starland.
1992 Splash Mountain.
1994 Legend of The Lion King replaces Magic Journeys, The Timekeeper replaces American Journeys.
1995 ExtraTERRORestrial Alien Encounter replaces Mission to Mars, Astro Orbiter replaces StarJets. WEDway PeopleMover renamed Tomorrowland Transit Authority.
1996 Ariel's Grotto. Grand Prix Raceway renamed Tomorrowland Speedway. Delta Dreamflight renamed Take Flight. Mickey's Toontown Fair replaces Mickey's Starland (adds Donald's Boat and The Barnstormer).
1998 Buzz Lightyear's Space Ranger Spin replaces Take Flight, Tropical Serenade becomes The Enchanted Tiki Room Under New Management.
1999 The Many Adventures of Winnie the Pooh replaces Mr. Toad's Wild Ride.
2000 Tomorrowland Speedway renamed Tomorrowland Indy Speedway.
2001 The Magic Carpets of Aladdin.
2003 Mickey's PhilharMagic replaces Legend of The Lion King.
2004 Stitch's Great Escape replaces ExtraTERRORestrial Alien Encounter.
2007 The Laugh Floor Comedy Club replaces The Timekeeper.

Shows and parades not included

Main Street U.S.A.

You enter the park with a stroll through a small, 1900s-era county seat. The past made perfect, Main Street U.S.A. is a world of Victorian buildings, barbershop singers, horse-drawn streetcars and horseless carriages. It's an ideal introduction to the Magic Kingdom.

A central Town Square green is surrounded by the town's key civic buildings — its courthouse (or city hall), firehouse, train station and exhibition hall. In the center is a statue of the founding father — in this case Roy Disney, who supervised Walt Disney World's creation after his brother's death.

Next is Main Street itself. Fronted with flowers and trees, the building facades use the motion-picture technique of forced perspective to appear larger than they are. Each has its first floor at full scale, its second at 80 percent, its third 80 percent of that. Upper story windows identify the offices of fictional business folk (actually Disney alumni).

Many of the 51 facades use Cape Cod-style clapboard and gingerbread trim;

Top: Main Street U.S.A. recalls a mythical Eastern seaboard town at the end of the 19th century. **Above:** Inspired by late-1800s street cars, a Main Street horse trolley pulls away from Town Square.

some include prefabricated metalwork, an Industrial Age invention. Each has its own window framing, frieze work and cornice. The interiors have tin ceilings, brick floors and some huge chandeliers.

It's a town in transition. Horse hitches are giving way to bus stops. Streetlights are changing from gas to electricity.

▶ Catch one of the first trolleys of the day and the Dapper Dans may serenade you.

The faces of Main Street. 1. A Casey's Corner pianist plays a ragtime number. **2.** Casey's pitcher holds a ball, ready to pitch the final strike. **3.** A huge bass saxophone adds depth to Mickey's Toontown Tuners. **4.** One of the street's many friendly cast members sells balloons. **5.** A spirited Trolley Parade performer. **6.** Effervescent Victoria Trumpetto belts out a song to passersby. **7.** A drumstick through the head hints at the wacky mentality of the Main Street Philharmonic. **8.** A cook at the Main Street Confectionery brings out a fresh batch of caramel apples.

OLD-FASHIONED ENTERTAINMENT Realistic down to their bells and horns, the **Main Street Vehicles** include trolleys, horseless carriages, jitneys, a double-decker bus and a small fire truck — all ready to take you down Main Street. There's never a line. *Typically out until 12:30 p.m. Duration: apx. 3 min., depending on traffic (and, with trolleys, the particular horse). Avg. wait: 5 min. Must be ambulatory. No horse petting. Debuted: 1971.*

The **Casey's Corner Pianist** ✔ bangs out honky tonk, rag and requests on an upright piano. The **Dapper Dans** ✔ barbershop quartet mixes its harmonically perfect repertoire with chimes, tap dancing and corny humor. They'll do "Happy Birthday" on request. Friendly, often silly, the **Citizens of Main Street** ✔ chat, sing, sometimes dance with guests. The **Main Street Philharmonic** ✔ often grabs a perky female out of its audience to help out with "Hold That Tiger." So strange but so Disney, the **Main Street Trolley Parade** ✔ consists of six Gay '90s couples who soft-shoe and *lip-synch* to "The Trol-ley Song" and a couple of service numbers. Sax quintet **Mickey's Toontown Tuners** ✔ appears on Main Street a couple of times each day, harmonizing deftly on ragtime, jazz and Disney tunes.

You can **watch cooks make candy** at the Confectionery until about 7 p.m. **Antique arcade games** inside the train station's second-floor waiting room include a mutoscope showing the San Francisco adventures of "The Goddess of the Silent Screen" (and Drew Barrymore's grandmother) Dolores Costello. In the back of the Exposition Hall, the **Milestones in Animation** exhibit includes a small padded-seat theater that shows a 25-minute loop of classic Disney cartoons. In the hall, a **Kodak camera display** shows two dozen models dating from 1889. Tucked between the Plaza Ice Cream Parlor and Cinderella Castle, the **Plaza Rose Garden** includes a number of Floribunda and Hybrid Tea prize winners. During the evening **Flag Retreat,** a guest military vet often helps a color guard lower Old Glory down the Town Square flagpole.

FUN FINDS ❶ "Well, howdy!" says a statue of Goofy every 30 seconds, on a bench in front of Tony's Town Square Restaurant. ❷ Lady and Tramp have put their paw prints in the sidewalk in front of Tony's patio. ❸ A window next to the front door of the Emporium identifies its proprietor as Osh Popham, the general-store owner played by Burl Ives in the 1963 film "Summer Magic." ❹ The sounds of a practicing singer and dancer come from two open Center Street windows marked "Voice and Singing Private Lessons" and "Music and Dance Lessons, Ballet Tap & Waltz." ❺ An 1890s mom and daughter complain that hamburger is at 5 cents a pound and discuss how to attract a man on a party-line call heard on the receiver of the wall-mounted phone next to the south Market House cash register. ❻ Antique baseball paraphernalia lines the walls of the Casey's Corner eating area. ❼ At night many second-story windows are lit. ❽ Swan topiaries mark the rose-garden entrance to the Plaza Swan Boats, a ride that closed in 1983.

Main Street west (above) and east (below)

FUN FACTS ❯❯ The entrance is designed to give the experience of going to a movie theater. The train station is the curtain. As it opens (i.e., as you walk through its tunnel) you see some Coming Attraction posters and smell popcorn. ❯❯ Belgian, Clydesdale and Percheron horses pull the trolleys. Each works a few mornings a week. The animals live at the Fort Wilderness Campground. ❯❯ The horseless carriages are modeled after 1903–1907 Franklins. ❯❯ The omnibus recalls New York City double-deckers of the 1920s. ❯❯ All vehicles are Disney's original machines from 1971. ❯❯ The Toontown Tuners saxophones include a 1926 curved soprano and a 1929 bass. ❯❯ The Harmony Barber Shop has 1920s barber chairs and a shoeshine chair from the 1870s. ❯❯ The symbol on Walt Disney's tie tack on the Partners statue is that of the Smoke Tree Ranch, a rustic Palm Springs retreat where he owned a cottage. ❯❯ Much of the background music is from the 1988 CD "The Whistler and His Dog" by the Paragon Ragtime Orchestra. The instrumental "Beautiful Beulah" comes from the soundtrack of the 1963 film, "Summer Magic." ❯❯ Exposition Hall replicates the look of the 1877 Adelphi Hotel in Saratoga, New York. ❯❯ The Crystal Palace combines the glass dome of San Francisco's 1879 Conservatory of Flowers with the greenhouse interior of London's Crystal Palace, an 1851 exhibition hall. ❯❯ The 850-foot-long street rises about 6 feet from the train station to the castle.

Walt Disney World Railroad

With stations at Main Street U.S.A., Frontierland and Mickey's Toontown Fair, this leisurely 1.5-mile trip offers a foot-free way to get around the park. The streetcar-styled cars are pulled by four steam locomotives, which chug along at 10 to 12 miles per hour. As you ride you get a heapin' helpin' of banjo pickin' and a folksy narrator. "Be on the lookout!" he warns along Adventureland. "You never can tell when a man-eatin' tiger, or train-chasin' tiger, might show up!"

The locomotives are actual antiques, assembled by Philadelphia's Baldwin Locomotive Works between 1916 and 1928. They were used by Mexico's United Railway of the Yucatan to haul passengers, jute, sisal and sugar cane.

20 min. Capacity: apx. 360. Avg. wait: 5 min. early morning, 10 min. peak afternoon. No service during parades, fireworks or thunderstorms. No Disney rental strollers; folding strollers are OK. ECV users must transfer. Handheld video captioning available. Debuted: 1971.

FUN FINDS ❶ Some characters have lost their luggage on the train. Items such as Pluto's bone, Capt. Hook's hook and Chip 'n' Dale's acorns are stored on shelves in the lower lobby of the Main Street depot. ❷ The red bridge between Main Street and Frontierland is from the old Florida Flagler line. It was originally two tracks wide. ❸ Some of the trees past the Indian village have charred trunks from falling Wishes fireworks.

Above: The Walter E. Disney locomotive blows off steam. **Below:** Indians build a fire along the track.

▶ Sit on the right for the best views, which include a couple of glances backstage.

Cinderella Castle. The two tallest spires, as well as the tops of several turrets and towers, are coated in real gold leaf.

Cinderella Castle

One of the most photographed buildings in the world, Cinderella Castle has its picture taken 30,000 times a day. And no wonder. A symbol of imagination, innocence and romance, the icon is not only a world-famous landmark but also quite a piece of fantasy architecture.

Its design combines the looks of a medieval fortress and a Renaissance castle. The heavy lower walls have sawtoothed battlements like those used to hide artillery atop 11th-century stone forts. The top has the turrets, spires and Gothic trim of French castles built in the 14th, 15th and 16th centuries. Accents include 13 winged gargoyles and a portcullis, an iron grate over the entrance

FUN FACTS ›› Two of the mosaic faces are those of real people. The page holding the slipper has the profile of castle artist Herb Ryman. His assistant is John Hench, who helped create the Walt Disney World master plan. **››** Until 2006 the castle's apartment was used as a radio room, a switchboard center and, finally, a dressing room for performers on the Castle Forecourt Stage.

that appears ready to drop at a moment's notice.

Though it's really a 189-foot steel frame covered in fiberglass, the castle appears to be a 300-foot-tall stone fortress. It was designed to be seen from a mile away, so guests arriving on ferries and monorails can spot it with anticipation.

Inside is a more traditional piece of art. Created out of 500,000 bits of glass in 500 colors, a five-panel mosaic tells the Cinderella story. The 15- by 10-foot arches were crafted by a team led by acclaimed artist Hanns-Joachim Scharff,* based on a design by Disney's Dorothea Redmond.

The mosaic took two years to make. Redmond's paintings were redrawn to life-size proportions on heavyweight brown craft paper. These images were cut up into 50 or so jigsaw-puzzle-like pieces. Scharff used smooth and uneven glass, a third of the pieces fused with silver and gold. Many were hand cut and shaped with a power grindstone. Thin glass strips were used to outline hands

---

* Scharff was a fascinating man in his own right. Born in Germany in 1907, he became a Luftwaffe interrogator of captured American Air Force fighter pilots during World War II. Still considered one of the best interrogators in the history of armed combat, he treated his prisoners with kindness and respect, which led them to unwittingly reveal pieces of military information which fit into a bigger strategic picture for the Germans. Scharff saved the lives of six U.S. prisoners from execution, by proving their innocence to the Gestapo. At one time, in fact, the Gestapo was investigating him for collaboration with the enemy because of his unusual treatment of prisoners. After the war Scharff met and befriended many of his former prisoners in the U.S. Scharff soon moved to New York, where out of a pre-war hobby he started a mosaic studio. A Neiman Marcus order of 5,000 mosaic tables gave the artist the funds to move to California and set up a new mosaic studio, where he was credited with introducing the smooth-surface Venetian glass form of mosaic art to this country in 1952. Scharff died in 1992, but his studio continues under the stewardship of his daughter-in-law, Monika, who started her mosaic apprenticeship on these five Cinderella murals. Scharff is still widely respected today, especially by U.S. military vets who argue against the torture of terrorist suspects.

▶ **Three windows of the castle apartment peer out from the right rear, halfway up.**

and faces. Multihued rods were chopped crosswise for other effects.

The interior also includes a restaurant and gift shop, security rooms, three elevators and an apartment that, though planned for the use of the Disney family, remained unfinished until 2006. Today it's the Cinderella Castle Suite, a fourth-floor foyer, salon, bedroom and bath that's often offered to guests.

The 650-square-foot suite combines Renaissance style with digital-age convenience. Above a fireplace, a portrait of Cinderella magically changes into a flat-screen television. The bedchamber includes a 17th-century desk with inlaid computer hookups. Bathroom sinks resemble wash basins; faucets look like hand pumps. A cut-stone floor recalls the castle mosaic.

Guests access the suite through a door in the breezeway. An elevator takes them to a foyer decorated with original movie concept art by the famed Mary Blair and a display case holding, of course, a glass slipper.

Above: Visiting from Toronto, Madison Greco and Shelby Devine, both 5, view the mosaic. **Below:** Artist Hanns Scharff compares a reference painting to his mosaic for Cinderella Castle, 1971.

FUN FINDS ❶ In the mosaic, stepsister Drusilla's face is green with envy, while Anastasia's is red with anger. ❷ Scharff and Redmond "signed" the mosaic's bottom-right corner. ❸ The columns alongside the mosaic are topped with molded sculptures of Cinderella's animal friends. ❹ Her wishing well is to the right of the castle, on a walkway to Tomorrowland. ❺ Her fountain is behind the castle to the left. Toddlers who stand in front of it see the princess wearing her crown.

HANNS-CLAUDIUS AND MONIKA SCHARFF

▶ Want to eat in the castle? Make your reservations months in advance.

Castle shows

DREAM ALONG WITH MICKEY When Donald Duck doesn't believe in dreams, Mickey Mouse and Goofy convince him otherwise in this 20-minute song-and-dance revue in front of the castle. An explosion brings forth Maleficent, the evil fairy from 1959's "Sleeping Beauty." "Nobody really believes in dreams any longer," she bellows. But Mickey, and the crowd, stand up to her. The cast also includes Minnie Mouse; princesses Aurora (Sleeping Beauty), Cinderella, Snow White and their princes; Peter Pan, Wendy, Captain Hook and Mr. Smee; and a dozen supporting players. Songs include "Some Day My Prince Will Come," "A Dream is a Wish Your Heart Makes" and "A Pirate's Life." *Debuted: 2006.*

LET'S HAVE A BALL Lady Lucinda and bumbling sidekick Simon lead young guests in a conga, freeze dance, Simon Says game and, for the finale, some waltz moves presided over by, as the narrator says, "the most well-rested royals in all of Fantasyland," Princess Aurora and Prince Phillip. Kids can meet the couple afterward. Held at the rear of the castle, the 20-minute show is presented about six times a day. Elementary-age girls especially like it. Show times are at Guest Relations. *Debuted: 2006.*

STORYTIME WITH BELLE The heroine from 1991's "Beauty and the Beast" is just a few feet away from you in this cozy show. Tucked into the secluded, shady Fairytale Garden Theater (along the walkway between Main Street and the Mad Tea Party), her stage sits just a couple of feet off the ground, in front of only four rows of benches. Six children and one adult join Belle onstage to act out her story. To give your child the best chance of getting picked, sit to the far left directly in front of the stage steps and have your child yell enthusiastic answers to Belle's early questions ("Who did I live with in my quiet little vil-

Top: Cinderella and Prince Charming in Dream Along with Mickey. **Above:** A court attendant leads future princesses in a freeze dance in "Let's Have a Ball."

lage?"). Sit at the far right to be among the first in line for Belle's autograph when the show ends. *15 min. Capacity: Apx. 75 seats, plus standing room for another 50. Arrive 30 min. early to pick your seats, 15 min. early to get any seat. Guests may stay in wheelchairs, ECVs. Best ages: 3–10. Debuted: 1999.*

▶ See Dream Along with Mickey after dark. Stage lights and pyro add theatrical flair.

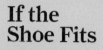

If the Shoe Fits

The classic rags-to-riches tale, Cinderella got its start as a **Chinese fable.** In the 9th-century "Yeh-Shen," a stepmother and two stepsisters humiliate a hard-working girl. But when a 10-foot fish gives her food, a beautiful dress and tiny slippers*, she gains confidence.

Often sweeping the fireplace, the girl gets so covered in ash her sisters call her Cinderella — the cinder girl — in **Charles Perrault's** French version of the tale, written to entertain the 17th century court of Louis XIV. When a king wants his son to wed, he has the prince invite all the land's maidens to a two-night ball. Cinderella's stepmom won't let her go, but then her fairy godmother (the spirit of her real mother) appears. Waving a magic wand, she turns a pumpkin into a coach, mice into horses, rats and lizards to footmen... and the girl's ragged dress into a ball gown, with glass slippers. Cinderella *can* go to the ball, the godmother says, but she must be home by midnight, as

* In ancient China tiny feet were a status symbol. The practice of foot binding started with palace dancers, but was soon used by wealthy parents to fashion their daughters for marriage. The painful process began when a girl was about 5 years old. Each foot was wrapped in a long bandage (compressing her arches and bending under all of her smaller toes) then jammed into a shoe far too small. As the girl grew, her feet could not. Eventually they would deform into hoof-like clubs just a few inches long.

that's when the magic wears off. The first night the girl mesmerizes the prince but never tells him her name. She leaves before midnight, but the next night stays until the clock strikes twelve. Rushing out, she drops her glass slipper, which the prince recovers.

Determined to find his love, the prince orders his Grand Duke (chief of staff) to try the slipper on every girl in the kingdom. On Cinderella's foot it slides on perfectly.

The story got bloody when Germany's **Brothers Grimm** published their own version, "Aschenputtel," in 1812. When the slipper won't fit the stepsisters, their mom has them slice off their heels and toes and try again. During Cinderella's wedding, birds peck out the sisters' eyes.

Disney's 1950 film gave Perrault's tale new life. Disney cleaned up the plot, added a supporting cast of animals and scored it all with catchy songs and doubled the drama. The stepmother locks Cinderella in her room when the Grand Duke arrives, but her mice pals unlock it. The stepmom trips the Duke so he drops the slipper and breaks it, but Cinderella pulls out the matching shoe from her pocket.

Walt Disney produced the first animated Cinderella in 1922, when his short-lived Laugh-O-Grams Co. used the fable for an **Alice comedy,** a silent cartoon with a live-action girl. **Betty Boop** danced her way through a 1934 color cartoon, "Poor Cinderella."

Rodgers and Hammerstein's 1957 musical "Cinderella" is still the most popular special in television history. Starring Julie Andrews, it drew 71 percent of all Americans with a TV set. It was remade as a colorful charmer with Lesley Ann Warren in 1965, and again as a colorblind clunker with Brandy in 1997.

Cinderella was, in essence, a boy in 1960's **"Cinderfella."** Jerry Lewis learns geeks, too, have charms when a Disney-like Cinderella pops out of the past to creepily flirt with him: "If I weren't a married woman," she purrs, "Grrrr!"

Hollywood ignored Cinderella for decades, but in the '90s she was back and always in charge. In 1998's **"Ever After,"** the princess-to-be (Drew Barrymore) escapes from her step family and enlightens the prince about social policy. A feisty "Ella" breaks out into Queen's "Somebody to Love" in the 2004 musical **"Ella Enchanted."** And she's no passive patsy in 2004's **"A Cinderella Story."** After dressing as Cinderella for a high-school ball, Hilary Duff gains the courage to simply walk out on her step family as well as her quarterback prince, until he decides to join her. Then they're off to their dream college: Princeton.

Cinderella's Golden Carrousel

A real antique, this 1917 merry-go-round was one of the fanciest of its day. One of only four five-row carrousels built by the Philadelphia Toboggan* Co., this "Liberty" model was adorned with carved flowers, medieval weapons and patriotic images. Its 72 hard-maple horses and six chariots rode under a lavish cresting featuring Miss Liberty, a crowned blonde in a robe and sandals. Craftsmen built five sizes of horses, and placed the largest and most ornate on the outside rim.

Built for the Detroit Palace Garden Park in Michigan, the ride moved in the 1920s to Maplewood, N.J.'s Olympic Park, where it stayed until Disney bought it in 1967. To follow Walt Disney's belief that every rider should feel like a hero, the company painted each horse white, repositioned its legs so it canters

* At the time, the word for a wooden roller coaster

Top: Visiting from Toronto, Elise Meiers, 2, rides the carrousel with her mom, Terri. **Above:** Miss Liberty.

instead of prances and took out the chariots to add more horses. It designated the steed with a gold ribbon on its tail (No. 37) as Cinderella's and themed everything to the princess, repainting the carrousel — including the patriotic pieces — gold, pink, purple and blue.

Today's 87 horses are fiberglass replicas, but one of the original wooden chariots has returned. Reinstalled in 1997, it offers the only truly antique seats on the ride.

By the way, the outside horses move at 7 mph; those on the inside at 3.5 mph.

2 min. Capacity: 91. Avg. wait: 5 min. early morning, 30 min. peak afternoon. Must be ambulatory. Debuted: 1971.

▶ Look up, down and to your left to see the original carvings and structural pieces.

Shopping guide

APPAREL Character Costumes: The Emporium *(Main Street U.S.A.)*, Tinker Bell's Treasures *(adjacent to Cinderella's Castle, Fantasyland)* and County Bounty *(Mickey's Toontown Fair)* have princess and other costumes. Pirate's Bazaar *(at Pirates of the Caribbean, Adventureland)* has the most pirate-costume items. **Children's Wear:** The best kids and babywear collections are at Disney Clothiers *(Main Street U.S.A.)*, Pooh's Thotful Shop *(at The Many Adventures of Winnie the Pooh, Fantasyland)* and County Bounty *(Mickey's Toontown Fair)*. **Fashion:** Disney Clothiers *(Main Street U.S.A.)* is the Magic Kingdom's main fashion store. Island Supply *(across from Swiss Family Treehouse, Adventureland)* has beach-themed apparel and purses. **Footwear:** Disney Clothiers *(Main Street U.S.A.)*, Island Supply *(across from Swiss Family Treehouse, Adventureland)* and Sir Mickey's *(adjacent to Cinderella Castle, Fantasyland)* sell sandals. **Sports Apparel:** Disney Clothiers *(Main Street U.S.A.)* is the park's sportswear shop. **T-shirts and headwear:** The Emporium *(Main Street U.S.A.)* has the most T-shirts. Attraction T-shirts are at the Briar Patch *(at Splash Mountain, Frontierland)*, Buzz Star Command *(indoors, at the exit to Buzz Lightyear's Space Ranger Spin, Tomorrowland)*, Fantasy Faire *(at Mickey's PhilharMagic, Fantasyland)* and the Space Mountain Shop *(at Space Mountain, Tomorrowland)*. Hats and caps are everywhere; monogrammed Mickey ears are sold only at The Chapeau (Main Street U.S.A.) and Sir Mickey's *(adjacent to Cinderella Castle, Fantasyland)*.

ART Fine Art: The King's Gallery *(inside Cinderella Castle)* sells Lexan china figures, glass art, swords and paintings. Other china figurines are at Uptown Jewelers *(Main Street U.S.A.)* and The Yankee Trader (Liberty Square). Crystal Arts *(Main Street U.S.A.)* and La Princesa de Cristal *(Caribbean Plaza, Adventureland)* offer crystal and glass figurines. **Posters and Prints:** The King's Gallery *(inside Cinderella Castle)* has the park's best poster and print collection. Small prints start at under $10.

BOOKS Disney titles are available at The Emporium *(Main Street U.S.A.)* and at County Bounty *(Mickey's Toontown Fair)*. Classic Pooh children's books are at Pooh's Thotful Shop *(at The Many Adventures of Winnie the Pooh, Fantasyland)*. Heritage House *(Liberty Square)* has United States history titles, while the Briar Patch *(at Splash Mountain, Frontierland)* has a small but satifactual selection of Brer Rabbit and Uncle Remus books.

CANDY The Main Street Confectionery *(Main Street U.S.A.)* makes its own fudge, Rice Krispy treats, candy and caramel apples, cotton candy and peanut brittle. The treats are also sold at County Bounty *(Mickey's Toontown Fair)* and Prairie Outpost & Supply *(Frontierland)*.

CHRISTMAS Ye Olde Christmas Shoppe *(Liberty Square)* is the Magic Kingdom's Christmas corner. You'll find "Nightmare Before Christmas" items at Madame Leota's Cart *(to the left of the Haunted Mansion, Liberty Square)*.

HOUSEWARES The most kitchen and cooking wares are at the Main Street Market House *(Main Street U.S.A.)* and The Yankee Trader *(Liberty Square)*. Pooh's Thotful Shop *(at The Many Adventures of Winnie the Pooh, Fantasyland)* has a few Pooh items.

JEWELRY AND WATCHES Uptown Jewelers *(Main Street U.S.A.)* draws personalized sketches of Disney characters and reduces them onto watch dials. The store also sells more conventional watches, fine jewelry, best-friend charms, name necklaces, birthstone necklaces and earrings. You'll also find watches at Disney Clothiers *(Main Street U.S.A.)*. The Emporium *(Main Street U.S.A.)* and Tinker Bell's Treasures *(adjacent to Cinderella's Castle, Fantasyland)* have costume jewelry. Island Supply *(across from Swiss Family Treehouse, Adventureland)* has casual beach-themed jewelry. Bwana Bob's cart *(at Adventureland's main entrance)* and Pirate's Bazaar *(at Pirates of the Caribbean, Adventureland)* have shell, skull and pirate jewelry.

PET PRODUCTS The Magic Kingdom's largest selection of pet products is at Engine Co. 71, the Firehouse Gift Station *(Main Street U.S.A.)*. It carries bandanas, bowls, clothes, collars, dishes, leashes, toys and treats.

PINS The Magic Kingdom's pin central is Frontier Trading Post *(Frontierland)*. Exposition Hall and Uptown Jewelers *(both Main Street U.S.A.)* have decent selections.

TOYS The big toy store is The Emporium *(Main Street U.S.A.)*. Among the lures: princess dolls, action figures and a wide range of plushies. County Bounty *(Mickey's Toontown Fair)* has just about every other Walt Disney World plaything. Pooh's Thotful Shop *(at The Many Adventures of Winnie the Pooh, Fantasyland)* carries Pooh toys and plushies. Pirate's Bazaar *(at Pirates of the Caribbean, Adventureland)* has a treasure trove of Pirates of the Caribbean toys. Pal Mickey is at Main Street Cinema *(Main Street U.S.A.)*.

© DISNEY

Mickey's PhilharMagic

✓ The most fun 3-D movie made to date, Mickey's PhilharMagic gives you the same delight you get from flipping through a Viewmaster — marvelous 3-D views that fill your field of vision. But here the scenes are videos, filled with beloved songs and characters. There's nothing scary for kids.

Many items seem to fly over your head, others hang in front of you. In-theater effects help immerse you in the action — you smell a fresh-baked pie, feel champagne corks pop, and get spritzed with water. Strobes flash when Donald kisses an eel, and when Simba's "in the spotlight" so are some audience guests.

The plot? When Mickey Mouse plans to conduct a magical orchestra, Donald insists on trying it himself. When his scheme fails, he (and you) are sent on a madcap adventure through the best scenes from Disney's best musicals, reprising songs such as "Be Our Guest," "Part of Your World," "I Just Can't Wait to be King" and "A Whole New World."

The animation is delightful, especially the first three scene transitions. The "Be Our Guest" feast falls into the "Sorcerer's Apprentice" workshop... where the water from the brooms' buckets washes into the sea of Ariel's grotto... where the sunlight at the surface turns into the sun of Simba's Africa. The following "Lion King" se-

quence is, as in the 1994 film, a kaleidoscope of flat 2-D cutouts, but here twisting and turning with 3-D realism.

Actor John Corbett compares the show to another Disney classic. "I loved the Tower of Terror," he says. "I did it three times. But after you get that thrill you don't think about it again. I'm still thinking about PhilharMagic. I've never experienced anything like it."

12 min. Capacity: 450. Avg. wait: 10 min. early morning, 30 min. peak afternoon. Fastpass available. Guests may remain in wheelchairs, ECVs. Assistive listening, reflective captioning. Debuted: 2003.

FUN FINDS ❶ There's a murmur in the theater crowd even when there's no one there. Faint audience noise plays from the loudspeakers. ❷ As Goofy walks behind the crowd, he hums the "Mickey Mouse March" and steps on a cat ("Sorry little feller!"). ❸ The instruments gasp when Donald grabs the flute, watch as he throws it into the audience and laugh when it whops him on the head. ❹ When Lumiere rolls out to you he's on a tomato that wasn't there a moment earlier. It arrived when Donald blocked your view to ask, "Where's my hat?" ❺ Ariel giggles as she swims onscreen. ❻ When a crocodile sends Donald flying (on the line

Above: Donald Duck searches for the Sorcerer's Hat in the Beauty and the Beast dining hall

▶ The best seats are in the middle rear, directly in front of the main projector.

"Everybody look right!") you hear him circle behind you before he returns to the spotlight. **7** A pull chain falls into view as Simba sings "I'm standing in the spotlight!" Zazu pulls it to turn the light off. **8** Jasmine waves to a guest as she starts to sing. **9** When she and Aladdin wave goodbye to Donald, so does their carpet. **10** Once Mickey regains control of the orchestra, the flute wakes up the tuba then trips Donald into it. **11** As you exit past the gift shop, Goofy says goodbye to you in five languages ("Sigh-a-NAIR-ee!").

CLASSIC DISNEY Enchanted as part of a spell on their owner, all of a castle's household objects — including the candelabrum — are alive in 1991's **"Beauty and the Beast."** When they get a visitor, they put on a floor show as they prepare a meal. In 1940's **"Fantasia,"** sorcerer's apprentice Mickey gets out of washing a floor by putting on his mentor's magical hat and casting a spell on a broom. At first it works: the broom marches out to a fountain, fills its bucket with water, marches back in and splashes it on the floor. Unfortunately, it never stops, and the workshop soon begins to fill with water. Desperate, Mickey chops the broom into

pieces, but each splinter turns into its own marching, splashing broom. Teenager Ariel collects every human object that floats down to her in 1989's **"The Little Mermaid."** Fish friend Flounder keeps her company, but she wants to be where the people are. A young cub just can't wait to be the king of beasts in 1994's **"The Lion King."** Simba's brushing up on looking down, but that's not enough to convince his father's advisor, the hornbill Zazu. In 1953's **"Peter Pan"** a boy can fly... and his friends can, too, if they get a sprinkling of dust from his pixie Tinker Bell. One night he convinces the children of London's Darling family to go with him to Never Land, a world where kids never grow up. "Here we go!" he yells, and they all soar over the moonlit city. They stop for a moment on the minute hand of Big Ben, the city's clock tower. **"Aladdin,"** a young streetwise commoner in 18th-century Iraq, falls in love with princess Jasmine in Disney's 1992 hit. To win her heart he disguises himself as "Prince Ali" and shows her a new, fantastic point of view as they ride on his magic carpet. Out to destroy his plans is Iago, the cranky red parrot of the king's advisor. **"The Mickey Mouse Club"** weekday TV show was a 1950s staple. Every kid knew the last line of its theme song: "M-I-C... See ya real soon!... K-E-Y... Why? Because we like you!... M-O-U-S-E."

FUN FACT » The screen starts out 16 feet high and 40 feet wide. It expands to 28 by 150.

Déjà Donald

With just a few exceptions (for example, his humming of "Be Our Guest"), Donald Duck's lines come from the master audio tracks of animated shorts of the 1930s and 1940s, as recorded more than 60 years ago by the original voice of Donald, Clarence "Ducky" Nash.

DONALD'S LINE...	COMES FROM...
"OH BOY OH BOY!," said when he realizes Mickey has left the Sorcerer's Hat unattended...	1942's "Sky Trooper," said when he realizes he can train to be a pilot if he peels some potatoes.
"ATTEN... TION!," said to the PhilharMagic orchestra as he begins to conduct it...	1940's "Fire Chief," said to nephews Huey, Dewey and Louie as he teaches them to be firemen.
"I'LL SHOW YOU WHO'S BOSS!," shouted at an unruly flute before he tosses it into the audience...	1941's "Early to Bed," shouted at a noisy alarm clock before he tosses it across his bedroom.
"WHO DID THAT?," said after the flute returns from its flight over the audience and hits him on the head...	1941's "Orphan's Benefit," said after a boy blows his nose during Donald's recitation of "Little Boy Blue."
"BLIBA-BLIBA-BLIBA," blubbered after the Sorcerer's brooms throw buckets of water on him...	1937's "Don Donald," blubbered after early girlfriend Donna Duck pushes him into a fountain.
"YOO-HOO!," yelled up to Ariel so the mermaid will slow down and wait up for him...	1940's "Window Washers," yelled down to Pluto so the dog will wake up and help him wash windows.
"NOTHIN' TO IT!," said after Peter Pan sprinkles Tinker Bell's pixie dust on him, allowing him to fly...	1944's "Commando Duck," said after he learns to bend his knees when he lands, allowing him to parachute.
"FASTER! FASTER!," said to his magic carpet while flying it through the narrow streets of Agrabah...	1937's "Don Donald," said by Donna Duck to Donald, while riding in his car through the desert.
"AH, PHOOEY!," said at the end of the show, after he falls through the back wall of the theater...	1942's "Donald Gets Drafted," said at the draft board, after he learns he has to pass a physical.

Guests on Peter Pan's Flight board miniature pirate galleons that fly over London and off to Never Land

Peter Pan's Flight

Originally built for Disneyland in 1955, this ride is timeless in its charm. Flying in a single-seat pirate ship, you swoop through scenes from 1953's "Peter Pan."

You start off in the upstairs nursery of the Darling home. As daughter Wendy reads her brothers a bedtime story, Peter beckons them (and you) to fly off with him to Never Land. Once Tinker Bell sprinkles you with pixie dust, you soar... over the Darling's back-yard and then the twinkling streets of London. The kids fly ahead of you; you can see their shadows on the moon.

Soon you come to Never Land, a lush island of mountains, waterfalls, flow-ers, even a volcano. But Captain Hook waits for you on his ship down below. "Fire, Mr. Smee!" he commands.

Rounding a corner, you pass the Lost Boys, dressed as animals, around a campfire. Three young sirens rest on the rocks of Mermaid Lagoon. At the In-dian Encampment, princess Tiger Lily sits with her dad and four braves. Then comes Skull Rock, a skeleton-faced cliff.

Next you set out to sea, to Hook's ship, where the pirate has kidnapped the Darling kids and the Lost Boys. Pe-ter is dueling the Captain on the mainsail; the crew is making Wendy walk the plank. As the ticking crocodile hints, however, Hook's time is up.

As you round a corner, Peter stands triumphantly at the ship's helm, with Wendy and her brothers alongside. Where's Hook? Behind the boat, in the water. "Help me Mr. Smee! Help me!" he calls, as he straddles the croc's snapping jaws. As you near the exit, a mural shows the ship again. Coated with pixie dust, it's flying the kids back home.

3 min. Avg. wait: 5 min. early morning, 90 min. peak afternoon. Fastpass available. Must be ambulatory. Handheld captioning. Debuted: 1971 (Disneyland, 1955).

FLIGHTS, FIGHTS AND TIGHTS Based on a 1904 play by English author James Matthew Barrie, Disney's 1953 film "Peter Pan" follows the adventures of a boy who refuses to grow up. One night he arrives at the London home of the Darling family and convinces daughter Wendy and her brothers John (who wears a top hat) and Michael to fly off with him to Never Land, a remote island where children don't age. Sprinkled with magic dust from moody pixie Tinker Bell, the kids join Peter's gang of Lost Boys (each lost by his parents when he fell out of his pram) for a series of adventures.

▶ Go first thing in the morning or use a Fastpass. The afternoon wait can be an hour.

"My favorite ride is Peter Pan's Flight. Of course, I always liked Peter best." — Maureen "Marsha Brady" McCormick

It's a Small World

✓ Filled with colorful dolls, fantastical animals, imaginative sets and layers of abstract art, this whimsical indoor boat ride promotes international brotherhood as it takes you on a trip around the world. Part baby mobile, part musical fantasy, part political statement, part pop art parade, It's a Small World has something for nearly everyone.

A true Disney classic, the beautifully restored attraction works on at least three levels.

First, it's terrific for children. To infants it's a world of their dreams — an exciting journey filled with happy, goofy faces and funny animals, accented with gentle music and the largest crib mobiles they've ever seen. To preschoolers it's a place to bond with their parents, as there's no narration and lots of time to chat ("Where are we now, mom?" "Hawaii!"). Artistic older kids will like the ride's conceptual playfulness and explosion of colors.

Second, it has a great message — honoring diversity while celebrating shared humanity. Color schemes underline regional differences, and each doll, with a skin tone that reflects its homeland, wears authentic cultural clothing. Yet the faces are more similar than different, and though the dolls speak different languages, they all sing the same song.

In today's times, the message is also one of reassurance. "It's a Small World

© DISNEY

It's a Small World's finale unites the world's children

portrays the world as we would like it to be," says Imagineer Jason Surrell. "It's a childlike view, yes, one which is pure and innocent and optimistic."

The ride also succeeds as a work of art. As created by illustrator Mary Blair — the artist behind the vibrant backgrounds of films such as "Alice in Wonderland" — the sets alone form a stylized pop-art collage that communicates a simple yet sophisticated innocence.

There is no color unused, no shading within a color. The shapes are both organic and geometric. The pieces combine cartoonish styles (such as the giant squiggle that forms the Swiss Alps) with cultural motifs (i.e., the patterns on the Mexican pyramids).

The elaborate costumes rival those of a Broadway show. Each is its own mix of embroidery, feathers, lace, satin, sequins and ribbons. There's nearly every type of hat and shoe known to man.

FUN FACTS)) The ride includes 289 human dolls and 210 animals and toys. **))** The dolls sing in English, Italian, Japanese, Spanish and Swedish. **))** The dolls wear 2,296 garments. **))** There are four types of Americans: cowboy, Hawaiian, Inuit and Native American. **))** Being a Small World ride operator was named one of the "Fifty Jobs Worse Than Yours" in the 2004 book by that title.

▶ Take your cruise before 10 a.m., when the wait rarely exceeds 5 minutes.

At home in the African jungle of It's a Small World, a bright-eyed hippo lets pick-pick birds rest on its back

A WORLD CRUISE You start off in Europe, a two-minute sensory overload filled with dozens, dozens, and more dozens of dancing, singing, swinging, marching, unicycling, even yodeling dolls and creatures. Then you cross Asia, a trip through oranges and yellows that passes belly dancers, Greek and Russian folk dancers, even an Indian snake charmer. Above you are Arabian flying carpets and Chinese kites. Cool blues and greens lead you into Africa, a hip jungle of wild animals diggin' a Dixieland band.

Chilean penguins welcome you to the Western hemisphere. Latin America is an orange-hot party spot. On your left it's Rio's Carnivale; on your right Mexico's Day of the Dead. Next is the blue and green Brazilian rainforest, a world of twirly-headed birds and nary a doll at all. As the rain falls (symbolized by hanging strips of clear plastic), a crocodile and jaguar bring out umbrellas.

Polynesian percussion takes you to the green and purple South Pacific (Australia, Easter Island, Hawaii and New Zealand) and finally you arrive back in Europe as all the world's children, now all dressed in the same pastel palette, sing in unison. Where exactly are you? Denmark's Tivoli Gardens, the world's oldest amusement park that's famous for its roller coaster, sparkling white lights — and as the inspiration for Disneyland.

Completely renovated in 2005, the ride now features smoother robotics, remastered music and modern lighting. Out front, a two-story clock comes to life every 15 minutes.

11 min. Capacity: 600. Avg. wait: 5 min. early morning, 60 min. peak afternoon.

"I WANT TO GET OFF!"
Despite its qualities, It's a Small World is so iconic many people love to poke fun at it. In "Selma's Choice," a 1993 episode of **"The Simpsons"** television program, Aunt Selma takes Bart and Lisa to the Disney World-like Duff Gardens, a park where every attraction is themed around Duff Beer. When they board the indoor boat ride Little Land of Duff, they find hundreds of manic dolls singing the one-verse theme song "Duff Beer for me, Duff Beer for you, I'll have a Duff, You have one, too!"

"I want to get off!" Bart yells. "You can't," says Selma. "We have five more continents to visit!" After Bart dares Lisa to take a drink of the water, she begins hallucinating that the dolls are coming after her. "They're all around me! There's no way out! No way out, I tell you! I am the lizard queen!"

Even Disney makes jokes. Some **Jungle Cruise** skippers tell their guests that any children left on board will be taken to It's a Small World, have their feet glued to the floor and be forced to sing the theme song "over and over for the rest of their lives." Small World dolls help destroy the theater during the **MuppetVision 3-D** finale at Disney-MGM Studios. The song is also dissed in the 1994 film **"The Lion King."** After evil lion Scar takes over the kingdom, Zazu the hornbill begins to sing "Nobody Knows the Trouble I've Seen." When the new king demands something more upbeat, the bird chirps "It's a small world after all; It's a small world after all..." "No, no, no!" cries Scar. "Anything but that!"

SECOND VERSE, SAME AS THE FIRST Lyrically, there's only one verse* and the chorus is simply three takes of "It's a small world after all" followed by "It's a small, small world." Musically, it's just ten notes that repeat twice, four that repeat four times, then seven that repeat three times. On the ride, though, the song "It's a Small World" isn't all that bad. Though it plays constantly, it's usually as an instrumental and sometimes just a rhythm track. When the dolls sing, half the time they're not speaking English. You hear the words "small world" only about every 30 seconds. * *The song actually has two verses, but only the first is used on the ride.*

▶ Sit in the front row of the boat. You'll see more details and have more legroom.

ECV users must transfer to a wheelchair. Handheld captioning. No flash photography. Debuted: 1971 (Disneyland 1966), refurbished 2005.

FUN FINDS Europe: ❶ A high-wire unicyclist crosses above you. ❷ A purple-haired clown floats in a wicker balloon basket. ❸ A diamond-eyed pink poodle wags its tongue as it watches the can-can girls. ❹ A British Bobby guards the Tower of London with a cork gun. ❺ One of Big Ben's hands spins backward. ❻ A Beefeater blinks as he guards the Tower. ❼ A bagpiper drones out the song. ❽ Three geese wag their tails and quack to the theme song. ❾ Crazy-eyed Don Quixote tilts at a windmill while his dismayed pal Sancho Panza looks on. ❿ An ax-wielding yodeler warbles the song. Asia: ⓫ Balkan folk dancers jig in a circle. ⓬ Three Russian boushka dancers perform at the Kremlin. ⓭ Israeli newlyweds dance in a tent. ⓮ One flying carpet has a steering wheel. Africa: ⓯ Cleopatra winks at you as she lies on a barge. ⓰ The eyes of three tongue-wagging frogs spring out of their sockets. ⓱ A pink elephant hoists a Dixieland trio. Latin America: ⓲ A pink pig piñata hangs above you. ⓳ Three butterflies flutter on a flower cart. ⓴ A horse and a cow sing along. ㉑ So does a ball-necked yellow, orange and turquoise ostrich. ㉒ Three singing basket people ride basket horses. ㉓ A saguaro cactus plays a guitar. Brazilian rain forest: ㉔ Three wind-up birds spin their cranks. South Pacific: ㉕ Eight lace-winged butterflies float above you. ㉖ Two purple Moais stand on Easter Island. Tivoli Gardens: ㉗ Four sparkly-eyed girls hold flowered umbrellas as they float above your boat. ㉘ Eleven flowered clouds turn like fans in the sky. ㉙ Two Asian plate spinners sing and dance as they perform. ㉚ A German band performs on top of a riverboat. ㉛ A jewel-eyed acrobat is hanging from an overhead unicyclist. ㉜ A bicycle act performs above you on a high wire.

BLAME IT ON RIO
The history of the ride dates back to 1941. Working on location in Brazil, Disney illustrator Mary Blair created dozens of concept paintings for the animated film "The Three Caballeros," which told the story of Donald Duck's visit to Central and South America. Filled with color, the abstract, collage-style pieces had a vibrancy rarely seen in commercial art. "Brazil is really a very colorful country," Blair said. "The jungle… the costumes and native folk art are really bright and happy."

Twenty-two years later, Pepsi-Cola wanted Disney to create its children-themed UNICEF pavilion at the upcoming 1964 World's Fair, which was only nine months away. "One of our executives actually declined," says Disney Imagineer Jason Surrell. "Walt found out about it and said 'I'm the one who makes these decisions. Tell Pepsi we'll do it.'"

Needing ideas quickly, Walt remembered Blair's work from "Caballeros." Though she had left the company in 1953, Blair returned to create dozens of collages of wallpaper cuttings, cellophane and acrylic paint. Disney animator Marc Davis added in his own playful mechanical animals. All of it was personally approved by Walt Disney. "Mr. Disney treats it like his baby," Pepsi President Donald Kendall told the New York Times, "because it is."

As for the dolls, Blair and Davis created three-dimensional versions of the "Mary Blair kid," a child with a large head and simple, smiling face that Blair had earlier used in the "Caballeros" sister film "Saludos Amigos" (1943) as well as 1950s advertisements for such products as Dutch Boy Paint and Meadow Gold Ice Cream.

At first, each of the doll groups was programmed to sing its own national anthem — the U.K. dolls sang "God Save the Queen," the French children "La Marseillaise," the Spanish kids the "Marcha Real." When that sounded awful, Disney songwriters Richard and Robert Sherman created a roundelay — a short, simple song with a catchy refrain that all the dolls could sing in unison.

To move its guests from scene to scene, Disney decided on a waterway, developing a new flume system that used tiny water jets to propel a series of free-floating, open-top boats.

The result was sensational. Though the World's Fair had more than 50 pavilions that charged a fee, It's a Small World accounted for 20 percent of the fair's total paid admissions (a Small World ticket cost 95 cents for adults, 65 cents for children). Guests voted the ride the "Most Charming" attraction at the fair, which drew 51 million people over its two-year run.

The ride even spawned its own non-Disney merchandise, including UNICEF-approved toy dolls that were sold by the Women's International League for Peace and Freedom in a fund-raising effort against the Vietnam War.

▶ **Place your children on the outside of your row so you don't block their view.**

Dumbo the Flying Elephant

✓ Cynics who dismiss this as just another carnival ride need to wake up and smell the elephant. As anyone with an inner child knows, *this is Dumbo*, the sympathetic star of Disney's touching 1941 classic. His story is so sweet, his face so cute, he transforms this basic attraction into something special.

But Dumbo or not, this is no midway ride. It's clean, free from grease or grime. The ride itself is not harsh but cushy, with a view not of weeds and trash but of flowers, trees and the carrousel. In fact, that's the best part. Strapped in with your kid, looking down at Fantasyland, you realize that you're finally here, on vacation, at the iconic epicenter of the Walt Disney World experience.

Designed for Disneyland Paris, the ornate hub is straight off the drawing board of Jules Verne. Details include spinning pinwheels, gilded trim, even hanging frames that show the stork delivering the baby. Atop it all, Timothy

Above, all ages enjoy the Dumbo experience.
At right, a clown-themed puzzle post in the queue.

holds Dumbo's feather. The surrounding trim features small elephant pyramids.

Come here during a busy, hot afternoon and it's nothing special; the long, sweaty wait just isn't worth it. But stop by first thing in the morning or late at night, when the air is cool and the line short, and Dumbo is magical.

90 sec. to 2 min. Capacity: 32. Avg. wait: 20 min. early morning, 90 min. peak afternoon. Shaded queue. Must be ambulatory. Debuted: 1971, revised 1993 (Disneyland, 1955).

JUMBO JR. When a stork delivers a baby boy to circus elephant Mrs. Jumbo in 1941's "Dumbo," she names him Jumbo Jr., but his huge ears soon earn him the nickname Dumbo. He fails at being the top of an elephant pyramid, but when his mouse friend Timothy convinces him that holding a feather will let him fly, Dumbo becomes the star of the circus. Later the elephant learns to fly whenever he wants, magic feather or not.

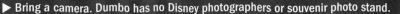

▶ Bring a camera. Dumbo has no Disney photographers or souvenir photo stand.

Snow White's Scary Adventures

Snow White's animal friends lift her spirits

Designed in 1954, this indoor ride is a Disney take on a carnival spook house, based on the 1937 film "Snow White and the Seven Dwarfs." Guided by a rail, a jerky wheeled vehicle takes you through a series of dark rooms filled with scary scenes. You travel through a predatory dark forest, see Snow White being offered the poisoned apple ("That's right dearie, take a bite...") and hear the old hag fall to her death. The effects are basic (the mouths of the "talking" characters don't move), but one illusion — when the Queen turns and becomes the hag — is a Disney classic.

Originally the ride was designed with the idea that guests are playing the role of Snow White, experiencing her adventures for themselves. The princess didn't appear until the last scene, where she's lying on the casket. But the ride didn't tell its guests they were Snow White, and many children thought the ride ended with the young girl dead. Disney redid the attraction in 1994, adding in the princess on the mural in the woods and standing next to the witch holding the apple. To clarify that Snow White doesn't die, Disney painted on a new final mural, showing her very much alive.

Still, much of the first-person terror remains — the crocodiles and trees still chase you through the woods — so some kids are still scared witless. As one dad told us, "My 2-and-a-half-year-old stomped up to a cast member and said, 'I did not like that! Not good! Bad ride!'"

2 min, 30 sec. Capacity: 66. Avg. wait: 5 min. early morning, 60 min. peak afternoon. Must be ambulatory. Handheld captioning. Fear factor: Can be terrifying for preschoolers. Many threatening scenes, some with loud screams. Debuted: 1971, revised 1994 (Disneyland, 1955).

ONE BITE, LONG NIGHT When a fair-featured girl's father dies, she's forced to contend with her evil stepmother, the Queen, and relegated to menial chores such as scrubbing the steps of the castle in Disney's 1937 film, "Snow White and the Seven Dwarfs." Obsessed with her own beauty, the Queen gets jealous when a magic mirror tells her Snow White has become "the fairest one of all." The Queen orders a huntsman to take the 14-year-old to a forest and kill her. Instead, he tells Snow White to "run away, and never come back!" She takes refuge in the cottage of the Seven Dwarfs, a group of men who work in a diamond mine. Learning of the girl's escape, the Queen transforms herself into an ugly old hag, tracks down Snow White and gives her a poisoned apple, which makes her appear to be dead. After the hag falls to her death while trying to crush the Seven Dwarfs with a boulder, they plan to bury the girl. Just in time, a prince arrives and gives Snow White "love's first kiss," breaking the spell.

Ariel's Grotto

You may wait an hour to see the star of 1989's "The Little Mermaid" at this outdoor meet-and-greet spot, but your line time can still be fun. The secret: use the queue as your break. Before you go in, stop at the adjacent Scuttle's Landing snack stand, then bring your food in with you as you sit along the line's low, shady side wall. As you eat, your kids can romp in the soft-floored water area. Finally, of course, you meet a girl with a tail (only at Disney!). When the grotto opens at 10 a.m. there's no wait at all.

▶ On your Scary Adventure, sit in the front seat. Most scenes are in front of you.

"They steal honey!" Tigger warns of hefflalumps and woozles on the Many Adventures of Winnie the Pooh.

The Many Adventures of Winnie the Pooh

✔ This storybook-style dark ride combines the cuteness and style of the Pooh films with imaginative visuals and effects. Hidden behind a swinging door, each scene comes as a surprise. You don't see another vehicle, which gives the ride a private feel.

The story comes, mostly, from "Winnie the Pooh and the Blustery Day," the 1968 featurette that was part of the 1977 film "The Many Adventures of Winnie the Pooh." As the ride starts, Gopher pops up

---

MR. TOAD'S WILD FANS You get drunk, steal a car, mouth off to a cop... then go to hell! That was the storyline of this building's former attraction, Mr. Toad's Wild Ride. The ride had ardent fans. In fact, when Disney announced its closing in 1997 some picketed inside the park. The last day of the ride, the Orlando Sentinel interviewed guests to get their feelings. One mom asked, "Who the heck is Mr. Toad?" Photos of Toad are still in the attraction. As you travel through Owl's house, look on the left wall for a picture of him handing over the deed to the space to Owl. Another picture, of Toad bowing to Pooh, rests on the right floor.

to greet you with "Happy Windsday!" Sweeping leaves, Piglet can barely hang on to his broom. Gardening Rabbit has been blown into his wheelbarrow. Roo swings gleefully from his scarf, which mom Kanga holds like a kite. Meanwhile, Pooh hunts honey. In a scene from the 1966 featurette "Winnie the Pooh and the Honey Tree," Pooh grips the string of a balloon, hoping to rise up to a beehive.

Next you enter Owl's toppling tree house. The walls are falling in, a limb has crashed through the roof, shelves and pictures are on the floor. Perched above, the oblivious Owl drones on about the big wind of '67 — or was it '76?

As night falls you're back outside, when suddenly up pops Tigger. "Come bounce with me!" he says. You rock as he trounces, flounces, pounces... and disappears for a second before dropping down from a tree. "I almost bounced clear out of the ride!" Tigger explains.

The bouncefest leads to Pooh's house, where Tigger warns of honey-stealing heffalumps and woozles. Pooh paces with his popgun, but dozes off —and then magically rises in the air.

▶ **Pooh's Thotful Spot gift shop carries hard-to-find heffalump and woozle plushies.**

As Pooh floats over your head, you enter his nightmare — a world of evil heffalumps and woozles. One heffalump blows a smoke ring at you, a woozle having lit its firecracker head. Another plays a honey harp. A third, now a hot-air balloon, blasts you with air. Finally, two watering-can heffalumps rise to start a storm.

Next is the Floody Place, a fiber-optic deluge that's all but real. As you sway in a loose glide Pooh wakes up, and uses the rising water to finally get to the top of that honey tree. The others rescue Piglet, who's about to tumble over a waterfall.

"At last the rain went away," the narrator says, "and everyone gathered together to say..." "Hooray!" the gang shouts, as a door opens onto a celebration. Where's Pooh? "Start the party without me," he calls, happily stuck in the honey tree.

3 min. 30 sec. Avg. wait: 5 min. early morning, 60 min. peak afternoon. Fastpass available. ECV users must transfer to a wheelchair. Debuted: 1999.

FUN FINDS ❶ Wind blows the words off the storybook page in the ride's first scene. ❷ As you enter the Floody Place, the air chills as words wash off another page. ❸ Items floating alongside you in the water include a once-bitten sandwich on your right, a rubber ducky on your left.

WINNIE, WINDY AND WET Based on an A.A. Milne story about the stuffed animals of his son Christopher Robin, the 1968 Disney featurette "Winnie the Pooh and the Blustery Day" tells of the group's adventure in a thunderstorm. Leader Pooh is a cheerful teddy who loves honey. His pals include excavation expert Gopher (a Disney creation), timid Piglet, fastidious gardener Rabbit, motherly Kanga and her adventurous son Roo, gloomy donkey Eeyore, self-important Owl and the ebullient Tigger, who loves to bounce. Pooh's enemies, he believes, are heffalumps and woozles, the elephants and weasles Tigger says steal honey. The chubby cubby has never seen one, but in his nightmares the crazy beasts blow smoke rings and morph into hot-air balloons and watering cans.

Mad Tea Party

This carnival ride whirls you around in a teacup that circles on a disk, which itself spins on the floor. Kids, of any age, love it. "My favorite Disney ride has always been the teacups," says NASCAR driver Kyle Petty. "From the time I was little I've loved to jump in and make people sick." It's based on 1951's "Alice in Wonderland," in which a prim and proper Alice eats a magic mushroom, shrinks, then attends the Mad Hatter and March Hare's Unbirthday Party, a nonsensical tea time in the woods that leaves her dazed and confused. Details include the film's soused mouse as well as its Japanese tea lanterns. The landscape features gigantic leaves, tulips and an Unbirthday Party topiary. *2 min. Capacity: 72. Avg. wait: 5 min. early morning, 30 min. peak afternoon. Must be ambulatory. Debuted: 1971 (Disneyland 1955).*

Raise your arms in the air on the Mad Tea Party and you'll slide right into each other, as New York's Jeffrey, Robin and Mikayla Reis demonstrate

▶ Watch the Blustery Day segment of the movie first to fully enjoy the scenery.

Swiss Family Treehouse

The ultimate treehouse — circa 1962 — this 62-step climb-through attraction is filled with ingenious ideas on how to live in the wild.

Some are obvious (the suspension bridge, the bamboo-and-barrel water system), some less so (the shell sinks, the vine handrails). The dining room's pull-stop organ is a real antique.

But the attraction does show its age. There are no interactive elements, and the climb can exhaust those who aren't fit.

Based on a banyan tree, a tropical variety that puts down vertical roots to support its outlying branches, the 60-foot "hardwood" is made from cement and steel. Its 15-foot trunk, nine main limbs and 600 branches are anchored by structural supports that extend 42 feet into the ground. The 330,000 leaves are polyethylene, but the Spanish moss is real, as are the lush and watery surroundings. The entire thing weighs about 200 tons.

Allow 15 min. Capacity: 300. Avg. wait: None; the walkway may be crowded. Must be ambulatory. Debuted: 1971 (Disneyland, 1962).

A HOMEMADE HIGHRISE In Disney's 1960 movie "Swiss Family Robinson," a dad, mom and their three sons — Fritz, Ernst and little Francis — are the sole survivors of an 1805 shipwreck on an uncharted tropical island. The dad and boys use the salvage from the boat to build an imaginative home in a huge tree. The story is based on an 1812 book, a compilation of morality lessons Swiss pastor Johann Wyss wrote for his sons, who themselves were fans of Daniel Defoe's 1719 novel "Robinson Crusoe."

A suspension bridge leads to the tree

▶ Go at night. It's more realistic.

© DISNEY

The Magic Carpets of Aladdin

Inspired by Disney's 1992 animated feature, this carnival-style hub-and-spoke ride is geared to young children. You circle around a giant genie bottle, flying a magic carpet which climbs, dips and dives at your command.

Just another Dumbo? Not exactly. Here the vehicles seat four, so the line moves twice as fast and small families can ride together. As you fly, a magic scarab controls both your height and pitch, which adds to the fun. Fly high enough and you can see over the Adventureland buildings, all the way to Big Thunder Mountain.

There are lots of extra touches. The base of the ride is a pool of water, so as you fly you look down at your reflection, just as Aladdin and Jasmine do in the

Kids of all ages enjoy the carpets' gentle thrills

film. Music — instrumental versions of the movie's best songs — fills the air. On the genie bottle, a sequence of Abu the monkey doing cartwheels is an homage to early zoetrope animation techniques. The best bonus: two golden camels spit water at riders and spectators alike. (Want to get spit on? Stand on the wet spots in the pavement in front of the attraction's sign. On the ride, fly about halfway high. You'll be in line for the camel who faces the genie bottle.)

90 sec. Capacity: 64. Avg wait: 5 min. early morning, 30 min. peak afternoon. ECV users must transfer to a wheelchair, then a carpet. Debuted: 2001.

FUN FACT » The camels are from Disney-MGM Studios. Part of Aladdin's Royal Caravan parade from 1993 to 1995, they sat outside the building that is today's Playhouse Disney theater until 1999.

A NEW FANTASTIC POINT OF VIEW In 1992's "Aladdin," a beetle-shaped amulet leads its holder to the Cave of Wonders, where street orphan Aladdin finds a magic carpet. Later, as it takes him and princess Jasmine on a flight above the city of Agrabah, they see their reflection in the water below.

▶ Sit in a front seat to control your carpet's height; in back to make it tilt.

Calm or crazy, Jungle Cruise skippers tell an endless stream of shameless jokes

Jungle Cruise

Sophomoric humor and, if you're lucky, a wild-eyed young skipper turn this dated river safari into a trippy tongue-in-cheek adventure. Spewing out a constant stream of puns, your guide leads you down the rivers of four continents. Exploring the South American Amazon, the African Congo, the Egyptian Nile and Southeast Asia's Mekong (all surprisingly narrow!) you learn such facts as "the Nile River goes for Niles and Niles and Niles. If you don't believe me, then you're in de-Nile."

You'll enter a Cambodian temple (its fallen beams are "man's first attempt at building a monorail") and encounter some threatening headhunters (their cache of skulls are "my last crew. They didn't laugh at my jokes, either!").

To a child the ride offers a lot, as it's fun but not scary. Many scenes are silly (the gorillas sacking the camp was re-created in the 1999 film "Tarzan"); the rising hippo heads and squirting elephants add some excitement.

Designed in the 1950s, the old-fashioned scenes have their flaws. Many of the animals don't move. The cultural stuff is often mixed up (the designs on the Congo canoes are Polynesian) and a theme of the attraction is colonialism.

Nevertheless, taken with a grain of salt the Cruise can be jolly good time. The best quips come at the end.

"After five years of college you too can become a Jungle Cruise skipper! My parents are so proud."

10 min. Capacity: 310. Avg. wait: 10 min. early morning, 60 min. peak afternoon. Fastpass available. Guests may remain in

▶ If you ask just as you board, your child may be able to help "steer" the boat.

wheelchairs, ECVs. Assistive listening; handheld captioning available. Fear factor: The right side of the boat comes close to some artificial snakes in the dark temple. Debuted: 1971 (Disneyland 1955).

FUN FINDS ❶ A queue sign honors the cruise company's latest Employee of the Month: E.L. O'Fevre. ❷ Toward the end of the queue, a cage holds a giant (pretend) tarantula that will occasionally jerk and rear up. Next to it are crates labeled "arachnid sedative." ❸ On the boarding dock, a chalkboard lists the crew's weekly lunch menu as fricassee of giant stag beetle, BBQ'd 3-toed skink, consomme of river basin slug and fillet of rock python. All are reported to taste like chicken. ❹ The invading headhunters end their chant with the phrase "I love disco!" (usually drowned out by the skipper's spiel). ❺ After you leave the dock, a chalkboard list of missing persons includes "Ilene Dover" followed by "Ann Fellen." ❻ Two crates just outside the exit were once part of the Swiss Family Treehouse landscape. One is addressed to "Thomas Kirk Esq." and "M. Jones" on the island of "Bora Danno," references to Tommy Kirk (a star of the 1960 film "Swiss Family Robinson" and the title character of the 1964's "The Misadventures of Merlin

Playful, water-squirting elephants are among the "hazards" along the banks of the Jungle Cruise

Jones") and James MacArthur (a "Swiss" star who went on to play "Danno" Williams in the 1968-1980 TV series "Hawaii Five-O"). The other is addressed to "Swiss" director Kenneth Annakin.

SHRUNKEN NED'S JUNIOR JUNGLE BOATS You steer a miniature Jungle Cruise boat through obstacles at this small diversion at the ride entrance. The boats are hard to control; if you play pick one that's already in a fun place and not stuck behind something. Use your forward gear. A $1 token buys two minutes.

FUN FACTS ❯❯ The plane is half of an old MGM stage prop. The other side is at Disney-MGM Studios in The Great Movie Ride's "Casablanca" scene. ❯❯ The river is 3 feet deep. ❯❯ The water is dyed its dark, murky color. ❯❯ Walt Disney originally wanted the trip to have live animals. The robotic versions were Plan B. ❯❯ The boat is on a track. Your skipper controls its speed, but not its course.

BUT SERIOUSLY, FOLKS... Premiering at Disneyland shortly after that park's opening in 1955, the Jungle Cruise was originally a serious attraction — an educational tour of regions most Americans had never seen in pictures. The humor began in the 1960s, with the addition of the playful bathing elephants (1962) and the safari party being chased up the tree (1964). By the time the Florida version opened in 1971, the whole thing was being played for laughs. In 1994 the queue got its radio broadcast and some new props. In 1998 the boats received their current vintage design, a look that includes cooking gear hanging from a roof net.

▶ **Try it at night. The lines are short and your boat's spotlight adds to the fun.**

Zazu looks on in disgust as Iago changes the show

Guests may remain in wheelchairs, ECVs. Assistive listening; handheld captioning available. Fear factor: Lightning and thunder scare some preschoolers. Debuted: 1998; original version 1971 (Disneyland 1963).

FOWL PHRASES ❶ Iago: Don't you guys ever fly to the movies? **José:** We don't get out much. **Pierre:** Oui, oui. We are... how do you say?... attached to the place. ❷ **Iago:** No more worries! **Zazu:** Well, where I come from, that's called Hakuna Matata. **Iago:** Hunky tuna tostada? What a stupid phrase! ❸ **Iago:** Come on, everybody out! Migrate people, migrate! **Birds:** Heigh ho, heigh ho! It's out the door you go! ❹ **Iago** (just before the exit doors close): Boy, I'm tired. I think I'll head over to the Hall of Presidents and take a nap.

The Enchanted Tiki Room — Under New Management

When new owners Iago (from 1992's "Aladdin") and Zazu (from 1994's "The Lion King") take over this show of singing birds and flowers, Iago wants to toss it out for something more current. But when he insults the Tiki gods he learns that, as Zazu says, "you cannot toy with the Enchanted Tiki Room." Songs include "Hot Hot Hot," "Conga," and, from the wooden mouths of the Tiki poles, "In the Still of the Night."

An outdoor preshow kicks off the fun, as two talent-agent parrots bicker over which one's client is the attraction's new owner. William (voiced by Don Rickles), representing Iago, and Morris (Phil Hartman), arguing for Zazu, trade bird-themed barbs: "Are you cuckoo?" "You birdbrain!" "Stop grousing!"

9 min. Capacity: 250. Avg. wait: 5 min. early morning, 15 min. peak afternoon.

FUN FACTS ❱❱ Does Pierre sound like Lumiere, the candelabrum from "Beauty and the Beast"? Both were voiced by Jerry Orbach, Det. Lennie Briscoe in television's "Law & Order." **❱❱** The bird sounds were all voiced by A. Purvis Pullen, a man known for his ability to imitate 1,000 creatures. He was the voice of Cheetah in the 1930s Johnny Weissmuller Tarzan films, the birds in Disney's 1937 "Snow White and the Seven Dwarfs" and 1959's "Sleeping Beauty," even Bonzo the chimp in the 1951 Ronald Reagan flick "Bedtime for Bonzo." Pullen was especially proud of his Tiki Room legacy. "It's my favorite accomplishment," he said, "the one that's gonna last." **❱❱** Conceived as a restaurant, the Tiki Room debuted at Disneyland in 1963 as the first Audio Animatronic attraction. After a bird barker out front enticed guests to "Come to the Tiki Room," they sang along to 18 minutes of "Let's All Sing Like the Birdies Sing" and other old-time tunes, while the walls' moving-mouth Tiki poles added some bizarre shouts. This duplicate version opened in 1971, but by the 1990s few guests bothered to see it. Disney redid things in 1998, creating today's shorter, sarcastic storyline with more familiar songs and characters. **❱❱** Once the cockatoos arrive and start singing "Conga" the parrot José says "I wonder what happened to Rosita," a reference to a bird from the original attraction who is no longer in the show. **❱❱** The upside-down masks on the walls depict Negendei, the Earth Balancer, who is always portrayed standing on his head. **❱❱** In Polynesian mythology, "Tiki" is the god who created man. The Maori people of New Zealand use the word to refer to a carved or sculpted human image.

▶ Sit on the left, three rows back. You'll face the goddess and see all the action.

Pirates of the Caribbean

✓ A rowdy, rum-soaked version of It's a Small World, Pirates of the Caribbean sends you on a slow-moving cruise through stage sets filled with robotic characters. But instead of cute little dolls, here you get big-boy pirates who, as the jaunty theme song reports, "pillage and plunder... rifle and loot... kidnap and ravage and don't give a hoot." A 2006 update added characters from the film series, including Captain Jack Sparrow.

AYE, A STORY THERE BE! When Captain Hector Barbossa invades a Spanish fortress looking for gold, he finds his crafty nemesis Captain Jack Sparrow one step ahead of him. Barbossa's men sack the town, but Sparrow sneaks a glance at their treasure map and discovers a room filled with gold.

You witness the fable firsthand, as despite the warnings of a ghostly Davy Jones — the octopus-faced ruler of the ocean who materializes here in a waterfall — you set sail back in time to explore the golden age of piracy.

Literally falling into an old Caribbean harbor, you sail into the middle of the first scene, smack between the battling cannons of an Audio Animatronic Barbossa and the stone fort. "It's Captain Jack we're after," Barbossa yells, "and a fortune in gold!" As music from the "Pirates" films plays in the background, cannonballs splash just a few feet from your boat.

Rounding a bend, you see Barbossa's men in a courtyard, interrogating the mayor by dunking him in a well.

"Where be Captain Jack Sparrow and the treasure, ya bilge rat?" the lead pirate demands. The robotic Sparrow (looking just like Johnny Depp) is hiding nearby, peering out from behind some dressmaker forms.

Meanwhile, other pirates are auctioning off some of the town's maidens to some raucous hecklers. Again you sail through the scene — women on your left, drunks on your right.

Another turn sends you into the village itself, where women are chasing pirates who have stolen some chickens and plates. In front sits an old salt holding a treasure map. As he rambles on ("What I wouldn't give to see the look on Captain Jack Sparrow's face when he hears tell tis only me that gots the goods..."), who should pop up behind him but Jack himself. Hiding in a barrel, Jack sneaks a peek at the map before ducking back out of sight.

The Pirates of the Caribbean building is based on El Morro, a 16th-century fortress in San Juan, PR

▶ **If you must wait in a line, this is a good one. It's covered, cool and moves quickly.**

〉 What is a pirate's favorite cookie? Ships Ahoy. 〉 What type of socks does a pirate wear? Aaaaarrrgyle. 〉 How much does a pirate pay for corn on the cob? A buck-an-ear.

More dioramas show pirates setting fire to the town's buildings, and, in perhaps the ride's best-known scene, trying to escape from a burning jail by luring a dog that holds its keys.

In the final scene a giddy Sparrow has found the village stash and basks in its glory. Lolling on an ornate rocking chair, leg draped over one of its arms, he sings, slurs, and chats with a parrot.

Other recent enhancements include a new sound system, which includes large subwoofers that add a distinctive "whumph" to each cannon shot, and digitally remastered vintage tracks that make the pirates' dialogue easier to understand. There's a new musical soundtrack, and new lighting. The Barbossa and Sparrow figures have modern movements, though the others still use their original 1960s technology.

As for flaws, there is a big one.

"There is nothing politically correct about Pirates of the Caribbean," says Disney Imagineer Eric Jacobson. "Much of it is patently offensive." It's also all in good fun, of course, but even the most carefree parent may wonder if scenes showing torture, heavy drinking and the selling of women are sending the best messages to young boys and girls.

In fairness, the attraction does show, vaguely, the results of such behavior (the pirates, as the first scene shows, end up dead) and Disney has gotten rid of the ride's most galling moments.

Where today's women are chasing pirates, pirates once chased them (what California-based Jacobson calls the old ride's "Schwarzenegger moment"). And that barrel that now holds Captain Jack? Originally a woman hid in there, while the pirate in front of it spoke not of a treasure map, but (as he held her shoe and

her slip in his hand) his desire to "hoist me colors on the likes of that shy little wench. I be willin' to share, I be!"

To many folks the revised attraction is a real hoot. As we heard one group of college girls sing as they waited in line:

"It's a world of fog and a world of caves.
It's a world of torture and of sex slaves.
But there's gold, and there's rum!
Johnny Depp? He's no bum!
It's the Disney Pirates ride!"

Originally developed and personally supervised by Walt Disney, the essence of the ride combines a Missouri farm boy's view of high-seas adventure with a Hollywood showman's use of theatrics. "Walt came from a world of movies," explains Imagineer Jason Surrell. "He wanted rides that use lighting and backdrops, establishing shots and lots of characters — up-close ones who are most important, and faraway characters who are less so."

9 min. Capacity: 330. Avg. wait: 10 min. early morning, 60 min. peak afternoon. ECV and wheelchair users must transfer. Handheld captioning available. Fear factor: The skeletons, dark drop, cannon fight and fire in some of the windows may scare toddlers. No flash photography. Debuted: 1973, revised 2006 (Disneyland 1967).

FUN FINDS Entrance: ❶ Visible through some windows on the right of the right queue, two chess-playing pirates in a dungeon apparently reached a stalemate some time ago. Their skeletons stare at the board. **Caverns:** ❷ A crab on your left rears as it moves its eyes, claws and pinchers. **Harbor attack:** ❸ A sign on the ship's stern reveals its name: the Wicked Wench. ❹ Barbossa yells "Strike yer colors, ye bloomin' cockroaches!" ❺ The Spanish speak *en español*: "¡Apenten! ¡Disparen! ¡Fuego!" ("Ready! Aim! Fire!"). **Interrogation:** ❻ The captain has a hook for a hand. ❼ When the pirates ask the mayor where Jack is, his wife calls from the window "Don't tell him Carlos! Don't be chicken!" ❽ He responds "I am

---

A GREAT BIG BEAUTIFUL SMALL SCURVY WORLD. Conceived as a wax museum, Pirates became an Audio Animatronic flume ride after the success of the Carousel of Progress robotics and It's a Small World boat system at the 1964 World's Fair.

▶ The right queue has the most fun detail, including some chess-playing skeletons.

Captain Jack's Pirate Tutorial. The famous Disney pirate instructs future swashbuckler Aiden Feeback of Vero Beach, Florida. The 20-minute show is held along the walkway to the left of the attraction.

no chicken! I will not talk!" ❾ Jack's hands rest on the derrieres of the female forms around him. **Bridal Auction:** ❿ A crate on your left is filled with bobbing, clucking chickens. ⓫ The first woman in line is beaming, happy to be sold. ⓬ The auctioneer refers to her overweight figure as "stout-hearted and cornfed" and asks her to "shift yer cargo, dearie. Show 'em yer larboard side." ⓭ Impatient to be next, a buxom redhead pulls up her skirt to show her leg. ⓮ The auctioneer tells her to "Strike yer colors you brazen wench! No need to expose yer superstructure!" ⓯ The second to last woman is crying. **Chasing scene:** ⓰ At the end of the scene, a drunken pirate to your right invites two gray cats to join him in "a little ol' tot of rum." **Burning town:** ⓱ On your left, a dog barks along to the cantina band. ⓲ On the right a drunk, snoring pirate lolls in the mud with three intoxicated pigs. His chest heaves. ⓳ As you leave the scene, the hairy leg of a pirate above dangles toward your face. ⓴ His parrot squawks "A parrot's life for me!" **Dungeon:** ㉑ Frustrated that the dog won't respond, a prisoner demands "Hit him with the soup bone!" ㉒ As the dog looks at you, another captive says "Rover, it's

us what needs yer ruddy help, not them blasted lubbers." **Treasure room:** ㉓ Jack says the loot is "my reward for a life of villainy, larceny, skullduggery and persnickety." ㉔ After he sings the "Yo, Ho" phrase "maraud and embezzle and even hijack" the parrot interrupts with "Hi Jack! Hi Jack!" ㉕ Jack refers to the bird as "my chromatic winged beast." **Exit area:** ㉖ On the exit ramp, a peg-leg print takes the place of the left shoe print.

FUN FACTS ❯❯ The fog screen of Davy Jones is built from microscopic droplets of water, each so small you stay dry as you pass through. The fog is held in place by columns of air. ❯❯ The fall drops 14 feet. ❯❯ The characters of Davy Jones and Captains Barbossa and Sparrow are voiced by their film counterparts — Bill Nighey, Geoffrey Rush and Johnny Depp. ❯❯ The auctioneer is voiced by Paul Frees, the Haunted Mansion's ghost host. ❯❯ The attraction has 125 Audio Animatronic figures: 65 pirates and villagers and 60 animals. ❯❯ The redhead is, in reality, little more than a pole from her waist down. ❯❯ Many of the ride's classic characters appear in the "Pirates" films, including the mayor, the redhead, the snoring pirate with the pigs, the jailed prisoners and their dog.

▶ The gift shop has treasures such as pirate hats, swords and plastic hand hooks.

THE COMPLETE WALT DISNEY WORLD **75**

© DISNEY

Left to right: John Quincy Adams (in brown), Thomas Jefferson (green) and John Adams (gold) listen to George W. Bush

democracy makes no inquiry about the color of the skin, or place of birth, or any other circumstance or condition."

The presidents stand like real people, shifting their weight from hip to hip, fidgeting, looking around, sometimes whispering to each other. Many look amazingly like their human subjects.

In fact, one Disney publicist used to tell members of the press that some of the presidents were real — that since there were always a few robots out for repairs, each show had at least one human stand-in. When he asked Walter Cronkite to spot the live actor, the veteran newsman just laughed. A minute later he turned back and said, "Jefferson?"

20 min. Capacity: 740. Avg. wait: 10 min. Guests may stay in wheelchairs, ECVs. Assistive listening; reflective captioning. No flash photography. Debuted: 1971; updated after the election of each new American president.

The Hall of Presidents

A bunch of old men stand there stoically. Two talk. That's the highlight — and it's a good one — of this inspirational movie and stage presentation. The patriotic show combines a decent video with Audio Animatronic versions of every United States president from George Washington to George W. Bush.

First is the film. Projected on a 180-degree screen that fills your field of vision, the 10-minute movie recounts how our country's early leaders argued about slavery, from the Constitutional Convention to the Lincoln-Douglas debates.

Then the screen slides apart to reveal our 42 commanders-in-chief. As a roll call introduces each president, each responds with a dignified nod or wave.

Next, Bush and Lincoln speak. "Let us do nothing that will impose upon another creature," Lincoln says. "True

FUN FACTS)) Each president's costume was hand-tailored with period techniques. **))** The Lincoln figure is a simplified remake of an ambitious, though problematic, creation that debuted at the 1964 World's Fair. Whenever there was a spike in current, Disney's first Abe would flail its arms, hit itself repeatedly in the head and then slam down in its chair. **))** The attraction was parodied on a 1993 episode of the television series "The Simpsons." In "Selma's Choice," Aunt Selma takes Bart and Lisa to the Disney World-like Duff Gardens, a theme park where every attraction is themed around Duff Beer. At the Duff Hall of Presidents, Lincoln says "Four score and seven years ago, our forefathers brewed a refreshing drink from hops and barley" as he holds up a can of the beer. Then he takes a swig and starts to rap — "We-e-ll, I'm Rappin' A.B. and I'm here to say, if you want to drink beer, well Duff's the only way! I said the only way!" — before mindlessly smashing the can on his head. Lisa calls the show a disgrace, but Selma has another view. "If it's this bad, it has to be educational."

▶ The Hall of Presidents opens at 10 a.m., with shows on the hour and half hour.

Liberty Square Riverboat

This steam-powered stern wheeler takes you on a slow cruise around Tom Sawyer Island and Fort Langhorn. The sights aren't that special (a burning cabin, an old fisherman, an Indian village and a few remarkably stoic moose and deer) but the boat's pretty cool. It looks like the real deal — a three-tiered vessel with a functioning boiler room, steam engine and paddle wheel on its first deck; a working smokestack and steam whistle up top. Wander around and you'll also find the captain's quarters and a small stateroom.

The half-mile trip is themed as a journey down the "Rivers of America" during the late 1800s. You hear imaginary captain Horace Bixby* direct his imaginary crew ("Steady as she goes!") as he navigates his Liberty Belle through the shallows and explains what you're passing. (The helmsman is exaggerating when he calls out "Mark Twain!" indicating the water is two fathoms — 12 feet — deep. These rivers are only 9 feet.)

Built by Disney at a backstage shop, the boat isn't free-floating. It rides on a steel rail on the bottom of the riverbed.

Some benches down in front offer a way to get off your feet, but the best views are from the top deck, where you can sometimes watch egrets and herons flying beneath you.

The boat was called the Richard F. Irvine until 1996. It originally had a twin, the Admiral Joe Fowler, which was dropped

A symbol of Americana, the Liberty Belle passes old-time settings (below) on the Rivers of America

by a crane during a 1980 refurbishment. Irvine and Fowler were Disney designers. Both names are now used by ferry boats in the Seven Seas Lagoon.

13 min Capacity: 400 Avg. wait 9 min. Guests may remain in wheelchairs, ECVs. Debuted: 1971.

* A real person, Bixby was the riverboat pilot who taught the skill to Mark Twain.

▶ Don't miss the engine. It's on the lower deck, just in front of the paddle wheel.

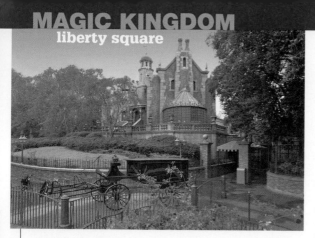

Nineteenth-century homes in New York's Hudson River Valley inspired the Mansion's exterior

The Haunted Mansion

✓ Packed with details and special effects, this tour of a ghostly retirement home is a campy Disney classic.

The show starts at the gate. You're received by a lifeless servant, a cast member trained not to smile. The grounds are unkempt. A hearse is there but its body is gone, and its horse invisible. A wolf howls in the distance. There's a black wreath on the door, coffin-shaped columns beside it and a bat weather vane.*

You enter through a side foyer. A voice says ghosts are present, "practicing their terror with ghoulish delight." Their first trick: aging the fireplace portrait's young squire into an old man, then a corpse.

Next up is a portrait chamber, where again the spirits are pulling pranks. When the door shuts, it disappears. Then the room starts to stretch. Can't find a way out? "There's always my way," the voice offers, as the ceiling reveals his hanging corpse. Fortunately, you find a less ghastly way to go, and board a "doom buggy" for the rest of your tour.

But the ghosts want someone to join them, and they've got their eyes on you. In a portrait corridor, the eyes watch you pass. In the library, the busts do.

Moving on, you see some of the ghosts' earlier attempts to land a new resident.

* After dark the street lights flicker and dim and the hearse lanterns are on.

In the conservatory, a live man is trapped in a casket. In a hall, you pass locked door handles that twist and turn, and hear increasingly desperate knocks, shouts, groans and moans behind them. One door flexes so much it appears to breathe.

Moments later you're at a seance, where a spiritualist — a disembodied head in a crystal ball — beckons serpents, spiders (and the tail of a rat) to "call in the spirits, wherever they're at." She wants the ghosts to materialize.

Once they do, the haunts get happy. The ghosts first appear in the ballroom, where they've gathered for a "death-day" party. A spooky trip through the attic (where a bride gives new meaning to the phrase "see-through dress") leads to the graveyard, where the midnight madness includes a Dixieland band, barbershop quintet, tea party, even some opera singers. As you enter a crypt a trio of spirits shows up to thumb for a ride. One appears to get in your vehicle.

Finally, the bride returns to seduce you to come visit again. Now just a few feet tall, she stands on a ledge above you. "Hurry back... hurry back..." she coos, a dead bouquet in her arms, her veil blowing in the breeze.

As you leave the mansion, the ghosts — again invisible — are sad to see you go. "Mortals pay a token fee," you'll hear them plead if you listen closely, "Rest in peace, the haunting's free. So hurry back, we would like your company."

Your tour also includes a music room (a spirit plays a piano) and an endless hallway (a chandelier floats in midair).

11 min. Capacity: 320. Avg. wait: 10 min. early morning, 45 min. peak afternoon. Must be ambulatory. Handheld captioning. Debuted: 1971.

▶ Is it scary? Only for preschoolers. There are no drops, chain saws or hockey masks.

Transforming before your eyes, a portrait in the foyer portrays a young man aging into a corpse

FUN FINDS Outside: ❶ Horseshoe prints and wagon wheel tracks lead from the barn to the hearse, which is hitched to an invisible horse. ❷ Dead roses lie inside the hearse. ❸ Madame Leota's eyes open and close on her sculpted tombstone face, which tilts toward you. **Foyer:** ❹ The fireplace grate forms a cross-eyed, arrow-tongued face. **Loading area:** ❺ Toothy brass bats top the waiting line's chain stanchions. **Portrait corridor:** ❻ Paintings on the right include Dracula and Jack the Ripper. ❼ Those on the left include the Greek goddess Medusa, her body covered with snake bites from her hair. **Library:** ❽ A bat face is carved into the paneling between each set of busts. **Music room:** ❾ The window frame is decorated with coffins. **Endless hallway:** ❿ Fang-baring serpents extend from the frame molding. **Conservatory:** ⓫ The coffin handles are bats. **Corridor of doors:** ⓬ The grandfather clock is a demon. The casing forms its hair and eyes; the clockface is its mouth. The pendulum is a tail. **Grand dining hall:** ⓭ On the mantle, a ghost in a top hat has his arm around a bust. ⓮ The fireplace grate includes the silhouettes of two black cats. ⓯ In front of the fireplace, an old woman knits in a rocking chair. ⓰ Five ghosts float in from a coffin, which has fallen out of a hearse that has pulled up to an outside door. ⓱ Mr. Pickwick (from the 1836 Charles Dickens novel "The Pickwick Papers") swings out from the chandelier. ⓲ Marc Antony and Cleopatra sit next to him. ⓳ Julius Caesar sits at the far left end of the table. ⓴ The sheet-music stand is a leering bat. **Graveyard:** ㉑ A band of medieval minstrels includes a flutist emerging from his tomb... ㉒ a drummer using bones to tap out a beat on the flutist's crypt cover... ㉓ a bagpiper in a kilt... ㉔ a soldier playing a small harp... ㉕ and a trumpeter wearing pajamas and a stocking cap. ㉖ When the trumpeter rears back, two owls perched above him do too. ㉗ Sitting on a tomb, five cats yowl and hiss to the beat. ㉘ A skeletal dog howls on a hill. ㉙ A ghostly king and queen ride a makeshift seesaw: a board balanced on a tombstone. ㉚ Swinging from a tree branch, a princess sips tea behind them. ㉛ A British duke and duchess toast each other at a candle-lit table. ㉜ Behind them four ghosts ride bicycles in a circle. ㉝ Wearing hoop earrings, a pirate near you raises his teacup, sometimes his head, from behind a grave. ㉞ Floating above the ground, a teapot pours tea into a cup. ㉟ Tracks from a hearse veer off your path. ㊱ The

MANY MANSION moments are inspired by films and literature. A tapping, thumping corridor of doors (with one that breathes) appears in the 1963 film **"The Haunting."** Statues follow guests with their gaze and wall sconces are held by human arms in the 1946 French **"La Belle et la Bete,"** a version of Beauty and the Beast. Oscar Wilde's 1890 novel **"The Picture of Dorian Gray"** includes a changing portrait in which a young man becomes old and disfigured, reflecting his damaged soul. Edgar Allen Poe fans will find Mansion allusions to 1843's **"The Black Cat"** (a wife's corpse is placed in a hidden room) and **"The Tell-Tale Heart"** (a murdered body is found by its loud heartbeat), 1845's **"The Raven"** and the 1846 novel **"The Cask of Amontillado"** (a man is entombed alive in a brick crypt).

▶ **For the shortest wait, go before 10:30 a.m. or late at night.**

driver chats with a duchess, who sits atop the hearse sipping tea. **③⑦** A ghost sits up from the hearse's coffin, which has fallen out the back. **③⑧** He's chatting with a sea captain. **③⑨** A dog sniffs an Egyptian sarcophagus. **④⓪** Its mummy is sitting up stirring his tea, mumbling through his bandages. **④①** "What's that? Louder! I can't hear you! Eh?" says an old bearded man to him, holding a horn to his ear. **④②** The Grim Reaper floats inside a crypt to your far right. His beady eyes stare at you from inside his hood. **④③** Dressed as Vikings, a male and female opera singer each belt out a loud, exaggerated solo. **④④** Holding his severed head in his hand, a knight cheerfully sings a duet alongside his gravelly voiced executioner. **④⑤** Shackled at his feet with a ball and chain, a pint-sized prisoner harmonizes with them. **④⑥** The party over, an arm of a ghost uses a trowel to brick itself back into its crypt. **Crypt: ④⑦** Human arms hold up the wall sconces here and in the unload area. **Outside the exit: ④⑧** Each of the 20 mausoleum occupants has a pun for a name. They include Hal Lucinashun, I. Emma Spook, Wee G. Bord. **④⑨** Dogs and snakes appear in the side frames of the benches in front of the pet cemetery. **⑤⓪** Mr. Toad is buried in the pet cemetery.*

* J. Thaddeus Toad is "dead" because his attraction, Mr. Toad's Wild Ride, is no longer at the Magic Kingdom. An original park attraction, it was replaced by The Many Adventures of Winnie the Pooh in 1998.

FUN FACTS ❯❯ Built during the Civil War, the hearse appeared in the 1965 John Wayne movie "The Sons of Katie Elder." ❯❯ The interior design comes from the 1874 Harry Packer mansion in Jim Thorpe, Penn. ❯❯ The soundtrack's only song, "Grim Grinning Ghosts," is performed in eight styles, including a dirge that plays as you walk in. ❯❯ The dust-like substance is made from fuller's earth, an ingredient in kitty litter. ❯❯ Except for a few books, the library bookcase is a flat, painted backdrop. ❯❯ So is the ballroom's rear wall, including its molding and woodwork. ❯❯ You never go in the home. The entire 960-foot ride takes place in a nondescript building behind the mansion facade.

Happy but haunted, a clerk sells Mansion merchandise at Madame Leota's cart

MANY OF THE VOICES are supplied by Hollywood talents. The ghost host is **Paul Frees,** who voiced Boris Badenov in the 1959-1964 television series "The Adventures of Rocky and Bullwinkle" and, incredibly, Pillsbury Doughboy Poppin' Fresh. He's also the Pirates of the Caribbean auctioneer, Carlos, concertina player, nearby dog and bridge parrot. The voice of the crystal ball spiritualist is **Eleanor Audley,** Lady Tremaine in 1950's "Cinderella" and Maleficent in 1959's "Sleeping Beauty." The group singing "Grim Grinning Ghosts" is the **Mellomen,** a quartet who sang on many 1940s and 1950s pop hits (such as Rosemary Clooney's 1954 "Mambo Italiano") and were Elvis Presley's backup singers in the 1963 movie "It Happened at the World's Fair," 1964's "Roustabout" and the 1966 film "Paradise Hawaiian Style." The graveyard's singing busts feature Mellomen lead **Thurl Ravenscroft** (second from left). Also the voice of Country Bear Jamboree buffalo head Buff and the Enchanted Tiki Room's Fritz the parrot, he sang "You're A Mean One, Mr. Grinch" in the 1966 TV special "How the Grinch Stole Christmas!" and was the voice of Tony the Tiger for Kellogg's Frosted Flakes cereal. The graveyard's singing executioner is voiced by **Candy Candido,** the man who played the angry apple tree in 1939's "The Wizard of Oz" ("Are you hinting my apples aren't what they ought to be?") as well as the Indian chief in Disney's 1953 "Peter Pan" and a goon in 1959's "Sleeping Beauty." *The corridor of doors' shrieks and screams are those of Disney's Jimmy MacDonald, the voice of Mickey Mouse after World War II.*

▶ **'DOOM BUGY' license plates are among the souvenirs at Madame Leota's gift cart.**

Restaurant guide

TABLE SERVICE Cinderella's Royal Table $$$$
✔ Would you pay $34 for Major Domo's Favorite Pie? Oh yes you would, if Cinderella is sitting across your table chatting with your daughter. Though expensive, breakfast or lunch at the castle can be a magical experience. Not just Cinderella, but often Ariel, Aurora, Belle, Snow White, even the Fairy Godmother will come by your table, all friendly and perfectly in character (no particular character, even Cinderella, is guaranteed). As for the food, breakfast is traditional American. Lunch includes an appetizer tasting plate and a choice of pasta, pork, salmon or the aforementioned pot pie, which is beef and vegetables topped with Cabernet sauce. Dinner *does not include the princesses,* but the food's good. Appetizers often include a tasty corn and crab soup; entrees can feature lamb and prime rib. All meals are all-you-can-eat, but brought to your table ("pre-plated," Disney calls it). The restaurant is always fully booked far in advance; to get in make reservations some (407-WDW-DINE, 407-939-3463) exactly 180 days early, right as the books for your day first open. Reservations must be guaranteed with a credit card; no-shows are charged the full amount of the meal. The Gothic dining hall overlooks Fantasyland. *184 seats. Inside Cinderella Castle.* **The Crystal Palace $$$–$$$$** ✔ Winnie the Pooh, Tigger, Eeyore and Piglet stop separately at your table at this buffet restaurant, set in an indoor Victorian garden. Breakfast is traditional American fare. Lunch offers some creative chicken and pasta dishes as well as beef and salmon (kids can get macaroni and cheese or chicken fingers); dinner adds prime rib and turkey. There's also an imaginative, fresh salad bar. As for value, having the characters here seems to add about $5 to each meal. Your inner Eeyore won't like the crowds, though, or especially the outdoor waiting line. The best bet: Breakfast at 8 a.m., an hour before the park opens. There's no wait, and the tab won't drain your bank account. *401 seats. Main Street U.S.A.* **Liberty Tree Tavern $$–$$$** ✔ This New England restaurant's Butter Griddled Pound Cake is the best dessert in the Magic Kingdom. It's covered in a warm pecan-caramel sauce and topped with vanilla-bean ice cream. The Maryland crab cake and signature pot roast fall apart in your mouth. The turkey is tender, too. Dinner is a family-style character meal with Minnie, Goofy, Pluto and Chip 'n' Dale. *250 seats. Liberty Square.* **The Plaza Restaurant $$** ✔ This comfortable Victorian room has good sandwiches, great ice cream and a calm, carpeted atmosphere. *94 seats. Main Street U.S.A.* **Tony's Town Square Restaurant $$–$$$** ✔ Cool, comfortable, lots of booths. Lunch is rarely crowded; choose from pasta and panini sandwiches. Thematically the Tony's of the 1955 movie "Lady and the Tramp;" the back right window looks into the alley. *286 seats. Main Street U.S.A.*

COUNTER SERVICE Casey's Corner $ Hot dogs, fries. *80 seats outside, 43 inside. Main Street U.S.A.* **Columbia Harbour House $** ✔ Good sandwiches, veggie chili. Nicest upstairs. *593 seats. Liberty Square.* **Cosmic Ray's Starlight Cafe $** Chicken, burgers, kosher choices, nice condiment bar. Robotic lounge singer. *1,162 seats. Tomorrowland.* **Main Street Bakery $** ✔ Yogurt parfaits, quiche, bagels. *29 seats. Main Street U.S.A.* **Pecos Bill Tall Tale Inn and Cafe $** Hamburgers, sandwiches. The two far-right rooms stay quiet. *1,107 seats. Frontierland.* **Pinocchio Village Haus $** Pizza, chicken, sandwiches. Crowded by noon. *400 seats. Fantasyland.*

OUTDOOR COUNTER CAFES Aunt Polly's Dockside Inn $ Desserts. *44 seats. On Tom Sawyer Island, Frontierland.* **Auntie Gravity's Galactic Goodies $** Soft-serve ice cream, smoothies. *12 seats. Tomorrowland.* **El Pirata y el Perico Restaurante $** Tacos, taco salads, chips and salsa. *Shares seats with Pecos Bill. Adventureland.* **Enchanted Grove $** ✔ Swirls and slushes. Also coffee, orange juice. *28 seats. Fantasyland.* **Liberty Square Market $** Whole fruit, corn on the cob, baked potatoes. *22 seats. Liberty Square.* **The Lunching Pad $** Turkey legs, pretzels, frozen drinks. *83 seats. Tomorrowland.* **Mrs. Potts' Cupboard $** Soft-serve ice cream. *53 seats. Fantasyland.* **Scuttle's Landing $** Bagels, muffins, pretzels. *80 seats. Fantasyland.* **Sleepy Hollow $** ✔ Funnel cakes, caramel corn, soft-serve ice cream. *51 seats. Liberty Square.* **Sunshine Tree Terrace $** Best treat in the park: Frozen OJ swirled with vanilla soft-serve ice cream. *46 seats. Adventureland.* **Tomorrowland Terrace Noodle Station $** ✔ Chicken with steamed rice, noodle bowls, teas. *500 seats. Dinner only, Tomorrowland.* **Village Fry Shoppe $** Fries, hot dogs. *Shares seats with Mrs. Potts. Fantasyland.*

SNACK STANDS ADVENTURELAND Aloha Isle $ ✔ Pineapple/vanilla soft-serve treats. Juice, pineapple spears. **Frontierland Fries $** French fries. **Westwood Ho Refreshments $** Muffins, hot dogs. MAIN STREET U.S.A. **Plaza Ice Cream Parlor $** Hand-dipped cones, floats, sundaes. MICKEY'S TOONTOWN FAIR **Toontown Farmer's Market $** Fruit, yogurt, frozen lemonade.

Country Bear backup band The Five Bear Rugs includes, from left: Tennessee, Fred, Zeke, Ted and Zeb. At far right is Zeb's young son, Oscar.

Country Bear Jamboree

City slickers may not cotton to it, and it hasn't aged well, but this Audio Animatronic hoedown is still loved by many. Set in an 1880s lumber camp union hall, it features 18 goofy, life-sized bears performing 14 songs.

Plump, tutu-clad Trixie performs the 1966 Wanda Jackson hit, "Tears Will Be the Chaser for my Wine." Lowered from the ceiling, temptress Teddi Barra performs "Heart, We Did All That We Could," a 1967 Jean Shepard hit. "Ya'll come up and see me sometime!" she coos, channeling Mae West. Replies the emcee: "As soon as I can find a ladder!" The best bear is sad-eyed, tone-deaf Big Al. He butchers the 1960 Tex Ritter dirge, "Blood on the Saddle."

Other songs include Ritter's 1950 "My Woman Ain't Pretty (But She Don't Swear None)" and Homer & Jethro's 1964 "Mama Don't Whip Little Buford (I Think You Should Shoot Him Instead)." Talking trophy heads Buff (a buffalo), Max (a deer) and Melvin (a moose) bicker and banter.

16 min. Capacity: 380. Avg. wait: 8 min. Guests may remain in wheelchairs, ECVs. Assistive listening; reflective captioning. Debuted: 1971.

Frontierland Shootin' Arcade

Filled with more than 50 silly sight and sound gags, this old-fashioned arcade is surprisingly fun. The infrared rifles are easy to hold, the targets easy to hit, and every hit causes something to happen — a prisoner escapes from his jail, an ore car comes out of its mine, a grave-digging skeleton pops out of his hole. You get 25 shots for a dollar. There's a bill changer on the side. Guns in the center have the best view of the most targets.

Capacity: 16. Avg. wait: None early morning, 5 min. peak afternoon. Guests may remain in wheelchairs, ECVs. Debuted: 1971.

➡ **Each gun is loaded with a secret free round to start the day.** A few remain as late as 10:30 a.m.

FUN FACTS ❱❱ Henry's introductory phrase "'cause we've got a lot to give" refers to the 1970s slogan of the show's original sponsor: "You've got a lot to live, and Pepsi's got a lot to give." ❱❱ Tex Ritter provides the voice of Big Al.

▶ Big Al's gift stand has Davy Crockett coonskin caps. Try one on for a fun photo.

Woody, Jessie and Sam the Singin' Cowboy invite children and adults to join them in Woody's Cowboy Camp, a 20-minute street hoedown based on the "Toy Story" films. Participants do the Hokey Pokey, sing along to "Hey Howdy Hey" and "You've Got a Friend in Me" and, led by Woody's trusty horse Bullseye, giddy-up their way through a cowboy obstacle course — maneuvering around parents donning hats shaped like cacti, mine shafts and mountains. Held at various Frontierland locations throughout the day, the performance also includes a dozen helpful cowboys and cowgirls.

Left: Roving Frontierland prospector Gold Dust Gus chats with a guest. **Above:** The wisecracking Notorious Banjo Brothers and Bob — he's the tuba-playing straight man — perform bluegrass, cowboy and a few Disney tunes during most afternoons.

Splash Mountain

✓ This half-mile flume ride in, out, around and down a man-made mountain is the most satisfactual, but least understood, ride in the park.

Lined with 68 Audio Animatronic creatures in cartoon-like musical scenes, it takes you through backwoods bayous, swamps, a cave and a flooded mine shaft. It includes five short drops and one five-story plummet.

Based on scenes from Disney's no-longer-sold 1946 film "Song of the South," Splash Mountain has a storyline that's fun and fascinating to follow. It's based on a series of American folk tales* popular with slaves in the antebellum South. Its obvious lesson: there's no place like home. Its subversive message: if they're crafty enough, the weak can do "pretty good, sure as you're born" against the strong.

You're in the story from the start. Climbing through some barns in rural Georgia, you come upon a secret passageway that leads to Critter Cave — the home of wise old storyteller Brer Frog.

"Mark my words," he says to two grandkids, in a shadow diorama on your left. "Brer Rabbit gonna put his foot in Brer Fox's mouth one of these days." Once in your log (hollowed out by sharp-toothed beavers, the story goes), you travel past the crafty rabbit's briar patch playground (around the ride's outdoor

Brer Fox uses a beehive to capture Brer Rabbit

drop), then head up Chick-A-Pin Hill, home to the tenacious but gullible Brer Fox and strong but stupid Brer Bear.

Floating into a magnolia bayou (i.e., once you go inside), you come upon Brer Rabbit packing up to leave. "I've had enough of this old briar patch," he sings. "I'm lookin' for a little more adventure."

Overhearing the rabbit, Brer Fox and Brer Bear scheme to catch the hare and cook him for dinner.

Trouble is, whenever they catch Brer Rabbit he always slips away.

First, Brer Fox captures him in a rope trap, but the bunny bamboozles Brer Bear into switching places.* Then, saying he's headed to a tempting "laughin' place," the rabbit leads the fox and bear far down the bayou and eventually into a hollow, fallen tree. It's not only filled with bees, it leads straight into a dark flooded mine. "I don't see no laughing place," the bear says. "Just bees!"

"I didn't say it was *your* laughin' place," the rabbit laughs, rolling on the ground. "I said it was *my* laughin' place!"

* "How Mr. Rabbit Was Too Sharp For Mr. Fox," "Mr. Rabbit and Mr. Bear" and "Brother Rabbit's Laughing-Place," as published in "The Complete Tales of Uncle Remus," an 1895 compilation of 185 African-American folk tales by Joel Chandler Harris, a columnist for the Atlanta Journal Constitution. Though the tales themselves have been widely embraced (Walt Disney loved "their rich and tolerant humor; their homely philosophy and cheerfulness"), Harris' book has not. In its forward, the white Harris described his created narrator, a freed slave named Uncle Remus, as "an old Negro... who has nothing but pleasant memories of the discipline of slavery." Disney's film basically ignored that premise but was still associated with it. The 1987 "The Tales of Uncle Remus" by Julius Lester offers most of the stories — which rival the best European folk tales for charm and meaning — in a more unadulterated state.

* In the film, Rabbit tells Bear he's a scarecrow, making $1 a minute. "Ya know, *you'd* make a mighty fine scarecrow, Brer Bear. How'd you like to have this job?"

▶ For the driest drop, duck down before the splash and stay down 'til after the slosh.

The final fall is 52 feet into, and under, a briar patch

In the mine shaft, Brer Fox slams a beehive over the rabbit and ties him up at his cooking pot. "Well Brer Rabbit, it looks like I'm gonna have to cook ya!"*

But the bunny has one more trick. "You can cook me," he yells, "but whatever you do, please don't fling me in that briar patch!" Brer Bear overhears this, so that's exactly what he does. Brer Rabbit escapes for good.

A singing showboat of friends welcomes him back home, but what's this? Brer Bear and Brer Fox are in the patch, too. Stuck in the thorns, the dim-witted bear is singing "Zip-A-Dee-Doo-Dah" along with the rabbit's friends.

"This is all your fault Brer Bear!" Brer Fox says, trying to pull the bear free while fighting off an alligator. "You flung us here. So stop that singing!"

12 min. Capacity: 440. Avg. wait: 10 min. early morning, 75 min. peak afternoon. Fastpass available. Must be ambulatory. Height restriction: 40 in. Fear factor: One small drop is completely dark. The big drop can scare even adults. Chicken exit. Best ages: 8 and up. Debuted: 1992 (1989 Disneyland).

FUN FINDS ❶ "Fleas, flat feet and furballs" are cured by the Critter Elixir trumpeted on a wagon past the second lift hill. **❷** Around the corner, Brer Bear snores in his house. **❸** "Time to be turning around... if only you could," say vultures above you before the drop. "If you've finally found your laughing place, how come you aren't laughing?"

* Alternates with "hang ya!" "roast ya!" and "skin ya!"

FUN FACTS » The logs reach 40 mph on the big drop, making it the fastest Magic Kingdom moment. **»** The ride uses 956,000 gallons of water, which is recycled every four minutes. **»** In 1993, Great Britain's Princes William and Harry, then ages 11 and 8, visited the park with their mother, Princess Diana. Splash Mountain was William's favorite ride, so Diana and her boys rode it twice more. **»** "Brer" is short for "Brother."

▶ **The front seat gets the wettest.**

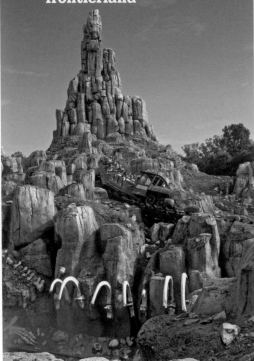

The peaks of Utah's Monument Valley inspired Disney's Big Thunder Mountain

more colorful, and every dip, drop and turn comes as a surprise.

Scattered around the set are hundreds of pieces of real mining gear, barbed wire, cactus and nearly 20 fairly realistic animals, including big-horned sheep, bobcats and javelinas.

The story is one of gods and greed. During the height of the Gold Rush*, men in the town of Tumbleweed were looking for gold on a nearby mountain, which was also an Indian burial ground. Though the mountain "thundered" whenever anyone prospected on it, these miners took ore trains deep down into its caverns and even dynamited new shafts. They removed the gold with glee and celebrated their finds with poker games and parlor girls. Acts of God struck back — mysterious spirits took control of the mine trains and spun them out of control, a flash flood hit the town and an earthquake struck. Everything was lost.

In reality, the mountain is a cement and wire-mesh skin over a concrete-and-steel frame. Inside are the ride's computers, electronics and pumps.

3 min. 30 sec. Capacity: 150. Avg. wait: 10 min. early morning, 60 min. peak afternoon. Fastpass available. Must be ambulatory. Height restriction: 40 in. Chicken exit. Debuted: 1980 (Disneyland 1979).

Big Thunder Mountain Railroad

✓ All curves all the time, this roller coaster is always exciting, but never scary. Three series of hairpin turns through caves, mine shafts, hot springs and a flooded town, the 36 mph ride slings you around but there are no big falls and you never go upside down. Sit in the back to go faster over the hills.

It's best at night. The dark track seems faster, its rattling louder, its sulfur pools

FUN FINDS ❶ Lights flicker and dim around the attraction. ❷ As you walk up to the building a box on your right reads "Lytum & Hyde Explosives Co." ❸ As you head down to the boarding area, a

FUN FACTS ❯❯ The trains are faster late in the day, after the track grease has melted. ❯❯ The train names are I.B. Hearty, I.M. Brave, I.M. Fearless, U.B. Bold, U.R. Courageous and U.R. Daring. ❯❯ The "Howdy partners!" announcer is Dallas McKennon, who voiced TV's Gumby and Archie Andrews; Rice Krispies characters Snap, Crackle and Pop; and Ben Franklin at Epcot's American Adventure.

* During the mid-1800s, a discovery of gold in a remote mountain area would often bring in a feverish migration of prospectors, who would search stream beds and canyon walls hoping to instantly find their fortune. Later a commercial company often arrived to mine for gold ore, chunks of rock with deposits of the precious metal.

▶ Hate long lines? Ride the rails before 10 a.m., during a parade or with a Fastpass.

Fun without the fear, Big Thunder Mountain pleases guests of all ages

box above you holds whiskey. ❹ In Tumbleweed, a bathtubbing prospector on your right has washed down from the hills. ❺ Rainmaker Prof. Cumulus Isobar bails himself out on your left. ❻ A whiskey-fueled poker match has been flooded out inside the Gold Dust Saloon. ❼ Once the sun sets, drunks and dance-hall dames still party upstairs. ❽ Around the bend, a "Floodometer" on your left reads "Flooded Out." ❾ Morris Code is the manager of a telegraph office behind a door along the left exitway. ❿ The right exit has a canary in a cage (he's not moving!) and, above a "Blasting in Progress" sign, a pushed-in plunger.

Tom Sawyer Island

Accessible only by a natural-gas-powered raft, this hilly, wooded island sits within the Rivers of America waterway of the Liberty Square Riverboat. Lined with paved, shady trails, it's filled with small adventures. Injun Joe's Cave is a cranny-filled cavern with a hidden scary face. Old Scratch's Mystery Mine is a creepy, twisting shaft with wailing winds and glowing crystals. Other spots include a climb-through grist mill (its creaks and groans subtly perform "Down By The Old Mill Stream;" the bird in the cogs is from the 1937 cartoon, "The Old Mill"), a barrel bridge and windmill. Atop a hill is a brook, duck pond, playground with a tiny rope swing and two picnic tables. Along the shore is Aunt Polly's Place, a shady snack bar.

A suspension bridge leads to calvary outpost Fort Langhorn. It has a snoring sentry, robotic horses and a "powder room" that's really the women's restroom. Kids love to find the "secret" escape tunnel at the back wall. Stairs lead to watchtowers with electronic rifles. *Allow 45 min. Capacity: 400. Avg. wait: 10 min. Must be ambulatory. Fear factor: The cave has side niches; preschoolers can get lost. Debuted: 1973.*

Barrels of fun. A bouncy bridge on Tom Sawyer Island.

▶ The mine water appears to run uphill.

Minnie's Country House

Though it looks a little like Barbie's Dream House (Minnie's signature red and white polka dots are nowhere to be found) this walk-through bungalow is a hands-on treat filled with Disney detail. The fun starts in Minnie's living room, where the chair and loveseat make good photo props. Children can climb on her potter's wheel in the craft room and check her answering machine in the hall. The best spot is the kitchen, where kids can bake a cake, heat up a teapot, wave some popcorn, open the fridge and try to grab a cookie.

It's all pretend, of course, but still fun. Silliness is tucked in everywhere. Attila the Mouse is the subject of a book on the coffee table, "Famous Mice in History." Written by Minnie, it's about a misunderstood invader who "merely came to taste the local cheeses." Another entry tells of Leonardo da Moussi, the inventor of the microwave cheese pizza.

The answering machine has a series of playable messages from Goofy, each time calling to say he forgot why he was calling. In the kitchen, the spice rack holds Thyme, Good Thyme, Bad Thyme and Out of Thyme.

The best gags are on the sun porch, where pun-prone plants include buttercups (teacups, each with a pat of butter) and palms (with hands for fronds). Each is explained in "Clarabelle's Big Book of Pun Plants," which sits on the room's wicker table.

No detail, it seems, was left out. The porch lamps are flower petals. Wall photos include a portrait of Minnie's great-grandparents, Milo and Mabeline. In the craft room, she's painting Wiseacre Farm, the scene that's visible out her window. Earlier she completed her own version of Norman Rockwell's "Triple Self Portrait."

Capacity: 125. No wait; a slow line takes 15 min. Guests may remain in wheelchairs, ECVs. Debuted: 1996.

➡ **Need to get off your feet?** The loveseat and chairs in Minnie's living room and sunroom are the only indoor spots to sit in Toontown.

FUN FACTS » The house has no bedroom. **»** It sits on the spot of Mickey's Hollywood Theater, a Meet Mickey building from 1988 to 1996.

Above: Rounded and out of proportion, Minnie's house (and Mickey's, at right) looks as if it was drawn by hand

▶ Out back, Minnie's garden gazebo makes a pretty photo spot.

Mickey's Country House

Two attractions in one, this walk-through House of Mouse is also the waiting line for the best place to meet Mickey.

First you tour the house. Mickey's just left, leaving on the television in the living room where he, Donald and Goofy have been watching football. In the bedroom hang many copies of his red-and-black tuxedo, while the den has seen Mickey beat his pals in ping pong. The kitchen is being "remodeled" by Donald and Goofy. Out back you walk through Mickey's appropriately shaped collection of cactus, pumpkins and tomatoes.

Then, if you like, you meet the mouse. He's always right next door, holding court in his Judge's Tent. The air-conditioned building entertains you with cartoons while you wait, and magically moves its line much faster than any other character location. (How's it done? Notice all the doors in the final hallway.)

Capacity: 125. Avg. wait: a slow-moving line can take 15 min. in the house; 30 more to see Mickey. Guests may stay in wheelchairs, ECVs. Debuted: 1988.

FUN FINDS ❶ A photo just inside the door shows Donald, Goofy and Mickey building the house. ❷ The bedroom has photos of Mickey as a baby, posing with Santa and as a Boy Scout. ❸ The bedroom also reveals a secret: Mickey wears glasses! ❹ Mail in the hall includes letters from Buzz Lightyear (return address: "Infinity and Beyond") and Ariel (from "Under the Sea"). ❺ The kitchen's plans are from the "Chinny Chin Chin Construction Co.; General Contractor Practical Pig," a reference to Disney's 1933 Silly Symphonies cartoon "The Three Little Pigs." ❻ The blueprints include a garbage disposal that is simply a pig under the sink. ❼ Scales on the plans read "16 parts = 8.9 parcels," "7 pinches = 2 dollops" and "1 smidgen = 4 oodges."

Above: A cartoon version of the archetypical American home, Mickey's house has a wooded yard wrapped in a picket fence and a workshop garage.
Below: Mickey-shaped tomatoes in the back garden.

▶ Want to meet Mickey? Stop by before 11 a.m. to avoid a long wait.

Goofy's plane crashes through a barn. **Below:** Laura Turner of Fort Myers, Fla., rides with her family.

The Barnstormer

With a short steep drop and a tiny tight spiral, this kid-friendly roller coaster is the perfect vehicle to introduce your kids to thrill rides. It's plenty zippy, but its tummy-tickling thrills are condensed into just 19 seconds of high-speed action.

The theme is fun, too. Taking off in a cartoon version of a 1920s crop-duster (Goofy's "Multiflex Octoplane") you immediately veer off course, turning, twisting and eventually crashing through a barn. It's the ideal spot to teach your tike to, in the words of '80s funksters Cameo, "wave your hands in the air like you don't care."

1 min. Capacity: 32. Avg. wait: 5 min. until 10:30 a.m., 30 min. after. Must be ambulatory. Height restriction: 35 in. Fear factor: Intense for toddlers. Best ages: 4 and up. Debuted: 1996.

FUN FINDS ❶ Goofy's pants fly above the silo. ❷ Real crops in the gardens often include beets, cabbage, corn, kohlrabi, squash and tomatoes. ❸ Cartoon crops

include "bell" peppers, popcorn, and squash that's been squashed by Goofy's feet. ❹ The giant jelly-jar lamps are "real" jelly jars. ❺ The chickens in the barn squawk after each plane passes. ❻ Behind them is a small "chicken exit." ❼ According to the plans on Goofy's drafting table (also reproduced in the boarding area), the crop-duster is powered by Dale running on a hamster wheel. ❽ Just outside the barn, a storage closet door labeled "Electrical Main" has been altered to read "Electrical Main Street Parade," a reference to the park's old Main Street Electrical Parade. ❾ A Goofy scarecrow is next, in the garden on your left.

FUN FACTS » The chickens once roosted inside Epcot's World of Motion (1982–1996), on the site of today's Test Track. **»** The first attraction here was Grandma Duck's Farm (1988-1995) a petting zoo with live pigs as well as Minnie Moo, a cow with Mickey-shaped spots. The pigs are now at the Fort Wilderness Campground. Ms. Moo moos no more.

▶ For a healthy treat grab some juice or fresh fruit at the Toontown Farmer's Market.

Donald's Boat

Here's where your toddlers and preschoolers can get soaked, and on a hot day they'll want to.

A leaky yacht-like tugboat, Donald Duck's yellow, blue and red S.S. Miss Daisy features a walk-in control room where pint-sized seafarers can clang a loud bell (by pulling on the right-hand rope) or secretly squirt water on others who have just gone out the back door (the left rope).

The big fun, however, is outside. The ship sits in a spongy duck pond filled with lily pads that spout jumping streams and spray without warning. Bring a swimsuit, or at least a change of clothes so your child can drench himself with abandon. The Pete's Garage restroom — to the left of Minnie's house — makes a good changing spot. Some parents just strip their kids down to their diapers and let 'em romp.

On the downside, the water is often turned off, due to drought conditions that have recently been common in Central Florida.

Even if you're just walking past you can still admire the boat. The two-story ship looks straight out of a cartoon. Its color scheme mimics Donald's sailor uniform and bill. The roof of the bridge resembles his cap.

Visiting from Naperville, Ill., 18-month-old Jessa Bergeron plays in one of the shooting fountains

Next door, Toon Park is a small covered play spot with small slides and tunnels as well as a handful of benches.

Capacity: 60. No wait. Guests may remain in wheelchairs, ECVs. Best ages: 18 months to 8 years. Debuted: 1996.

How to meet the characters

A variety of characters await you inside the Toontown Hall of Fame tents. One line leads to classic stars such as **Chip 'n' Dale**, **Goofy** and **Minnie Mouse**; another has princesses such as **Aurora** (Sleeping Beauty), **Belle**, **Cinderella** and **Snow White**; a third goes to **Winnie the Pooh** and friends that may include **Eeyore**, **Piglet** or **Tigger**. As the fair's presiding judge, **Mickey Mouse** is in the Judge's Tent — accessible through Mickey's Country House — surrounded by prize-winning fruits and vegetables. Waits for each room can be up to 30 minutes, but the lines are air conditioned and your child will get all the one-on-one time she wants with each star. The princesses are happy to chat. *There are no lines at 10 a.m., when this section of Magic Kingdom first opens. The adjacent County Bounty shop sells autograph books.*

© DISNEY

Stitch isn't happy in the Prisoner Teleport Center

Stitch's Great Escape!

Featuring elaborate robotics and sound effects, this theater-in-the-round show is geared to those familiar with the 2002 movie "Lilo & Stitch." In a story that takes place before the film, when Planet Turo's Prisoner Teleport Center receives an especially naughty detainee (Experiment 626), he breaks free and seems to skitter around in the dark.

The show begins as a sergeant tells you that most prisoners come in two types, and that you, as a new security guard, will be guarding the Level Ones, the "common criminals of the cosmos."

Then an alarm sounds. Arriving any second is a rare Level Three! Agent Pleakley orders you into a high-security chamber. As two DNA-tracking cannons zero in on the little guy, the quick-witted monster breaks free and shorts out the power. Sounding as if he is roaming around the audience, he eats a cell phone, then a chili dog, before escaping to Cinderella Castle.

The Audio Animatronic technology is impressive. The preshow sergeant shifts his weight from foot to foot and counts down on his fingers. Stitch's ears have multiple, simultaneous movements just like those of a dog; his eyes, arms, fingers and spine move fluidly.

18 min. Capacity: 240. Avg. wait: 10 min. early morning, 30 min. peak afternoon. Fastpass available. ECV users must transfer to a wheelchair. Handheld captions, assistive listening. Height restriction: 40 in. Fear factor: The harnesses and dark periods scare some kids. Best ages: 8 and up. Debuted: 2004.

IN "LILO & STITCH," a mad scientist on the planet Turo uses the genes of ferocious creatures to create Experiment 626, a tiny monster. Programmed to destroy everything it touches, the six-limbed alien can see in the dark and think faster than a supercomputer. When the Grand Councilwoman asks it to "show us there is something inside you that is good," 626 responds with the defiant yell "Meega, nala kweesta!" As it licks its holding glass, the monster is exiled to an asteroid, then guarded by robotic cannons that track genetic signatures. The ingenious creature, however, coughs on the floor. When the guns stalk the spit, 626 breaks loose, knocks out the power grid and escapes to Earth. Landing in Hawaii, the creature is adopted, and named Stitch, by Lilo, a lonely 7-year-old misfit. Other characters include Pleakley, a panicky government science advisor; and Gantu, a military captain whose face resembles a largemouth bass.

▶ Sit in back for the best view of Stitch. His platform sits high off the floor.

The Laugh Floor Comedy Club

✓ Sitting in a theater, you'll laugh, joke, sing songs and match wits with on-screen animated characters in this amazing theatrical show. Based on the 2001 Disney-Pixar film "Monsters, Inc.," it uses transparent technology and hidden backstage comedians to create improvisational exchanges between its characters and audience.

It's quite an experience.

The setting: the city of Monstropolis, where eyeball-on-legs Mike Wazowski has a big new idea: Since laughs contain 10 times the power of screams, he wants to generate electricity by gathering laughter in bulk. To do it, he's turned the laugh floor of utility company Monsters Inc. into a comedy club for people.

Wise-cracking Roz isn't sold on the idea, so Mike has booked a full slate of acts — slapstick comedian Buddy who's basically just arms and hands; two-headed comedy team Mac and Jeeze; and Melvin, Mike's look-alike nephew.

The monsters chat with the audience ("So, where you from?"), playfully tease some visitors and read jokes that guests provide via, among other methods, text messaging (a preshow film explains how to do it).

The performers often choose elementary and 'tween-age children to speak with. To increase the odds of your kids getting picked, have them dress with a big hat or colorful shirt.

The new attraction takes the place of the Timekeeper, in the building that also holds the attraction Buzz Lightyear's Space Ranger Spin.

15–20 min. Capacity: 400. Avg. wait: 30 min. early morning, 60 min. peak afternoon. Guests may stay in wheelchairs, ECVs. Reflective captioning, assistive listening. Best ages: 6 and up. Debuted: 2007.

Astro Orbiter

The most thrilling of Disney's four hub-and-spoke rides, Astro Orbiter is fast, high and a little scary. Sitting low in a one-person-wide rocket, you soar up into a tight banked circle 55 feet above the ground. Top speed is 20 mph, plenty fast when you're at a 45-degree angle.

You pass within a few feet of a huge kinetic model of rings, planets and moons (one with its own moon) and look down on everything from the Tiki Room to Toontown. You can even spot the Tower of Terror, five miles away at Disney-MGM Studios.

The line is usually awful, but first thing in the morning there's no one here and you can often ride twice in a row without getting off. After dark the rockets' green nose cones and red engine fires light up and the huge central antenna flashes in blue, red and pink neon. The rockets run during drizzles, but are grounded by lightning and downpours.

The ride's green, steel-mesh elevator is meant to resemble a Cape Canaveral rocket gantry.

2 min. Capacity: 32. Avg. wait: 10 min. early morning, 60 min. peak afternoon. Must be ambulatory. Fear factor: The height and steep angle scare even some adults. Debuted: 1971 (Disneyland, 1955).

Retro rockets. Astro Orbiter's Art Deco vehicles soar within a ring of twirling planets and moons.

Buzz Lightyear's Space Ranger Spin

✓ This addictive, goofy ride turns the concept of a shooting gallery inside out: the targets stand still while you travel on a track. Piloting an open-cockpit "space cruiser," you use a laser gun to fire at more than a hundred targets. You spin your vehicle to help your aim, while a dashboard display tracks your score. The point? To help Buzz Lightyear, the deluded toy space ranger from the "Toy Story" films, save the galaxy from the Evil Emperor Zurg.

It's more fun when you know the story. As you enter Star Command Headquarters, Buzz thinks you're a new recruit in his Galactic Alliance. And you're just in time: Zurg's robotic henchmen are stealing all the "crystallic fusion power cells" (batteries, in Buzz-speak) from the world's toys to power his new secret weapon. Buzz orders you out to destroy the robots, and his claw-worshipping little-green-alien buddies to go recapture the batteries.

Flying into space, you and a partner battle two huge robots then land on Zurg's volcanic home, Planet Z. You fight his monsters (including the bendy snake from the "Toy Story" bedroom), then

"Stop that! I'm invincible!" Zurg bellows as the squeakies take apart his secret-weapon scooter

sneak onto his ship and face Zurg head-on. Luckily his weapon won't fire — his aides have knocked the batteries loose. When Zurg sneaks out an escape hatch you follow him, shifting into hyperdrive.

Suddenly Zurg and his scooter reappear, this time as a video image. "Prepare for total destruction!" he bellows, darting in front of you. You fire (whether you pull the trigger or not) and the blast spins him out of sight... and right to the squeakies, who capture Zurg and then leave him hanging — from a claw.

The whole thing takes place in a world of toys. Buzz gets his information from a Viewmaster and Zurg's lead henchman is a Rock 'Em Sock 'Em Robot. With batteries on its back, your space cruiser is a remote-controlled toy. Its remote sits to your right as you enter the exit area.

4 min. 30 sec. Capacity: 201. Avg. wait: 10 min. early morning, 60 min. peak afternoon. Fastpass available. ECV users must transfer to a wheelchair. Handheld captioning. Debuted: 1998.

HOW TO SCORE BIG There are five secrets to getting a high score: ❶ Call dibs on the joystick, so you can keep your vehicle aimed at the right targets. ❷ Let your partner board first, so you sit on the right, the side with two-thirds of the targets. ❸ As soon as your gun is activated, pull the trigger and hold it in for the entire ride. The gun will automatically fire about once per second, and the flashing effect of its laser beam will make it easy to track your aim. ❹ If the ride stops, keep your blaster fixed on a target. You'll rack up points in a hurry. ❺ Aim only at targets with big payoffs: As you enter the first room, aim for the left arm of the left robot (each hit is worth 100,000 points). As you pass the robot, turn your vehicle to the left and hit the other side of that same arm (25,000). As you leave the first room, face your vehicle backwards and aim at the overhead claw of the other robot (100,000). As you enter Planet Z, aim at the top and bottom targets of the large volcano (25,000). As soon as you see Zurg, hit the bottom target of his space scooter (100,000) by firing early and late; your gun can't aim low enough to hit it straight on. Finally, as you go into hyperspace, aim about six feet to either side of the top of the exit tunnel to hit a circle sitting in the middle of a rectangular plate (25,000). *Maximum points possible is 999,999.*

Walt Disney's Carousel of Progress

Part of the General Electric pavilion at the 1964 World's Fair, this Audio Animatronic show traces how electricity has improved family life. Personally developed by Walt Disney, its theaters rotate around a central stage, like horses on a carousel.

The first scene takes place before electricity, on Valentine's Day, 1904. "Things couldn't be any better," a father proclaims, as he shows off his cast-iron stove which "keeps five gallons of water hot all day on just three buckets of coal" and icebox that holds so much ice that "milk doesn't sour as quick as it used to." Scene two takes you to the Fourth of July, 1927. "Mr. Edison sure added life to our home," the 'droid daddy says, sitting in a firetrap of cords as he points out his electric oven, refrigerator and vacuum cleaner. "It just can't get any better!" Next it's Halloween, 1949. "Everything is better than ever now," he says, amazed his new fridge "holds more food than ice cubes." Finally it's the future, a world of laser discs and other wonders from, well, the tomorrow of 1994, the last year this scene was updated.

The vintage script is not exactly PC — son Jimmy installs fuses and carves the jack-o-lantern while daughter Patty does little but get ready for dates — but it is funny. When Jimmy looks through his dad's stereoscope the boy exclaims, "Ooh la la! So that's the Norwegian doing the hoochie-koochie?" When Patty tells her 1940s friend Babs that she's going to a party with "that dreamboat, Wilfred," Babs replies "Wilfred?! What a slug!"

21 min. Capacity: 1,440. Guests may remain in wheelchairs, ECVs. Assistive listening; handheld and activated video

I, Robot. Built in 1964, the Carousel of Progress host was Disney's first Audio Animatronic human.

captioning. No flash photography. Debuted: 1964 at the New York World's Fair, installed at Disneyland in 1967, moved to Walt Disney World in 1975; revised 1994.

FUN FACTS » The father is voiced by Jean Shepherd, the narrator of 1983's "The Christmas Story." **»** His face was modeled from that of actor Preston Hanson, who starred as Marilyn Monroe's manager in the 1975 film "Goodbye, Norma Jean." **»** The grandpa is voiced by 1950s singing cowboy Rex Allen. **»** Grandma is voiced by Janet Waldo, teenager Judy in the 1960s cartoon series "The Jetsons" and Josie in the 1970s "Josie and the Pussycats." **»** Cousin Orville is Mel Blanc, the longtime voice of Warner Bros. cartoon characters. **»** Songwriters Richard and Robert Sherman had Walt Disney in mind when they wrote their "Great Big Beautiful Tomorrow" lyrics: "Man [Walt] has a dream and that's the start. He follows his dream in mind and heart..." **»** The 1904 grandma also rocks in front of the ballroom fireplace at the Haunted Mansion. **»** The building has an outer doughnut of six theaters which rotate on railroad-style wheels and tracks. **»** The theaters weigh 375 tons. **»** They move at 2 feet per second.

▶ Sit in the center of a back row. Many sound details come from the rear speakers.

The ride is pure joy. You never know where you are going, and rarely know where you are. Projected onto the underside of a smooth dome, twinkling stars and shooting comets have no beginning and no end. Pinpoint projectors and hidden mirror balls put some stars right in your path. In fact, you have no reference points at all. You can't even see the sides of your rocket. It's all sensation, no thought required.

2 min. 30 sec. Capacity: 180. Avg. wait: 10 min. early morning, 60 min. peak afternoon. Fastpass available. Must be ambulatory. The Fastpass queue is wheelchair accessible. Height restriction: 44 in. Fear factor: Many dark drops and turns, but you don't go upside down. Chicken exit. Best ages: 8 and up. Debuted: 1975.

Space Mountain

✓ "I want to go again! I want to go again! I want to go again!" said the 8-year-old boy to his parents. "That! Was! Cool!" said the 18-year-old college dude, here on Spring Break. "I rode it daddy! I rode it!" said a fully gowned Cinderella, age 6.

Where are these people? Climbing out of their rockets at the Space Mountain exit dock. Now *this* is the happiest place on earth.

And no wonder. The world's first indoor roller coaster when it debuted in 1975, this rocket-in-a-planetarium is still a delight. A series of surprises, its dips and whips leave you in seventh heaven.

Half the fun is the vehicle itself. One of the narrowest coaster cars ever built, your rocket is only slightly wider than you are. The sides are ridiculously low. They're at the waist of most people, just thigh-high for taller folks.

A FUTURISTIC SPACE FLIGHT The story begins as you walk into the building — a futuristic spaceport and repair center that's orbiting high above the earth. Passing the departure board, you walk down a long corridor to the launching platform, an open-air loading zone with its own control tower.

Once you climb into your rocket, a sign to your side flashes "All Systems Go." This activates the rocket transporter, which takes you through the energizing portal, a flashing blue tunnel of ever-louder "whoops" that powers up your machine and ignites your engine.

Climbing the launch tower (the chain lift), you pass under robotic arms that secure a large ship that has come in for service. As two mechanics work on its ion engines, two control-room operators monitor their progress.

Then you blast off — on a journey through, according to Disney, "the void of the universe." Zooming through space, "you become engulfed in a spectacular spiral nebula with flashing com-

▶ Ask for the front row. You'll fly through the air with a breeze on your knees.

ets and a whirling galaxy." (Apparently you lose your bearings, as halfway through you fly right back through the launch bay.) Finally you return to the spaceport, creating your own sonic boom in a red de-energizing tunnel before you dock in the entry bay.

FUN FINDS ❶ Just inside the building, departure board destinations include Star Sirius, Real Sirius, World Ceres and Beta Beleevit. ❷ As you walk along the corridor, the music changes from a light melody to an ethereal mix of harmonics, chimes and pings.

FUN FACTS ❯❯ The left track is a little darker, has a longer first drop and covers a slightly greater distance: 3,196 feet compared to the right track's 3,186. The final drop of both tracks is 35 feet. ❯❯ The meteorites projected on the ceiling are not pictures of chocolate-chip cookies. They just look that way. ❯❯ The energizing portal has a practical function: its flashing blue strobes shrink your pupils, which makes your space flight seem darker than it really is. ❯❯ Why do the docked ship's engine nozzles look like the plastic caps of spray-paint cans? Because they are! Used by an artist on a pre-production model, they were mistakenly reproduced as-is on the full-scale prop. ❯❯ Your rocket's top speed is only 28 mph. ❯❯ The "sonic boom" in the red re-entry tunnel is the reversed sound of a jet engine starting up. ❯❯ There are 30 rockets, numbered 1 through 31. There is no rocket 13. ❯❯ The building is 183 feet tall with a 300-foot diameter. It covers about two acres. Each of its 72 exterior concrete "ribs" weighs 74 tons, is 117 feet long and narrows from 13 feet wide at its base to 4 feet wide at its top. ❯❯ Much of the attraction is a subtle tribute to the seminal 1969 film, "2001: A Space Odyssey." The entranceway's eerie music recalls that of the film's early scenes of a moon transport shuttle, while the hall's angled plastic clapboard walls duplicate those of the transport's interior. The movie's Discovery One spacecraft shows up three times. In the ride's boarding area, the spool-like corners the rockets pass look just like the axle area of Discovery One's rotating living quarters. The blue strobe tunnel recalls its hexagonal corridor that leads to its EVA pods. On the lift hill, the docked ship has the craft's unique head-spine-and-hip shape. (The docked ship also appears earlier in the ride, outside an entranceway window.) ❯❯ The building gets its sweeping-pillar look from Israel's Kennedy Memorial. Its shape comes from Japan's Mt. Fuji.

"WHERE'S TINKER BELL?"
With its first passengers NASA astronauts Scott Carpenter, Gordon Cooper and Jim Irwin, Space Mountain opened with an elaborate ceremony on January 15, 1975, with Disney officials declaring the world's first indoor roller coaster "the nation's most breathtaking thrill ride." But not everyone got the message. As regular guests climbed into their rockets, many expected — since at the time Disney didn't do roller coasters — something along the lines of Peter Pan's Flight.

A few minutes later, up came their lunches and out flew their hats, purses, eyeglasses and, on more than one occasion, false teeth. Disney's response included posing two of the ride rockets in a dive up on the attraction's entrance tower, and putting a video in the queue in which Cooper told guests it was A-OK with him if they would rather just head for the exit ramp (or as cast members called it, the "chicken exit") but if not, to "be sure to hang onto anything that's not fastened down: eyeglasses, hearing aids, hats, and even wigs." (Meanwhile, Disney discreetly ironed out some of the ride's most violent jerks and jolts.)

Though it opened during a recession, Space Mountain was an instant smash. By Easter every Central Florida hotel and motel was full, and passenger traffic at the Orlando airport was up 14 percent. When summer came, families with teenagers — many of whom would have never previously considered a Disney vacation — began crowding Magic Kingdom turnstiles early each morning, running straight to Space Mountain as soon as the park opened. Afternoon waiting times at the ride would be two, sometimes three hours. By the end of 1975 Magic Kingdom attendance — down 17 percent the year before — was up 20 percent, giving the park its busiest year yet.

Three decades later the only real difference is the postshow. Originally the elaborate RCA Home of Future Living, dioramas along the exit ramp showed a dad in a patio chair engaged in a teleconference while kids inside watched videodiscs. In 1985 the area became the more spare RYCA-1 Dream of a New World, where robots inhabited a pod city on a "hostile planet." The goofy Federal Express FX-1 Teleport took over the planet from 1993 to 1998, as "teleportation units" digitized and transported alien fossils back to earth. Remnants of the FedEx scenes remain today, though the robot boy and dog have been around since the beginning. Originally known as Billy, the boy used to film guests for their television appearances on the Speedramp.

The FedEx years also had a preshow, as monitors in the boarding area aired the futuristic "SMTV" network. Commercials had Crazy Larry selling used spaceships, while a space newscast featured ditzy weather girl Wendy Beryllium: "Our extended forecast: giant comet. Wow, scary!"

▶ Not sure? Sneak a peek at the ride on the Tomorrowland Transit Authority.

Tomorrowland Indy Speedway

Yikes! Your child is at the wheel at this old-fashioned "race" track — and, if he or she can reach it, on the gas pedal, too. This winding, wooded course puts your little boy or girl at the controls of a 5-year-old's dream machine — a free-wheeling racer with a rough ride and a rumbly, smelly engine. Top speed is 7.5 mph; you stay in your lane thanks to a rail underneath your car (expect to hit it every few seconds). The one-lap trip takes you under and over a bridge.

If your child can't reach the gas pedal, have her steer while you work the pedal.

5 min. Capacity: 292. Avg. wait: 5 min. early morning, 60 min. peak afternoon. Must be ambulatory. Height restriction: 52 in. to take a car out alone. Debuted: 1971 (Disneyland 1955). Revised 1996.

FUN FINDS ❶ Speakers around the track feature famed Indy announcer Tom Carnegie calling your "race." ❷ A brick from the 1909 pavement of the real Indy Speedway is embedded in the "starting line" between lanes 2 and 3, close to the elevated exit walkway.

Above: Jeff Turner of Fort Myers, Fla., cheers on his son, Andrew, 6, as they head for the Indy Speedway finish line

Terry's Teen Troupe of Avon, Connecticut, is among the hundreds of bands, choirs, orchestras, dance troupes, and other amateur groups that have appeared at Tomorrowland's Galaxy Palace Theater. They entertain as part of Disney Magic Music Days, an ongoing performance series.

▶ Take your spin early in the morning or late at night to avoid a long wait.

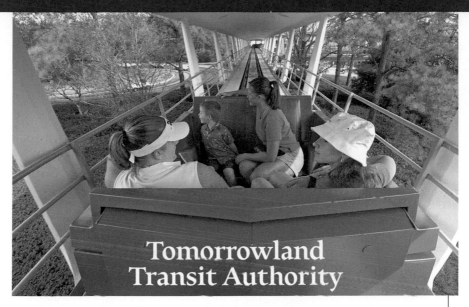

Tomorrowland Transit Authority

There are no big thrills, no special effects, not even a story, but this breezy elevated tour of Tomorrowland is still a nice way to get off your feet. You get a great view of Cinderella Castle, travel over the Indy Speedway and through Space Mountain.

Anytime is good to go. During a rain the covered route protects you from all but a windy downpour. At night the track glows red. A weird time to ride is when Space Mountain shuts down for repairs and its interior work lights are on. (Like seeing your grandma naked, it's interesting, but you learn things you didn't need to know.)

There's never a wait.

A far cry from its original purpose (see right), today the ride is presented as a mass-transit system for a silly future world, with scenes of a wacky hair salon and rocket port. A narrator says that the center section of an early diorama of Walt Disney's proposed EPCOT community is a relic from the "Metro Retro Historical Society;" a page tells Mr. Tom Morrow his "party from Saturn has arrived; please give them a ring."

10 min. Capacity: 900. Must be ambulatory. Handheld captioning. Debuted 1975 as the WEDway PeopleMover, revised 1996.

TRAIN IN VAIN

Today's Tomorrowland Transit Authority began life as a sketch drawn by Walt Disney in the mid-1960s. Planning for his Experimental Prototype Community of Tomorrow (EPCOT), he thought a system of small, narrow, electric trains would be ideal for people to run errands or go to work, as it could snake alongside or circle over convenience stores, offices and monorail stations without creating pollution or traffic problems. Though Walt died just as the idea was getting off the ground, his team developed it fully. Loading is fast, as each train slows but never stops. Clean, efficient and easy to maintain, the power system has no engines and no moving parts except for its wheels. The trains move via an electrical system in the track. Every six feet or so a coil embedded in a shoebox-size rectangle pulses with electricity, turning on to pull the next car to it (its magnetism attracts a steel plate in the car's floor) then turns off to let that vehicle pass over it. These on-and-off bursts continue around the track (there are 533 numbered electromagnets in its 4,574 feet) moving the trains in a smooth glide of linear induction. The concept won a design achievement award from the National Endowment for the Arts and the U.S. Dept. of Transportation. Disney believed in the system so much that it formed a separate division, Community Transportation Services (CTS), to market it to other municipalities. But without Walt, the dream died. EPCOT the city was abandoned, and CTS only sold the idea once: to the Houston International Airport in 1981. A modern version of the system powers the Rock 'n' Roller Coaster at Disney-MGM Studios.

Above: Guest Carol Ravenhorst (in orange) rides with daughters Andrea and Pam and grandson Van

▶ Ride it at dusk for a great view of a colorful sight: Astro Orbiter in front of a sunset.

Disney Dreams Come True Parade

Filled with Disney stars all ready to wave, this character cavalcade is your kids' chance to wear out their arms.

First up is Walt Disney, shown as a young animator drawing Mickey Mouse. Then it's Mickey Mouse. Riding on a "It Was All Started by a Mouse" platform, he's surrounded by statues that show how he evolved from a gloveless black-and-white imp in 1928's "Plane Crazy" to the colorful cherub of 1983's "Mickey's Christmas Carol." Behind him are his brooms from 1940's "Fantasia."

A "Wish Upon a Star" float has characters from 1937's "Snow White and the Seven Dwarfs" and 1940's "Pinocchio," followed by those of 1951's "Alice in Wonderland." Then stars such as Aladdin, Mary Poppins and Winnie the Pooh (about to lift off with a balloon) celebrate "A Hundred Thousand Dreams to See."

Other floats include "Face the Darkest Fears" (Disney villains), "As Long as There is Imagination Left in the World" (1953's "Peter Pan") and "A Dream is a Wish Your Heart Makes" (princesses). Additional characters include Minnie Mouse, Donald Duck, Goofy, Chip 'n'

Dale, and the cartoon stars of the 1946 film "Song of the South." The procession is an update of the Share a Dream Come True snowglobe parade (2001–2006), a rolling tribute to Walt Disney.

Route: Starts in Frontierland; travels Liberty Square and down Main Street. The 3:00 parade gets to Liberty Square at 3:07, the castle at 3:15, Town Square at 3:25. 15 min. Arrive 30 min. early for a good seat. Special areas for those in wheelchairs and ECVs. Debuted: 2001, revised 2006.

Main Street Family Fun Day Parade

You'll join Pluto and other characters in a stroll down Main Street if you're picked to be in this brief patriotic procession. Held two or three times a day, it also includes small floats, a marching band and the avenue's old-time fire truck. Nearly anyone can be in it: there's even a stroller drill team. Disney selects participants 10 to 15 minutes before it starts, from a queue line in front of Cinderella Castle.

Above: Tigger greets happy fans on Main Street

▶ The best viewing spot: On the curb on the shady western side of Main Street.

park puzzler

How much do you really know about the Magic Kingdom?

1) The girl at right is dressed as which princess?
a. Ariel.
b. Aurora.
c. Cinderella.

2) The flying Tinker Bell at the beginning of Wishes is portrayed by...
a. An Audio Animatronic robot.
b. A beam of light.
c. A cardboard cutout.
d. A real person.

3) Which former attraction star is buried in the Haunted Mansion's pet cemetery?
a. The ExtraTERRORestrial Alien Encounter alien.
b. Minnie Moo from Grandma Duck's Petting Farm.
c. Mr. Toad from Mr. Toad's Wild Ride.

4) At the Pirates of the Caribbean, the auctioneer tells the redhead to...
a. "Bury your treasure!"
b. "Cover your cargo!"
c. "Lower your sails!"
d. "Strike your colors!"

5) In the Enchanted Tiki Room, after Iago hears "In the Tiki Tiki Tiki Tiki Tiki Room" he threatens to...
a. Spill his beans.
b. Toss his crackers.
c. Cut his cheese.

6) The interior decor of Space Mountain re-creates the look of what classic film?
a. 1968's "2001: A Space Odyssey."
b. 1968's "Barbarella."
c. 1971's "The Andromeda Strain."

7) The exterior of Cinderella Castle is made of what material?
a. Concrete.
b. Fiberglass.
c. Stone.

Answers, page 319

Cinderella's twinkling pumpkin transforms into an all-white carriage during the SpectroMagic finale

SpectroMagic

✓ Like a Christmas tree in a dark living room, just the sight of this nighttime light parade makes you feel good. It's a cavalcade of colorful lights, many of which animate into synchronized patterns. Everything is lit — the floats *and* the characters — but since it all comes from within it's all against a pitch-black backdrop.

But it's more than just lights. Set to a symphonic score and filled with twirling butterfly girls, spinning fish and dancing ostriches, SpectroMagic is like a hallucinatory dream — you can't understand it, but it sure is interesting.

The theme? Disney's cartoons and musicals from the 1930s, '40s and '50s, accented with a couple of modern milestones. The parade features more than 80 characters, 90 percent of them from works released before 1960.

Smoke and disco balls add to the fun, as does the mischief of the performers. The "Fantasia" ostriches peck, kick or slap each other. The Three Little Pigs taunt the Big Bad Wolf. Peter Pan has been known to kick Mr. Smee.

A good place to sit is in front of Tony's Town Square Restaurant on Main Street, where the parade comes at you and then turns. You're also next to the park exit. Running late? Front-row seats are often available in front of the Town Square firehouse until just before showtime. You'll be directly across from the barber shop, where celebrities often watch.

A bad spot to sit: In Frontierland, facing the Rivers of America. A spotlight by the riverboat shines right in your face.

FLOATS The procession begins with the exuberant SpectroMen, a group of green-, orange- and purple-haired trumpeters and whirlyball riders who are literally light-headed.

After Mickey Mouse casts his spell over a lightning ball, Genie conducts a three-float symphony. Goofy, playing the timpani, rides with the Golden Harp from "Mickey and the Beanstalk" (from the 1947 film "Fun and Fancy Free"). Also on board: the bass violins from the 1935 Silly Symphony "Music Land" and a Liberace-like, bench-gliding Chip 'n' Dale playing a grand piano.

A peacock leads in the three-float flower garden of Disney's 1959 princess "Sleeping Beauty." Good fairies Fauna

▶ Let your kids play in the dark street before the parade. Where else can they?

(wearing green), Flora (in blue) and Merriweather (red) turn a multicolor day to a blue and green night. Alongside dance human butter- and dragonflies.

A 12-foot fish escorts three more to lead in "The Little Mermaid" float. From the 1989 film comes a spinning Ursula, swimming Ariel and singing Sebastian, followed by a sea-horse-drawn King Triton. Also floating by: two flashing, twirling fish. (Watch for the bubbles!)

Next it's back in time to 1940's "Fantasia." Ben Ali Gator, Hyacinth Hippo and the dancing ostriches entertain Bacchus with their "Dance of the Hours" routine. Then Chernobog, the monstrous bat-winged demon from the film's "A Night on Bald Mountain" segment, is escorted by five winged horses that fly above some dry-ice clouds.

The finale tops it all. Poised before six floats, the Three Little Pigs (stars of the 1932 "Silly Symphony" cartoon) flick paint brushes to change the convoy — including Cinderella's coach and castle, a rotating carousel, Captain Hook's ship and every character's costume — from a silvery white to the full color spectrum.

It's not just color changes. The coach converts from a carriage to a pumpkin. And the Cheshire Cat, riding on the back of an "Alice in Wonderland" float, disappears except for his mouth and eyes.

Route: Starts on Main Street U.S.A. between the Town Square firehouse and car barn. Continues to the castle hub, through Liberty Square and Frontierland. 20 min. Arrive 30 min. early for a decent seat, an hour early for the best spots. Special viewing areas for guests in wheelchairs and ECVs. Fear factor: The Chernabog float has spooky music and a 30-foot-tall animated monster. Debuted: 1991, revised 2001.

FUN FINDS ❶ The SpectroMen's horns light when they're played. ❷ Mickey's 24-tier cape extends up over his float. ❸ His electricity ball sizzles when he touches it and adds rays to his cape. ❹ Other lights on the cape sync to the music. ❺ The bass violins pluck themselves. ❻ Notes project on the ground around them. ❼ A sun changes to a moon on the first garden float. ❽ The insect girls have painted faces. ❾ A waterfall cascades down the back of the last garden float. ❿ Each pair of eyes in the fish school moves differently. ⓫ Ursula stops to chat with some guests ("Hello handsome!"). ⓬ Ariel does the breast stroke. ⓭ The spinning fish wink. ⓮ The ostriches wear tuxedo jackets and eyeliner. ⓯ The red-lit Chernabog turns into the pink Bald Mountain. ⓰ Two buzzards guard him. ⓱ Lightning strikes under Chernabog's horses and on the mountain. ⓲ A crown spins above Cinderella. ⓳ Tinker Bell appears in the castle windows. She flies outside of them. ⓴ Two mechanical "Alice in Wonderland" playing cards paint their roses red. ㉑ Mary Poppins' umbrella lights up with her jacket. ㉒ Dumbo is one of the carrousel animals. ㉓ The stars of 1945's "The Three Caballeros" appear on the merry-go-round's rear top panel. ㉔ The hook of Captain Hook lights up. ㉕ Hook's cannons fire in time with the music. ㉖ Flying on the mast, his Jolly Roger flag always has red eyes. ㉗ Riding with Hook, the Evil Queen has her magic mirror. ㉘ Tinker Bell appears again in the Evil Queen's castle. ㉙ Lights circle the ground around Minnie and Donald. ㉚ Facing backward, a Jiminy Cricket puppet waves "So long! See ya later!"

FUN FACTS 》 The floats are covered in scrim, a transparent black gauze. **》** The drivers' faces hide behind mesh screens. **》** The parade uses 2,000 car batteries. Walking performers wear battery packs. **》** There are 600,000 miniature lights; 100 miles of fiber-optic cable. Some floats and costumes use fiber-optic thread. **》** The floats carry 204 speakers with 72,000 watts of power. **》** Soundtrack composer John Debney also created the scores for the motion pictures "Elf," "Bruce Almighty," "The Scorpion King," "Spy Kids (1 & 2)" and "The Passion of the Christ." **》** The Sebastian and Jiminy Cricket puppets were added to the parade in 2001, when it returned to the Magic Kingdom after a two-year hiatus.

▶ At Town Square? Get snacks at the line-free locker shop *outside* the train station.

Pyro shoots wildly during the villains segment of Wishes, Walt Disney World's largest fireworks show

Wishes

✓ Every! Other! Fire! Works! Show! Emphasizes! Every! Explosion! Not this one. Disney's signature fireworks show is artistic, even subtle.

Though it includes 683 different pieces of pyro in just 12 minutes, Wishes paints delicate strokes as well as bold. Sometimes the sky sparkles, sometimes it explodes. Some explosions form stars, hearts, even a face. Some bursts dribble away, others disappear. Comets shoot off solo and by the dozen.

But that's just the half of it. Synchronizing its visuals to a symphonic score, Wishes packs an emotional punch. Narrated by Jiminy Cricket with help from the Blue Fairy, it teaches a heart-tugging lesson about believing in yourself.

The show starts softly, as a quiet chord grows louder and the castle begins to glow and sparkle. Then you hear the Blue Fairy: "When stars are born they possess a gift or two... They have the power to make a wish come true."

Right on cue, a lone star arcs across the sky. *"Starlight, star bright, first star I see tonight,"* a chorus of little girls sings. *"I wish I may I wish I might, have the wish I wish tonight..."* Blue stars — not star bursts but actual five-pointed stars — explode above Cinderella Castle.

"I'll bet a lot of you folks don't believe that, about a wish coming true, do ya?" Jiminy asks. "Well I didn't either. But lemme tell you... the most fantastic, magical things can happen, and it all starts with a wish!"

And with that, the spectacle begins. First Tinker Bell (a real person) steps off the top turret of Cinderella Castle and glides over the crowd to Tomorrowland. Major explosions fill the air as the voices of Cinderella, Ariel, Pinocchio and other Disney stars recall their

IN 1940'S "PINOCCHIO," the Blue Fairy (a symbol of kind, patient wisdom) appoints Jiminy Cricket to serve as the boy's official conscience

▶ Watch the show from in front of the castle. Main Street doesn't fill until showtime.

wishes, then medleys of fireworks (each in its own color palette) express courage and love.

"Fate is kind," a choir sings. *"She brings to those who love... the sweet fulfillment of... their secret longing."*

A fan of comets wipes the sky clean, then shooting fountains dance to the opening notes of "The Sorcerer's Apprentice." Later, a villains segment features chaotic, crackling bursts, some as bright as strobe lights.

"Wishes can come true," the cricket says. "And the best part is, you'll never run out. They're shining deep down inside of you."

WHERE TO WATCH IT With fireworks that launch directly behind Cinderella Castle as well as symmetrically alongside, Wishes is best seen from in front of the castle, anywhere on Main Street.

The perfect spot is on the crest of the Main Street bridge (between the tip board and the hub), where you'll be close enough to see all the castle effects, but far enough away to see all the pyrotechnics. There's always room here, as cast members don't let people stand in this area of the street until just minutes before showtime.

Avoid Town Square (where the lights stay on) and especially the train station balcony (where there's no audio). Want to dash out of the park as soon as the show ends? Stand in front of the Emporium — the closest dark spot to the exit.

But why fight the crowd? Instead, why not embrace the magical mood you'll be in to get an ice cream and relax. Your kids will be happy; why not talk with them? Ask about their dreams and wishes. Tell them about yours.

"STARLIGHT, STAR BRIGHT," a 19th-century American nursery rhyme, is based on the notion that if you see the first star of the night sky before any others have appeared, any wish you make will come true. (In reality, an evening's first visible "star" is often the planet Venus.)

12 min. Special viewing areas for wheelchair and ECV guests if arranged 30 min. early. Debuted: 2003.

FUN FINDS **❶** Blue stars appear above the castle during the opening verse, just after the lines "When you wish upon a star..." "makes no difference who you are..." and "anything your heart desires will come to you..." **❷** Tinker Bell starts her flight from the castle just after Jiminy Cricket says "...and it all starts with a wish!" **❸** As each Disney character says their wish, the accompanying fireworks are the color of his or her famous wardrobe (i.e., Cinderella's are blue, Ariel's green). **❹** After Aladdin tells Genie "I wish for your freedom!" a shout of "Wishes!" brings out another blue star. **❺** Red hearts appear above the castle at the end of the song "Beauty and the Beast." **❻** More blue stars explode as Jiminy sings "...when you wish upon a star, your dreams... come true!" **❼** "Whoa!" Genie says as his fireworks appear. "Ten thousand years can give ya such a crick in the neck!" **❽** During the "Sorcerer's Apprentice" sequence, the castle turns into the blue Sorcerer's Hat, with its white stars and moons. **❾** A red explosion introduces the villains. **❿** Images of the Evil Queen's mirror appear on the castle as she commands "Slaves in the magic mirror, come from the farthest space..." **⓫** A frowning face appears in the sky, and the castle mirrors become faces, when the queen commands "Let me see thy face!" **⓬** Meanwhile the castle glows in dark greens, oranges and purples and is flashed with lightning. **⓭** It turns blue again as the Blue Fairy returns.

FUN FACTS ❯❯ The fireworks launch from 11 locations. **❯❯** Tinker Bell is sometimes a man. The role's physical requirements are only that the performer weigh no more than 105 pounds and be no taller than 5 feet 3 inches. **❯❯** Wishes replaced Fantasy in the Sky, the park's fireworks show from 1976 to 1993. Though only five minutes longer, Wishes uses almost three times the fireworks.

▶ Keep an eye on the castle. It sparkles, flashes and changes colors.

The symbol of Epcot, Spaceship Earth is a 180-foot geosphere covered in 11,000 triangular facets

Epcot

Where can you talk with a sea turtle, crash through test barriers, soar over California, take a rocket ride to Mars, be chosen King of England, buy some exclusive French perfume and feast at a German Oktoberfest? At Epcot, a unique theme park that puts a Disney spin on the science expositions, national pavilions and large, iconic structures of a classic world's fair — all set in a relaxing, if huge, musical garden.

TWO PARKS IN ONE The world's fair theme kicks off in **Future World,** a science-and-technology zone themed to subjects such as agriculture, automotive safety, fossil fuels and geography.

Sound dull? It isn't. Each of those topics is the theme of a ride — a greenhouse boat cruise (Living with the Land), a spin around a General Motors proving ground (Test Track), a moving-theater trip through a dinosaur swamp (Ellen's Energy Adventure) and a hang-gliding flight over California (Soarin'). Other highlights: the interactive "Turtle Talk with Crush" and the ultra-realistic Mission Space. In the middle is Innoventions Plaza, a hub with two exhibit halls.

You'll travel around the world (and stop only in friendly countries) when you take the 1.3-mile trek around Epcot's **World Showcase.** Circling a 40-acre lagoon, 11 national pavilions are filled with native entertainment, food and merchandise. Most offer an attraction or small museum. Best of all, each is staffed by young natives of its country. Chosen for their outgoing personalities, these participants in Disney's Cultural Representative Program are always willing to chat.

THE LAYOUT OF FUTURE WORLD mimics the left-right division of the human brain. As you enter the park, pavilions on your left are themed to analytical, linear or engineering issues (i.e., energy, space travel, automobile) and sit within a landscape of straight-lined walkways. Those on the right cover more natural topics (seas, land) and rest in a hilly, meandering, watery landscape.

Eleven international pavilions line a 1.3-mile promenade that circles the World Showcase Lagoon

HISTORY Epcot opened Oct. 1, 1982. For its first four years it was called EPCOT Center. Four pavilions were added during the park's first decade — Morocco (1984), The Living Seas (1986, now The Seas with Nemo & Friends), Norway (1988) and Wonders of Life (1989). Its biggest change came in 2000, when its futuristic Horizons pavilion was demolished to make way for Mission Space.

The word Epcot comes from the acronym for Walt Disney's Experimental Prototype Community of Tomorrow, a working model city of the future he envisioned would be centered on this site. After his death, the company took two of Walt's ideas — a science center that would show ways to improve existing communities, and an international exposition that would showcase the culture, history and goals of other nations — and reworked them into a theme park.

A TWO-DAY TOUR With nearly two dozen pavilions over 260 acres, Epcot takes two days to fully enjoy. As shown on the next page, an easy plan is to spend one day in Future World, another at

Spaceship Earth (left) was inspired by the Perisphere (above) of the 1939 World's Fair

▶ Rain cancels most of Epcot's live entertainment but only one attraction: Test Track.

Epcot has two entrances. The main gate is at the front of the park, next to the parking lot and monorail station. A second entry, called the International Gateway, lies between the World Showcase pavilions of the United Kingdom and France. It provides access to guests staying in the Epcot Resort Area hotels — Disney's BoardWalk, Yacht Club and Beach Club; and the Walt Disney World Swan and Dolphin.

World Showcase. The two areas keep separate hours. Future World closes at 7 p.m. except for major attractions; World Showcase doesn't open until 11 a.m. The park typically closes at 9 p.m.

FUN FINDS ❶ The central Innoventions fountain offers a five-minute show choreographed to music every 30 minutes. ❷ An upside-down waterfall propels water into a pool in front of the Imagination pavilion. ❸ A single splash of water appears to hop from pad to pad at the Leap Frog Fountain, directly in front of the Honey, I Shrunk the Audience attraction. ❹ Meanwhile, jelly-like blobs of water hang in mid-air after they break off from the streams of the nearby Jellyfish Fountain. ❺ Three Future World drinking fountains imitate submarine sounds, sing opera and offer wisecracks such as "Hey, save some for the fish!" when water hits their drains. One sits in front of MouseGear along the east side of the Innoventions fountain. ❻ A second is near the play fountain between Future World and the World Showcase. ❼ A third fountain sits close to the restrooms behind Innoventions West. ❽ Voices inside a trash can talk to you inside the Electric Umbrella. Swing open the lid of the receptacle marked "Waste Please" (next to the topping bar to the left of the order counter) and you may hear a surfer dude complain "Like, your trash just knocked off my shades!" or a Frenchman exclaim "This is my lucky day! French fries!" ❾ Fiber-optic lights are embedded in the sidewalks in front of the Innoventions buildings. Pinpoints of shimmering, flickering stars hide in

BY THE NUMBERS ⟩⟩ **260** Number of acres in Epcot. **162** Number of acres in the Epcot parking lot.

Two Magical Days

DAY 1: FUTURE WORLD

8:30 Arrive at the park

9:00 Test Track

9:30 Get Fastpasses for Soarin'.

9:45 The Seas
See Turtle Talk with Crush, then the 10:30 marine biology presentation.

12:00 The Land
Buy tickets to the 2 p.m. Behind the Seeds tour, ride Soarin', have a 1 p.m. lunch at Garden Grill.

3:00 Mission Space

4:30 Innoventions

6:00 Spaceship Earth

7:00 Dinner at the Coral Reef.

DAY 2: WORLD SHOWCASE

10:30 Arrive at the park

11:30 U.K. See World Showcase Players.

12:00 France
Impressions de France, lunch at Chefs de France.

1:30 Japan See Miyuki.

2:15 Italy See Masquerade.

3:15 Germany See the miniature train.

3:45 Outpost See OrisiRisi.

4:15 China See Dragon Legend Acrobats.

5:30 Norway Ride Maelstrom.

6:30 Mexico
Mariachi Cobre, dinner at San Angel Inn.

8:30 Illuminations

EPCOT
park map

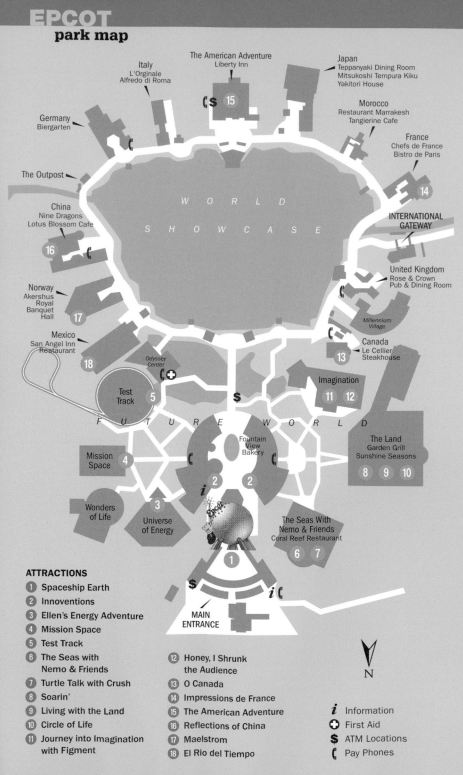

Italy
L'Orginale
Alfredo di Roma

The American Adventure
Liberty Inn

Japan
Teppanyaki Dining Room
Mitsukoshi Tempura Kiku
Yakitori House

Germany
Biergarten

Morocco
Restaurant Marrakesh
Tangierine Cafe

The Outpost

France
Chefs de France
Bistro de Paris

China
Nine Dragons
Lotus Blossom Cafe

WORLD SHOWCASE

INTERNATIONAL GATEWAY

United Kingdom
Rose & Crown
Pub & Dining Room

Norway
Akershus
Royal
Banquet
Hall

Millennium Village

Mexico
San Angel Inn
Restaurant

Odyssey Center

Canada
Le Cellier
Steakhouse

Test Track

Imagination

FUTURE WORLD

Fountain View Bakery

Mission Space

The Land
Garden Grill
Sunshine Seasons

Wonders of Life

Universe of Energy

The Seas With Nemo & Friends
Coral Reef Restaurant

MAIN ENTRANCE

ATTRACTIONS

1. Spaceship Earth
2. Innoventions
3. Ellen's Energy Adventure
4. Mission Space
5. Test Track
6. The Seas with Nemo & Friends
7. Turtle Talk with Crush
8. Soarin'
9. Living with the Land
10. Circle of Life
11. Journey into Imagination with Figment
12. Honey, I Shrunk the Audience
13. O Canada
14. Impressions de France
15. The American Adventure
16. Reflections of China
17. Maelstrom
18. El Rio del Tiempo

i Information
✚ First Aid
$ ATM Locations
℄ Pay Phones

N

Kids make their own souvenirs at Epcot's Kidcot Funstops, located in pavilions throughout the park

Park resources

The park has three **ATMs:** outside the gate near the kennel, at the bridge between World Showcase and Future World near the Disney Vacation Club kiosk and at the American Adventure near the restrooms... The **Baby Care Center** *(inside Future World's Odyssey Center)* has changing rooms, nursing areas and a microwave; and sells diapers, formula, pacifiers and over-the-counter medications... Gateway Gifts Camera Center *(underneath Spaceship Earth)* sells **cameras and accessories** and burns photo CDs... The **First Aid Center** *(inside Future World's Odyssey Center)* handles minor emergencies and has registered nurses on hand... The park's **Guest Relations** center *(to the left of Spaceship Earth, and at the far right of the park entrance)* has cast members ready to answer any question or help with any problem. It has maps and Times Guides for all the theme parks, exchanges foreign currency and stores items found in the park that day... **Lockers** can be rented at Gateway Gifts Camera Center *(underneath Spaceship Earth)* for $5 per day plus a $2 deposit. The lockers are immediately to the right of Spaceship Earth.... Report **lost children** to Guest Relations or any cast member. Children who lose their parents should tell a cast member... Anything you buy can be sent to **Package Pick-Up** *(park entrance or International Gateway)* for you to get as you leave. Purchases can also be delivered to your Disney hotel or shipped.... For day guests **parking** is $10 a day. Those staying at a Disney resort (and annual passholders) get free parking. A tram takes you to the park entrance... The **Pet Care Kennel** *(Entrance Plaza, 407-560-6229)* has clean cages in air-conditioned rooms (see the chapter "Practical Information" for details)... **Security guards** inspect all bags and purses outside the park entrances... Stands at both entrances rent single **strollers and wheelchairs** ($10 per day), double-passenger strollers ($18) and Electric Convenience Vehicles ($35)... A **tip board** *(Innoventions Plaza)* displays waiting times for top attractions... As for **transportation,** boats lead to Disney-MGM Studios and the BoardWalk, Dolphin, Swan and Yacht and Beach Club resorts. A monorail connects to the Contemporary, Grand Floridian and Polynesian resorts and to Magic Kingdom. Buses run from Animal Kingdom, Blizzard Beach, Disney-MGM Studios and every other Disney hotel. Epcot has no direct transportation to Downtown Disney or Typhoon Lagoon.

dozens of small squares. ❿ Larger, colorful changing patterns appear in three 6-foot squares in front of Innoventions West. The lights are on all day, but only noticeable at night. ⓫ Thirty-eight discoveries and inventions are honored in the rarely noticed Epcot Inventor's Circle, five concentric rings embedded into the walkway that leads from Innoventions Plaza to The Land pavilion. Inner-ring discoveries lead to outer-ring ones (i.e., the inner Alphabet leads to the outer World Wide Web). ⓬ The Tower of Terror at Disney-MGM Studios appears to be a part of the Moroccan skyline when seen from the promenade area to the right of the Mexico pavilion. The structures share a Spanish influence.

FUN FACTS ❱❱ The park has 3.5 acres of flowers and plants, 70 acres of lawn, 12,500 specimen trees and 100,000 shrubs. ❱❱ There are nearly 300 optical, motion and sound effects at Epcot, more than five times the number in the Magic Kingdom. ❱❱ The construction of Epcot was the largest private construction job in U.S. history. The $1 billion project involved 7,500 people (3,000 designers and 4,500 construction workers), and the movement of 54 million cubic feet of dirt.

You enter Spaceship Earth from underneath the ball

Spaceship Earth

That huge silver sphere is more than the park icon. It's also a ride: a time trip through the history of communications. A four-seat vehicle spirals you slowly past detailed Audio Animatronic dioramas of everything from early cave paintings to the birth of television. The narrator is Jeremy Irons, the voice of Scar in 1994's "The Lion King."

The first scene is the dawn of human language, about 10000 BC. As a Cro-Magnon man recounts a hunt, those around him draw images of it on a wall.

An Egyptian smashes papyrus stems into a thin paper scroll during 1500 BC, then a scribe records the words of a Pharaoh using symbolic hieratic writing.

The next diorama shows early widespread trade, a benefit of the first alphabet (800 BC). Two seafaring merchants from Phoenicia (today's Lebanon and coastal Syria) keep track of sales with letters instead of symbols as they travel through the Mediterranean.

Language becomes an art form as Greek theater emerges (450 BC), as two actors perform Sophocles' "Oedipus Rex." Around the corner are the first

highways, roads that let Romans spread their rule over three continents. A centurion delivers news to a civilian.

You move forward 1,000 years to the Dark Ages, as you see — and smell — the smoky aftermath of the 5th- and 6th-century invasions of Rome by German Ostrogoths. Religious scholars discuss and read ancient texts, then Benedictine monks hand-copy pages of a Bible.

As the Renaissance begins, you pass Johann Gutenberg examining his newly printed bible, from his new moveable-type press (invented in 1456, it signaled the dawn of mass communication by printing 500 pieces of paper per day). You pass poets and musicians practicing their crafts and then, in the ride's best scene, Michelango flat on his back above you painting the Sistine Chapel.

Then it's the age of mass communication, the 19th and 20th centuries. You pass William Bullock's 1863 steam-powered printing press (it made possible the mass distribution of newspapers, printing 15,000 huge, two-sided sheets per hour) a telegraph (1830; transmitting a sequenced series of beeps initially along a network of electrical wires, it allowed

▶ Hop on after 5 p.m. when the line is short. After dark there's usually no line at all.

for near-instant messaging), a telephone switchboard (1876; central exchange operators plugged connecting cords into recipient sockets), a radio network broadcast (1928; programming mixed comedy, news and drama), a movie theater (1895, silent films; 1929, talkies; 1935, color) and lots of TV broadcasts (1936, black and white; 1954, color).

Finally, having been "electronically transmitted aboard a burst of telemetry," you end up in space. As you gaze upon our planet, Irons asks you a question: "Will these seemingly infinite communications become a flood of electronic babble — or will we use this power to usher in a new age of understanding and cooperation on Spaceship Earth?"

Extra touches are everywhere. An Egyptian's torch smokes, the monks' candles flicker, the steam press steams. The Roman horses look real, with perfect manes and subtle movements.

Calls from the switchboard operators travel visually on fiber-optic wires. Behind them, silhouettes show people chatting on phones.

14 min. Capacity: 308. Avg. wait: 45 min. peak morning; 20 min. mid-afternoon. Must be ambulatory. Handheld captioning; handheld translation available. Fear factor: Low. Debuted: 1982, revised 1994.

FUN FACTS)) Serious research went into the show. Science-fiction author Ray Bradbury ("The Martian Chronicles," "Fahrenheit 451") helped design the attraction, along with consultants from the Smithsonian Institution, the University of Southern California and the University of Chicago. The caveman is speaking a Cro-Magnon language. The drawings on the cave walls are based on actual images found in the Salon-Niaux cave in Ariège, France. The hieroglyphics in the Egyptian temple are reproductions of drawings found in the Middle East. The pharaoh's words come from a real letter.)) Rumors persist that some of the figures in the attraction have heads that were once used in the Magic Kingdom's Hall of Presidents. The bald Egyptian slave is said to be William Howard Taft; the sleeping monk Woodrow Wilson. Disney denies it.)) The call letters of the radio station are WDP, a reference to Walt Disney Productions.)) The movie clips include 1928's "Speedy," the last silent film of Harold Lloyd, as well as 1954's "20,000 Leagues Under the Sea."

BUILDING THE BALL
A 180-foot-high geodesic sphere, Spaceship Earth took 26 months to build, from August 1980 to September 1982. It was created without scaffolding or temporary supports.

First, a foundation team poured over 100 steel pilings into the ground, to depths of 150 feet. Three pair of angled legs were placed on top, themselves topped with a six-sided platform about 45 feet off the ground. Secured on that platform, adjustable cranes built a circular frame around themselves, using hundreds of metal-strut triangles. After an outside crane hoisted the preconstructed, 50-foot-wide dome, workers built the bottom, a separate piece that is not load-bearing. Next, rubber-coated panels were secured onto the triangles, creating a giant waterproof black ball. A separate, decorative outer sphere was then added, set off two feet from the core by 4-inch aluminum pipes. The outer sphere is made up of 11,324 triangles of Alucobond*, a rustproof material made of polyethylene plastic bonded to two layers of anodized aluminum.

Spaceship Earth does not drip water: a 1-inch gap between each panel allows the triangles to expand and contract in the Florida heat and lets rainwater flow into two interior gutters that drain through the building's support legs into canals that run alongside the park.

The building weighs 16 million pounds. That's 158 million golf balls.

New York style. Disney got the idea for the structure from the entrance icons of the New York World's Fairs of 1939 and 1964, both held in Flushing Meadows, New York. The 1939 event featured the Perisphere, a 180-foot-tall sphere which held a slow-moving, educational ride (a six-minute film portrayed Democracity, a "perfectly integrated garden city" from the year 2068). The focal point of the 1964 fair was the Unisphere, a 140-foot open-grid Earth that symbolized global interdependence. It's still standing.

Spaceship Earth can also trace its parentage to the 1940s geodesic domes designed by visionary engineer R. Buckminster Fuller. Billed as homes of tomorrow, his futuristic half-circles were composed of self-bracing triangles. They had no internal supports, got stronger as they got bigger and could be built in one day. The "Bucky balls" caught on as weather stations and airport radar shelters, but never got beyond a cult following as private homes (one reason: they leaked water). Fuller also coined the name "Spaceship Earth." His 1963 treatise, "An Operating Manual for Spaceship Earth," argued that all the world's peoples must work together as a crew to guide our planet's future.

* A brand name of Alcan Composites, the word is a contraction of "aluminum composite bond." First used in 1978, the material today covers more than 50,000 buildings, including many Honda automobile dealerships.

Performing on Innoventions Plaza, Kristos features former Bulgarian National gymnast and Ringling Bros. contortionist Nellie Ivanov (bottom left) and her two sons

The Kauffman Foundation's **Opportunity City** teaches what it's like to be an entrepreneur. Video screens help you decide what product to sell and how to market it. Overhead lights project "Be The Boss" onto the floor around you; "Ka-Ching!" rings out from your screen when you make a sale. Underwriters Laboratories' **Test the Limits** lab lets you hammer a TV screen and smash a 55-gallon drum onto a helmet. What happens to a house in a hurricane? It depends how it's built, as you'll see at **Weather the Storm,** a Mercedes Homes exhibit.

INNOVENTIONS WEST The American Farm Bureau's **Great American Farm** includes a lesson about what goes into pizza and a tunnel filled with bugs. Kuka's industrial

Innoventions

Housed in two 50,000-square-foot buildings, this collection of corporate-science demonstrations and hands-on displays is fun, though much of it has a promotional feel. The exhibits change often.

INNOVENTIONS EAST Younger children will go for the video games at **Disney's Internet Zone.** You can make a piece of paper from wood pulp at the **Environmentality Corner.** The building's most popular exhibit is the 25-minute **Fantastic Plastics Works,** sponsored by the Society of the Plastics Industry. You build a virtual robot, race it against others by running in place on an electronic pad and make a plastic robot to take home. The **House of Innoventions** is an 18-minute tour of near-future appliances and electronics. Included is a refrigerator that shops for itself online and a Jacuzzi with a built-in 43-inch television.

Rockin' Robots tap out fun tunes with your choice of car parts. If you're over 16 you can ride a Segway Human Transporter, the one-axle gyroscopic electric scooter, at **Segway Central.** Some afternoons have free 30-second tryouts. Extra-cost tours should be booked in advance (407-939-8687). IBM's **Thinkplace** lets you e-mail a video postcard, build a virtual scavenger vehicle and play video games. **Tom Morrow's Playground** is a free video arcade. Developed by Cornell University and the National Science Foundation, **"Too Small to See"** allows you to manipulate "atoms," magnify a computer chip 100,000 times and see how your movements affect molecules. Liberty Mutual's **Where's the Fire?** has kids search for fire hazards in a six-room miniature home. Nearby, a real fire truck has a hands-on switch panel.

Allow 90 min. if you stop at each exhibit. Guests may stay in wheelchairs, ECVs. Assistive listening. Debuted: 1994.

▶ The nearby **Club Cool** shop lets you sample Coke products from around the world.

Ellen's Energy Adventure

This complex, 45-minute multi-media presentation about the history and future of energy stars Ellen DeGeneres and combines three large theaters with Audio Animatronic dinosaurs.

Appearing on a series of large video screens, DeGeneres displays the same loopy wit she used as Dory in 2003's "Finding Nemo." You meet her in her apartment when Bill Nye* stops by to ask for some aluminum foil, a clothes pin and a candle (she replies "Another hot date, huh?"). Once Nye leaves, she falls asleep while watching her snooty old college roommate Judy Peterson (Jamie Lee Curtis) compete on the game show "Jeopardy!"

Dreaming she's a contestant on the show, Ellen discovers that all the categories deal with one thing she knows nothing about: energy. So she "freezes" her dream and asks Nye for help. He takes Ellen, and you, back in time for a crash course in Energy 101.

Moving into a large theater, you watch as three huge screens dramatically display the Big Bang and the creation of the Earth — billions of years compressed into one stunning minute.

As the seating area breaks apart, you travel to the Mesozoic Era — a swamp filled with Audio Animatronic dinosaurs. Ellen is afraid ("Why don't we just skip to the air-conditioning and Jacuzzi period?"), but Nye wants her to get a close-up look at all the flora and fauna that will later turn into fossil fuels.

Arriving in yet a third theater, you're brought back to the present through a series of radio broadcasts, then watch as Ellen learns about man's energy use.

* A former mechanical engineer, Nye hosted "Bill Nye the Science Guy," a 1992-1998 PBS preteen program which Disney later sold as a video series.

Jumping for joy in a Future World fountain

Finally you return to the first theater, where Ellen unfreezes her dream and becomes the "Jeopardy" champion.

Produced back when the average price of a gallon of gasoline was $1.30, the show seems unaware of the problems of fossil fuels. There's no mention of the Middle East, no talk of global warming or even fuel efficiency. The attraction was created in cooperation with Exxon-Mobil, its sponsor until 2004.

Universe of Energy pavilion. 45 min. (new shows every 17 min.). Capacity: 582. Avg. wait: 10 min. ECV guests must transfer. Assistive listening; handheld captioning. Fear factor: Intense for preschoolers; the Big Bang is loud. Debuted: 1996.

FUN FINDS ❶ After Trebek says to Ellen, "Your first correct response!" her lips don't move when she yells "Freeze!" ❷ Nye's lips stay zipped when, in front of a solar mirror, he says "all right."

▶ Sit in the theater's back far right. You'll be with the dinos more and go under a few.

Mission: Space

✓ So intense it includes motion-sickness bags, this flight simulator provides realistic sensations of space travel. Developed with NASA, it's Disney's most advanced attraction ever.

Why do people get sick? Because you spin. You can't tell it when you're in your vehicle, but the ride is a centrifuge, a circular machine with a series of rapidly rotating containers on its spokes. As it spins, it applies centrifugal force to its contents (that's you) that mimic the G-forces of a rocket launch and then the weightlessness of space. The spinning creates forces up to 2 Gs, or twice that of the Earth's gravity. That may not sound like much — it's actually less than many roller coasters — but this force is sustained; you feel it continually throughout the ride. It's one of the ways NASA trained astronauts for decades. "Mission Space is my favorite ride at Disney," says Lance Bass, the former member of the pop group N'Sync who trained to be a Russian cosmonaut. "The experience here is 100 percent on target."

BYE BYE BYE! The story begins as soon as you enter the building. You're in the year 2036 at the International Space Training Center, where astronaut hopefuls come to see if they have the right stuff. You're there to train for an upcoming mission to Mars. (Robots, you soon learn, have been established on the Red Planet. You are training to be one of the first humans.)

The first room is the Space Simulation Lab. Alongside you is a 35-foot model of a Gravity Wheel, a slowly rotating prop from the 2000 film "Mission to Mars" that's complete with exercise rooms, offices, work areas and sleeping cubicles. Nearby is a Lunar Roving Vehicle display unit, a real one essentially identical to those used on the moon, on loan from the National Air and Space Museum.

After the voice of Mission Control ("CSI" actor Gary Sinise, also known for his roles in 1995's "Apollo 13" and 2000's "Mission to Mars") introduces you to your vehicle, you climb in your trainer and buckle in.

Once a cast member seals the door, an elaborate control panel pivots into place. As you angle up into launch position, you look out into a beautiful blue (video) sky, complete with birds passing overhead. Then the engines power up and the countdown begins.

"3... 2... 1... Zero!" The earth begins to rumble, white clouds of exhaust start to

▶ Disney also offers a mild version of the ride, in which the centrifuge does not spin.

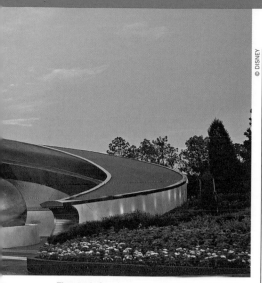

The steely facade has no straight lines. Spheres symbolize Earth, Jupiter, Mars and the moon.

billow and then, in a moment that seems absolutely real, you launch straight up. As the G-forces push your body back into the seat, it truly feels like you're on your way to Mars.

Soon Mission Control breaks in with instructions. "Initiate first stage separation, now!" Sinise tells the mission commander. The others get similar orders.

You head past the space station, are slingshot around the moon, feel weightless for a moment, then go into hypersleep. But your three-month nap seems to take only a few seconds, as alarms wake you up. Not only are you in a meteor storm, but your autopilot has broken and Mars is coming up fast.

Your team performs with flying colors. Attempting to follow the instructions of Mission Control, the four of you barely miss some canyon walls, crash through some barriers and nearly go over a cliff, before landing safely.

In reality, two hidden computers on the centrifuge control everything in your capsule — regardless of what you do.

Many adults have no problem with the ride, and children often fare better than their parents. Still, the side effects have landed some riders in the hospital. A few

have died, though in each of those cases the rider had existing health problems and ignored the warning signs. The most common troubles are dizziness and a lingering headache. To avoid getting sick, continually stare straight at your monitor and do not close your eyes. Don't eat or drink alcohol before you go. Afterward, get lots of fresh air, take it easy and have some saltine crackers or a soda.

6 min. Capacity: 160. Avg. wait: 10 min. early morning, 30 min. peak afternoon. Fastpass available. ECV and wheelchair guests must transfer. Activated video captioning. Height restriction: 44 in. Fear factor: Intense, can cause disorientation, headaches, nausea. Take the warnings seriously: don't ride if you have any serious health issues or a head cold. Chicken exit. Best ages: 8 and up. Debuted: 2003.

MISSIONS FOR ALL With entrances from both the exit area and the gift shop, the Advanced Training Lab post-show area is a series of calm, interactive experiences designed for every age group, even toddlers. **Mission Space Race** is a group video game where two teams (each with up to 25 guests) race spaceships from Mars back to Earth. **Space Base** is a preschooler climbing area with a crawl-through rocket, some zany mirrors and a lookout tower. The **Expedition: Mars** video game lets you test your joystick skills as you navigate through dust devils, polar ice and quicksand to rescue fellow astronauts. Everyone will get a kick out of **Postcards from Space,** a video booth which puts your animated face into an alien abduction, saucer invasion or other goofy space scenes and e-mails the results anywhere you choose.

FUN FACTS 》》 The logo for Horizons, the attraction previously at this site, appears on the hub of the Gravity Wheel. 》》 The Mission Space music was composed by Trevor Rabin, who, as a member of the rock band Yes in 1983, wrote the song "Owner of a Lonely Heart." 》》 Besides training astronauts, centrifuges are used to separate fluids of different densities, such as cream from milk.

▶ To avoid getting sick, stare straight at your monitor and do not close your eyes.

© DISNEY

The fastest ride at Walt Disney World, Test Track includes a final 50-degree banked turn where vehicles reach 65 mph

on how you and your vehicle hold up," Bill adds, "we'll even throw a few surprise tests in there."

"Surprise tests?" Sherry asks.

"Yeah. Pick one."

With a grin, Sherry chooses the Barrier Test — which slams its test dummies into a wall. Before you can protest, the doors open and you board your vehicle.

Heading to the (indoor) testing grounds, you rumble over some blocks, skid through some cones and twist up a hill.

Then things go wrong. Did Sherry forget to turn off those Environmental Test robots? Oh no! You get sprayed with acid! Miss that sign that said to turn on your headlights? Oh no! Here comes a truck! Remember that surprise test? Oh no! You're heading right into a massive...

At the last second, the wall slides open and outside you fly for the Handling Run, an elevated series of banked corners that culminate in a burst around the building at 65 mph.

In the post show, a house of mirrors re-creates GM's truck-assembly plant in Shreveport, La. (can you spot the real walls?), a Fuel for Thought display promotes hybrids, then a showroom holds eight or so current vehicles, unlocked to inspect without any sales pressure.

Test Track

✔ Think of it as Snow White's Scary Adventures with a $60 million budget. Resembling an automobile proving ground, Test Track is an elaborate version of a classic dark ride. Riding in a small vehicle, you speed around corners, through obstacles and over hills. With 34 sharp turns but no corkscrews, falls or loops, the mile-long course is perfect for those who like excitement but hate roller coasters.

A catchy mechanical soundtrack fills the waiting area. Its 22 testing demonstrations make even a 30-minute wait pass quickly. Next, a Briefing Room introduces you to track engineers Bill and Sherry, who appear on a video link (the monitor displays the current time and date, making it seem live). As he determines your test schedule, she programs it into a computer and you watch a short clip of what to expect. "And depending

5 min. Capacity: 192. Avg. wait: 20 min. early morning, 90 min. peak afternoon. Fastpass available usually until 1 p.m. Must be ambulatory. Assistive listening; activated video captioning. Preshow: 4-min. video. Height restriction: 40 in. Fear factor: Intense for those scared by high speeds or sharp turns. Chicken exit. Debuted: 1999.

FUN FINDS ❶ The left anticorrosion robot is labeled "CRUS-T." **❷** The right one is marked "RUS-T."

▶ The adjacent gift shop offers a unique souvenir: a remote-control Test Track car.

park puzzler

How much do you really know about Epcot?

1) The acronym "EPCOT" stands for...

a. Experimental Polyester Costumes of Torture.

b. Experimental Prototype Community of Tomorrow.

c. Every Person Comes Out Tired.

2) According to the Maelstrom narrator, where is the spirit of Norway?

a. In its kjottkaker.

b. In its people.

c. In its skolebrød.

3) What goes wrong on your Mission Space flight?

a. Zurg steals your batteries.

b. You hit a meteor storm.

c. You're forced to learn the history of communication.

4) The top speed of your Test Track vehicle is about...

a. 55 mph.

b. 65 mph.

c. 75 mph.

5) The man at right is...

a. Failing to greet guests in "the Disney Way."

b. A drummer in the Epcot street-band Jammitors.

c. Picking up park trash.

6) In the American Adventure attraction, Mark Twain says no dynamic people have ever survived...

a. "Without justice and equality guaranteed forever."

b. "Drought, disease, avalanches and floods."

c. "Success, plenty, comfort and ever-increasing leisure."

7) On Spaceship Earth, one scene depicts...

a. William Bullock's steam-powered printing press.

b. Alexander Graham Bell's early telegraph.

c. Johann Gutenberg's first television.

Answers, page 319

The Seas with Nemo & Friends

✔ There's a lot to like in this revamped pavilion, which is themed to the 2003 Disney/Pixar film "Finding Nemo." Quality attractions combine with live marine-life aquariums, exhibits and demonstrations.

First you take a little ride. At the end of the entranceway you board a "clammobile" that roams past three-dimensional video-based scenes from the movie. Its finale takes you alongside the pavilion's large aquarium, where, in a jaw-dropping moment, the animated fish appear to swim with the real ones.

You exit on the first floor of the two-story pavilion, which includes a stunning video attraction and some exhibits.

The headliner is **Turtle Talk with Crush,** a theater in which the animated sea turtle interacts with the audience in real-time spontaneous conversations. Appearing on what appears to be a window into the sea, he addresses guests individually ("Elizabeth, your polka-dot shell is totally cool!"), asks specific questions ("Is that your female parental unit in the fourth row? She's a total babe!"), reacts to their responses. As the chat progresses, the reptile also works in some turtle trivia and welcomes a visit by Dory, who can speak some mighty mean whale. To have Crush speak to your child, give her a funny hat to wear and have her sit in the front center on the floor. Sometimes a cast member will also bring the microphone to guests along the center aisle. *15 min. Capacity: 130. Avg. wait: 30 min. early morning, 90 min. peak afternoon. Guests may remain in wheelchairs, ECVs. Reflective captioning, assistive listening. Debuted: 2004.*

The **Nemo and Friends** room features live versions of the movie's creatures. Walk-around tubes and wall tanks hold clownfish (Nemo), regal blue tangs (Dory), Moorish idols (Gill), rays (Mr. Ray) and jellyfish, as well as sea horses, camouflaged frogfish and venomous lionfish and scorpionfish.

Bruce's Shark World has kid-friendly displays and photo props. It's housed in the submarine home of shark stars Bruce, Anchor and Chum.

On the second floor, a huge **saltwater aquarium** is filled with blacknose, brown and sand tiger sharks; some angelfish, cobia, snapper and tarpon; schools of

A bottlenose dolphin swims past an aquarium guest

▶ To avoid a long Turtle Talk line see the first (10 a.m.) or last (apx. 8:50 p.m.) show.

lookdown; a Goliath grouper; sea turtles; and a few rays. Built to resemble a Caribbean coral reef, the tank has an observation tunnel that extends into it.

A side area holds a bachelor herd of dolphins — Rainer (born in 1986), Calvin and Kyber (1997) and Malabar (2001). Huge bars keep the guys in their area; otherwise they'd play with and, yes, eat the fish. Stop by at 10:45 a.m., 2:15 p.m. or 4:15 p.m. to see a marine-biology demonstration, which is often a dolphin training session. These 20- to 30-minute presentations include identity-matching, rhythm-identification and echolocation lessons. There are also three fish feedings, at 10 a.m., 1 p.m. and 4 p.m. A diver unloads his pouch in front of you while a narrator adds educational trivia.

A **manatee aquarium** holds two Florida sea cows. You can watch them from above the surface or below. Five-minute presentations are given at 15 and 45 minutes after each hour.

A **mariculture room** is devoted to fish farming techniques. Large tubes and cylinders hold species that can be commercially raised for food, medicine and the aquarium industry.

FUN FINDS ❶ The Audio Animatronic gulls on the rocks outside the pavilion squawk "Mine! Mine! Mine!" **❷** "Hey wait! Take me with you!" says sea star Peach as you exit the entranceway ride, as the animated fish continue to sing "Big Blue World." "It's a nice song but it just won't stop!" **❸** Rub Bruce's sandpapery skin in Bruce's Shark World and he'll say "Ooooooo! That's good!"

FUN FACTS ❯❯ The creatures are fed 400 pounds of food a day. Since the parrotfish naturally eat coral, Disney plants synthetic coral (dental plaster) into the artificial reef. ❯❯ Why don't the sharks eat the other fish? Because Disney feeds them tilapia every day, which it raises in the adjacent Land pavilion. ❯❯ The aquarium has 3,500 inhabitants, representing 65 species. ❯❯ The observation area has 61 acrylic windows that are 4 to 8 inches thick. Each of the central panels are 8-by-24 feet and weighs 9,000 pounds. ❯❯ Like all manatees in U.S. waters, these are controlled by the Fish & Wildlife Service. Both are candidates for release.

Under the Sea

A saltwater mollusk related to a squid, the soft **cuttlefish** has an internal shell (the "cuttlebone"), eight short arms and two long tentacles. The tentacles can be pulled into pockets behind the eyes... One of the world's smartest animals, the **bottlenose dolphin** has the largest brain, in proportion to its body size, of any mammal besides man. It takes in air through a blowhole on top of its head, which is, in essence, a nose with only one nostril. The mammal "holds its nose" underwater by shutting a valve near the blowhole's opening... Related to sea bass, **grouper** have large heads and broad, down-slanted mouths. The black grouper can lighten or darken its color to suit its environment. The goliath grouper can be up to 5 feet long and reach 700 pounds... A **jellyfish** is like a floating stomach. Coated with a clear, thick flesh, it uses the same orifice for both food intake and waste expulsion. The animal has no heart, blood or bones, and nerves but no brain... Perhaps drinking a little too much rum, sailors thought they saw a beautiful, naked woman when they saw a **manatee**, a mammal with the shape of a cow and the skin of an elephant, its closest relative. Its rear legs have evolved into a beaver-like tail; its front legs have become flippers... Known as the Flower of the Sea, the carnivorous **sea anemone** looks like a plant. It feeds by stinging passing small fish with its tentacles then pushing the prey up into its mouth. After hatching from an egg inside its mother's body, a newborn will swim out of its mom's mouth, attach itself to a rock or piece of coral, and stay there forever... Is there anything stranger than a **sea horse?** This small pipefish has the head of a horse, the tail of a monkey and the pouch of a kangaroo. Its body has prickly, spiny plates instead of scales. To top it off, the male gives birth! Simply put, she has the eggs, but he has the uterus... Related to a shark, the nonaggressive **stingray** appears to fly through the water. It moves by flapping its wing-like side fins. The unusual fish feeds by sucking up small fish and other sea life into its mouth, which is on the underside of its body... The huge silver **tarpon** can breathe air. It can get oxygen by rising to the surface, rolling on its side, filling its swim bladder with air, then absorbing it through its flesh... **Green sea turtles** can live approximately 150 years. Their ancestors evolved on land... Finally, don't flush your pet **clownfish** down the toilet. Despite Gill's belief in "Finding Nemo" that "all drains lead to the ocean," they don't — and no fish can survive a trip through a sewage plant.

Soarin'

✔ This one may take you by surprise: it really does give you the feeling of flight. Far more than just a 5-minute film, the attraction uses an innovative theater to immerse you in its experience. Exhilarating but not scary, the ride is a smooth, fun fantasy everyone will love.

After you board a multi-seat "hang glider," Soarin' lifts you up to 40 feet into an 80-foot projection dome. From all sides your vision is filled with the beauty of California. You get the impractical delight of gliding over the Golden Gate Bridge and El Capitan, floating over an aircraft carrier in San Diego Harbor, skimming along the foamy waves of Malibu and soaring through the night lights of downtown Los Angeles.

You also get a bird's-eye view of Redwood National Park and the Anza-Borrego Desert State Park, near Mexico.

"You're seeing the world from a totally different vantage point than you'll ever be able to in real life," explains executive producer Kathy Mangum.

Your glider tilts as you sweep, your legs dangling underneath.

But that's not all. The theater is filled with effects that make your flight seem *really* real.

Hidden fans put wind in your hair. Unseen odorizers let you smell pines and oranges. Surround-sound speakers re-create a crashing surf and a thunderous waterfall.

There's plenty of detail. The entrance, waiting area and theater resemble an airport. Cast members dress as airline employees, with shoulder boards and brass buttons. The gift stand looks like a ticket counter; the ride's walkway is a concourse; its boarding areas gates. The theater has runway lights; the gliders navigation lights.

The Land pavilion. 5 min. Capacity: 174. Avg. wait: 20 min. early morning; 180 min. peak af-

Providing the sensation of flying over sites in California, Soarin' surrounds you with a huge movie screen

© DISNEY

Living with the Land's quonset hut uses red light to keep its animals calm and reduce algae growth

ternoon. Fastpass available until about 1 p.m. ECV and wheelchair users must transfer. Handheld captioning. Height restriction: 40 in. Fear factor: Those with a fear of heights could be bothered by the actual (40 feet) and virtual (800 feet) distances off the ground. Debuted: 2005 (Disneyland 2001).

FUN FACTS ⟩⟩ Soarin' cast members may call your flight "number 5 5 0 5," a reference to the ride's opening date of May 5, 2005. ⟩⟩ The boarding video features Patrick Warburton, who played Puddy on "Seinfeld" and was the voice of Kronk in Disney's 2000 film, "The Emperor's New Groove." ⟩⟩ The river is Redwood Creek. ⟩⟩ The vineyards are in Napa Valley. ⟩⟩ The mountains are the Sierras, near Lake Tahoe. ⟩⟩ At Yosemite, the sheer cliff on your left is El Capitan. Once you turn, the peak in front of you is Half Dome. The waterfall is Bridalveil Fall. ⟩⟩ The orange groves are outside of Camarillo. ⟩⟩ The surfers are off the shore of Malibu. ⟩⟩ The golf course is the PGA West golf complex in La Quinta. ⟩⟩ The jets are the U.S. Air Force Thunderbirds. ⟩⟩ The largest carrier in the U.S. fleet, the USS Stennis is maneuvering at the San Diego Naval Air Station. ⟩⟩ The film is projected at 48 frames per second, twice the speed of a normal movie. ⟩⟩ The hang glider you see flying over Yosemite is computer generated. So is that errant golf ball. ⟩⟩ Why California? Because this is the same film used at Disneyland's Soarin' Over California attraction. Notice the little boy in the preshow wears a Disneyland, not Disney World, T-shirt.

Living with the Land

This indoor boat ride takes a subject usually thought of as dull as dirt — agricultural science — and presents it as an entertaining attraction. A trip through four working greenhouses, the tour is filled with weird plants most Americans never see, as well as some unusual growing techniques. Your slow-moving boat meanders within a few feet of the plants; you can often smell the leaves and fruit.

The crops include four types of banana palms, including the Indonesian "monkey finger" which bears a slender fruit. Papayas, some the size of bowling balls, cover their trees, while 2-foot jackfruit hang from theirs. Vanilla orchids climb trellises. Other sights include 3-foot-long winter melons and pummelos, the world's largest citrus fruit.

Some plants are here only for their looks, such as the "nine pound" (ponderosa) lemons in the Temperate Greenhouse that resemble lumpy grapefruit and the nearby 500-pound Atlantic gi-

▶ **The best Soarin' seats are top-row center. Ask the gate attendant for Row 1, Gate B.**

ant pumpkins. The Creative Greenhouse always has at least one three-sphered (i.e., Mickey-shaped) cucumber, pumpkin or watermelon, each grown in a specially shaped plastic mold.

Many plants hang from strings or trellises, roots in the air. Some are on overhead conveyor belts, touring their greenhouse like suits in a dry cleaner.

An aquaculture hut includes elevated, clear-sided tanks of catfish, sturgeon, shrimp, eels, even young alligators.

The ride begins with a trip through three habitat dioramas — a rainforest, a desert and a farm.

The Land. 14 min. Capacity: 20 people per boat. Avg. wait: None early morning; 60 min. peak afternoon. Fastpass available. ECV users must transfer to a wheelchair. Handheld captioning. Debuted: 1982 (as Listen to the Land); revised 1993.

Circle of Life

Subtitled "An Environmental Fable," this 13-minute movie uses the stars of 1994's "The Lion King" to teach environmental protection. When Timon and Pumbaa start to clear their savannah to build a tourist resort, Simba tells the story of a creature (man) who at first lived in harmony with nature, but now often forgets that everything is connected in the great circle of life. Live-action sequences show smokestacks, clogged highways, trash dumps and an oil-soaked cormorant, but also wind turbines, electric cars and recycling efforts.

The Land. 13 min. Capacity: 482. Avg. wait: 7 min. early morning; 15 min. peak afternoon. Guests may remain in wheelchairs, ECVs. Handheld and reflective captioning, assistive listening. Debuted: 1995.

Behind the Seeds

✔ A complement to the Living with the Land boat ride, the extra-cost Behind the Seeds 1-hour walking tour is a fascinating botany lesson. Leaving the main building through a backstage door, your guide takes you into a pest-management room and biotechnology lab before giving you a close-up tour of the greenhouses and fish farm.

Your first stop is the Integrated Pest Management lab, where you see one way Disney controls pests: by using tiny parasitic wasps that hatch within the crop-killing bugs and then eat them (yucko!) from the inside out.

Next is the biotech lab, where scientists from the U.S. Dept. of Agriculture are breeding pear trees. A second program tests reproducing plants without seeds, an idea developed here with NASA to create dwarf wheat that could be grown in space.

Then you head to the greenhouses, where your tour includes some fun, hands-on activities. Behind the Seeds is conducted a few times each day. The charge is $12 for adults; $9 for children. For reservations stop by the registration desk (the Soarin' "ticket counter") or call (407) WDW-TOUR.

Tour guide Rachel Naegele holds a fluted pumpkin

Journey into Imagination ...with Figment

A tour through the Imagination Institute, this tongue-in-cheek indoor ride starts as Dr. Nigel Channing (Eric Idle, left) shows how human senses control the imagination. He's interrupted by Figment, a dragon who believes an imagination works best "when it's set free." Eventually you go to Figment's house, an upside-down world. There is one great effect: in a cage past the Sight Lab, a huge butterfly appears to disappear as you go by. Post-show activities include a chance to conduct music by waving your arms.

Imagination pavilion. 6 min. Avg. wait: 5 min. early morning, 20 min. peak afternoon. Guests may remain in wheelchairs, ECVs. Handheld captioning. Fear factor: A dark room has the loud clamor of an oncoming train; a blast of air smells like a skunk; the last room has a sudden flash. Debuted: 1983, revised 1998, 2002.

FUN FINDS The office doors of ❶ 1997's "Flubber" inventor Dr. Phillip Brainard and ❷ 1969's "The Computer Wore Tennis Shoes" principal Dean Higgins line the entrance hall. ❸ There's a page for 1965's "The Monkey's Uncle" chimp-teacher Merlin Jones ("Your monkey is on the loose"). ❹ A door looks into the distorted Dimension Hall. The opposite window (an unmarked pane just to the left of the "Magic Photo Studio") exposes the trick. ❺ On the ride itself, red tennis shoes sit outside the computer room, another reference to that 1969 film.

Honey, I Shrunk the Audience

"Everybody either hates the mice or hates the snake." That's what a cast member says about this theatrical attraction, which features Disney's scariest 3-D effects. The story seems innocent. You're in an auditorium to see Professor Wayne Szalinski (Rick Moranis, reprising his role from 1989's "Honey, I Shrunk the Kids") accept the Inventor of the Year Award. But when he gets lost in the wings, everything goes wrong. The auditorium fills with scurrying rodents (some convincing effects under your seat), then a holographic house cat gets too much power and lunges right into your face first as a lynx, then a lion. The professor returns, only to reduce the theater to the size of a bread box. Then a huge snake slides in and bares its fangs and, finally, a curious canine looks in, sniffs, and sneezes.

Imagination pavilion. 15 min. Capacity: 570. Avg. wait: 7 min. early morning, 15 min. peak afternoon. Fastpass available. Guests may remain in wheelchairs, ECVs. Assistive listening; reflective captioning. Preshow: 5 min. Kodak slide show. Fear factor: Some children will be terrified by the effects. Debuted: 1994.

A giant dog greets the audience during the Honey I Shrunk the Audience finale. *Photo illustration.*

▶ The "Honey" screen has the best focus if you sit in the center rear of the theater.

Clockwise from top left: The grand gardens and architecture of Canada; a symbolic tori gate fronts Japan; the estate-like structures of the United Kingdom; an authentic French restaurant; signing a young guest's "passport" at Italy's Kidcot station; a saddle-ridged roof line in China. Center photo: Two Norwegian cast members.

World Showcase

Eleven countries, one mile

You can cheer for young acrobats. Down some brews at an English pub. Dine on gourmet French food, see Viking swords, shop for a Moroccan lamp — and all the while chat with young adults from around the world at these 11 pavilions, which represent countries from Asia, Europe, North America and North Africa as they sit in a circular 1.3-mile promenade. Three offer travelogue films, two have indoor boat rides, six have cultural exhibits.

Although the World Showcase is Disney's most adult land, every pavilion has a Kidcot crafts table, and most offer chances to meet geographically appropriate characters — from the stars of 2003's "Brother Bear" at Canada to those of 1945's "Three Caballeros" at Mexico.

'Free beer!' A World Showcase Player gathers a crowd at the U.K. pavilion.

guitars, a bagpipe and a sense of humor into a 20-minute show. Often guests twirl with Deadhead joy. **DINING** The popular Le Cellier steakhouse is cool, dim and quiet. **SHOPPING** Northwest Mercantile has Roots apparel; colorful Linda Edgington ceramics, real maple syrup, candy and cream cookies from Ontario; and sweaters and caps from Prince Edward Island. The adjacent Trading Post stocks cute moose and reindeer plushies.

United Kingdom

You can spend hours at this pavilion. It includes a park and two gardens, seven stores, lots of entertainment and a real British pub.
ENTERTAINMENT The **World Showcase Players** ✔ butcher English Lit with improvisational street skits. The **British Invasion** ✔ plays spot-on Beatles classics. Evenings in the Rose & Crown Pub feature magician **Jason Wethington** ✔, pianist **Leon Gregory** ✔ or bon vivant storyteller, piano-player and Epcot institution **Pam Brody** ✔. Kids will love the hopscotch game, chalked fresh each morning by U.K. cast members. **DINING** The Rose & Crown offers fare such as bangers and mash and beef stew; its small pub has live nightly entertainment (see above). The Yorkshire County Fish Shop window serves fish and chips. **SHOPPING** There are so many tempting British goods here. Walk through the shops and you'll find elaborate chess sets; Bronnley, Burberry and Taylor of London perfume, powders and soap; Dunoon and Royal Patrician fine bone china; Lochcarron of Scotland tartan purses, scarves and sweaters; Jacksons of Piccadilly and Twinings teas — and for kids, ELC Pony Club horses and Jellycat plushies. There's much more, too, from Beatles goods to rugby balls.

Canada

A hillside garden, a tumbling waterfall, an immense French Gothic hotel... it's all part of the landscape at Disney's salute to our northern neighbor. **ATTRACTION O Canada!** Nine screens wrap around you in a stand-up theater for this 1982 travelogue of Canadian cultural icons, landscapes and fast-action sports. During the hockey game the camera is just inches above the ice. You ride in a Calgary Stampede buckboard race and on a dogsled and toboggan. Some aerial sequences were filmed with a camera hanging from a helicopter. The 25-year-old film shows its age. The best place to stand is in the middle center, about a third of the way back. *17 min. Capacity: 600. Avg. wait: 10 min. Guests may remain in wheelchairs, ECVs. Assistive listening, reflective captioning. Debuted: 1982.* **ENTERTAINMENT** Kilt-wearing Celtic rock band **Off Kilter** ✔ combines electric

▶ The hidden garden behind Tudor Street has a few private, shady tables.

France

Artistic parks, refined rooflines, and yes, even the Eiffel Tower let you know you've arrived in Paris, circa 1900. It's the home of the best film in the World Showcase, and some of the best food.

ATTRACTION Impressions de France ✔ Set to an ethereal classical score, this movie fills your field of vision with the fairy-tale grandeur of the French landscape. Accompanied by a digitally-perfect soundtrack, the 200-degree screen packs over 40 scenes into 18 minutes. Starting off over the cliffs of Normandy, your trip includes stops at chateaus, a church, marketplace, a vineyard, the gardens of Versailles, a rural bicycle tour and race of Bugattis through Cannes. And that's just the first five minutes. Based on Napoleon III's theater in Fontainebleau, the intimate Palais de Cinema has padded, though petite, seats. *18 min. Capacity: 325. Avg. wait: 9 min. Guests may remain in wheelchairs, ECVs. Assistive listening, reflective captioning. Debuted: 1982.*

ENTERTAINMENT Everyone likes the **Serveur Amusant** ✔ (comical waiter). He juggles vegetables, then gets a "volunteer" to climb a tower of tables and chairs.

DINING Chefs de France features creations by Paul Bocuse, Gaston Lenotre and Roger Verge. Bistro de Paris is pure gourmet. Sidewalk shop Boulangerie Pâtisserie has indulgent treats.

SHOPPING Perfume brands include Chanel, Celine, Jean Patou and Guerlain. Also here: French wine (bottle and glass) and housewares; the Galerie des Halles has authentic berets.

Morocco

Nineteen Moroccan artists installed nine tons of tiles to help create this unique pavilion, the indoors of which are a work of art in themselves.

ENTERTAINMENT Sting's 1999 hit "Desert Rose" is among the tunes performed by **Mo'Rockin** ✔, a six-piece band that's fronted by a contemporary belly dancer. The musicians create a hypnotic sound by blending Moroccan instruments, such as the darbouka goblet drum, with a violin and keyboards.

EXHIBIT Used in possession rituals, a guitar-like gimbri is among the antique musical instruments and other artifacts in the three small rooms of the Gallery of Arts and History, an often-overlooked treasure to the left of the front courtyard. In a sense the entire pavilion is an exhibit, created with pride by

▶ Need a break? Try an indoor table in the Galerie des Halles in the back of France.

the Kingdom of Morocco. Its Fez House even has the sounds of its family.

DINING Belly dancers perform at the Restaurant Marrakesh, which serves dishes such as couscous and stewed chicken. The counter-service Tangierine Cafe offers lamb and chicken sandwiches, couscous and a tea-and-pastry counter.

SHOPPING Casablanca Carpets has rugs from Casablanca, Rabat and Tangier; lamps that filter light through camel skin; and some handmade Fez furniture. The Brass Bazaar offers detailed brass goods from Fez and Marrakesh, ceramics, rosewater bottles and aromatic burled-root thuya wood bowls, boxes and pencil holders. The open-air Marketplace in the Medina has scarves, seagrass baskets and two drums: ceramic tam-tams covered in stretched camel skin and open-top darbukas with bottoms of flounder skin. Tangier Traders has robes, wraps and handmade slippers. Out front, the Souk-Al-Magreb ("The Flea Market of Northern Africa") offers a little of everything. Next door, a henna artist will decorate your hands, feet or neck with your choice of designs that last about 10 days.

Japan

Dominated by a department store, this pavilion focuses on modern-day Japan. Except for its architecture and drum show, everything is post-World War II.

ENTERTAINMENT The intense **Matsuriza Taiko Drummers** ✔ pound out hypnotic rhythms on their hand-made instruments. Arrive early for **Miyuki** ✔. At each performance, she makes free candy animals for lucky children standing right in front of her. Grabbing a taffy-like ribbon of soft rice dough, the Tokyo native quickly snips out a child's choice of colorful animals, each with surprising detail. She performs outside the front entrance of the Mitsukoshi department store. Also here: Japanese storyteller **Honobono Minwa** ✔.

Japanese candy artist Miyuki gives away her imaginative, yummy creations to lucky children

EXHIBIT Wind-up robots, spaceships and other wobbly treasures fill the dozen display cases of the Tin Toy Stories exhibit in the Bijutsu-kan Gallery at the rear of the pavilion. There's video narration by Pixar's John Lasseter.

DINING Tableside chefs entertain at the Teppanyaki Dining Room. A horseshoe-shaped bar, Tempura Kiku has batter-dipped selections and sushi. The Matsu-No-Ma Lounge offers tempura and sushi with a second-story view of the lagoon. The counter-service Yakitori House has beef, chicken and shrimp bowls, as well as a good miso soup.

SHOPPING A Mitsukoshi department store is divided into four sections — Festivity (cooking products, teas, sweets, dishes and a sake tasting bar), Silence (home items such as bonsai trees, rice paper and kimonos), Harmony (a blend of Japanese and Western cultures with Chirimen cloth handbags and Tombo-Dama glass-bead jewelry) and Interest (kitschy Lucky Cats, transforming clocks and lots of quirky kids stuff). *Founded in 1673, the Mitsukoshi company runs the entire Japan pavilion.*

▶ Raining? Duck into one of the World Showcase's authentic shopping areas.

The American Adventure

The focus here is purely on the attraction: a great Audio Animatronic show.

ATTRACTION The American Adventure ✔ The only World Showcase attraction that is critical of its country, this theatrical show combines film footage with robotic versions of historical figures to review the triumphs, flaws and challenges of the United States. Ben Franklin and Mark Twain lead you from the time of the Pilgrims through World War II.

The robots move convincingly — Franklin appears to walk, Frederick Douglass stands on a rocking raft. Some movements are subtle. In Valley Forge a guard takes just a split second to raise his head and look at his partner. George Washington shifts his weight in his saddle, and his horse twitches and pulls like a real animal. Each character has its own speaker; its voice projects from it.

The film, a combination of real and re-created images, pans across paintings and photographs in a style later made famous by documentarian Ken Burns.

The presentation addresses both proud and ugly episodes of the American story. Chatting with Franklin after the Revolutionary War, Twain says "You Founding Fathers gave us a pretty good start... [but then] a whole bunch of folks found out that 'We the People' didn't yet mean all the people." Civil War images include a close-up of a dead soldier.

A photomontage finale covers historic events and cultural leaders of the past 50 years. Images include artist Jasper Johns and golfer Babe Didrikson Zaharias.

29 min. Capacity: 1,024. Guests may remain in wheelchairs, ECVs. Assistive listening, reflective captioning. Debuted: 1982; revised 1993.

ENTERTAINMENT Performing in the rotunda, the a cappella **Voices of Liberty** ✔ do more than patriotic numbers; the group's harmonies on songs such as "Amazing Grace," "Ol' Man River" and

The tricorn hats, white wigs and regimental coats of the Spirit of America Fife and Drum Corps recall the formal dress of the Revolutionary War era

"This Land Is Your Land" bring to life aspects of U.S. history that are often forgotten. The five-person **Spirit of America Fife & Drum Corps** ✔ marches into the promenade to play "Battle Hymn of the Republic" and other inspiring tunes.

EXHIBIT Five display cases explore how historic African art has influenced modern artists in Echoes of Africa, in the American Heritage Gallery. Some pieces use human skin. They come from the Disney-Tishman African Art Collection.

FUN FACTS ❯❯ The show uses three Franklins and three Twains. ❯❯ Twelve statues on the sides of the auditorium represent the Spirits of America. ❯❯ The show uses 35 Audio Animatronic characters on a multi-plane stage. ❯❯ Hidden from view, the staging system is a mechanical marvel. Just beneath your sight line is a mass of wiring and hydraulic-fluid lines which give movement to the figures. Underneath that is a 175-ton scene changer, a steel frame that's 65 feet long, 35 feet wide and 14 feet high. Operated by computer, it wheels in each of the 13 three-dimensional sets horizontally, then raises them into view on telescoping hydraulic supports. Other devices bring in side elements. Behind all that is a 155-foot rear-projection screen that shows the 70-millimeter film.

▶ Stand under an edge of the rotunda. A whisper will carry to the other side.

Italy's Character Masquerade roams through the pavilion's outdoor areas most afternoons

every hour or so. They'll pose for your camera. Comedic juggler **Sergio** ✔ appears weekdays in the courtyard. His 20-minute shows include audience volunteers. The **World Showcase Players** ✔ (see United Kingdom) often appear.

DINING An offshoot of the Roman eatery that invented Fettuccini Alfredo, L'Originale Alfredo di Roma has a spirited warmth at dinner, when an accordion player often strolls among the diners. Want a treat? Try the vanilla gelato at the donkey cart.

SHOPPING The La Bottega store has candy, chocolates, cookware, wines and wine sampling. Don't miss the papier-mâché and fabric Carnivale masks; each is a festive piece of art. Il Bel Cristallo offers leather goods, silk scarfs and ties; Armani, Bulgari, Dolce e Gabbana and Gucci perfumes; Giuseppe Armani figurines; gold, sterling silver and Venetian glass jewelry; and decorative watches.

DINING The Liberty Inn is a good place to get out of the sun. The counter-service spot serves cheeseburgers, hot dogs, apple cobbler and a kosher meal. Stands out front sell turkey legs and ice-cream funnel cakes you can bring in to eat.

SHOPPING Heritage Manor Gifts sells patriotic clothing and some fun items that can help your kids learn history.

Italy

Gold-leafed ringlets decorate an angel atop the Campanile. Gondolas are tethered to barbershop-striped poles. Where are you? Venice. Or at least, Disney's Venice, one of the World Showcases most beautiful, intricate facades.

ENTERTAINMENT Performers of the **Character Masquerade** ✔ silently, dramatically roam through the outdoor areas

Germany

An animated glockenspiel comes to life every hour at this picture-perfect pavilion that seems straight out of "Snow White and the Seven Dwarfs."

DINING An indoor buffet, the Biergarten celebrates Oktoberfest every day. A live oompah band entertains. Just outside, the Sommerfest counter serves good bratwurst, other treats and beer, with tables on a covered patio. The courtyard Bierline walk-up stand has beer, pretzels and wine.

SHOPPING Nice German imports include handcrafted Black Forest cuckoo clocks, made-to-order dolls, hand-painted eggs, Steiff teddy bears, Christmas pickle ornaments, Steinback nutcrackers and limited-edition beer steins. There's also German schnapps and wines by the glass and bottle.

▶ The promenade's American Gardens Theatre often hosts complimentary concerts.

A **horticulturist** plants "trees" in Germany's miniature train village

China

While Germany celebrates, China reflects. This serene pavilion combines a thoughtful exhibit, poetic film and calm restaurant and department store. The landscape looks naturally placed. It includes a weeping mulberry, a runner bamboo and tallow tree — a plant with a waxy fruit long used to make candles. **ATTRACTION Reflections of China** ✔ is the best of Disney's CircleVision 360 movies. A well-lit, in-focus experience, the film takes you to ancient areas such as Inner

The Outpost

This enclave between Germany and China has some terrific African entertainment and folk art. You drum along with **OrisiRisi** ✔, an engaging pair of storytellers who teach timeless truths of life as they relate Nigerian folktales, myths and legends. Don (right) and Tutu Harrell are masters of their craft. And no wonder: he's a music researcher and folklorist; she's a Nigerian native who heard many of these tales as a child. Children love the drumming experience, of course, but you'll be surprised how much you'll like it, too. Showtimes are available at Guest Relations; arrive 15 minutes early to get a seat. Unified families with intertwined arms are the signature sculptures of African wood and soapstone artist Andrew Mutiso at the open-air **Village Traders.** Other pieces include animals, busts, canes and masks. The **Refreshment Cool Post** offers soft-serve ice cream, frozen yogurt and soft drinks.

Mongolia and Tibet, as well as modern spots like Hong Kong, Macao and Shanghai. The host portrays 8th-century Chinese poet Li Bai. You stand up to watch. *20 min. Capacity: 200. Avg. wait: 10 min. Guests may stay in wheelchairs, ECVs. Assistive listening; reflective captioning. Debuted: 1982, updated 2003.*

ENTERTAINMENT The **Dragon Legend Acrobats** ✔ are a terrific troupe of children. Inside the Temple of Heaven, Chinese harpist **Si Xian** ✔ performs before most screenings of Reflections of China.

EXHIBIT You'll see how archeologists uncovered thousands of full-size terra cotta soldiers and horses from a lost tomb in Tomb Warriors: Guardian Spirits of Ancient China, in the House of the Whispering Willows gallery. Adjacent cases hold authentic tomb sculptures.

DINING Choose from the table-service Nine Dragons Restaurant or the counter-service Lotus Blossom Cafe.

SHOPPING The Yong Feng Shangdian department store is filled with apparel, food, furniture, housewares and jewelry.

Norway

Welcome to Norway, where men are menn and women are kvinner and meatballs are kjottkakers and all in all there are just way too many consonants. Pronunciation differences aside, this beautiful country is the basis of one of Epcot's most interesting pavilions.

ATTRACTION The **Maelstrom** ✔ indoor boat ride has a quirky appeal. After you set sail in a dragon-headed longboat, an ancient god urges you to seek the spirit of Norway. Your journey starts off peacefully, as your search first takes you past a quaint fishing village, but then things turn into a confused chaos (a "maelstrom") as trolls commandeer your ship. A three-headed ogre sends you backward past some polar bears and nearly off a cliff. Then another troll pops up to send you forward down a waterfall and into a stormy North Sea. You make land-

Typically 9 to 12 years old, students from the PRC's Puyang Acrobatics Center perform daily

fall at a modern fishing village.

Climbing out of your boat, you head to a small theater to watch "The Spirit of Norway," a 5-minute film that portrays the daydreams of a young boy. As he examines an old Viking ship, he imagines seafarers, oil riggers, ski jumpers, scientists, businessmen and a Constitution Day parade. The point? "The spirit of Norway... is in its people!"

15 min. (5 min. ride, 5 min. wait, 5 min. film). Capacity: 192. Avg. wait: 5 min. early afternoon, 30 min. peak afternoon. Fastpass available. Wheelchair, ECV users must transfer. Assistive listening; handheld and reflective captioning. Fear factor: The ride is often completely dark and has scary faces. In the film, two opening loud flashes will jolt those of any age. Debuted: 1988.

ENTERTAINMENT Mix an accordion and a couple of fiddles with an acoustic guitar and bass and you've got... hand-clapping country music, in this case the Norwegian sounds of **Spelmanns Gledje** ✔. Performing outside, the five-piece group plays short sets of dance and gypsy tunes. Its hoedown sound will show you where American country got its start.

▶ Giant bullfrogs live in China's reflecting pool. Their heads poke out of the water.

EXHIBIT A lifesize Rögnvald the Raider stares at you with axe in hand in The Vikings: Conquerors of the Seas, a five-display exhibit inside the Stave Church Gallery. The display also includes Erik the Red and King Olaf, as well as authentic swords, arrows and axe blades.

DINING The Akershus Royal Banquet Hall is all princess all the time. Its character meals feature an American breakfast, a Norwegian lunch and dinner. The Kringla Bakeri Og Kafe serves open-faced sandwiches (including smoked salmon) and tasty pastries such as coconut-dusted, custard-filled School Bread.

SHOPPING Finds include stylish Helly Hansen apparel, Dale of Norway blankets and ski sweaters, Geir Ness perfume — and silly plastic Viking helmets, all with horns, some with braids.

Disney sells alcohol throughout the World Showcase, including frozen margaritas at the Mexico pavilion

Mexico

A great place to get out the sun, the Mexico pavilion is, for the most part, totally enclosed. Housed in what appears to be a small pyramid, its large marketplace and attraction are cool and dark.

ATTRACTION A peaceful indoor boat tour that surveys Mexico's cultural history, the earnest **El Rio del Tiempo** ("The River of Time") offers no thrills or modern magic, but there's never a wait. You start off in a dark Mayan night, then drift into a foggy temple where video-screen dancers demonstrate Mayan moves. Next it's a world of laughter, it's a world of tears... well it's really the Day of the Dead, but these two dozen dolls will surely remind you of those in It's a Small World. Finally you're in modern Mexico. You float along Acapulco's cliffs and grottos (watch for the "underwater" snorkeler on your left), pass some street merchants, and arrive at Mexico City's Reforma Boulevard. Many scenes have a breeze. *8 min. Capacity: 250. No wait. ECV users must transfer. Handheld captioning. Debuted: 1982.*

ENTERTAINMENT Epcot's best live band, **Mariachi Cobre** ✔ is an 11-piece group led by trumpets, violins and confident vocals and backed by harmonizing guitars. Formed in Tucson in 1971, the band has often played with Linda Ronstadt.

EXHIBIT Wild styles dominate the painted wood carvings of Animalés Fantásticos: Spirits in Wood, a collection of modern Mexican folk-art animals, humans and mythical creatures just inside the pavilion entrance. The copal-wood creatures are carved with machetes and pocketknives then painted with brushes, cactus spines and syringes. Most are for sale. A series of push-button displays introduces you to the art, food, music and regions of modern Mexico at Casa Mexicana, a large room off the indoor courtyard.

DINING Inside, the San Angel Inn offers real Mexico City cuisine in a tranquil setting overlooking the Rio del Tiempo. Outside, the counter-service Cantina de San Angel serves fast food and drinks.

SHOPPING The indoor bazaar has everything you expect and plenty you don't, including silly hand-painted piggy banks, impossibly vivid ceramics and pure-silver Taxco jewelry.

▶ Sit on the left side of the El Rio del Tiempo boat. Most scenes are on the left.

World History

WORLD SHOWCASE ARCHITECTURE

The pavilions of the World Showcase represent the architectural, cultural, and sometimes political history of Europe, Asia and North Africa.

At the entrance courtyard to the **Canada** pavilion, a log cabin, trading post and 30-foot totem poles represent the country's frontier culture. Carved by a Tsimshian Indian in 1998, the left totem depicts the magical Raven releasing the sun, moon and stars from a carved cedar chest. Up the steps, a stone building reflects the British styles of Canada's east coast. On the right, the French Gothic Hotel du Canada recalls Ottawa's Chateau Laurier, a 19th-century railroad hotel. In back it's the mountains, complete with a 30-foot waterfall and a mine entrance adorned with shoring and Klondike equipment.

The **United Kingdom** pavilion re-creates many historic sites of Olde England. Out front, the red-brick turrets and medieval crenellation of the Sportsman's Shoppe mimic Henry VIII's 16th-century Hampton Court. The white-stone side of the building is Abbotsford, the 19th-century Scottish estate where Sir Walter Scott wrote many of his novels. Across the street is the 16th-century thatched-roofed cottage of Anne Hathaway, the wife of William Shakespeare. Also on this street: a half-timbered 15th-century Tudor (leaning with age), a plaster 17th-century pre-Georgian, an 18th-century stone Palladian, even an angled-brick home. The lakeside Rose & Crown Pub combines a medieval rural cottage, a Tudor tavern and an 1890s Victorian bar.

France depicts the Paris of La Belle Epoque ("the beautiful time" from 1870 to 1910). Walking across a replica of the Pont des Arts footbridge that crosses the Seine, you view a park that recalls Georges Seurat's 1884-1886 painting "A Sunday Afternoon on the Island of La Grande Jatte." Sites in the city include the Les Halles market (the Galerie des Halles shop), an iron-and-glass-ceilinged structure that stood from 1850 to 1971. In the distance is the Eiffel Tower, with a period-correct tawny finish.

Designed by the Kingdom of Morocco, the **Morocco** pavilion is divided into the Ville Nouvelle (new city, in front) and the Medina (old city). Anchored by two fortress-like sandstone towers, the new city recalls Casablanca and Marrakesh. Towering over the courtyard is a replica of North Africa's most famous building, the Koutoubia Minaret prayer tower in Marrakesh.

The Medina of Fez lies in back, behind that city's 8th-century Bab Boujouloud Gate. On the left is the Fez House, a courtyard of a traditional Moroccan home. On the right is an open-air market. Past the restaurant (a Southern Moroccan fortress) stands a reproduction of the Nejjarine village fountain. Rising above it all is a 14th-century minaret from the necropolis of Chellah.

Graceful architecture and landscaping harmonize in the symbolic **Japan** pavilion. Elements to the left represent culture and religion, including an 83-foot pagoda that recalls the 8th-century Horyuji Temple in Nara (its five stories represent the five elements from which Buddhists believe all things are created — earth, water, fire, wind and sky), a hill garden with evergreens (a symbol of eternal life), rocks (the long life of the earth) and koi-filled water (the brief life of animals and man), and the rustic Yakitori House, modeled on Kyoto's 16th-century Katsura Imperial Villa.

Elements on the right represent commerce. Housing the store and restaurants, its architecture recalls the ceremonial Shishinden Hall at the 8th-century Gosho Imperial Palace at Kyoto.

The rear of the pavilion symbolizes politics and history. You first come upon the massive wood and stone Nijo castle, with its huge sculptures of mounted samurai warriors. You then cross a moat to the Himeji (White Heron) castle. Recalling feudal Japan, its curved stone walls, white plaster structures and blue tile roof are modeled after Shirasagijo, a 14th-century fortress which overlooks the city of Himeji.

The English Georgian style of the **American Adventure** recalls the look of many public buildings built in the colonies just before and after their independence. Its walls use 110,000 hand-formed bricks, laid with an old-fashioned one-then-a-half technique.*

Ah, Venice! The icons of *La Serenissima* welcome you to the **Italy** pavilion. Along the lagoon are the city's bridges, gondolas and striped pilings; the front of the pavilion re-creates the Piazza San Marco. The two freestanding columns mimic the square's two 12th-century monuments, one topped by the city's guardian, the winged lion of St. Mark the Evangelist, the other crowned by St. Theodore, the city's former patron saint (shown killing the dragon that threatened the city of Euchaita, an act that gave him the courage to declare himself a Christian). The 10th-century Campanile (bell tower) dominates the skyline, though this version is just 100 feet tall, less than a third the height of the original. At the left is the square's 14th-century Doge's (leader's) Palace. The most elaborate World

---

* One of the few Disney buildings that uses a reversed forced perspective, the structure appears just three stories tall though it actually rises more than 70 feet to accommodate the large theater. The illusion only works from a distance; up close the second-story windows look huge.

Showcase facade, it replicates nearly every detail of the original. The first two stories rest on realistic marble columns that front leaded-glass windows. The third floor of tile is topped by marble sculptures, statues, reliefs and filigree.

Inside the piazza are styles found throughout Italy. The stairway and portico adjoining the palace reflect Verona. On the right, the first shop (La Bottoga) is themed to a Tuscany homestead. Sculptures include a large heroic version of Neptune with his dolphins, recalling Bernini's 1642 fountain in Florence.

The facade of the first building in the **Germany** pavilion (the Das Kaufhaus shop) was inspired by the Kaufhaus, a 16th-century merchants' hall in the Black Forest town of Freiburg. Three statues on its second story recall the rule of the Hapsburg Emperors. The huge backdrop combines the looks of two 12th-century castles, the Eltz on the Mosel river and the Stahleck Castle on the Rhine. The centerpiece of the plaza is a sculpture of St. George, the patron saint of soldiers, with the dragon that legend says he slayed during a trip to the Middle East. Inside, the Biergarten imagines medieval Rothernberg.

China is anchored by a colorful welcoming gate with banners that translate to "May good fortune follow you on your path through life" and "May virtue be your neighbor." The triple-arched gateway and three-tiered, blue-roofed (and half-sized) Hall of Prayer for Good Harvests are based on the main gate and building of Beijing's Temple of Heaven, a summer retreat for Chinese emperors built during the Ming dynasty in 1420. The area also includes facades of an elegant home, a school house, a city gate and shop fronts reflecting European overtones. The art gallery has a formal saddle-ridge roof line.

The colorful inner rotunda alludes to the cycles of nature. The 12 outer columns represent the months of the year and the years in a cycle of the Chinese calendar. Four central columns denote the four seasons, a central beam represents earth, a round topping beam is heaven. On the floor, the center stone is cut into nine circling pieces, reflecting the fact that, to the Chinese, nine is a lucky number.

Simulating those found in Suzhou, the gardens and reflecting ponds symbolize the order and discipline of nature. Keeping with Chinese custom, most of the garden appears old and in a natural state. At the lagoon, large pockmarked boulders demonstrate the Chinese tradition of

The faux marble columns of Disney's Doge's Palace have detailed filigree and realistic veining

designing surprising views in landscapes by creating holes in waterside rock formations.

Standing at the **Norway** pavilion's entrance is a replica of the 13th-century Gol Church of Hallingdal, one of Norway's stavkirkes ("stave churches") which played a key role in the country's movement from the Viking Age to Christianity. Next door, the bakery has a sod roof, a traditional way to insulate homes in Norway's mountains. The gift shop facades recall coastal cottages. Finally, the pavilion's castle-like restaurant and rear facade re-creates Akershus, a 14th-century fortress that stands in the harbor of the city of Oslo.

The **Mexico** pavilion's facade is that of a small pyramid, modeled after the Aztec temple of Quetzalcoatl (honoring the feathered-serpent god of life) in the ancient city of Teotihuacan. The god itself is depicted by heads along the priests' steps. Inside, the entry portico to the Plaza de Los Amigos is that of a Mexican mayor's mansion. The market area was inspired by the 16th-century silver mining town of Taxco, south of Mexico City.

Back outside, the Cantina de San Angel waterside restaurant has the look of Mexico City's original 17th-century San Angel Inn.

IllumiNations: Reflections of Earth

✓ The lights go dark, then a fireball explodes over the huge stage as thousands stare in awe. As the music begins, fireworks erupt and lasers shoot out from backstage.

Baby boomers may think they're at a Pink Floyd concert, but it's actually the beginning of IllumiNations: Reflections of Earth, Disney's dazzling spectacle of "Wow, man!" effects that concludes every Epcot day. Synchronized to a symphonic world-music score, the extravaganza uses the entire World Showcase lagoon as its stage. Much more than a fireworks show, it includes strobe lights on — and laser beams from — the pavilions. A rotating Earth moves across the water, shows moving images on its continents and unfolds to reveal a torch.

Though there's no narration, the show tells the history of the world in three acts: Chaos, Order and Celebration. It begins with the dawn of time — the Big Bang and the creation of Earth — symbolized by a lone shooting star that explodes into a fiery ballet of chaos.

Act Two starts as the planet is brought under control and gains order. As the spinning globe appears, scenes on it depict primal seas and forests; the development of famous cultural landmarks including the Sphinx, the Easter Island statues and Mount Rushmore; and key historical figures such as Muhammad Ali, the Dalai Lama, Albert Einstein, Martin Luther King Jr., Jonas Salk, Mother Teresa and, if you look closely, Walt Disney. The coolest image: video of a running horse that transforms into a cave painting.

The third act begins as the globe unfurls into a lotus flower and a 40-foot torch rises from its heart. Celebrating both human diversity and the unified

IllumiNations' lasers and fireworks light up the sky over the World Showcase Lagoon

▶ Pick out a viewing spot at least 30 minutes early to get a good view.

spirit of humankind, this segment features a colorful fireworks finale that heralds a new age of mankind, originally the new Millenium. It ends with a loud crackle, sending you off to embrace the future (as you leave, the exit music is "We Go On").

The show is directed to the front of the park (directly at Spaceship Earth) so the best seats are those at the World Showcase Plaza, where you'll see everything symmetrically, as the designers intended it (the photo on the opposite page was taken there).

An added plus: the plaza is the closest viewing spot to Epcot's main exit, so you'll be ahead of the masses when the show ends.

Many places have a fine view of all the effects, but watching IllumiNations from another location is like sitting at the side, or rear, of a concert stage. It may be interesting, but you really don't get the same show.

If you can't make it to the plaza, better spots include the promenade along the Canadian waterfront; the waterside tables at the U.K.'s Rose and Crown, though they are notoriously tough to snare (you can't reserve one); and the bridge between the U.K. and France, which gives you a more elevated view.

Other good spots include Japan, especially on the balcony above the Mitsukoshi department store; the bridge between China and Germany; and the Cantina de San Angel cafe at Mexico, where you can munch nachos while you watch.

The music can be heard everywhere, as speakers surround the lagoon.

On, above and around the World Showcase Lagoon. 15 min. Guests may remain in wheelchairs, ECVs. Preshow: 30 min. of instrumental music from Japan, Scandinavia, South America and Spain. Fear factor: The loud, bright explosions and fire can be too intense for toddlers and some preschoolers. Debuted: 1988; revised 1997, 1999.

Loading the guns. A cast member packs mortar tubes with fireworks for an IllumiNations show.

FUN FACTS ❯❯ The 2,800 fireworks launch from 34 locations that house 750 mortar tubes. Some ring the shore, just a few feet from unsuspecting guests. ❯❯ The four fountain barges pump 5,000 gallons of water per minute. ❯❯ The 150,000-pound "Inferno barge" has 37 propane nozzles. ❯❯ The 28-foot steel globe rotates on a 350-ton barge that houses six computers, 258 strobe lights and an infrared guidance system. Wrapped in more than 180,000 light-emitting diodes, the globe is the world's first spherical video display. ❯❯ The performance uses 67 computers in 40 locations. ❯❯ The pavilions are outlined in more than 26,000 feet of lights — nearly 5 miles worth. ❯❯ For religious reasons, the Morocco pavilion does not participate in the show. ❯❯ The music supervisor was Hans Zimmer, the composer for the 1994 film, "The Lion King." ❯❯ The songs "The Promise" and "We Go On" are performed by country singer Kellie Coffey. ❯❯ There are 19 torches around the lagoon, symbolizing the first 19 centuries of modern history. The 20th torch, in the globe, represents the Millennium. ❯❯ Disney occasionally tests IllumiNations after midnight. If you stay up late at one of the Epcot resorts (the BoardWalk, Swan and Dolphin or Yacht and Beach Club) you may see, or hear, an unscheduled explosion or two.

APPAREL Children's Wear: Morocco offers caftans, tunics and belly dancer outfits in children's sizes. Japan offers Hello Kitty outfits for girls. The American Adventure has patriotic shirts. China stocks infant and children's embroidered pajamas, dresses, dynasty sets and slippers. Mexico carries child-sized peasant blouses and skirts. **Cold weather:** Canada sells Roots cold-weather gear and Margaret McEachern merino-wool sweaters and caps. The U.K. stocks tartan scarves and sweaters. Norway offers vivid Helly Hansen jackets as well as thick wool sweaters and caps from Dale of Norway. Mexico has ponchos and scarves. **Fashion:** In Future World, Cargo Bay *(Mission Space)* sells women's knit shirts with sayings such as "Space Cadet." In the World Showcase, Canada sells Roots apparel. Morocco offers traditional caftans, dfinas, gandouras and complete tenue outfits; embroidered sweaters; and all the elements of a belly dancing outfit. Japan has a huge selection of kimonos; a smart collection of women's shirts, skirts, belts and embroidered jackets that mix Asian and Western influences; and traditional men's caps and tenugui head coverings. The American Adventure has patriotic clothing. Italy offers scarves and ties. China stocks embroidered dresses, jackets, robes and wraps. Norway offers stylish Helly Hansen apparel. Mexico has peasant blouses and skirts, as well as leather belts with silver accents. **Footwear:** Canada sells Roots slippers. Morocco offers Babouche slip-ons. Japan deals in Tabi split-toe cotton socks and their accompanying Zori rice-straw house shoes, the traditional Geta wood platform sandals, and tennis shoes. China stocks embroidered slippers and sandals. Norway offers Helly Hansen sandals and athletic shoes. Mexico carries leather sandals and woven huaraches. **Headwear:** Canada sells Roots caps and novelty moose hats. France often has Beatex berets. Morocco offers Fez hats. Japan has men's caps and tenugui head coverings. Norway offers novelty Viking helmets. Mexico stocks straw sombreros. **Sportswear:** The U.K. has soccer jerseys and shirts from Great Britain. Germany sells Adidas soccer jerseys, women's jersey-like tops and dresses and duffel bags. **T-shirts:** In the World Showcase, all pavilions sell T-shirts with their country name. Other adornments include Canadian NHL logos (Canada), vintage Beatles art (U.K.), Kanji symbols (Japan) and Chinese astrological animals (China).

ART Disney: In Future World, The Art of Disney *(to the right of Spaceship Earth)* has lithographs, posters, prints and two-foot figurines of Disney characters. At times an artist will sketch a character for you. **Folk art:** Germany has hand-painted eggs by Jutta Levasseur. Italy offers Carnival Masquerade masks made on-site. The Outpost sells wood and soapstone carvings by Kenyan and Nigerian artists. Mexico sells vivid Animalés Fantásticos woodcarvings from Oaxaca; piggy banks and purses by Yucatan artist Carlos Millet. **Posters and prints:** France has small prints and photos, with frames to fit.

BOOKS The Seas With Nemo & Friends gift shop carries books on sea life. Each World Showcase pavilion has a selection of books on its sponsoring country. Japan has the most.

CANDY AND TREATS Canada sells maple candy and cookies, thick-wafer Coffee Crisp bars and Smarties, an M&M-like candy with a thicker coating and better chocolate. The U.K. stocks the creamy Aero Bubbly and yummy Cadbury dairy milk caramel, as well as two spot-on McVitie's tea choices: milk-chocolate caramel digestives and knobbly oaten Hob Nobs. France carries Lu butter biscuits and fruit-filled Pims. Japan offers jelly-bean-like Botan Rice Candy, each piece wrapped in a melt-in-your-mouth wrapper. Italy has Perugina Baci kisses filled with crushed hazelnuts. Germany sells Milka Alpine-milk-chocolate bars. China stocks ginger candy and some peanut-brittle-like nutcakes. Norway sells the creamy Melkesjokolade chocolate bar or the toffee-like D'aim. Mexico has Obleas wafers, a caramelized sweet made with burnt goat milk. Want something American? In Future World, MouseGear *(Innoventions Plaza)* offers Goofy's Candy Co.

CHRISTMAS DECOR Canada sells hand-blown glass ornaments from Fergus and Ontario's Kitras shop. Germany has glass pickle ornaments and nutcrackers by the renowned Christian Ulbricht. Norway offers unique figurines.

DISNEY MERCHANDISE In Future World, the huge MouseGear *(Innoventions Plaza)* is Epcot's headquarters for items themed to Disney characters or with Epcot or Walt Disney World logos. The store has Disney character costumes, children's wear, costume jewelry, housewares, pet products, T-shirts, toys, watches and more. At the entrance to World Showcase, the twin stores of Disney Traders and Port of Entry *(World Showcase Plaza)* offer Disney fashion apparel.

FOOD In Future World, Cargo Bay *(Mission Space)* sells astronaut food, including ice cream. In the World Showcase, the U.K. stocks teas. Japan offers teas, soup mixes, rice crackers and nut and roasted-green-pea snacks. China stocks jasmine and green tea, as well as red panax ginseng extract and ginseng royal jelly. Norway offers Löfbergs Lila Swedish coffee. Mexico carries salsa, seasonings and jalapeño jelly.

HOUSEWARES Canada sells Linda Edgington ceramics from Ontario and Artables hand-painted clay plates and tiles from Alberta artist Debra Cherniawsky. The U.K. stocks Belleek parian china from Northern Ireland, Royal Albert floral bone china and Dunoon mugs and tea pots. France carries large wooden rolling pins and spoons. Morocco offers tables, lamps, rugs, leather cushions, baskets, pillows, small wall mirrors, thuya-wood boxes and game boards, silver tea pots, brass genie lamps and incense. Japan deals in china, chopsticks, knives, sake cups and pots, sushi serving dishes and Seiko Melodies in Motion and Rhythm Small World clocks. Italy has Murano glass, alabaster and marble accessories and Bialetti coffee makers. Germany sells Schneider Black Forest cuckoo clocks, collectible beer steins and Hummel figurines. China stocks a range of jade furniture, including dining tables and chairs, tables and desks; elaborate lamps, rugs and vases; china; decorative tea sets; sometimes jade chopsticks. Norway offers thick wool Dale of Norway blankets, teeny pewter figurines and huge resin troll statuettes. Mexico carries thick table glasses, pitchers and margarita goblets; wool blankets; and many house accent pieces.

JEWELRY In Future World, The Seas with Nemo & Friends gift shop carries shell necklaces. In the World Showcase, Morocco offers bracelets, earrings and necklaces. Japan has a cultured pearl shop. Italy has lovely charm bracelets. The Outpost sells hand-carved wood and bead bracelets and necklaces. China stocks coral and jade jewelry, including pins and pendants. Norway offers fine jewelry of silver, gold and porcelain. Mexico carries silver and turquoise items.

PERSONAL CARE The U.K. stocks perfume, cologne, after shave, lotions and room mist by Taylor of London, Bronnley, Burberry and Dunhill. France carries Guerlain perfume and a mix of other brands that usually includes Azzaro, Chanel, Annick Goutai, Givenchy and Thierry Mugler, as well as E. Barrett shea butter soap. Italy typically has scents by Giorgio Armani, Bulgari, Salvatore Ferragamo, Acqua di Parma and Emanuel Ungaro. Norway offers two fragrances by Geir Ness: Laila for women and Geir for men. Mr. Ness is sometimes on hand.

PINS Epcot's Pin Central is an open-air shop in the center of Future World, adjacent to the large information board (Innoventions Plaza).

PLANTS In Future World, the Soarin' counter (The Land) and Cargo Bay (Mission Space) have Mickey's Mini Garden plants grown from tissue cultures. In the World Showcase, Japan deals in

Fashionable finds. Boston's Grace Kim shops in the Morocco pavilion.

bonsai trees and novelty children's plants. China often has lucky bamboo trees.

PURSES The U.K. stocks tartan purses by Lulu Guinness. Italy has classic leather clutches and handbags. China stocks traditional embroidered purses, some encrusted with stones. Mexico carries hand-tooled leather purses and hand-painted handbags by Yucatan artist Carlos Millet.

SPORTING GOODS The U.K. has quality shin guards as well as soccer and rugby balls.

TOYS In Future World, Cargo Bay (Mission Space) sells astronaut and space toys and a toy version of the ride's X-2 rocket. Inside Track (Test Track) has remote-control and die-cast automobiles. The Seas with Nemo & Friends gift shop carries plushie sea creatures. In the World Showcase, Canada sells reindeer and moose plushies and Anne of Green Gables dolls. The U.K. stocks ELC Pony Club horses and Jellycat plushies. France carries Madeline dolls and Babar plushies. Japan has Hello Kitty, Pokemon and similar items, model cars, Monchhichi monkeys and Tamiya mechanical models. Germany sells Schleich medieval toys, Steiff teddy bears and custom Engel dolls. China stocks marionettes and puppets, panda plushies, Diabolo games and magic sticks. Norway offers huge-haired Good Luck Trolls. Mexico has Jacob's ladders, spinning tops and string puppets.

WATCHES Japan has J-Axis and EOS timepieces. Italy has watches trimmed in Murano glass.

WINE AND SPIRITS France, Italy and Germany sell native wine by the glass and bottle. Japan offers plum wine and lots of sake, including sweet varieties. Mexico stocks tequila.

A world's fare

TABLE SERVICE FUTURE WORLD **Coral Reef $$$** ✔ Eight-foot-tall viewing windows look into a huge aquarium at this modern seafood restaurant. Lunch: sandwiches, fish, salmon, steak, salads, prime rib. Dinner: fish, salmon, steak, prime rib. Creative recipes. Great appetizers include tasty lobster soup. Kid's meals include grilled fish. Ask for a table by a window. *275 seats. The Seas.* **Garden Grill $$** ✔ Farmer Mickey Mouse, Pluto and Chip 'n' Dale are your hosts at this character buffet. Roasted meats, catfish, vegetarian selections. Much of the food, including the catfish, comes from the pavilion greenhouses. *232 seats. The Land.* WORLD SHOWCASE Four to five crowned and gowned heroines are on hand for every meal for Princess Storybook Dining at the **Akershus Royal Banquet Hall $$,** meeting guests, signing autographs and posing for pictures at every table. Breakfast is a family-style American affair. Lunch and dinner offer Norwegian fish, lamb, venison and kjottkaker (fried patties of beef, pork and diced beets). Don't worry; the kids menu has American standards. Princesses can include Ariel, Aurora (Sleeping Beauty), Belle, Jasmine and Snow White; sometimes Mary Poppins drops by. Each seating area is a replica of a real room in Oslo Harbor's 13th-century Akershus castle. (It's pronounced "ocker-shoos.") *255 seats. Norway.* It's always Oktoberfest at the **Biergarten $$,** an indoor buffet restaurant with the look of an outdoor garden. A band plays polkas. The hearty buffet has sausages, red cabbage, sauerkraut, spaetzle, schnitzel and more. *400 seats. Germany.* **Bistro de Paris $$$** ✔ Gourmet French seafood (fish, lobster, scallops) and meats (duck, beef, lamb, venison, veal.) Outstanding appetizers. Quiet, intimate atmosphere. On the second floor; overlooks promenade. Ask for a window table. Dinner only. *120 seats. France.* Rich creams and soft cheeses dominate many of the provincial dishes at the airy, bustling **Chefs de France $$** ✔, which features the creations of the renowned Paul Bocuse, Gaston Lenotre and Roger Verge. The menu includes beef, chicken, salmon and seafood dishes; sandwiches at lunch. Don't overlook the Gruyere-topped French onion soup or the rich creme brulee. Great wine list. *266 seats. France.* The stone-walled, low-ceilinged **Le Cellier Steakhouse $$** ✔ resembles a chateau wine cellar. The Alberta-beef steaks are aged 28 days; the best is the filet mignon (dinner only). Made with Moosehead beer, the cheddar-cheese soup makes a great dip for the complimentary soft breadsticks. Other options include salmon, seafood, chicken, entree salads and sandwiches. Young, friendly staff. The toughest World Showcase reservation. *156 seats. Canada.* **L'Originale Alfredo di Roma $$** is an offshoot of the Roman restaurant that invented Fettuccini Alfredo. Order it and you'll get a dish where the taste is in the pasta; the light, sharp Parmesan sauce is a complement. The menu also includes individual pizzas, roast lamb, veal stew and steak. The trompe l'oeil ("trick the eye") paintings, deeply upholstered armchairs and, at night, strolling musician create a relaxing, memorable atmosphere. *300 seats. Italy.* The wonton soup is good at the Chinese **Nine Dragons $$** ✔ — its strong, clear broth is topped with floating scallions. Two nice dinner choices are the Sichuan seafood casserole in a spicy red rice spice and the Beijing duck. For dessert the thick ginger ice cream tastes like a whipped gingerbread cookie in a wash of thick cream. Have kids sample the Dim Sum list instead of the kids menu. As you enter the lobby look up; a golden dragon is staring at you. *300 seats. China pavilion.* An entertaining tableside chef may juggle knives or even make a "smoking Mickey train" out of onion stacks at the Japanese **Teppanyaki Dining Room $$.** Using a grill set into the table, the chef's hands fly fast as they slice, dice and stir-fry your choice of beef, seafood or chicken. You'll probably share your 8-seat table with other guests. *330 seats. Japan.* **Mitsukoshi Tempura Kiku $$** This counter offers batter-fried beef, chicken, scallops, shrimp and vegetables, served with soup and steamed rice. Also good sashimi, sushi. *25 seats. Japan.* A belly dancer often entertains at **Restaurant Marrakesh $$,** which serves traditional foods such as roast lamb, kebabs and couscous, a tiny steamed pasta served with lamb, potatoes or other vegetables. The traditional soup is harira, a smooth blend of lamb, lentil and tomatoes. Green tea, liqueur coffees. *255 seats. Morocco.* Hope you like mashed potatoes! The British **Rose & Crown Pub & Dining Room $$** includes them with most of its entrees, such as bangers and mash (sausages and mashed potatoes, with cabbage), cottage pie (ground beef with carrots and mashed potatoes) and Guinness-flavored beef stew. Steak, fish, sandwiches. Good appetizers: a fruit and cheese plate (with seven cheeses including creamy blue Stilton); lamb and barley soup. Brews: Bass, Boddingtons, Guinness, Ireland's Harp, even Australia's Strongbow Cider. The pub has live evening entertainment. The restaurant has indoor and covered-outdoor (lakefront) seating.

Avg./adult: **$** <$10. **$$** <$20. **$$$** <$30. **$$$$** <$40. Reservations: 407-WDW-DINE

242 seats, including 40 outside. *U.K.* You sit on padded chairs around a lamp-lit table at **San Angel Inn Restaurant $$ ✔**, a cool Mexican cafe that overlooks a passing waterway (the Rio del Tiempo), glowing pyramid and rumbling volcano. The tortilla soup is a tasty tomato-based broth filled with stringy cheese and vegetables. The smoky, boneless carne asada tastes like it's from a backyard grill; the Chef's Special version is a filet. On-the-rocks margaritas are dashed with lots of lime juice and Triple Sec. Ask for a table on the water. Run by the same family as its Mexico City namesake. *156 seats. Mexico.*

Princess Storybook meals at Restaurant Akershus

COUNTER SERVICE FUTURE WORLD **Electric Umbrella $** Breakfast: Omelettes, bagel sandwiches, cereals. Lunch, dinner: Cheeseburgers, sandwiches, wraps. Good vegetarian chili. A talking trash can (marked "Waste Please") sits next to the topping bar left of the ordering counter. *426 seats. Innoventions East.* **Fountain View Espresso and Bakery $** Pastries, desserts, coffees, smoothies. *45 seats inside, 59 outside. Innoventions West.* WORLD SHOWCASE **Liberty Inn $** Cheeseburgers, chicken strips, hot dogs. Kosher meal. *710 seats. American Adventure.* **Sunshine Seasons $$ ✔** Food court with five separate stations serving sandwiches (thick deli and a grilled vegetable Cuban), Asian noodle plates and bowls, grilled entrees (beef or chicken on flat bread, grilled salmon), creative soups and salads (soups such as beer and Tillamook cheddar cheese; salads such as seared tuna or roast beet and goat cheese) and bakery items. Cold-case offerings include whole fruit, sushi, beer, wine. Nothing's fried. Disney's best fast food. *707 seats. The Land pavilion.* **Tangierine Cafe $ ✔** Chicken and lamb sandwiches and platters with hummus and couscous. Coffee and pastry counter offers baklava, Moroccan mint tea, liqueur coffees, frozen daiquiris, beer. *101 seats. Morocco pavilion.* **Yakitori House $** Beef, chicken and shrimp bowls. The sushi plate and miso soup are bargains. Garden setting. *58 seats inside, 36 outside. Japan.* **Lotus Blossom Cafe $** Egg rolls, grilled chicken, stir-fried entrees, specialty drinks. *100 seats. China pavilion.*

OUTDOOR COUNTER CAFES WORLD SHOWCASE **Yorkshire County Fish Shop $** Harry Ramsden-brand fish and chips, Bass ale. *31 seats. U.K.* **Boulangerie Patisserie $ ✔** Pastries, croissant sandwiches, quiche, cheese plates. Over two dozen choices. Also coffees, wines, beers. *24 seats. France.* **Sommerfest $ ✔** Bratwurst, frankfurters, pretzels, cake, strudel, beer. *52 seats under a covered patio. Germany.* **Lotus Blossom Cafe $** Rice bowls, vegetable lo mein, salads, egg rolls, red bean or caramel ginger ice cream, peach oolong iced tea. *107 seats. China.* **Kringla Bakeri Og Kafe $ ✔** Open-faced sandwiches, pastries, desserts. Try the School Bread or Kringla. *51 seats. Norway.* **Cantina de San Angel $** Burritos, tacos, quesadillas, nachos, guacamole, frozen margaritas, beer. Good Conga fruit drink. *150 seats. Mexico.*

SNACK STANDS PARKWIDE **Joffrey's Coffee.** Coffees, pastries, muffins, smoothies, tea, hot chocolate. *Future World between Innoventions East and the Universe of Energy; World Showcase between Canada and U.K.; at American Adventure.* FUTURE WORLD **Cool Wash.** Sodas, chips, bottled water. *Test Track.* **Pizza Cart.** Pizza. *Test Track.* WORLD SHOWCASE **Refreshment Port** McDonald's snacks. *Near Canada.* **Crepes des Chefs de France** Crepes, waffle cones, beers, coffees. *France.* **Les Vins des Chefs de France** Champagne, wine, cheese. *France.* **Kaki Gori ✔** Shaved ice topped with fruit syrups; Kirin beer. *Japan.* **Funnel Cake Kiosk ✔** Funnel cakes with ice cream, fruit, chocolate sauce; fried ice cream. *American Adventure.* **Pasticceria Italiana di Alfredo di Roma** Coffee, desserts, beer, wine. *Italy.* **Donkey Cart ✔** Gelato, ices. *Italy.* **Bierline** Pretzels, beers, wine. *Germany.* **Das Kaufhaus Cart $** Soft pretzels, beer, wine. *Germany.* **Refreshment Cool Post $** Soft-serve ice cream, coffee, beer. *Outpost.* **Margarita kiosk** Frozen margaritas. *Mexico.*

BARS **Rose & Crown Pub ✔** Beer, mixed drinks, appetizers, sandwiches (try the London broil). Live evening entertainment. *20 seats. U.K.* **Matsu-No-Ma Lounge** Plum wine, sake, mixed drinks. Good sushi (try the Niji Maki), tempura. Overlooks lagoon. *52 seats. Japan.*

© DISNEY

Disney-MGM
Studios

Celebrating the diverse world of show business, this intimate park is one the whole family can enjoy. From preschoolers who love Disney television shows to seniors who long for the days of James Cagney and Humphrey Bogart, all ages can have a good time.

Boys are especially well served. There are two stunt shows, two big thrill rides, a motion simulator, a roving rock 'n' roll band and even appearances by the Power Rangers. Other attractions include stage shows that recreate the best moments from Disney films and downright kooky creations such as the Great Movie Ride and MuppetVision 3-D.

EASY DOES IT With the smallest public area of any Walt Disney World theme park, Disney-MGM Studios is easy to tour. Though the park encompasses more than 150 acres, much of that is backstage. The main thoroughfare, Hollywood Boulevard, is just 500 feet long, and from there nearly every attraction is, at most, just a few minutes away. What's more, you sit down a lot. There are no stand-up theaters and only one walk-through attraction. You may find a long line every now and then, but taken as a whole this is the one Disney park that won't wear you out.

The park is divided into two areas.

The front is Old Hollywood. This 1940s world features palm-lined streets with period-specific shops, signs and stoplights as well as re-imagined landmarks. The entranceway, Hollywood Boulevard, includes an authentic Brown Derby restaurant and authentic-looking Chinese Theater, which houses the Great Movie Ride. On your right is Sunset Boulevard, a trolley-line theater district that leads to the glamorous Hollywood Tower Hotel. This area is home

Below: Detail from the back studio archway.
Opposite page: A Citizen of Hollywood emcees an audience-participation Dating Game.

Authentic down to its warning bell, a two-color traffic light sits alongside Hollywood Boulevard

to the popular Beauty and the Beast and Fantasmic stage shows, the Rock 'n' Roller Coaster starring Aerosmith and the Twilight Zone Tower of Terror.

To your left is Echo Lake, with its Indiana Jones Epic Stunt Spectacular.

The rear is movie-studio land, with areas that resemble a production center and backlot. Its entrance arch resembles Hollywood's Paramount Studio gate, while side streets are marked by (always open) security gates. Many buildings look like soundstages. The best attrac-tions include the Playhouse Disney, Lights Motors Action and Voyage of the Little Mermaid shows, the Star Tours simulator and the film-based fun of MuppetVision 3-D.

The park is dotted with curving, shady side streets and hidden garden spots. In fact, its friendly feel is a lot like that of the first park Walt Disney himself drew up more than 50 years ago: California's Disneyland.

Posing for pix in front of the Sorcerer's Hat

HISTORY Disney-MGM opened as a production facility in 1988 and to the public on May 1, 1989. "Welcome to the Hollywood that never was and always will be," then-CEO Michael Eisner said at the dedication. A Hollywood-style gala, the park's Grand Opening featured legends Lauren Bacall, George Burns, Audrey Hepburn and Bob Hope. "Who says

© DISNEY

▶ Rain? No problem — nearly every attraction is inside or under a covered pavilion.

Eyeing an old LaSalle on Sunset Boulevard

money can't buy happiness?" said television star Morey Amsterdam after touring the grounds. "With this much money you can build happiness."

Alas, the park is no longer a production center. The company once used the soundstages and backlot streets for movie and television work. Regulars on the lot included Britney Spears, Christina Aguilera and Justin Timberlake.*

The animation building was the East Coast home of Disney Feature Animation. It created the Roger Rabbit shorts "Tummy Trouble" and "Roller Coaster Rabbit;" painted cels for "The Little Mermaid;" produced segments of "Beauty and the Beast," "Aladdin" and "The Lion King;" and created the films "Mulan," "Lilo & Stitch," "Brother Bear" and "Home on the Range" in their entireties. At its peak the animation studio had a staff of 350.

FUN FINDS Hollywood Boulevard: Second-story offices include those of ❶ tailor Justin Stitches and of ❷ Allen Smythee

Productions,* both above the second entrance to Keystone Clothiers. **Echo Lake:** Offices around the right of the pond include ❸ acting-and-voice studio

Petite prints. The authors' daughter compares her hands with those of legend Audrey Hepburn.

* As cast members of The Disney Channel's "New Mickey Mouse Club," filmed here from 1989 to 1994. Among those who auditioned for the show but didn't make it: Jessica Simpson and Matt Damon.

▶ Disney's most zany restaurants are the '50s Prime Time Cafe and Sci-Fi Dine-In.

overview

Hollywood Redux

ARCHITECTURAL INFLUENCES

A tribute to Hollywood in its heyday, the architecture of the park re-creates the look of Los Angeles during the mid-20th century. At the **entrance area,** the turquoise color and white-ringed flag pylons of the bus station, security gate and ticket center are in the style of 1935's Pan Pacific Auditorium, a sports and concert hall.

Hollywood Boulevard is a dreamlike 500-foot version of its namesake. Each of its 15 facades is modeled on an actual structure.

Kicking things off is the Crossroads of the World gift kiosk, a replica of a Streamline Moderne stand at the 1937 Crossroads of the World shopping center. Sid Cahuenga's is a tribute to the Craftsman bungalows that became Hollywood tourist shops during the 1930s and 1940s. The Disney & Co. store brings back the black-marble-and-gilt Security Pacific Bank building, itself a copy of downtown L.A.'s Richfield Oil Building whose black and gold trim represented the "Black Gold" of the oil industry, and a Hollywood veterinary clinic. Keystone Clothiers includes the scaled-down facades of Hollywood's Max Factor Building and Jullian Medical Building.

The right side of the street is equally inspired. The photo center is a clone of The Darkroom, a 1938 Hollywood photo shop known for its front window trim that looked like a giant camera. Celebrity 5 & 10 evokes an Art Deco building that once housed a J.J. Newberry five and dime. Next door, Adrian and Edith's Head to Toe and the adjacent L.A. Cinema Storage recall a two-block Spanish Colonial Revival area. Finally, the Hollywood Brown Derby is modeled from the 1929 second location of the famous restaurant, a legendary dining spot for hundreds of movie stars.

Inside the buildings is a ceiling lover's paradise. Cover Story's film-roll theme recalls the style of Frank Lloyd Wright. The tiny Head to Toe foyer towers almost 30 feet.

At the end of the road is a full-scale model of a famous Hollywood landmark: Grauman's Chinese Theatre. The front is designed from the same blueprints as the 1927 building and has essentially all the original's soaring trim pieces and intricate detailing. The only real difference: this one has its ticket booth off to the side.

To the left of Hollywood Boulevard, **Echo Lake** recalls downtown L.A.'s Echo Lake Park, where 1920's silent-movie czar Mack Sennett shot many of his Keystone Comedies. Two snack stands re-create that era's programmatic architecture, when buildings were designed to look like giant objects. Appearing to be a tramp steamer is Min & Bill's Dockside Diner. What appears to be an apatosaurus is Dinosaur Gertie's Ice Cream of Extinction. This tribute to 1914 cartoon star Gertie the Dinosaur includes her footprints in the sidewalk. Nearby, the Hollywood & Vine restaurant evokes a cafeteria that once stood on North Vine, near the actual Hollywood Boulevard.

Sunset Boulevard begins with a replica of the 1940 Mulholland Fountain in Griffith Park. On your left, the Colony Sunset gift shop is New York City's Colony Theatre as it appeared in 1928, when it premiered

Hollywood's Carthay Circle Theatre (top); Disney's visual tribute (above)

the cartoon "Steamboat Willie," the public debut of Mickey Mouse. The Sunset Ranch Market recalls the 1934 Los Angeles Farmers Market, where Walt Disney himself often ate.

On your right, the Legends of Hollywood store features the front facade and spiral corkscrew tower of the 1938 Academy Theater. A few doors down, the Once Upon a Time gift shop is a dead ringer for the 1926 Carthay Circle Theatre, which hosted the premiere of Disney's "Snow White and the Seven Dwarfs" in 1937. Next up, the Theater of the Stars is an homage to the 1922 Hollywood Bowl. The entrance to Fantasmic's Hollywood Hills Amphitheater draws its design from the Los Angeles Ford Amphitheater that's nestled in the Hollywood Hills.

The stone structures that form the entrance to The Twilight Zone Tower of Terror are nearly exact replicas of the Hollywood Gates, the 1923 entrance to the Hollywoodland real-estate development. The ride's Hollywood Tower Hotel gets its Spanish Revival look from the 1902 Mission Inn in Riverside, Calif.

The park's "studio" buildings were inspired by the Walt Disney Studios in California.

The entrance to the park's studio-themed area

Sights and Sounds (motto: "We've Finished Some of Hollywood's Finest"), run by master thespian Ewell M. Pressum, voice coach Singer B. Flatt and account executive Bill Moore (the door to the left of Keystone Clothiers), ❹ a dentistry office run by doctors C. Howie Pullum, Ruth Canal and Les Payne (to the left of Peevy's Polar Pipeline), ❺ Holly-Vermont Realty, the name of a real business that in 1923 rented its back room to Walt and Roy Disney to use as their first office (to the right of Peevy's) and ❻ grumpy gumshoe Eddie Valiant from 1988's "Who Framed Roger Rabbit" (above the Hollywood & Vine restaurant). Valiant's workplace has two windows; Roger has crashed through one. ❼ A billboard for Roger's employer Maroon Studios sits on the roof above Peevy's. Three crates to the left of Min & Bill's snack stand refer to classic films: ❽ One addressed to "Charles Foster Kane, Xanadu Compound, Gulf Coast, Florida, to the Rosebud Sled Co." refers to 1941's "Citizen Kane." ❾ A "Casablanca" crate marked "From Curtiz Wine & Spirits Ltd. to Rick Blaine, Rick's Cafe Americain, 112642 Rue Renault, Casablanca Morocco," includes references to the film's

A Magical Day

Can you *absolutely, positively* get to Disney-MGM Studios by 8:30 a.m.? If so, here's an easy, non-hurried way to have a great day.

8:30 Arrive at the park
As you wait for the gates to open (typically at 8:45 a.m.), visit the adjacent Guest Relations window to pick up a Times Guide and get show times for the Citizens of Hollywood. Confirm show times for Beauty and the Beast — Live on Stage. If you haven't already, make your meal reservations. When the turnstiles open, be among the first at the Sunset Boulevard rope barrier.

9:00 Get Fastpasses
for the Rock 'n' Roller Coaster Starring Aerosmith.

9:05 Tower of Terror

9:30 The Great Movie Ride

10:10 Rock 'n' Roller Coaster

10:30 Beauty and the Beast
Be among the first in line for the 11 a.m. Beauty and the Beast — Live On Stage show. Sit in the center of one of the first non-handicapped rows.

12:00 Lunch
At the Brown Derby. While you eat make a specific afternoon plan. Use your Times Guide to find the exact show times for the following attractions and put them in the order that works best.

2:00 Playhouse Disney

3:00 Street performers

4:00 Indiana Jones stunts

5:00 Parade

6:00 Dinner
at '50s Prime Time Cafe. Share s'mores for dessert.

7:30 MuppetVision 3-D

8:30 Fantasmic
You should get there right on time to get a great seat for the 10 o'clock show.

Assumes operating hours of 9 a.m. to 10 p.m.

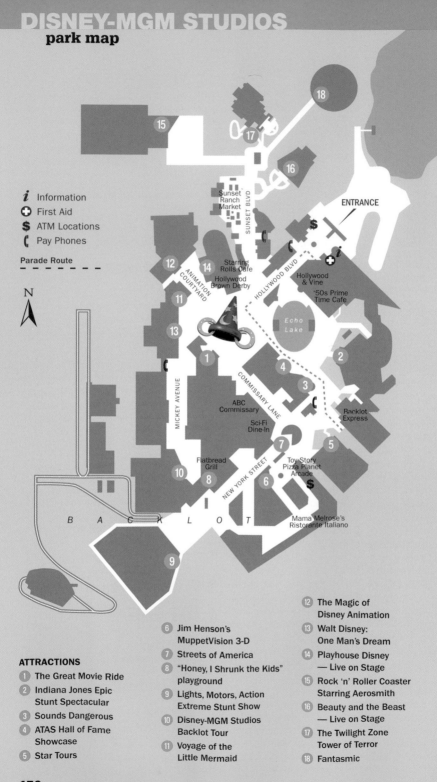

i Information

✚ First Aid

$ ATM Locations

☎ Pay Phones

Parade Route

N

15

18

17

16

Sunset Ranch Market

SUNSET BLVD

ENTRANCE

12

14

Starring Rolls Cafe

Hollywood Brown Derby

ANIMATION COURTYARD

11

HOLLYWOOD BLVD

Hollywood & Vine

'50s Prime Time Cafe

13

Echo Lake

1

4

2

3

MICKEY AVENUE

COMMISSARY LANE

ABC Commissary

Sci-Fi Dine-In

Backlot Express

7

5

Flatbread Grill

10

8

NEW YORK STREET

6

Toy Story Pizza Planet Arcade

9

Mama Melrose's Ristorante Italiano

B A C K L O T

ATTRACTIONS

1. The Great Movie Ride
2. Indiana Jones Epic Stunt Spectacular
3. Sounds Dangerous
4. ATAS Hall of Fame Showcase
5. Star Tours
6. Jim Henson's MuppetVision 3-D
7. Streets of America
8. "Honey, I Shrunk the Kids" playground
9. Lights, Motors, Action Extreme Stunt Show
10. Disney-MGM Studios Backlot Tour
11. Voyage of the Little Mermaid
12. The Magic of Disney Animation
13. Walt Disney: One Man's Dream
14. Playhouse Disney — Live on Stage
15. Rock 'n' Roller Coaster Starring Aerosmith
16. Beauty and the Beast — Live on Stage
17. The Twilight Zone Tower of Terror
18. Fantasmic

A **"High School Musical"** skit at the Sorcerer's Hat

director (Michael Curtiz), Claude Rains' character Capt. Renault and premiere date (Nov. 26, 1942). ❿ A third crate, marked "From Fleming Fashions Ltd., Atlanta to Scarlett O'Hara, Tara Plantation, 121539 Mitchell Lane, Jonesboro County, Georgia," alludes to the director, premiere city, lead character, main setting, premiere date, novelist and inspiration (Jonesboro, Ga.) for "Gone With the Wind." ⓫ On Sunset Blvd., an office above Villains in Vogue is the home of the International Brotherhood of Second Assistant Directors (IBSAD, say it carefully), a union with the motto "We're standing behind you."**

* "Allen Smythee" was an official pseudonym-credit used by film, television and music-video directors between 1968 and 1999 when they did not want to be associated with a production. ** During the Great Depression, "Second Assistant Director" was a mercy title given to studio go-fers, who were often told to "Get coffee and stand behind me."

BY THE NUMBERS ❱❱ **122** Height, in feet, of the Sorcerer's Hat. **350** How tall, in feet, Mickey would have to be to wear it. ❱❱ **25,000** Number of outfits created each year by Disney's costuming department, seen on the Backlot Tour. **3.4** Height, in miles, a year's supply of the shop's buttons would reach, if stacked. ❱❱ **300,000** Gallons of water that will fit in the water tower. **0** Gallons of water in the tower, which is just a prop.

Park resources

ATMs are located outside the gate by the package-pickup window and inside in the Pizza Planet restaurant. All restaurants, stands and stores accept plastic and traveler's checks... Inside Guest Relations (see below), the **Baby Care Center** has a microwave and nursing areas and sells supplies and over-the-counter medications... The Darkroom *(Hollywood Blvd.)* sells **cameras and accessories** and burns photo CDs... Next to Guest Relations, the **First Aid Center** handles minor emergencies and has registered nurses on hand... Staffed by cast members ready to answer any question or help with any problem, **Guest Relations** *(park entrance)* has walk-up windows to the left of the gate and a walk-in office off Hollywood Blvd. It has maps and Times Guides for all parks, exchanges foreign currency and stores items found in the park that day... The Crossroads of the World kiosk *(Hollywood Blvd.)* rents **lockers** ($5 per day plus a $2 deposit) which are located behind Oscar's Super Service... Report **lost children** to Guest Relations or any cast member. Children who lose their parents should tell a cast member... Anything you buy can be sent to **Package Pick-Up** *(park entrance)* for you to pick up as you leave. Purchases can also be delivered to your Disney hotel or shipped to your home.... For day guests **parking** is $10 a day. Those staying at a Disney resort (and annual passholders) get free parking. A tram takes you to the park entrance... The **Pet Care Kennel** *(park entrance)*, 407-560-4282, has clean cages in air-conditioned rooms. See the chapter "Practical Information" for details... **Restaurant reservations** can be made at Hollywood Junction *(Hollywood Blvd. at Sunset Blvd.)* and Guest Relations or by calling 407-WDW-DINE... **Security guards** inspect all bags and purses at stations outside the park entrance... Oscar's Super Service *(Hollywood Blvd.)* rents single **strollers and wheelchairs** ($10 per day), double-passenger strollers ($18) and Electric Convenience Vehicles ($35). The ECVs book quickly; many are used by overweight guests... The **tip board** *(Hollywood Blvd. at Sunset Blvd.)* displays waiting times for popular attractions... As for **transportation,** boats and walkways bring guests from Epcot and the BoardWalk, Dolphin, Swan and Yacht and Beach Club resorts. Buses run from every other Disney hotel, and from Animal Kingdom, Blizzard Beach and Epcot. Magic Kingdom guests take a monorail to the TTC, then a bus to the park. Service from Downtown Disney and Typhoon Lagoon connects through the TTC.

Off to see the Wizard, Dorothy and her pals chat in a Great Movie Ride diorama

The Great Movie Ride

✓ Still Disney's grandest and most complex indoor ride, this fun tram tour is the Studio's original showcase attraction. Filling 95,000 square feet, it has more than 60 Audio Animatronic characters and nearly 3,000 special effects.

Portraying 16 movie sets that have come to life, full-size dioramas create a dreamlike tribute to the Golden Age of Hollywood. Your tram passes Gene Kelly "Singin' in the Rain" (1952), travels alongside "The Public Enemy" James Cagney (1931), gets stuck in the middle of gangster and Old West shootouts, goes under Sigourney Weaver's stalking "Alien" (1979) and then heads into "The Wizard of Oz" Munchkinland to confront the Wicked Witch of the West (1939).

Additional sets portray scenes from 1933's "Footlight Parade," 1934's "Tarzan and His Mate," 1940's "Fantasia," 1942's "Casablanca," 1964's "Mary Poppins" and 1981's "Raiders of the Lost Ark." Other Audio Animatronic celebrities include Julie Andrews, Humphrey Bogart, Clint Eastwood, Harrison Ford, John Wayne and Johnny Weissmuller.

The best is the witch, a piece of magic that reincarnates Margaret Hamilton. With a life-like face, she quickly flexes her backbone, swivels her hips and points her finger as she confronts your guide. "I'll get you my pretty..."

Your trip takes in nearly every movie genre. Comedy comes from two live characters. The guide is a self-absorbed projectionist who, inspired by Buster Keaton's character in 1923's "Sherlock Jr.," magically takes you into some of his (or her) favorite films. Channeling actor Jeff Daniels in 1985's "The Purple Rose of Cairo," a second performer steps out of the set and takes over your tram.

Sometimes your hijacker is a 1930s gangster, sometimes a Wild West outlaw.

The ride concludes in a dark theater, with a three-minute montage of 247 film clips. The snippets include everything from the 1925 Charlie Chaplin vehicle "The Gold Rush" to modern-day hits.

For the best trip, sit next to the tram guide (ask the cast member at the boarding entrance for the first seats in either the first or second row). You'll have to wait a few minutes for the next tram, but it's well worth it. Not only will the guide's

▶ Take your ride before 10 a.m. or at the end of the day, when crowds are light.

spiel make sense (you'll always be viewing the same scene), but you'll get an up-close-and-personal encounter with the hijacker, who may direct a few scripted lines your way ("What are you lookin' at?") or even talk with you off mic. Once in the "Alien" scene the gangster glanced at the monster, looked over at us and whispered, "I would shoot that but it looks too much like my Aunt Chloe."

The entrance facade and lobby are picture-perfect, full-scale reproductions of Hollywood's Grauman's Chinese Theatre, an over-the-top example of La-La-land architecture that has been a focal point of Hollywood since 1927.

Almost two decades after they created it, Disney Imagineers look back on their Great Movie Ride work with fondness. "It's really dear to my heart," says show producer Eric Jacobson, "not only because of all the effects, but also because of all the work we did. Getting the rights to those movies was not a simple task."

22 min. Capacity: 560. Avg. wait 25 min. late morning, 60 min. peak afternoon. ECV users must transfer. Assistive listening, handheld captioning. Preshow: Highlights from classic movie trailers. Fear factor: Intense for preschoolers. The "Alien" creature moves toward you from the ceiling and then appears suddenly out of the right wall. The Wicked Witch looks real. Best ages: 6 and up. Debuted: 1989.

FUN FINDS ❶ Lobby props include a monkey head used in the palace dinner scene in 1984's "Indiana Jones and the Temple of Doom" (it held the dessert: chilled monkey brains) and ❷ Andrews' carousel horse from 1964's "Mary Poppins" (it also appears in the preshow trailers). ❸ The actual Chinese Theatre appears in the trailer for 1952's "Singin' in the Rain." ❹ In Gangster Alley, an argument is taking place in the second-floor flat above Patrick J. Ryan's Bar. One man has a gun. ❺ The Western scene's "Sheriff's Office" sign swings when it gets hit by an illusionary bullet.

"Maybe nobody will get hoit." Before hijacking the tram, Mugsy the gangster fights off a mob ambush.

FUN FACTS ❭❭ Replicas of statues at the actual Chinese Theatre, two Fu Dogs sit alongside the central entrance doors. On the left is a female, with a pup under her paw. On the right is a male, with a ball. Fu Dogs were used in early China to ward off evil spirits. ❭❭ The Cagney robot wears one of the star's actual tuxedos. It was donated by his family. ❭❭ The Gangster Alley buildings and signs refer to scenes from classic movies. Ryan's Bar, J.L. Altmeyer & Sons Novelty Manufacturing, the Red Oaks Social Club and Western Chemical Co. are settings in 1931's "The Public Enemy." The signs "Dead End" and "Society for Juvenile Delinquents" refer to the 1937 Bogart film "Dead End." ❭❭ The Ransom Stoddard placard alludes to the attorney played by Jimmy Stewart in 1962's "The Man Who Shot Liberty Valence." ❭❭ Historical references include the "021-429" license plate on the gangsters' 1931 Chrysler (the Feb. 14, 1929, St. Valentine's Day massacre) and the Western town's Monarch Saloon (the Leadville, Colo., home to outlaw gambler Doc Holliday) and Cochise County Courthouse (the site of Tombstone, Ariz.'s gunfight at the O.K. Corral.) ❭❭ The "No Help Wanted" and "Sheriff's Office" signs are old props from the MGM California backlot. ❭❭ The attraction was built to portray three "Wizard of Oz" scenes. The "Fantasia" room was to be Dorothy's tornado; the video screen still sits in a sepia-toned funnel. You'd wake up in Munchkinland then travel to the Emerald City, where the Wizard would tell you to "pay no attention to that man behind the curtain." Last-minute copyright snags forced the cutback.

▶ Want the outlaw? Tell the cast member at the entrance to the boarding area.

6 Along the left floor of the Nostromo spaceship, inside jokes on the first video screen include its "estimated time till next special effects failure" and **7** a "welcome to all aliens visiting from the Glendale galaxy."* **8** The third screen lists an astronaut as "still programming the witch." **9** After it captures its victim, the eyes of the Anubis statue glow red. **10** Along the left wall of the skeleton room, a snake squirms out of the eye of a sarcophagus and **11** a pharaoh pets a mummified cat. **12** A Munchkin pops out of a manhole next to the swirly start of the yellow brick road at the beginning of "Ding Dong the Witch is Dead" — just as in the film. **13** After the Wicked Witch warns "Just try to stay out of my way — just try," a Munchkin hiding behind her peeks out for a moment.

* Glendale, California, is the home of Walt Disney Imagineering.

TIME LIFE PICTURES / GETTY IMAGES

Celebrity Impressions

Many Hollywood celebrities have placed their hands and feet into Studios concrete. The Chinese Theatre courtyard has more than 100 prints. Front and center is the work of Warren Beatty (shown above making his mark in 1990), nearby are the marks of Bob Hope, Jim Henson (who brought Kermit) and Dustin Hoffman and Robin Williams (who brought their kids). Others on hand: George Burns, Tony Curtis and George Lucas. On Sunset Blvd., 30 TV stars have left impressions at the Theater of the Stars in a small plaza next to the rear bleachers. "Star Trek's" Scotty, James Doohon, added "Beam Me Up" while "Jeopardy" host Alex Trebek wrote "Who is Alex Trebek?" Also here: Morey Amsterdam from "The Dick Van Dyke Show," Imogene Coca from "Your Show of Shows," Bob Denver from "Gilligan's Island," June Lockhart from "Lassie," George Wendt from "Cheers," even journeyman Martin Mull.

Most prints are from the early 1990s, made at ceremonies during the park's old "Star of the Day" events. During Charlton Heston's 1995 ceremony, a photographer yelled "Charlton!" just as the Hollywood legend was drawing out the "R" in his first name, causing him to look up. When the then-72-year-old star got back to work, he accidentally skipped the next letter of his name, creating a signature that reads "Charton" Heston.

Not all of Disney's prints are on display. Some, including those of Johnny Depp, are stored backstage. All are real except the impressions of Judy Garland's ruby slippers from "The Wizard of Oz," which are replicas of those in the concrete slab at the California theater.

A Cavalcade of Classics

'FOOTLIGHT PARADE'

When talking pictures put Broadway producer Chester Kent (James Cagney) out of business, he hits upon a swell idea: he'll stage musical "prologues" at movie theaters throughout New York. That's the plot of 1933's bawdy, gaudy "Footlight Parade." The highlight is "By a Waterfall," a 15-minute aquacade that concludes in a huge twirling fountain of bathing beauties. The segment has influenced dozens of modern commercials, stage shows and movies, including the "Be Our Guest" sequence of Disney's "Beauty and the Beast."

'SINGIN' IN THE RAIN'

Silent-film star Don Lockwood (Gene Kelly) has such a glorious feeling (not only has his career been saved, but he's fallen in love with a beautiful ingenue) he doesn't mind getting wet as he swings from a lamppost in 1952's "Singin' in the Rain," often called the greatest musical ever. Built around the transition to talking pictures, the movie is filled with updated versions of early-talkie songs. The title number debuted in "The Hollywood Revue of 1929" as a tune by Ukulele Ike, AKA Cliff Edwards, the voice of Jiminy Cricket in Disney's "Pinocchio."

'MARY POPPINS'

When two Victorian London children are scolded by their father in Disney's best live-action musical, 1964's "Mary Poppins," chimney sweep Bert (Dick Van Dyke) takes them and their nanny (Julie Andrews) up on the rooftops to see the sights and sing "Chim Chim Cher-ee." When other sweeps arrive, they break out into "Step in Time," a huge dance number.

'THE PUBLIC ENEMY'

Based on the true story of 1920s bootlegging murderer Hymie Weiss, 1931's "The Public Enemy" invented (along with that year's "Little Caesar") the gangster genre. In an early Prohibition scene, Tom Powers (James Cagney) threatens a speakeasy owner with violence if he doesn't become a customer: "When Dutch comes around he's gonna leave you some beer. And you're gonna take it. And you're gonna kick in with the dough. If you don't, somebody's gonna drop by here and kick your teeth out one at a time." The film made Cagney Hollywood's first antihero. Its most famous scene — Cagney shoving a grapefruit into the face of nagging Mae Clarke — flashes past in the Great Movie Ride's film-clip finale.

JOHN WAYNE

Western legend John Wayne appeared in nearly 250 movies, many of epic proportions. He once said his favorite film was 1953's "Hondo," in which he starred as a half-breed who befriends a married white woman. Just after they meet, Hondo kisses the woman and has no regrets — because he knows she wanted it. "A long time ago, I made me a rule," he says, "let people do what they want." Wayne's Great Movie Ride character repeats that line, and wears a costume from the film.

CLINT EASTWOOD

Credited with re-establishing the American Western, Clint Eastwood starred as the quiet, stone-hearted antihero lead character (the Man with No Name) in the trilogy "Fistful of Dollars" (1964), "For a Few Dollars More" (1966) and "The Good, The Bad and The Ugly" (1967). Produced in Italy by director Sergio Leone, the darkly comic films were known as Spaghetti Westerns.

'ALIEN'

Hiding in ventilation chambers, a bloodthirsty beast stalks, and sometimes lays eggs in, the crew of 1979's "Alien" space freighter Nostromo. After the rest of the crew dies, Warrant Officer Ellen Ripley (Sigourney Weaver) rigs the craft to self-destruct, but the monster pursues her as she tries to escape. The film's tension and heart-stopping surprises make it a modern horror classic.

'RAIDERS OF THE LOST ARK'

In 1981's "Raiders of the Lost Ark," the U.S. government enlists archaeology professor Indiana Jones (Harrison Ford) to help keep the golden Ark of the Covenant out of the hands of Hitler's Nazis. When Indy asks his old friend Sallah (John Rhys-Davies) to help him find it, they do — in the Well of Souls, an ancient Egyptian tomb outside of Cairo. The film was director Steven Spielberg's effort to recapture the fun of early Saturday matinee serials.

'TARZAN AND HIS MATE'

1934's "Tarzan and His Mate" is the best, and most provocative, of the Tarzan films. Having met Tarzan (Johnny Weissmuller) in 1932's Tarzan the Ape Man, Jane (Maureen O'Sullivan) now lives with him. The film includes plenty of action, some smoldering glances, racy dialogue, revealing loincloths and even a nude swimming scene. The couple uses an army of elephants to scare off attacking natives and lions, and has, for the first time, a pet chimp, Cheeta. According to film lore, an MGM sound technician created the Tarzan yell by combining a camel's bleat, hyena's howl, plucking violin string and yodeling soprano.

'CASABLANCA'

When expatriate American Rick Blaine (Humphrey Bogart) meets old flame Ilsa Lund (Ingrid Bergman) in 1942's "Casablanca," the cynical former freedom fighter must choose between love and honor: though the couple is still in love, she's married to a Resistance hero and Rick has only two Letters of Transit to escape the Nazi-controlled city. Rick makes his decision at the airport: he stays behind. Considered the best-loved American movie, "Casablanca" has been shown on American broadcast television more than any other film.

'FANTASIA'

When a magician's student (Mickey Mouse) has to wash a floor in "The Sorcerer's Apprentice" (a segment of 1940's "Fantasia"), he gets out of it by putting on his mentor's hat and conjuring up powers of his own. Soon he learns you shouldn't start something you can't finish. The film debuted a new-look Mickey with pupils in his eyes.

'THE WIZARD OF OZ'

After a tornado knocks a farm girl unconscious in 1939's "The Wizard of Oz," she dreams she travels with her dog to the magical land of Oz, a colorful world of friendly Munchkins, yellow brick roads and wicked witches. Farm hands appear as a courageous lion, smart scarecrow and kind tin man. Initially panned by critics (The New Yorker labeled it a "stinkeroo"), the film became a cherished American icon starting in 1956, when it began playing yearly on television. During a rehearsal of the Munchkinland scene, the copper-oxide-based green makeup on Wicked Witch of the West Margaret Hamilton caught fire, putting the actress in the hospital for six weeks.

Indiana Jones punches a sword-wielding assassin

Indiana Jones Epic Stunt Spectacular

✓ Seventeen performers re-create the physical stunts of three scenes of 1981's "Raiders of the Lost Ark" in this timeless outdoor stage show.

First you relive the opening scene, as the actor playing Indiana drops, literally, into a Mayan ruin. Pursuing a golden idol, he dodges spears, hatchet-slamming statues and a giant rolling boulder.

Next, Indy and Marion take on a village of Cairo bad guys. Indy fights 'em off with his bullwhip (and, of course, gun), lots of folks fall off buildings and Marion makes a death-defying escape out of a flipping, flaming truck.

For the finale, our heroes are at a Nazi airfield in a North African desert. When a Flying Wing taxis in for fuel, Indy and Marion try again to escape. They fight Nazis in, on and around the spinning plane (its iron-fisted mechanic gives Indy quite a battle), fleeing to safety just as leaking fuel sparks a huge explosion.

MEAT, WITH CHEESE Basically the same since 1989, this show hasn't lost its appeal. Most of the stunts look real (notice the face punches as Indy battles the mechanic), there's always something to watch and there's plenty of humor. Audience volunteers are made fun of throughout the show, as are some of the cast. The fighting is punctuated by cartoonish sound effects. Listen for the clang-clang of the frying pan when Marion whacks it into two heads.

Between scenes you learn how sets can be quickly dismantled, how heavy-looking props can be feather-light and how to throw a fake punch.

To add to the show, Disney pretends it is a real film shoot. Mock cameramen peer through mock cameras; a pretend director barks out pretend directions. When the Assistant Director of the Second Unit explains "We're going to shoot 36 instead of 24 frames per second," his boss declares "I like it!"

The creation of the attraction was overseen personally by George Lucas. The stunts were designed by the late Glenn Randall, one of Hollywood's most

▶ Get here early to sit in the first few rows. You'll feel the heat from the fires.

famous stuntmen and horse wranglers, and the stunt coordinator for "Raiders."

The first performance of the day is usually the least crowded. The last show is often the best looking, when the darker sky makes the pyro more visible. *32 min. Capacity: 2,000. Avg. wait: 10 min. early morning, 30 min. peak afternoon. Fastpass available. Guests may remain in wheelchairs, ECVs. Assistive listening; handheld captioning. Preshow: Selection of audience volunteers. Fear factor: None unless kids think the action is real. Best ages: 8 and up. Debuted: 1989, revised 2000.*

FUN FINDS ❶ One of the volunteers is really a professional stuntman. Can you spot him before everyone else catches on? ❷ "I have a bad feeling about this." Indy says this signature George Lucas line during the Cairo street scene as he and Marion become surrounded by bad guys with swords. ❸ At the end of the Cairo scene Marion is kidnapped and taken away in a truck. Apparently the truck circles behind a building, reappears, then flips and catches fire. In reality it stops behind the building and a second, empty truck finishes the circle. Attached to the building, this second truck simply rotates over. As for Marion, though she appears to run out of that burning truck, she actually comes back onstage through a small gray crate just to the right of the vehicle. ❹ The sidecar motorcycle is a reproduction of the one Harrison Ford commandeered in the 1989 film "Indiana Jones and the Last Crusade." It even has the same front fender license: WH38475. ❺ In the last scene the German mechanic is supposedly chopped up by one of the plane's propellers; in truth he falls through an easily visible trapdoor. ❻ Behind the adjacent Outpost gift shop are three vehicles that were used in the filming of the

"Last Crusade," in the scenes where Indy and the Nazis are racing to find the Holy Grail. Just off the sidewalk you'll find the film's Nazi staff car and truck, as well as its "Steel Beast" tank (its side gun barrel still "exploded" from Indy stuffing it with a rock). Each vehicle still displays the symbol of the film's Republic of Hatay. ❼ Just to the left of the Fastpass machines, a British chap has dug a hole and lowered himself down to the bottom of it. Pull on his rope and the irritable archeologist will talk to you ("I say! Stop mucking about up there!").

A CLASSIC ADVENTURE

A rollicking throwback to the movie serials of the 1930s and 1940s, 1981's "Raiders of the Lost Ark" is a true adventure epic. The story begins in 1936. Beleaguered New England archaeology professor Dr. Indiana Jones has just returned from the jungles of Peru, where he has failed to recover a sacred idol from the Temple of the Chachapoyan Warriors. Then the U.S. Army calls. It tells the professor that Germany's Adolf Hitler has plans to find the Ark of the Covenant, the golden casket used by ancient Hebrews to hold the Ten Commandments. Not only is it a revered Jewish artifact, its supernatural powers, legend says, can wipe out entire armies.

Uncle Sam wants Indy to find it first.

So off he goes — to Nepal, to reunite with young Marion Ravenwood, a gutsy old girlfriend who owns a precious medallion that can reveal the Ark's location. Then the two head off to Cairo, to enlist the help of a trusted archeological digger. But the Nazis have beat them there, and recruited henchmen to kidnap Marion and steal her medallion. The couple puts up a brave defense (he fights off a gang of assassins; she knocks one out with a handy frying pan) but Marion is captured and taken away in a truck. When Indy sees the truck explode, he assumes she's dead.

In fact she's alive, sound but bound in the desert at a Nazi excavation camp that's searching for the sacred relic. Indy arrives and frees her, then they learn the Nazis are about to load the Ark on a Flying Wing aircraft bound for Germany. The couple tracks down the plane and, while it's fueling, takes it over: she shoots Nazis from the cockpit while Indy's fight with a mechanic ends when that Nazi is shredded by a propeller. Then, when leaking fuel catches fire, Indy and Marion run to safety just before everything blows up.

Eventually the Nazis do open the Ark, only to be burned alive as they face the Wrath of God.

FUN FACT ⟩⟩ The sound of the airplane is that of a Ford Tri-Motor, the aircraft used in an early scene of 1984's "Indiana Jones and the Temple of Doom."

▶ To be in the show, jump and scream when the "casting director" asks for volunteers.

There's no wait for Sounds Dangerous

The show's OK, but the postshow is better. A collection of old but engaging activity stations, **Sound Works** lets you dub your voice to classic cartoon and movie characters and make your own sound effects with video help from Disney effects legend Jimmy MacDonald. The walls are lined with gadgets MacDonald used to create effects for 20 classic films. To see Sound Works by itself enter through the Sounds Dangerous exit, the doors to the right of the entrance.

If you're nursing, Sounds Dangerous offers good privacy. For seven minutes the theater is totally dark and, with your headphones off, quiet. But be aware: After a minute and 45 seconds the screen comes on for 15 seconds, throwing a dim light on the seats. Then it's dark again for five minutes.

When you get sprinkled with water you have 15 seconds before the lights come on for good.

12 min. Capacity: 240. Avg. wait: 6 min. Guests may stay in wheelchairs, ECVs. Assistive listening. Preshow: Video trivia about ABC television shows. Fear factor: Some sound effects mimic scary encounters. Debuted: 1999.

Sounds Dangerous

When television's "Undercover Live" incognito investigator Drew Carey shorts out his tiny spy cam, the theater of his test audience — that's you — goes completely dark. You're at the mercy of your imagination when he opens a jar of bees, gets a shave and bumps an elephant.

ATAS Hall of Fame Showcase

To the right of Sounds Dangerous, this small plaza has 15 bronze busts of television stars, all members of the Academy of Television Arts and Sciences Hall of Fame. Included are Lucille Ball, Andy Griffith and Mary Tyler Moore. Plaques along the back wall list all the inductees for each year. Ignored by most visitors, the plaza seems more suited to a museum than a theme park, or perhaps too many of these once-household names are now just ancient history. As one 9-year-old boy said while eyeing a nameplate, "Hmmm... 'Sid Caesar.' Probably the brother of Julius Caesar." Disney stopped adding busts and plaques in 1996.

Restaurant guide

TABLE SERVICE **50's Prime Time Cafe $$** ✔
This surreal re-creation of a 1950s home kitchen serves comfort food but has rules — no elbows on the table and you must eat your vegetables. Break them at your own risk. You sit at a Formica table. Extras include black-and-white counter TVs and "mom" as your waitress. Ask the host for a TV table and an extra-schticky server. 225 seats. *Echo Lake.* **Hollywood & Vine $$** Breakfast and lunch character buffets with Playhouse Disney stars JoJo and Goliath from "JoJo's Circus" and June and Leo from "Little Einsteins." 468 seats. *Echo Lake.* **The Hollywood Brown Derby $$$** ✔ With the best food at any Disney theme-park restaurant, the Brown Derby is a terrific break from the theme-park grind. A faithful re-creation of its 1929 Hollywood namesake (complete with leather booths and a white-tuxedoed wait staff), the Derby offers a classic American menu that's modern but not trendy. The famous Cobb Salad was created when theater owner Sid Grauman had a toothache. The grapefruit cake was first made for gossip columnist Louella Parsons during a 1930s Grapefruit Diet craze. Even the rolls have a celebrity connection: they're the same German Spitzwecks that an angry Lucille Ball once tossed at "Wizard of Oz" tin man Jack Haley. Another throwback: tableside phone service. Arrange it with the host and you can relive another Old Hollywood tradition: getting a phone call at your booth. Just as California servers did in the 1930s and 1940s, yours will bring a corded phone to your table, because you (or your child) have an important call — from Goofy, who congratulates you on your anniversary, birthday or other magical moment. Gawrsh! 224 seats. *Hollywood Blvd.* **Mama Melrose's Ristorante Italiano $$** This dimly lit restaurant has good individual pizzas, tasty pasta and comfortable booths. You can write your name on the walls. Also on the walls are autographed photo cards from the park's 1980s Star of the Day program, which show many female celebrities with huge permed and teased hair. The 'do on Mary Ann Mobley makes her look like Marge Simpson; each side of Sally Struthers' hair is as wide as her face. 250 seats. *Backlot.* **Sci-Fi Dine-In Theater $$** This re-created 1950s drive-in movie theater puts you under the stars in a classic convertible as a carhop serves you. Up front the giant silver screen shows a never-ending assortment of science-fiction shlock. Not all the tables are cars; ask for one for the full effect. 252 seats. *Backlot.*

COUNTER SERVICE **ABC Commissary $** ✔ This comfortable cafe has cushioned booths and chairs, a carpeted floor and live palms. Try the Cuban sandwich: pressed roast beef, pork, cheese and a pickle. There's breakfast, too. 562 seats. *Backlot.* **Backlot Express $** Decked out as a backlot crafts shop, this burger and sandwich joint is filled with the down-and-dirty clutter of a real production area. Taped on the window of the paint department office are actual call sheets for the "Cheers" television series and the 1989 movie "Star Trek V." Bigger finds include the Bennie the Cab stunt car from 1988's "Who Framed Roger Rabbit." Sitting in the outdoor patio is that film's Toon Patrol truck. Try the turkey or grilled vegetable sandwich. 600 seats. *Backlot.* **Toy Story Pizza Planet $** This arcade has individual pizzas, salads. Bring change for the Space Crane. *Backlot.*

OUTDOOR COUNTER CAFES **Flatbread Grill $** Nice offerings include grilled chicken, a barbecued-pork sub and chicken stew. Most seats are shaded. 498 seats. *Backlot.* **Starring Rolls Cafe $** ✔ Why do these deli sandwiches taste so good? They're made next door at the Brown Derby. Breakfast offerings include smoked salmon on a bagel. Coffee, pastry, wine too. The best counter service food at Disney. Typically closes about 3:30 p.m. 10 tables. *Hollywood Blvd. at Sunset Blvd.* **Sunset Ranch Market $** This food court has six stands and umbrella-sheltered tables. Food options include fresh fruits and vegetables; individual pizzas and salads; cheeseburgers, chicken strips and salads; turkey legs and hot dogs; and hand-dipped ice cream (Edy's). 400 seats. *Sunset Blvd.*

SNACK STANDS ECHO LAKE **Dinosaur Gertie's $** Soft ice cream, waffle cones. **Dip Site $** Philly cheese steaks, beer, soft drinks. Seasonal. **Min & Bill's Dockside Diner $** Soft ice cream treats, beer, pretzels and other snacks. An outdoor patio seats 140. **Peevy's Polar Pipeline $** Good Slushie-style frozen treats made from Coca-Cola, lemonade and other drinks. BACKLOT **Herbie's Drive In $** Steamed buns (three-bite, dinner-roll mounds of stuffed dough), frozen drinks. **The Writer's Stop $** ✔ A bagel, cookie, pastry and drink counter hides in this small shop that was modeled to be Buy the Book, the bookstore in the 1990s television sitcom "Ellen." Tucked in the back is a small two-person table; there's also a comfy cloth chair and sofa. Try the Cafe Cooler, an iced mix of chocolate milk and coffee. SUNSET BLVD. **KRNR The Rock Station $** Frozen lemonade, smoothies, soft ice cream.

BAR ECHO LAKE **Tune-In Lounge $** ✔ This well-stocked bar has friendly bartenders and creative specialties. It also offers the full menu from the adjacent 50's Prime Time Cafe — without a wait! BACKLOT **High Octane Refreshments $** An alcoholic oasis with beer, wine, margaritas.

It's got legs. You enter under an All Terrain Armored Transport.

the galaxy. R2-D2 and C-3PO are working for intergalactic airline Star Tours. You're there to board a tourist shuttle to the Ewoks' moon of Endor.

You're first in the maintenance bay, where 3PO and R2 repair a shuttle. Then you step into the "Droidnostics Center," as a mechanic assembles pilots and navigators. Finally you board your shuttle, a StarSpeeder 3000. R2 is its navigator but a rookie, RX-24, is at the controls.

"Rex" makes mistakes immediately, sending your ship off its docking ledge and down through a repair bay, barely missing a swinging crane before flying out a side door — then past Endor into a field of ice crystals. You tunnel through the biggest crystal and smash your way out.

But an enemy destroyer is nearby, and is pulling you toward it. "Oh no!" Rex yells. "We're caught in a tractor beam!" A rebel fighter pilot breaks in on your video monitor. "Star Tours?!? What are you doing here? This is a combat zone!" You get free but then get hit, and fall toward a Death Star.

R2-D2 repairs your ship just in time.

But it's not over. "I've always wanted to do this!" Rex says as he dives toward the Death Star. "We're going in!" You swoop along the surface, zooming under bridges and into a trench, blasting bad guys along the way. Trailing the lead fighter, you watch as he drops two torpedoes down the Star's exhaust port.

You rocket away just as it explodes.

Despite nearly skidding into a fuel tanker on the way in, you return to your Star Tours hangar shaken but sound.

Star Tours

You journey into space in this elaborate "Star Wars" attraction, which features an early motion simulator.* For a Lucas project it's surprisingly unrestored, but it does have the same mix of wit and action of the early "Star Wars" films.

The story begins as you enter the building. You're in deep space, inside a spaceport during a time after the 1983 movie "Return of the Jedi." Darth Vader is dead and the Republic and its rebels (the good guys) have a tentative hold on

---

* Used by airlines and militaries to train pilots, these enclosed, garbage-truck-like machines create a sensation of flight by synchronizing their tilts, dives and other movements to films that simulate the view out of windshields.

Choose a middle row for a fun ride that won't make you sick, the back seats for lots of rock 'n' roll. The front row is the most calm. Perfect for photos, a climb-on replica of a Speeder Bike (the woods-weaving vehicle of "Return of the Jedi") sits across from the ride entrance.

7 min. Capacity: 240. Avg. wait: 10 min. early morning, 45 min. peak afternoon. Fastpass available. ECV guests must transfer to an available wheelchair. Guest-activated captioning. Height restriction: 40 in. Fear factor: The vehicle's unpredictable sways and dives can cause motion sickness in guests of any age. Chicken exit. Debuted: 1989 (Disneyland 1987).

FUN FINDS ❶ The entrance area is the "stage set" of a village of Ewoks, those teddy-bear creatures that helped save the day in 1983's "Return of the Jedi." Redwood, sequoia and pine "props" are all just tall enough for a film scene (at night you can hear the Ewoks in their tree huts, talking and drumming). The set also includes a captured, 35-foot-tall Imperial Walker, a woodland path (the brown sidewalk) and, just inside, the directors chairs of stars C-3PO and R2-D2. ❷ "Don't insult me, you overgrown scrap pile!" 3PO snaps to R2 in the maintenance bay. ❸ Pages call "Egroeg Sacul" ("George Lucas" backward), Dr. Tom Morrow (the host of 1970s Magic Kingdom attraction Flight to the Moon) and the owner of a vehicle with the ID "THX-1138" (the first Lucas film, 1971). ❹ Little red men chase each other across the bottom of the large video screen. ❺ A watermelon-sized robot circles the left floor of the Droidnostics Center. ❻ The mechanic asks for your help ("Could you tell me where this goes?") and gets offended by your attention ("Take a pic-

ture, it will last longer"). ❼ A wiggling hand and foot hide in a pile of robotic junk on your right. ❽ "Excuse me but you'll have to check the excess baggage," the gate attendant tells you. "Oh, I'm sorry, I didn't realize that was your husband." ❾ As you leave the Center, two robotic hawks above you tend their nests. ❿ Inside your shuttle, a red plastic strip attached to Rex reads "Remove Before Flight." ⓫ "I have a bad feeling about this!" Rex yells as you fly into the crystals, repeating a line used in nearly every Lucas film. ⓬ As you re-enter the maintenance bay Lucas himself appears as a control-room operator. He's standing in an office in front of you. ⓭ Just before the gift shop, a glass case on your right displays some character sketches and a page of the script from 1999's "Star Wars Episode 1: The Phantom Menace."

A SPACE FANTASY that takes place "a long time ago, far, far away," the "Star Wars" films tell a timeless story of good versus evil. Combining a space-opera plot like those of the Buck Rogers serials of the 1930s and '40s with the use of special effects and modeling similar to the 1968 film "2001 A Space Odyssey," the films created a mix of wit, mythology and simulated reality that has entranced audiences worldwide for decades.

Some classic "Star Wars" vehicles and weapons play key roles in your Star Tours flight. You become caught in an Imperial Star Destroyer's tractor beam, an invisible force field that can capture and redirect rebel ships. Rebel forces fly the X-Wing starfighter. The symbol of the rebel fleet, its double-layered wings separate into an "X" formation during combat. Luke Skywalker flew one in the first "Star Wars" trilogy. The bad guys use the TIE starfighter, named for its twin ion engines. These bare-bolts machines lack hyperdrives and deflector shields. The Empire's most horrific weapons are its Death Stars. Powered by a fusion reactor in its center, each of these moon-sized space stations is staffed with over a million troops. Its main weapon is a superlaser housed in a crater-like cannon well. There have been three Death Stars. The first destroyed Princess Leia's home planet of Alderaan in 1977's "Star Wars," then fell victim to Luke Skywalker when he dropped a pair of proton torpedoes into its exhaust port. The second was never finished; the rebels destroyed it in 1983's "Return of the Jedi." The third appears during your flight. It's destroyed by the X-Wing in front of you.

FUN FACTS ❯❯ Anthony Daniels provided the voice of C-3PO in the maintenance bay as well as the alien voice. ❯❯ In the Droidnostics Center, two of the droids behind G2-9T were background extras in the first "Star Wars" film.

▶ The Tatooine Traders gift shop often carries Darth Tater, a special Mr. Potato Head.

A revolving brass fountain re-creates one of Miss Piggy's roles in MuppetVision 3-D

then nearly sucks up the theater when he tries to fix things with a VacuuMuppet. Miss Piggy storms off the set when she learns her special effects are nothing more than plastic butterflies on sticks.

The finale nearly destroys the theater. When patriotic Sam Eagle tries to condense his three-hour extravaganza ("A Salute to All Nations But Mostly America") into 90 seconds, all the performers end up onstage at once. The result is a chaos of falling, tripping, shooting and, in one case, stripping.

Created in 1990, the theater effects look their age, but the show has so much wit it doesn't matter. Despite Kermit's assurance that "at no time will we be stooping to cheap 3-D tricks," his cast does exactly that. (When Sweetums walks on screen and, for no reason, starts knocking a paddle ball into the audience, he's channeling a famously pointless scene from the classic Vincent Price horror film, 1953's "House of Wax.") The film uses its 3-D technology creatively. Its scenes often have enormous depth.

Even those who have never heard of the Muppets will like the show. Miss Piggy's offended rage is funny the first time you see it, as is Honeydew's thick-rimmed, eye-free, melon head. Kermit and the gang peaked on the pop-culture radar decades ago, but, as always, it takes no time to fall in love with them.

Don't miss the preshow, 12 minutes of backstage banter, musical numbers and general confusion that plays out over a synchronized set of monitors in a backstage warehouse. The best moment comes early, when Sam Eagle introduces his special guest Mickey Mouse.

Even the rarely-used outdoor waiting area is worth your time. Wrapping around the right rear of the building, this

Jim Henson's MuppetVision 3-D

✓ Built around a funny 3-D film, this inspired attraction mixes vaudeville humor with silly effects. As you sit in the red-velvet theater from the 1970s television series "The Muppet Show," you watch a typical Muppet misadventure that's accented with bubble showers, cannon fire, even Statler and Waldorf.

The Muppets have renovated the auditorium to debut a new film technology. Nicki Napoleon and his Emperor Penguins tune up in the orchestra pit as the Swedish Chef readies the haphazardly assembled projection equipment. As the film begins, Kermit takes you to the lab of Dr. Bunsen Honeydew, the scientist who has created the devilish Waldo, a "living, breathing 3-D effect."

But everything goes wrong. Assistant Beaker gets caught in the machinery,

▶ Save this for the middle of the day. Most of your wait will be watching the preshow.

covered walkway is lined with zany drawings and wacky posters.

Little kids have little to fear. Nothing scary jumps out at you, there are no floor or chair effects and the only explosion (from the Chef's cannon at the end of the show) is telegraphed well in advance.

The attraction was Jim Henson's last major project, and his lavish magical touch is everywhere. That's him voicing Kermit and the Swedish Chef.

25 min. Capacity: 584. Avg wait: 15 min. Guests may remain in wheelchairs and ECVs. Assistive listening; reflective and activated video captioning. Fear factor: A few dark moments. Debuted: 1991.

FUN FINDS ❶ Director Gonzo and cameraman Fozzie are filming a brassy Miss Piggy in the courtyard fountain. Clad in a flowing gown and laced sandals, she's re-creating her role as the Statue of Liberty in the MuppetVision finale. She stands on a half shell, an homage to the 1879 William Bouguereau painting "The Birth of Venus." ❷ Underneath are three rats in the fountain: Rizzo and two friends snorkeling for coins and fishing for dollars. ❸ An outdoor staircase leads to the projection room, where the Swedish Chef is running a combination editing and catering business (its slogan: "Frøøm Qüick Cüts tø Cöld Cüts"). ❹ In a tribute to Harold Lloyd's 1923 silent black-and-white film "Safety Last!" a black-and-white Gonzo hangs from the clock tower. ❺ Around the corner is a reference to classic *Warner Bros.* cartoons: an ACME anvil. ❻ Atop the brick wall to the right, two of the large round planters are actually ice cream sundaes. One is half-eaten. ❼ Signs lining the little-used outdoor queue area that winds around the right of the building include movie posters for such films as "Beach Blanket Beaker" and "Kürmet the Amphibian" ("So Mean He's Green") and ❽ placards created by Honeydew's MuppetLabs that help you get from "here" to "there" (an eight-step process), perform experiments

OF MAN AND MUPPETS
Jim Henson invented the Muppets when he was a teenager. As a senior at a Washington, D.C., high school in 1954, the 18-year-old combined the features of a marionette with those of a hand puppet.

Success came fast. While attending the University of Maryland Henson got his own local television show

GETTY IMAGES

Jim Henson

("Sam and Friends," a 5-minute daily program), appeared on NBC's "Tonight" show and became a hot commodity in the advertising world. Out of college he landed a weekly spot on NBC's "Today" show. In 1962 Jim had his first full-time national gig: performing the piano-playing dog Rowlf on ABC's "The Jimmy Dean Show." In 1966 the Muppets began a series of appearances on the CBS "Ed Sullivan Show."

Then the Children's Television Workshop called. It wanted Henson to create characters for its new show, "Sesame Street." He had mixed feelings — he feared it could pigeonhole him as a kiddie act.

He was right. Though his "Sesame Street" characters were instant superstars, Henson soon learned that no U.S. network would give him a show of his own. In 1975 NBC gave him a limited role on its new "Saturday Night Live," but when he pitched ABC on a half-hour comedy-variety show starring Kermit and a cast of new, more adult-oriented characters, it turned him down flat.

British producer Lew Grade came to the rescue, giving Henson the money to produce 24 shows to syndicate. Hosted by a who's who of 1970s movie and television stars, "The Muppet Show" soon became an international hit. At its peak it was watched by 235 million viewers a week. After a few years Henson moved to films, and by 1989 the world was at Jim Henson's doorstep.

Specifically, the world of the Walt Disney Co. That August he and Disney announced a partnership: Disney would purchase the rights to certain Muppets and Henson would make movies, television shows and specials exclusively for Disney, working from the backlot of the just-opened Disney-MGM Studios. Henson bought a house just a few miles north of Disney property.

By the spring of 1990 he was immersed in projects. Filming the new attraction MuppetVision 3-D in California, he simultaneously worked in Florida shooting "The Muppets at Walt Disney World," a TV movie that would be the first public celebration of the new Disney-Henson relationship. It aired on a Sunday night, May 13.

Two days later Henson contracted an aggressive form of pneumonia, and was rushed to a hospital. He died within 24 hours. He was 54.

▶ The Stage 1 Co. Store has Beaker, Dr. Bunsen Honeydew and Swedish Chef plushies.

WHO'S WHO IN MUPPETVISION 3-D

The show combines characters from "The Muppet Show" with stars from other Jim Henson productions from the 1980s. Known for his shock of red hair and scared-witless stare, squeaky meep **Beaker** is the victim of Professor Honeydew's inventions... Known for his big imagination, **Bean Bunny** debuted in the 1986 TV special "The Tale of the Bunny Picnic" and starred in the 1984-1991 kids' show, "Jim Henson's Muppet Babies"... The head of MuppetLabs, good-natured inventor **Dr. Bunsen Honeydew** creates elaborate gadgets most people don't know they need... Named for his puppeteer Frank Oz, sweetly insecure **Fozzie Bear** never gives up in his quest to be funny, often accenting his routines with a shout of "Wacka! Wacka!"... A skittish perfectionist, beaked mutant **Gonzo** loves to perform stunts and collect fungus, and has an affection for chickens... Named for rock icon Janis Joplin, hippie chick **Janis** played rhythm guitar and tambourine in the Electric Mayhem, the "Muppet Show" house band led by Dr. Teeth, and starred as the wisecracking nurse in the recurring skit "Veterinarians' Hospital"... The first Muppet, **Kermit the Frog** was created by an 18-year-old Henson in 1954 using two halves of a ping-pong ball and his mom's old green coat. He was named for Henson's childhood friend Theodore Kermit Scott, who later became a professor of philosophy at Purdue University... A Rubenesque starlet that loves to kick butt, **Miss Piggy** is the Muppet's diva, or at least thinks she is. She flies into a rage whenever she thinks she has been insulted. During the first year of "The Muppet Show" she was known as Miss Piggy Lee, a reference to purring pop songstress Peggy Lee... Inspired by Ratso Rizzo, Dustin Hoffman's homeless con man in the 1969 film "Midnight Cowboy," streetwise **Rizzo the Rat** has a grating personality and New Jersey accent... Stiff and censorious, patriotic **Sam Eagle** is the group's self-appointed moral watchdog. He wants every Muppet production to promote conservative values and stay orderly... The nephew of the theater's owner, **Scooter** is the group's inept stage manager and all-purpose go-fer... Sitting in a balcony box in the theater, curmudgeons **Statler and Waldorf** heckled Kermit and the gang throughout "The Muppet Show." Statler wears the three-piece suit; Waldorf has the mustache... Lovable but short-tempered, the **Swedish Chef** speaks in nearly indecipherable mock-Swedish. From 1988 to 1989 he had his own General Foods breakfast cereal, Cröonchy Stars... Genial monster **Sweetums** was created for the 1971 television special "The Frog Prince," in which he was the pet ogre of a wicked witch... The world's first digitized puppet, **Waldo C. Graphic** made his debut on the "Jim Henson Hour." His movements were created by a puppeteer wearing an electronic glove, which transmitted signals to a computer to generate a wire-frame image.

such as "How to Stick Out Your Tongue and Touch Your Ear" and understand the surprisingly complex 3-D glasses. Drawn by the doctor himself, these last diagrams include doodles. **9** The outdoor waiting area and adjacent covered bus shelter are trimmed out as a salute to a closet Jim Henson, Frank Oz and others decorated in 1963 when the Muppets were booked on "The Jack Paar Program" at NBC Studios in Radio City. Mistakenly arriving six hours early, they killed time by decorating their dressing room's utility closet with some Muppet touch-up paint. Henson and his pals covered the walls with loopy designs and faces, incorporating pipes as noses. **10** In the entryway the sign at the Security Office saying "Key Under Mat" isn't lying. **11** Inside the office there's a wanted poster for Fozzie (for impersonating a comic) and a Miss Piggy cheesecake calendar. **12** The directory case includes listings for Statler and Waldorf's Institute of Heckling and Browbeating and Gonzo's Dept. of Poultry and Mold Cultivation. **13** A sign above the 8-foot archway reads "You must be shorter than this to enter." A chip at the top indicates someone didn't see it. **14** A hall door leading to the MuppetLabs' Department of Artificial Reality reads "This is not a door." **15** Hanging from the waiting room ceiling is a net full of Jell-O, a reference to 1950s Mouseketeer Annette Funicello. **16** Next to it is a bird cage with a perch — a fish, not a pole. **17** Down front a crate labeled "2-D Fruities" is filled with flat cutouts of a cherry, lemon and banana. **18** Among the items in a wooden box addressed to the Swedish Chef from Oompah, Sweden's "Sven & Ingmar's Kooking Kollection" is "Der Noodle Frooper." **19** A box holding Gonzo's stunt props identifies its contents as "mold, fungus, helmets, helmets covered with fungus and mold, helmets with mold — no fungus" and "fungus and mold — no helmets." **20** Frankie's Formal Wear has sent "emergency tuxedos" for the penguins in a crate stamped "Open in the event of an event." **21** The birds' food has arrived, too, in a box from Long Island

Sound and Seafood Supplies ("Everything from Hearing to Herring"). ㉒ Catwalks above include the SwineTrek spaceship used in "Pigs in Space" skits of "The Muppet Show" as well as the frontiersman and some wooden soldiers used in the 3-D film's finale. ㉓ At the front is a hydraulic tube from the MuppetVision machine. ㉔ Along the walls are large reprints from the Kermitage Collection, a series of photo portraits issued as a calendar in 1984. They include parodies of Henri Rousseau ("The Sleepy Zootsy") and Hans Holbein ("Jester at the Court of Henry VIII," a portrait of Fozzie holding a banana to his ear. Its Latin phrase "Bananum In Avre Habeo" translates to "I'm holding a banana in my ear."). ㉕ A photo hanging from the ceiling of a banjo-holding, Henson-like Muppet shows a character in a "Muppet Show" Muppeteer band. ㉖ In the front of the room, a sarcophagus peers through a pair of 3-D glasses. (In the movie, a bust of Beethoven in the lab wears a pair on its head. In the next scene, just after Kermit says "This way, folks," a brass bald eagle has them on.) ㉗ In the theater, the penguin orchestra cackles at Statler and Waldorf's barbs (especially when Waldorf says the penguins "probably took the job for the halibut") and cough when they get squirted by Fozzie's boutonniere. One gets sucked up by Beaker's VacuuMuppet. ㉘ Statler and Waldorf gape in amazement at the MuppetVision machine, nod as Waldo bounces off people's heads, duck from the VacuuMuppet and hide when the Swedish Chef brings out his cannon. ㉙ A chicken wanders behind Kermit as the frog begins the tour of Muppet-Labs. Later, another flies off its perch. ㉚ In the lab, two goldfish eventually swim in the beaker just above the

Instructions from Dr. Honeydew along MuppetVision's back queue

Chinese-food takeout boxes. ㉛ When Kermit returns, the theater go-fer Scooter and wanna-be rock star Janis ride a bicycle behind him. ㉜ Miss Piggy loses her head during her waterskiing moment. Watch closely and you'll see it ease backward off her body as she is pulled into the lake. ㉝ In the finale, some members of the marching band aren't wearing pants. ㉞ Manning the projection room, the Chef reassures Kermit that "der machinen is goin' der floomy floomy" as the show begins. After the penguins fire their cannon at the projector, he yells "Schtupid crazy birds!" ㉟ As you leave the theater, the eight holes created by his cannon fire disappear. (Changes in lighting expose, then conceal, these real holes.) ㊱ Exit posters outside the building include ads for Fozzie Bear ("your full-service funny bear"), penguin outfitter Frankie ("Large formalwear for the hard-to-fit. Small formalwear for the hard-to-find.") and a record album by Rowlf ("the critics are howling!"). ㊲ The adjacent Stage 1 Co. Store gift shop includes the Muppet lockers and Happiness Hotel registration area from the 1981 film "The Great Muppet Caper" as well as nearly two dozen silly signs. One over a doorway reads "Absolutely no point beyond this point."

Streets of America

This collection of backlot-style streets and building facades is dominated by Beaux Arts-style New York Street, a 500-foot thoroughfare based on West 40th St. in the Big Apple. The north end, a three-dimensional background piece, includes flat representations of the Chrysler, Empire State and Flatiron buildings. Details include graffiti, soot stains and a sidewalk stairway that appears to lead to a subway terminal. The stoplights were used on New York City roadways during the 1930s. Background noises include honking horns, playing kids, screeching buses, talking crowds and whistling police. The best find is the "Singin' in the Rain" umbrella. Hanging off a lamppost off the southern end of the street, it will often mist you with rain when you stand under it. The crossing road recalls Chicago, London and San Francisco.

The Naked City. Building facades expose their framing along the Streets of America.

'Honey, I Shrunk the Kids' Playground

This soft-floored outdoor playground lets children pretend they're the size of bugs, lost in a suburban backyard. Grass blades tower above kids while they climb over a spider web and explore ant tunnels. A hose drips on unaware heads, grass stalks sound off when stepped on, a giant dog nose sniffs passersby.

Kids love it all but parents can get cranky —the playground is crowded and there's almost no place to sit. Come early when the mobs aren't here yet. The playground is based on the 1989 film "Honey, I Shrunk the Kids," in which an inventor mistakenly shrinks his children who then get lost in their own yard. *Capacity: 240. Guests may remain in wheelchairs, ECVs. Debuted: 1990.*

Racing 'round the Doh at the "Honey" playground

▶ Bring a camera. The oversized playground props make great photo backgrounds.

An Opel Corsa leaps across the stage.

Lights, Motors, Action Extreme Stunt Show

"That was AWESOME!"
"That was BEAUTIFUL!"
"That was GOOD-LOOKIN' STUFF!"

The hosts sure are enthusiastic at this outdoor stage show, and it is unique. Cars and motorcycles fly through the air — and barely miss each other as they skid and spin on the ground — as skilled stunt drivers demonstrate how chase scenes are created for modern action-adventure films. The premise is the filming of a European spy thriller, with a working film crew on a live set.

There are four scenes. First, six Opel Corsas race around in a choreographed ballet chase. The cars return to dodge, weave and jump over a blockade of produce stands and trucks (one car appears to jump backward). Then three motorcycles arrive, one jumping through what appears to be a plate-glass window as the cars drive on two wheels and, for a moment, two guys end up on Jet Skis. This scene ends as a motorcyclist falls and, thanks to a special jumpsuit, catches fire. For the finale, a car jumps directly at the audience as 40-foot fireballs billow in the air.

After each scene unfolds, the director combines shots into the completed scene that is played on a large video screen.

There's also a car that breaks in half.

The set resembles a seaside village marketplace in southern France (one shop is the Café Fracas, the "restaurant of the noisy rumpus"). The show premiered at Disneyland Paris, hence the French connection.

If you can, sit low in the stands, just in front of the columns. You'll get an unobstructed, fairly close view that's still within range of the large overhead fans.

40 min. Capacity: 5,000. Avg. wait: 20 min. Arrive 30 min. early for a good seat. Fastpass available. Guests may remain in wheelchairs, ECVs. Assistive listening devices. Fear factor: Low. All the action is away from the seating area. Debuted: 2005.

FUN FACTS)) Custom-built in Europe, each car has a 150-horsepower motorcycle engine with four forward gears and four reverse gears, which lets it reach the same speed in either direction.)) Each car weighs 1,300 pounds, less than half that of a similar production vehicle.)) Drivers wear the same suits as professional racecar drivers.)) The stage is 6.5 acres.)) All the "live" video was filmed before the show opened in 2005.

▶ Sit on the left and when you leave you'll pass some interesting backstage sights.

backlot

© DISNEY

Flood watch. An oil tanker threatens to overturn in Catastrophe Canyon.

Disney-MGM Studios Backlot Tour

A pet project of then-Disney-chair Michael Eisner, this tour originally featured a walk-through of working soundstages and a tram trip along real production shops and through a working backlot, passing home facades used in the television shows "The Golden Girls" and "Empty Nest."

Today that's all been eliminated, as Disney has shut down its Florida filmmaking. The soundstages are dark and the backlot has been demolished. What's left is a water-effects demo, a glimpse into a staged prop room, a peek into costume and set-building shops now used mostly for theme-park work and a stop at a make-believe disaster-effects set.

The tour begins with the filming of a faux movie ("Harbor Attack"), a demonstration of how water cannons and fire bursts can simulate torpedo and bombing attacks. As volunteers get splashed on a PT boat, the scenes are filmed and edited into a comical video.

After a quick walk through the prop room you're off on the tram tour. You see the park's Mickey-eared water tower, rumble past the costume and scenic shops, then head out to Catastrophe Canyon, a Mojave-Desert-themed special-effects area that puts you in an earthquake, fire and flood all within a minute (sit on the left to get sprayed with

water). As you head back you pass some actual movie vehicles and Walt Disney's real 1960s jet.

Once off the tram you exit through the American Film Institute (AFI) Showcase. This walk-through exhibit most recently has featured costume pieces of movie villains, including a witch hat worn by Margaret Hamilton in 1939's "The Wizard of Oz." A display case is filled with ten antique film cameras and projectors.

To make the tour more fun tell a cast member you'd like to be in the Harbor Attack demonstration. The first show of the day usually begs for volunteers, as crowds are light. You can see the AFI exhibit without going on the full tour: its back entrance (its store) is behind the Prop Shop gift shop.

30-40 min. Capacity: 1,000. Avg. wait: 5 min. early morning, 20 min. peak afternoon. Guests may remain in wheelchairs, ECVs. Handheld and activated video captioning. Fear factor: The water demo has fire. The Canyon simulates an earthquake, fire and flood. Debuted: 1989, revised 2004.

SCREEN GEMS Real movie props line the Backlot Tour walkways. In the queue is the Black Pearl figurehead from 2003's "Pirates of the Caribbean: Curse of the Black Pearl" and a wooden model of the sunken USS Oklahoma used in 2001's "Pearl Harbor." The prop warehouse is filled with fun stuff, though little of it is identified. Look closely to find cans of eyeballs and glue from 1988's "Who Framed Roger Rabbit," the shrinking machine and a giant shoe from 1992's "Honey, I Blew Up The Kid," the Austin of England taxi from 1984's "The Muppets Take Manhattan," an 18-foot Holy Temple statue from 1989's "Indiana Jones and the Last Crusade," furniture from the 1990s television show "Dinosaurs," even props from Epcot's old World of Motion attraction: a hang glider and balloon basket with its pilot and chicken.

▶ Want to be in the Harbor Attack demo? Tell the cast member at the entrance gate.

Shopping guide

APPAREL Character Costumes: In Character *(at Voyage of The Little Mermaid, Animation Courtyard)* has princess costumes and a create-your-own-crown station. **Children's Wear:** The best collections are at L.A. Cinema Storage *(Hollywood Blvd.)* and Stage 1 Co. Store *(next to MuppetVision 3-D, Backlot)*. The Playhouse Disney stands *(Animation Courtyard)* and the Sound Stage Trailer *(Mickey Ave.)* have a few shirts. **Fashion:** Keystone Clothiers *(Hollywood Blvd.)* is the Studios' main fashion store. Legends of Hollywood *(Sunset Blvd.)* has stylish Tinker Bell apparel. **Footwear:** Keystone Clothiers *(Hollywood Blvd.)* sells sandals. Stage 1 Co. Store *(at MuppetVision 3-D, Backlot)* has infant and kids shoes. **Sports Apparel:** Mouse About Town *(Sunset Blvd.)* is the park's sports shop. **T-shirts and headwear:** Mickey's of Hollywood *(Hollywood Blvd.)* has the most. Sunset Ranch Souvenirs *(Sunset Blvd.)* has lots of hats.

ART Custom Sketches: Artists at Sunset Club Couture and Once Upon a Time *(both Sunset Blvd.)* will sketch a personalized Disney character as you watch. **Other Art:** The Animation Gallery *(Animation Courtyard)* sells glass vases, decorative plates and stemware, ceramics, quality lithographs, posters and prints and commercial sericel art.

BOOKS The tiny Writer's Stop *(adjacent to the Sci-Fi Dine-In Theater, Backlot)* has a small selection of paperbacks, hardcovers, cookbooks, and Disney titles. Movie and TV books are at Sid Cahuenga's One-Of-A-Kind *(Hollywood Blvd.)* and the AFI Showcase *(Backlot Tour exit, Backlot)*. Tower Hotel Gifts *(Tower of Terror exit, Sunset Blvd.)* has Twilight Zone titles. Tatooine Traders *(Star Tours exit, Backlot)* has Star Wars books. Animation books are at the Animation Gallery *(Animation Courtyard)*.

CANDY Sweet Spells *(Sunset Blvd.)* makes its own chocolate-covered strawberries and caramel apples. Other treats include cotton candy, fudge, lollipops and cookies.

CHRISTMAS Once Upon a Time *(Sunset Blvd.)* is the Disney-MGM Studios' Christmas corner. You'll find "Nightmare Before Christmas" items at the nearby Villains in Vogue *(Sunset Blvd.)*.

HOUSEWARES The park's housewares headquarters is Celebrity 5 & 10 *(Hollywood Blvd.)*. The Writer's Stop *(adjacent to the Sci-Fi Dine-In Theater, Backlot)* has a few unique items.

JEWELRY AND WATCHES Artists at Sunset Club Couture *(Sunset Blvd.)* draw personalized sketches of Disney characters and reduce them onto watch dials. The store also sells more conventional watches, fine jewelry, Lenox china figurines, snow globes and statuettes. You'll also find watches at the adjacent Mouse About Town. Across the street, Sunset Ranch Souvenirs and Gifts has costume jewelry. The open-air Indiana Jones stand *(at the Indiana Jones Epic Stunt Spectacular, Echo Lake)* has a nice collection of casual jewelry.

PET PRODUCTS The Studios' largest selection of pet products is at Legends of Hollywood *(Sunset Blvd.)*. It carries beds, bowls, clothes, dishes, leashes, toys and treats. The Writer's Stop *(Backlot)* has a nice variety.

PINS The Studios' pin central is the open-air shop underneath the Sorcerer's Hat *(Hollywood Blvd.)*. The Hollywood Junction kiosk *(Hollywood Blvd. at Sunset Blvd.)* has a decent selection.

TOYS The biggest toy store is L.A. Cinema Storage *(Hollywood Blvd.)*. Among the lures are Disney princess dolls and a create-your-own Mr. Potato Head station. Across the street, Mickey's of Hollywood is packed with just about every other Walt Disney World plaything. The Stage 1 Co. Store *(Backlot)* has Muppet action figures and plushies. Indiana Jones action figures, guns and snakes await you at the Indiana Jones Adventure Outpost *(Indiana Jones Epic Stunt Spectacular, Echo Lake)* and the nearby Indiana Jones stand *(next to the Backlot Express restaurant)*. May the force, or at least willpower, be with you at Tatooine Traders *(at the Star Tours exit, Backlot)*. It's filled with "Star Wars" temptations, including miniature versions of the attraction's Starspeeder 3000 spacecraft. A few Playhouse Disney toys are sold at the Playhouse Disney stands *(Animation Courtyard)*.

A Hollywood Tower Hotel door hanger from the Tower of Terror gift shop

She wants more. Gadgets and gizmos aplenty aren't enough for Ariel.

The lyrics alone make the show worthwhile. "Out in the sun they slave away," Sebastian the crab sings, "while we devotin' full time to floatin'." After Ariel's dad forbids her to go to the surface, the teen sulks "Betcha on land they understand. Bet they don't reprimand their daughters." The theater's high-backed cloth seats, dark ambiance and cool breezes make it a great place to relax.

17 min. Capacity: 600. Avg. wait: 10 min. early morning, 45 min. peak afternoon. Fastpass available. Guests may remain in wheelchairs, ECVs. Assistive listening, reflective captioning. No flash photography. Fear factor: Ursula causes some toddlers to cry. Debuted: 1992.

FUN FIND Hanging over the right door to the theater is a Disney-fied replica of P.T. Barnum's 1842 "FeJee Mermaid," which the huckster claimed was a mermaid caught off the Fiji Islands. In truth it was the shriveled body of a monkey stitched to the dried tail of a fish.

Voyage of the Little Mermaid

Puppets, live actors and imaginative effects tell the story of Ariel in this condensed version of Disney's 1989 animated movie, "The Little Mermaid."

As a water curtain opens across the stage, the show begins with a rousing blacklight-puppet version of "Under the Sea." Then you meet Ariel — she wants legs, and Prince Eric — who belts out "Part of Your World" like a Broadway star. Ursula the Sea Witch (a parade-float-sized Audio Animatronic octopus) slithers in to trick Ariel out of her voice, singing "Poor Unfortunate Soul."

Video clips advance the plot to the finale, where the live actress grows her gams and hugs her honey.

REBEL REBEL The 1989 film "The Little Mermaid" broke new ground for a Disney heroine: Ariel's dream comes true because she rebels against her father and takes action herself. Her problem: She wants legs, and the human Prince Eric. Ursula the Sea Witch offers to make the girl human — if Ariel will give up her voice and agree to get it back only if she kisses Eric within three days. Then Ursula transforms herself into a rival beauty — with Ariel's voice — and nearly marries the prince herself. A singing crab and a friendly fish help Ariel land her man. The movie leaves out some grim moments of Hans Christian Andersen's 1836 fable. In that version, when a grandmother puts flowers in the mermaid's hair for her 15th birthday she also clasps eight oysters on the girl's tail, as "pride must suffer pain." The Sea Witch takes the girl's voice by cutting out her tongue. The mermaid and the prince don't live happily ever after; he dumps her for the girl next door. Heartbroken, the mermaid dissolves into the sea foam and becomes a spirit.

▶ The best seats are in the middle. The front row sits too low to see onto the stage.

The Magic of Disney Animation

This lightweight attraction consists of a short movie, a hands-on drawing lesson, some computer games, an air-conditioned chance to meet characters and some art exhibits.

The film presentation, "Drawn to Animation," shows how Disney created Mushu, the dragon sidekick in 1998's "Mulan." A large open area is filled with preschooler-friendly computer games. Nearby, stars from a recent Disney movie meet, greet and pose for pictures.

You learn to draw a Disney character at the Animation Academy, a classroom setting in which you sit at a drafting table, follow step-by-step instructions from a live artist and keep your sketch.

The final area is the Animation Gallery, a few small rooms filled with conceptual models and drawings, including Tinker Bell as a redhead and Buzz Lightyear with a pompadour. A glass case holds a dozen Oscars. The one for "It's Tough to be a Bird" is the actual award from the 1970 ceremony.

Film: 10 min. Animation Academy: 10 min. Rest self-guided. Capacity: Theater: 150; Animation Academy: 50. Avg. wait: 10 min. early morning, 30 min. peak afternoon. Typically no wait after the characters leave (about 5:30 p.m.). Guests may remain in wheelchairs, ECVs; lap boards available for drawing. Reflective, video captioning. Debuted: 1989, revised 2004.

FUN FIND Take too long to make your choices at the Soundstage screens and Ursula, the "Little Mermaid" Sea Witch, will shout "Hurry and make a choice! I have fish sticks in the oven!"

Walt Disney: One Man's Dream

A salute to the life of Walt Disney, this Mickey Avenue exhibit combines a memorabilia museum with a short film. It includes the desk Walt used (and carved "wd" into) as a Missouri second-grader, his studio desk from the 1930s and his (re-created) 1960s office.

Disney's hand in theme-park history is well represented. Built by Walt himself in 1949, a hand-wired wooden diorama displays his early ideas for multiple-room attractions such as Peter Pan's Flight. Nearby, the "Dancing Man" electronic mari-

Early bird. One of Disney's first Audio Animatronic figures, Pierre the toucan was the co-host of the Enchanted Tiki Room when he debuted at Disneyland in 1963. Built by motion-picture engineers, the bird was controlled with 24 electronic signals a second, much like a movie projector flickers its film at 24 frames a second.

onette tested figure-movement techniques that led to Audio Animatronic robots. Display cases include tabletop models of Disneyland's Main Street U.S.A. and Peter Pan's Flight. A simulated TV studio shows Walt filming a video to interest investors in his ultimate dream: the Experimental Prototype Community of Tomorrow. The rear room has two Audio Animatronic creatures you can control yourself: a robotic man and Tiki bird. A 200-seat theater shows a moving biographical film. Narrated by Disney himself through an assemblage of audio clips, the inspirational 16-minute film explores his never-ending drive and the hardships he overcame.

Next to the Voyage of the Little Mermaid. Duration: Allow at least 35 min. Theater capacity: 200. Avg. wait: None. Access: Guests may remain in wheelchairs, ECVs. Assistive listening, handheld and reflective captioning available. Best ages: 8 and up. Debuted: 2001.

Playhouse Disney — Live on Stage

✓ Engaging for kids, charming for adults, this interactive stage show speaks to preschoolers on their own level. Stars from the Playhouse Disney television shows "Bear in the Big Blue House," "JoJo's Circus," "Stanley" and "The Book of Pooh" dance, sing, act out stories and even teach a few life lessons. The plot concerns the importance of friends. When Tutter is too bashful to dance, the show's perky live host Jamie brings out a giant storybook full of tales that teach that, with friends, anything is possible.

Above: Winnie the Pooh, Stanley and JoJo are featured in the storybook segments of Playhouse Disney — Live on Stage. **Below:** Ella Cottle, 2, enjoys the show with her parents.

JoJo and Skeebo help Goliath get rid of his hiccups. Dennis helps Stanley value good grooming. In a chapter from "The Book of Pooh," Winnie the Pooh, Tigger, Eeyore and Piglet learn that friends can get along together even when they like different things (even though Tigger once refers to Eeyore as "Donkey Boy"). As the storybook closes Tutter feels better and bops along with the others. The show ends as Luna the moon slides down to lead everyone in "The Goodbye Song."

As soon as the lights dim children sense this is a show all their own. Little faces beam as cast members encourage kids to clap to the theme song. Children eagerly call Bear in to start the show, and reach out when bubbles float down from the ceiling. When the characters invite the kids to dance many joyously do, sometimes with their parents joining in.

Best of all, the show treats its young audience with respect. The stories are lessons, not lectures, showing characters solving problems on their own. And

▶ The stands out front often stock JoJo, Goliath and Skeebo plushies.

the host speaks to the children as equals, bouncing into the crowd throughout the performance to meet a few kids face-to-face.

Production values are the equal of any Disney show. Most of the puppet eyes blink, and many of the mouths open. The studio sound is crisp, and the video version of Luna is almost eery in its clarity. The stage features an innovative sliding walkway that lets the human performers magically walk on the same floor as the puppets. Nearly a hundred spotlights hang from the ceiling, not only illuminating the stage but also shining down on the kids whenever it's their turn to participate.

You sit on a flat, carpeted floor, which makes it easy for kids to get up and boogie. The stage curves into the seating area, so even those in the back are still close to the action.

A few tips: The first show of the day is the least crowded, with the shortest wait. Sit in the middle, not the front, so your child can see all the action (the stage is raised a few feet high). If you sit by an aisle your child may get a chance to dance with the host.

By the way, the host, played by various male and female actors, is always named "Jamie." They have no choice: the voice of Bear is prerecorded, and the big lug refers to his human pal by name.

20 min. Capacity: 600. Avg. wait: 25 min. Guests may remain in wheelchairs and ECVs. Assistive listening, reflective and activated captions. Preshow: Outdoor monitors show Playhouse Disney characters. Fear factor: The hoots of Stanley's friendly gorilla pal may scare an infant. Best ages: 2–6. Debuted: 2001, revised 2005.

FUN FIND Taller adults standing along the back of the theater can often see the heads and arms of the puppeteers.

Dancing Bear. Looking identical to his TV image, the 7-foot Bear performs an energetic cha-cha-cha as he welcomes guests to his Big Blue House.

BIG SHOTS FOR LITTLE TOTS Can't tell your Pip from your Skeebo? Here's a quick primer: "Jim Henson's Bear in the Big Blue House" stars Bear, a gentle patriarch of all the Muppet-like critters who live around him, including Tutter, an impatient blue mouse who lives in Bear's kitchen; and ornery otters Pip and Pop. Luna, a motherly moon, stops by each evening. Enthusiastic 6-year-old clown JoJo Tickle and her best friend Skeebo Seltzer learn gentle life lessons in "JoJo's Circus." JoJo often loses track of Goliath, her pet lion. In "Stanley," curious Stanley Griff, also 6, has a secret life away from his parents: he can talk with his pet goldfish, Dennis, and can transport them both to the lands of exotic animals using his Great Big Book of Everything. You will recognize insecure Piglet, playful Tigger, pessimistic Eeyore and honey-sweet Winnie the Pooh from "The Book of Pooh," a puppet series based on the beloved Disney films.

▶ Sit in the middle so your child can see all the action. The stage is a few feet high.

Max axe. A 40-foot guitar decks out the Rock 'n' Roller Coaster entrance. Its 320-foot neck becomes a coaster track that rolls out above the walkway.

Rock 'n' Roller Coaster Starring Aerosmith

✓ This popular thrill ride has a lot going for it — a high-speed launch that blasts you to 57 mph in just 2.8 seconds, rock music blaring in every seat, two loops and a tight corkscrew. But like other good Disney attractions, what makes it special is a detailed, fun theme.

The grins begin as you enter the building. Step through the cool lobby — mimicking guitar necks, its foyer columns are complete with fret boards and strings — and you're off on a time-warp back to the rockin' world of the mid-1970s. As you walk through the halls of G-Force Records, you pass displays of authentic vintage recording and playback gear. Soon you enter Studio C, where you find Aerosmith mixing the rhythm tracks to "Walk This Way."

Suddenly the guys have to leave — they're late for a show. But you're in luck: they want to give you backstage passes, so their manager phones for a limousine to take you to the concert. "We're going to need a stretch," she says, counting the crowd. "In fact, make it a super stretch."

"The show is all the way across town," she tells you, "but I got you a really fast car."

You're ushered into the grimy back alley, where up pulls your baby-blue, 24-seat 1959 Cadillac convertible. In you climb and off you go, rocketing into the Los Angeles night with Aerosmith blasting on the car stereo. You zoom through the "Hollywood" sign, through a giant billboard doughnut, through a half-mile of twists, turns and loops.

Plenty thrilling for most folks, the ride gets mixed reviews from coaster freaks. The launch is exhilarating — some of the most exciting seconds in all of Walt Disney World — but everything after that is rather mild. You slow down after the first few turns, and average just 28 miles per hour. The ride has no steep drops and you're not jerked around in your seat. But the turns are tight, the tunes rock and it's all in the dark.

In other words, you won't get sick, but your palms may sweat.

1 min. 22 sec. Avg. wait: 30 min. early morning, 60 min. peak afternoon. Fastpass available. ECV users must transfer. Height restriction: 48 in. Fear factor: Anticipating the launch scares even most adults. Chicken exit. Debuted: 1999.

FUN FINDS ❶ Equipment in the first display case includes a disc cutter, which,

FUN FACTS ❯❯ The manager is played by actress Illeana Douglas, perhaps best known as Angela on the HBO series "Six Feet Under." ❯❯ The car radio's DJ is voiced by longtime Los Angeles rock jock Uncle Joe Benson. ❯❯ The squeal you hear as each limo peels out is fake. It's coming from barely visible speakers under the driveway. ❯❯ Most of the ride takes place inside "Stage 15," the structure behind the G-Force headquarters building.

▶ Ask to sit in the front row. With nothing in front of you the launch is hard to predict.

in the days of vinyl, etched sounds from a mixing console onto a master disc, thus creating the phrase "cutting a record." Nearby is a 1958 Gibson Les Paul Standard guitar. ② The second case holds vintage record players, from a 1904 external-horn Edison Fireside to a 1970s "Disc-O-Kid." ③ Put your ear to the doors marked "Studio A" or "Studio B" and you'll hear Aerosmith rehearsing. ④ The concert posters include one for a 1973 concert from Aerosmith's first national tour, as the opening act for the New York Dolls. It's midway down the right wall. ⑤ The alley is full of puns. Signs on the rear of the G-Force building indicate work has been done by Sam Andreas and Sons Structural Restoration. ⑥ The parking garage is run by Lock 'n' Roll Parking Systems. ⑦ The Dumpster is owned by the Rock 'n' Rollaway Disposal Co. ⑧ As you near your limo a glass case lists rates for the Wash This Way Auto Detail. ⑨ Each of the limos' license plates sports an apt message, such as 2FAST4U and UGOBABE. ⑩ Once you arrive at the show, watch the concert video to see Tyler scream "Rock 'n' Roller Coaster!!!"

ALL-AMERICAN ROCK 'N' ROLL Known for its spare, driving riffs and suggestive lyrics, Aerosmith formed in Boston in 1970. Its raunchy swagger, highlighted by singer Steven Tyler's prancing stage antics, drew comparisons to the Rolling Stones. Tyler and Mick Jagger even looked similar. Early hits included 1975's "Walk This Way," which, like the Stones' earlier "Satisfaction," used a groove so strong the words didn't matter. Aerosmith also created the first power ballad in 1973, adding strings to the piano-based "Dream On." Plagued by drugs in the late 1970s, the band got back on track in 1986: Tyler and lead guitarist Joe Perry appeared on rap group Run D.M.C.'s cover of "Walk This Way" and the video became an MTV staple.

Your Rock 'n' Roll limo loops just after launch

▶ Long legs? Ask for an odd-numbered row. They have far more legroom.

park puzzler

How much do you really know about Disney-MGM Studios?

1) In the Great Movie Ride, what does Clint Eastwood say as you pass him?
a. "Do you feel lucky?"
b. "Go ahead, make my day."
c. He doesn't speak.

2) In Star Tours, your planned destination is...
a. The moon of Endor.
b. The rings of Naboo.
c. The jowls of Jar Jar.

3) The MuppetVision 3-D finale is titled...
a. "A Salute to All Nations."
b. "A Salute to America."
c. "A Salute to All Nations but Mostly America."

4) The Lights, Motors, Action stunt show is introduced as:
a. Bippity Boppity Bang.
b. When You Wish Upon a Car.
c. Voyage of the Little Mermaid.

5) The man at left is...
a. Angry at the price of his turkey leg.
b. A star of the new Studios stage show "Pirates of the Caribbean: Dead Man's Dinner."
c. An actor taking a break from filming a commercial on New York Street.

6) According to its elevator signs, how many floors are in the Hollywood Tower Hotel?
a. 12.
b. 13.
c. 14.

7) What company do you tour at Rock 'n' Roller Coaster?
a. G-Force Records.
b. Fly-By-Night Music.
c. Twist 'n' Shout Studios.

8) What do the initials "MGM" stand for?
a. Mickey's Got Money
b. Minnie's Got More
c. Metro-Goldwyn-Mayer

Answers, page 319

Beauty and the Beast — Live on Stage

✓ This uplifting show re-creates the spirit of Disney's 1991 animated film by focusing entirely on its music. "Belle," "Gaston," "Be Our Guest," "Something There," "The Mob Song," "Beauty and the Beast" — they're all here. Most lead vocals are live.

The supporting cast is terrific. When Gaston struts on stage the village girls fight over him with flirty passion; when he chooses Belle they stalk off in a huff. The "Be Our Guest" maids squeal in delight when Lumiere announces dinner. Two tickle Belle with feather dusters; later a pair whispers to each other, leaves the stage and returns with a sundae that transforms into a warbling diva.

Colorful costumes and extra lighting effects add to the theatrical feel. In the first scene the supporting cast wears six different hues. In the ballroom scene Belle's gold gown is offset by the other girls' vivid pink dresses. The stage arch flashes during "Be Our Guest." Dappled lights color "The Mob Song."

25 min. Capacity: 1,500. Guests may remain in wheelchairs and ECVs. Assistive listening. Fear factor: During "The Mob Song" Gaston stabs the Beast, but you don't see the wound. Debuted: 1991, revised 2001.

FUN FINDS ❶ The show begins with a pun: a ringing bell. ❷ As Gaston incites the mob, one couple remains skeptical. One of them never joins in.

FUN FACT ⟩⟩ "The Mob Song" includes a quote from Shakespeare. "Screw your courage to the sticking place" Gaston says as he rallies the villagers to kill the Beast — the same phrase Lady Macbeth uses to urge her husband to kill Duncan.

Top: Belle yearns for "adventure in the great wide somewhere." **Above:** From stage hands to stage hams, a group of "stage workers" walks on stage 15 minutes before showtime to become the crowd-pleasing a cappella group Four for a Dollar.

▶ For a full experience, get in line 45 minutes before showtime and sit down front.

Tale as Old as Time

"Beauty and the Beast" got its start in Roman mythology. In **"Cupid and Psyche,"** philosopher Lucius Apuleius told the tale of Psyche, the youngest of three mortal sisters. Incredibly pretty, Psyche earns the envy of Venus, the goddess of beauty. But when Venus orders her son, Cupid, to make the girl fall in love with a castle-dwelling snake, Cupid himself falls in love with her, and secretly turns himself into the snake. Cupid gives Psyche a great life in the castle, including invisible servants who prepare her dinner, and eventually turns himself back to a young man.

The story spreads as societies became mobile, and eventually over 200 Eurasian folk tales have a similar plot: a beautiful girl with two mean sisters finds herself living with a beast, who becomes human once she cares for him.

A Chinese version makes a few changes — including a "golden shoe" — and becomes the first "Cinderella."

The love of a good woman turns a pig into a prince in the first published beauty-and-beast fable. Produced soon after printing presses became widespread in 1553, **"The Pig King"** was one of many folk tales transcribed by Italian novelist Giovanni Straparola. This beast marries all three sisters, one at a time. He kills the oldest two because they don't like him "climbing into bed stinking with filthy paws and snout."

The Beast is a snake again in 1650, when the story becomes a popular parlor tale among French aristocrats. In this, the first story named **"Beauty and the Beast,"** a king has three daughters, and one day he leaves to get them each a gift. When he comes upon a deserted castle he plucks a rose for his youngest, named Beauty. "Who said you could take my flower?" a voice asks. "I will kill you for that, unless you bring me one of your girls." Beauty volunteers. She doesn't see anyone when she arrives at the castle, but the next morning wakes up to find a serpent in her lap. "You must marry me," it hisses. Beauty says no, but the snake persists. It orders its servants to starve her, and each day repeats its demand. Finally, she gives in. "I won't marry a serpent," she says, "but I will marry a man." The snake turns itself into a handsome prince.

There are oodles of *oo-lá-lá* in the fable after French blueblood **Gabrielle de Villeneuve** gets hold of it in 1740. Writing for the pleasure of her salon friends, she turns the tale into a 362-page bodice-ripper. The prince is turned into a beast after he turns down a promiscuous fairy. When Beauty arrives, he doesn't ask "Will you marry me?" but "Will you go to bed with me?" He stays a beast until after the wedding night.

The story becomes a child's fable 16 years later. In 1756, French tutor **Jeanne-Marie Leprince de Beaumont** publishes her version, a tale she had written to prepare her young charges (girls 5–13) for arranged marriages. She bases her story on the earlier serpent tale, but makes the Beast a humble, gentle mammal. Wanting her girls to believe that love can make any man princely, Beaumont contrasted Beauty's beastly fate with that of the girl's two sisters: The first is matched with a handsome man who thinks only of himself. The second gets a smart man who belittles his bride. "Many women," this Beauty ponders, "are made to marry men far more beastly than mine." Beaumont's own arranged marriage had been annulled when

Better than Bambi. Beast Jean Marais gives up deer hunting after he meets Josette Day in the 1947 French film.

her philandering husband contracted a venereal disease. To encourage girls to read, Beaumont makes Beauty a book lover. Her story becomes the definitive "Beauty" fairy tale.

The love of a beauty rescues the soul of a bloodthirsty beast in the first "Beauty and the Beast" motion picture, a 1947 French film by avant-garde artist **Jean Cocteau**. The adult melodrama grows tedious in its second act (40 minutes of little more than the Beast bellowing "Belle!") but its surreal images — living busts and candelabras and a disembodied arm that pours wine — make it an arthouse favorite.

Its Beauty is no role model. She faints when she first sees the Beast and shudders ecstatically when she sees him again. A remake of the film appears in 1983 as an episode of the Showtime television series "Faerie Tale Theatre." Directed by French auteur Roger Vadim, it stars a blond Susan Sarandon as Beauty.

Can a man sleep in a sewer and still hook up with a society gal? That's the premise of the 1987–1990 **CBS television series** "Beauty and the Beast." Linda Hamilton plays Catherine Chandler, a wealthy New Yorker who wants more out of life. Ron Perlman is Vincent, her beasty boy beneath the streets.

It's no wonder **Disney's** animated "Beauty and the Beast" was nominated for a Best Picture Oscar. Packed with life, humor and music, it also has a great message: A girl can be herself, speak her mind and still end up with a prince of a hubby. Smart, gutsy and with plans for her life, this Belle is no pushover. The villagers say she's a "most peculiar mademoiselle" but she couldn't care less; while street tarts swoon for the town hunk she pushes him off. And when the Beast yells at her, she yells back.

Disney keeps the meat of Beaumont's tale but cuts the fat, eliminating the sisters and downplaying the dad. And it adds a villain: the handsome Gaston, who grows beastly as the Beast grows human.

On a different note, Disney's production is also an homage to Broadway and Hollywood.

The song "Belle" gets its bickering villagers and throwaway jokes from "Tradition," the rousing introductory number to 1964's "Fiddler on the Roof." Its "Bonjour! Bonjour!" refrain comes from the "Good Morning! Good Day!" opener to the 1963 stage play "She Loves Me."

"Be Our Guest" is a tableware take on Busby Berkeley's "By a Waterfall" sequence in 1933's "Footlight Parade." And the title-song waltz features its couple like "Shall We Dance" portrays Anna and her King in 1951's "The King and I."

The enchanted objects have their own ancestors. Mrs. Potts is a jollier version of Mrs. Bridges, the cook from the 1970s British TV drama, "Upstairs Downstairs." Lumiere blends dashing Maurice Chevalier from 1958's "Gigi" with Pepé Le Pew, Warner Brothers' scent-imental skunk created in 1945 for a few Looney Tunes cartoon shorts.

A VOICE OF LIFE The lyrics in Disney's "Beauty and the Beast" show a poet at the top of his game. "Belle" is a prologue, filled with story details that typically take up a first act. "Gaston" is a silly pub song — *"No one's slick as Gaston, no one's quick as Gaston, no one's neck's as incredibly thick as Gaston's"* — while "Be Our Guest" bubbles with swing: *"Try the gray stuff, it's delicious! Don't believe me? Ask the dishes!"* The title song is elegant: *"Ever just the same, ever a surprise. Ever as before, ever just as sure as the sun will rise."*

Howard Ashman

Ironically, these lyrics, so full of life, were written by a man on his deathbed. Howard Ashman penned them while dying of AIDS.

A New York playwright, Ashman had his first success in 1982. Working with composer Alan Menken, his musical version of "Little Shop of Horrors," a quirky story of a flower-shop worker and a man-eating plant, became the top-grossing off-Broadway musical ever. Ashman later wrote the screenplay for the movie.

After penning "Once Upon a Time in New York City" for Disney's 1988 "Oliver and Company," Ashman was hired as the lyricist for "The Little Mermaid." His witty wordplay *("bright young women, sick of swimmin'")* helped make the film Disney's first animated blockbuster since Walt Disney died of lung cancer in 1966. In response, the company made Ashman the executive producer (as well as the lyricist) of its next major film, "Beauty and the Beast." Just after production began in 1989, however, Ashman learned he had contracted HIV.

This being the eighties, Ashman kept the news to himself. He had loved Disney's musicals since he was a kid (you can hear the influence of songs such as "Cruella de Vil" in his lyrics) and wanted to continue his work. When he acknowledged his illness a year later, two days after winning the Best Song Oscar for "Under the Sea," Disney stuck by him. When he could no longer travel it moved the film's development from California to New York, setting up shop at a hotel near Ashman's home.

The dying artist gave it his all. To offset a strong Belle, Ashman built a better Beast: a creature with a clear reason to be cursed (he's selfish) and a deadline to fix it (his 21st birthday). He focused the script on men (the Beast and Gaston) as much as women. And he fixed what had always been the fairy tale's fatal flaw as a screenplay: it's dull-as-dirt second act. To add life to the scenes where Beauty and Beast do little but have dinner, Ashman created a comic Greek chorus of enchanted objects. Even when he could no longer leave his bed Ashman still kept working, finishing the project over the phone.

Then he died. At age 41 in March 1991, six months before the film was released. Awarded a year later, his second Oscar (Best Song for "Beauty and the Beast") was the first given to a known AIDS victim.

Some believe Ashman built the story as an AIDS allegory. In 1992 CBS newsman Dan Rather wrote that you could think of Ashman's Beast as a metaphor for an AIDS victim: "He's just a guy trying as hard as he can to find a little love, a little beauty, while he's still got a little time left." In "The Mob Song" some listeners find a commentary on gay bashing. *"The Beast will make off with your children,"* Gaston warns the villagers, who then chant *"We don't like what we don't understand, in fact it scares us, and this monster is mysterious at least.* Sally forth, tally ho, praise the Lord and here we go: Kill the Beast!"*

Regardless of how you interpret his work, Howard Ashman was undeniably a creative genius, cut down at his most productive time by a preventable disease.

Just like Walt.

* This line is omitted from the theme park show.

Ready to crumble at the next lightning strike, the Hollywood Tower Hotel looms above Sunset Boulevard

of the Tower lounge, many guests check in for the night. But then a freakish thunderstorm sweeps in across the hills and, at 8:05 p.m., a huge bolt of lightning electrifies the hotel. It hits with such force it eliminates two wings and two elevator shafts of the structure and dematerializes the guests in those areas, including five who had just boarded an elevator — a child actress with her nanny, a glamorous couple of young rising stars and a hotel bellhop.

The remaining guests run out in horror, leaving their luggage and other belongings behind.

The hotel stands deserted for more than 50 years, but mysteriously reopens in 1994. Strangely, the staff from that fateful night is still there, unaged, and has no memory of the disaster.

The Twilight Zone Tower of Terror

✓ Loaded with spectacular effects and detail, this attraction is designed to freak you out. Checking in to an otherworldly hotel, you climb into a freight elevator as souls of earlier guests beckon you to join them. Then you enter the dark, supernatural Fifth Dimension, where you fall up to 130 feet.

And it's never the same ride twice.

Meant to recall the peculiar look and feel of the classic television series "The Twilight Zone," the attraction is even more fun if you know its story.

According to Disney lore, the luxurious, 12-story Hollywood Tower Hotel first opened in 1917. Famous for its service, it soon became a gathering place for the Tinseltown elite.

Fast forward to Oct. 31, 1939. As the hotel hosts a Halloween party in its Top

As you walk through the entrance gate, you're a guest of the hotel and are arriving to check in. But immediately you sense something is wrong. The misty entrance garden is lush but overgrown. The fountain has no water. The lobby is covered in dust and cobwebs. A bellhop notices you and prepares to take you to your room. Since the lobby elevators aren't working (behind an "Out of Order" sign, their doors hang crooked in their tracks), he asks you to wait for a moment in the library.

Then things really get creepy.

The library power goes out, but then on comes its television set, a black-and-white model that seems to have been built about 1959. Rod Serling appears, describing "tonight's story on 'The Twilight Zone'," a "somewhat unique" fable about a maintenance service elevator. He shows you those five guests, boarding their elevator car just before the flash. When it hits, they appear to disappear.

▶ The gift shop offers thick, comfortable "Hollywood Tower Hotel" bathrobes.

"We invite you if you dare to step aboard," Serling says, "because in tonight's episode, you are the star."

Suddenly a rear door opens, and you're directed into a back boiler room, an industrial area clearly not meant for guests. Still trying to get to your room, you board a service elevator. But as soon as the doors close you learn it, too, has a mind of its own.

First the lights go out. Then it whisks you to the fourth floor, where its doors open to reveal a typical hotel corridor. Do Not Disturb signs hang on most of the doors, while shoes and wine bottles sit outside them.

But as lightning flashes in the hall window, who should flicker into view but those five guests from 1939. They beckon you to follow them but, wrapped in a net of cackling electricity, disappear.

Then the walls disappear, revealing a clear night sky. The hall window floats, then shatters.

You've entered the Twilight Zone.

The doors close and up you go again, to the 13th floor — a level that supposedly doesn't exist. When the doors open, Serling speaks again: "One stormy night long ago, five people stepped through the door of an elevator and into a nightmare. That door is opening once again, and this time it's opening for you."

Your cabin moves forward, out of its shaft and alongside the glowing, moving silhouettes of those same spooky five. Directly ahead is a star field, but it too moves, forming a line which separates with a bright flash. That becomes the edge of another opening door — into one of those shafts that no longer exists.

You move into the space and the doors slam shut. It's completely dark.

Silent. Tense.

Then you move — violently — up, down — down, up — up, up, down — no telling which way. Occasionally doors in front of you open, revealing the open sky. You may see the figures again, or hear rainfall. After about a minute, however, the madness stops, and the elevator settles down into the basement. "The next time you check into a deserted hotel..." Serling says, "make sure you know just what kind of vacancy you're filling. Or you may find yourself a permanent resident... of 'The Twilight Zone.'"

The Twilight Zone Tower of Terror is an outstanding attraction — thrilling, full of surprises and with theming that fills every square inch.

4 min. Capacity: 84. Avg. wait: 20 min. early morning, 60 min. peak afternoon. Fastpass available. ECV guests must transfer to a wheelchair. Activated captioning available. Height restriction: 40 in. Fear factor: Mighty frighty. The drops are smooth, but Disney's mind games start as soon as you come through the entrance gate, when the friendly theme park completely disappears. By the time the library lights go out you'll be ready to scream — and you're still at least five minutes from, as one child called it, "being electrified." Chicken exit. Best ages: 8 and up. Debuted: 1994; revised 1996, 1999, 2002.

FUN FACTS ❯❯ When you see Serling speak on the library TV, you're actually watching him introduce the 1961 "Twilight Zone" episode, "It's a Good Life." In that introduction, Serling said "This, as you may recognize, is a map of the United States..." On the video, however, the camera cuts away just as he pronounces the word "map," and you hear him say "maintenance service elevator..." All of Serling's lines are dubbed by impersonator Mark Silverman. (Serling died in 1975, and there never was a "Twilight Zone" episode about a Hollywood Tower Hotel.) ❯❯ The lobby in the video is not the one at the attraction. Disney filmed the shoot on a California soundstage, using an identical set. ❯❯ The elevators have four loading areas but only two exits. The initial four shafts merge into two paths on the top floor. ❯❯ The cast members' break room is between the elevator shafts. When you scream, they hear you. "It's very difficult to relax," one says. ❯❯ The ride's engines hide at the top and bottom of the shafts. Each develops 110,000 foot-pounds of torque, uses regeneration for deceleration control and is 35 feet long, 7 feet wide, 12 feet tall and weighs 132,000 pounds. ❯❯ The Tower is 199 feet high, just short enough to *not* have aircraft warning lights. ❯❯ It really was struck by lightning, as it was being built in 1993.

▶ Your fall is over when you see the turning spiral from "The Twilight Zone."

The Twilight Zone Tower of Terror features a high-speed drop into the dark mysterious realm of the Twilight Zone.

WARNING!

For safety, you should be in good health and free from high blood pressure, heart, back or neck problems, motion sickness, or other conditions that could be aggravated by this adventure.

Expectant mothers should not ride.

Supervise children at all times.

Persons who do not meet the minimum height requirement may not ride.

Must transfer

If you dare. A cautionary notice at the ride entrance.

FUN FINDS ❶ To the right of the reception desk, a AAA plaque honors the hotel's "13-diamond" status. An actual award, it was presented by the American Automobile Association when the ride opened in 1994. ❷ Abandoned items at the desk include a fedora, topcoat, folded newspaper, open registration book, alligator-skin luggage and mail-slot mail and messages. ❸ A bag, cane and white fedora lean against the concierge desk.

❹ A diamond ring, white glove and two glasses rest on a table on the left. Next to it is a champagne bucket. ❺ A mah-jongg game is in progress on a nearby table.* Tea has just been served to the players; a cart holds cups ready for pouring, roses and a newspaper. ❻ Another teacup rests on the end table in front of a fireplace; a goblet and small plate sit on a table to the right. ❼ The message EVIL TOWER U R DOOMED is formed by letters at the bottom of the hotel directory (between the lobby's two passenger elevators) that ap-

TRANSCENDENTAL TV "There is a fifth dimension beyond that which is known to man… a middle ground between light and shadow, between science and superstition… it is an area which we call The Twilight Zone." Along with a four-note theme song ("do-do-do-do, do-do-do-do…"), those classic words welcomed viewers to "The Twilight Zone," an imaginative CBS television anthology that aired from 1959 to 1964. Placing ordinary people into extraordinary situations, the episodes often had mind-bending twists, with confused characters in unfamiliar, sometimes supernatural surroundings. Host Rod Serling created the show after getting fed up with censorship hassles at his job as a writer of the dramatic series "Playhouse 90." Though "The Twilight Zone" was as popular as today's "American Idol" (each episode was watched by about one in 10 Americans) Serling had to fight hard to keep it on the air. In the pre-cable world of the 1960s, an audience that size was considered pitiful. Though the show made him a giant in the TV industry, Serling stood only 5-foot-5 and weighed just 137 pounds. A chronic smoker, he died from complications of heart surgery in 1975, at age 50.

A HAUNTED HISTORY While planning the attraction Disney considered a variety of themes. At first it was to be housed in the "Haunted Hollywood Hotel," a real resort with rooms guests could stay in. One idea featured actor Mel Brooks as a madman hotel owner who chased guests into an elevator. Another had movie stars filming a horror picture, with a walk-through segment narrated by Vincent Price. The attraction was built with a reprogrammable ride system, which has let Disney update it three times. At first it was just one gut-grabbing plummet of more than 100 feet. A 1996 revision made it three tumbles, adding a half drop and a false fall. Three years later Disney debuted a seven-fall experience that also brought faster acceleration, more weightlessness and a lot more shaking. Finally, on New Year's Eve 2002, the company introduced "Tower of Terror 4," the current mix of random drops enhanced with physical, sound and visual effects. "We can reinvent the experience as often as we want," says Imagineer Theron Skees. "We can add effects, change timing sequences and alter the way the elevator moves."

parently shook off during the lightning strike. **8** The footage of Serling has been altered to remove a cigarette from his right hand. **9** The little girl sings the nursery rhyme "It's Raining, It's Pouring" on the video and on the fourth floor. **10** Though the service elevators' tracking dials only go to "12," their arrows go to an unmarked "13." **11** As your doors close, a hint at your destination — a "1" on the left door and a "3" on the right — disguises itself as a "B," the elevator's letter. **12** The clock in the basement office is stuck on 8:05, the time of the lightning strike. **13** The gift shop windows are still decorated for the Halloween of 1939.

* It's a real game, in progress. "One of our designers actually learned to play mah-jongg," Imagineer Eric Jacobson says, "so he could make sure the game pieces would be in a proper position."

PROPS AND ALLUSIONS References to "The Twilight Zone" are scattered throughout the hotel. A poster at the **concierge desk** promotes a show by Anthony Freemont, the name of a 6-year-old boy in a 1961 "Twilight Zone" episode ("It's a Good Life") who uses telepathic powers to terrorize his neighbors. In the **library**, the bookcases hold such items as the devil-headed, "Ask Me a Yes or No Question" fortune-telling machine from the 1960 episode "Nick of Time" (a story of a man unable to make decisions for himself) and the tiny silver robot featured in the 1961 episode "The Invaders" (a tale of a farm woman who kills what appear to be small invading aliens). As you board the **elevator**, the small inspection certificate on its wall is signed by "Cadwallader," a jovial character in the 1959 episode "Escape Clause" who secretly is the devil. Dated Oct. 31, 1939, the certificate has the number 10259, a reference to the date the TV program premiered: Oct. 2, 1959. When your elevator finally stops to unload, you sit next to a basement **storage area** that includes a "Special Jackpot $10,000" slot machine from the 1960 episode "The Fever" (a story of a talking slot that drives a tightwad crazy), two ventriloquist dummies used in 1962's "The Dummy"(a dummy switches places with its human owner) as well as 1964's "Caesar and Me" (a ventriloquist uses his cigar-smoking dummy to commit crimes) and a silver spaceship, the home to the library's "Invaders" robot. Finally, the **bulletin-board** notes to the right of the basement office (the "Picture If You Will" souvenir-photo area) seek finders of items such as a "Pocket watch, sentimental value, broken crystal" a reference to the 1963 episode "A Kind of Stopwatch" (in which a bank robber stops time forever when he breaks an unusual timepiece).

THE SCIENCE OF SPOOKY What makes the Tower so fun? In part it's the science. Hidden behind all the theming is a unique mix of innovative engineering, classic special effects and modern math. Combining three distinct ride systems, the mechanics of the attraction represent a novel achievement of applied science. Its "elevator" goes up, moves forward, then plummets down — and soars up — a second shaft, all in one seamless experience.

The first system is obvious: an elevator. When you leave the boiler room, you're traveling in a standard, 50-foot elevator shaft, with typical sliding doors and two distinct stops. The second kicks in at the top of the shaft. As your elevator car (actually an independent vehicle, which rode up the shaft in a cage) moves forward, it's using the technology of a self-guided palette driver, an automated machine used by companies such as Anheuser-Busch, JC Penney and Sony to move inventory around large warehouses. Controlled by an unseen computer, it rolls on wheels and gets its power from an on-board battery.

The third system is Disney's own, and is a real innovation. Once your cabin enters the drop shaft, it's silently locked into a second cage that is tightly suspended on a looped steel cable. Pulled by high-speed winches and motors, the cage "falls" faster than the pull of gravity — you reach 37 mph in just 1.5 seconds, about a quarter of a second faster than if you were falling freely — and shoots up with similar speed. The result: though you never actually fall and are never truly free of the ride's grasp, you feel completely out of control.

Though often stunningly realistic, most of the elevator effects are created by simple, time-tested methods.

At your first stop, a long corridor filled with translucent people, disappearing windows and sudden star fields is really a shallow area filled with transparent screens, which show images from hidden projectors. Though it looks far away and 8 feet tall, the end of the hall is actually just a few feet in front of you, and only 4 feet high.

Once your elevator moves forward, mirrors on the floor and ceiling make it seem those planes have disappeared. The characters to your side are simply independently moving plastic cutouts, split down the middle to make them look warped. In front of you, the changing star field comes from synchronized fiber-optic lights built into the doors to the final drop zone.

Each ride is different, as the attraction's computer system chooses the particulars of your fall using a random-number generator that's based on modulo functions (calculations that search for two numbers that, when divided by a third number, have the same remainder). "The very moment that the elevator is entering the shaft, the computer decides what is going to happen," explains Disney software engineer Michael Tschanz.

Top to bottom: Lilo and Stitch, Mike, Snow White wave; a classy chassis poses

Disney Stars and Motor Cars Parade

✓ Stars such as Lilo and Stitch, JoJo and Kermit are among the newer Disney characters who greet you in this up-close-and-personal parade. Half ride in customized convertibles from Hollywood's Golden Age; the others dance alongside looking to shake your hand. It's easy to make contact with the car stars: they're right at eye level.

Most of the vehicles are heavily modified. One 1951 Mercury has become Andy's bed from 1995's "Toy Story;" another has been transformed into Genie from 1992's "Aladdin;" a '33 Ford has been converted into a stretched open-air hearse. The strangest car is nearly stock. Looking like something from a long time ago in a galaxy far, far away, the "Star Wars" vehicle is really just a 1949 Studebaker.

Good viewing spots include the ATAS Hall of Fame Showcase near Echo Lake (the narrow road brings the cars especially close and the short wall makes a good seat); the nearby ABC Theater steps; or the tiny Crossroads of the World gift stand (a shady spot where the parade comes straight at you). The best spots are taken 30 minutes early.

Parade route: Enters between Star Tours and the Backlot Express, goes past Sounds Dangerous to the Sorcerer's Hat then down Hollywood Blvd. Exits between Mickey's of Hollywood and Sid Cahuenga's gift shop.

Outstretched arms await JoJo

(To exit the park during the parade, stay on the Sunset Blvd. side of Hollywood Blvd. and walk through the shops). 15-20 min. Special viewing areas for ECV and wheelchair guests. Debuted: 2001, revised 2005.

FUN FINDS ❶ Mary Poppins' hood ornament is a penguin. ❷ Snow White's is an apple with a bite out of it. ❸ Goofy honks his horn whether or not he touches his steering wheel.

STARS...	MOTOR CAR...
GRAND MARSHALLS (guest family)	1934 Ford
"TOY STORY" (1996) characters Woody and Buzz Lightyear, escorted by three Green Army Men, Bo Peep, and, from 1999's "Toy Story 2," Jessie the cowgirl	1951 Mercury
"MARY POPPINS" (1965) and Bert the chimney sweep on "Jolly Holiday" carrousel horses, escorted by three penguin waiters	1934 Ford
MUPPETS Kermit and Miss Piggy, escorted by Sweetums	1932 Ford
"STAR WARS" (1977-2005) characters Luke Skywalker and Princess Leia, escorted by Darth Vader and R2-D2	1949 Studebaker
"MULAN" (1998), escorted by masked warriors and friendly dragon Mushu	1939 Ford
"MONSTERS, INC." (2001) characters Mike and Sulley	1940 Ford
"ALADDIN" (1992) and Jasmine, escorted by four happy harem girls	1951 Mercury
VILLAINS Hades (1997's "Hercules"), Jafar ("Aladdin"), Maleficent (1959's "Sleeping Beauty"), Frollo (1996's "The Hunchback of Notre Dame"), and Cruella De Vil (1961's "101 Dalmatians")	1933 Ford
"LILO & STITCH" (2002)	1940 Ford
"THE LITTLE MERMAID" (1989) stars Ariel and Sebastian, escorted by fish	1939 Ford
"POWER RANGERS" — one each from the TV show's "Time Force," "Ninja Storm," "Wild Force," "Dino Thunder," and "Space Patrol Delta" incarnations	1940 Ford
PLAYHOUSE DISNEY characters Bear, Treelo, Pip and Pop (from "Bear in the Big Blue House") and Stanley (from "Stanley"), escorted by JoJo and Goliath (from "JoJo's Circus") and Rolie and Zowie (from "Rolie Polie Olie")	1934 Ford
"SNOW WHITE" (1938) and Dopey	1951 Mercury
CLASSIC STARS Mickey Mouse, Minnie Mouse, Donald Duck and Goofy, escorted by Chip 'n' Dale, Pluto, Pinocchio and Geppetto (from 1940's "Pinocchio"), Alice and the White Rabbit (from 1951's "Alice in Wonderland")	1929 Cadillac

Rockin' out with Mulch, Sweat and Shears on the Streets of America

Street performers

✓ The Studios has more street theater than any other Disney park, most of it geared to adults and older kids.

A troupe of professional improvisational actors, the **Citizens of Hollywood** roam the park as the living, breathing residents of this 1940s Tinseltown, chatting with guests and holding audience-participation skits. They appear as a variety of stereotypical characters, including "America's favorite childhood star" Dainty Debbie, boy-off-the-bus Francis Floot, starlet Gracie Flutterbuck (the "extra with something extra"), silent movie great Dame Sadie Whimsey and rich socialite Polly Wolly Doodle.

The performers never break character, a fact that impresses even other actors. "These guys have way more commitment than I do," says John Corbett, known for his roles in television's "Northern Exposure" and "Sex and the City" and the 2003 film "My Big Fat Greek Wedding." "I'm supposed to be the 'real' actor, but in my job when they say 'action' I stay in character for about a minute and a half, just until they say 'cut.'"

Up to 17 Citizens are on the streets at a time. If you see one, strike up a conversation. You'll quickly find yourself in one of the most memorable moments of your vacation. To be picked for a staged routine, smile and make eye contact. You'll often find the characters on Hollywood and Sunset boulevards after 2 p.m.

Driving into the Streets of America a few times each day as a truckful of landscape workers, **Mulch, Sweat and Shears** is actually a hilarious live rock band. As its vehicle transforms into a stage and power source, the group cranks out a 25-minute set of classic tunes and medleys, grabbing audience members to play cow bells and air guitars in a show that rocks hard but never takes itself seriously. The group changes some lyrics to make them more family-friendly: lead singer and wannabe comedian Morris Mulch delivers a line from the Eagles' 1977 hit "Life in the Fast Lane" as "They had one thing in common, they were good... at sports!" As for Aerosmith's raunchy 1975 classic "Walk This Way," this version has more than one strategic mumble.

Following the park's parade route along Echo Lake and down Hollywood Boulevard, the **High School Musical Pep Rally** stops at the Sorcerer's Hat for an 11-minute show. It's short, but has all the spirit of the popular television movie.

Juggler, magician, mime and general guest pest **Rockin' Rob** appears in the courtyard of the Rock 'n' Roller Coaster. Beware: he'll sneak up on you.

▶ Guest Relations has the daily showtimes for all Studios street performers.

Fantasmic

The kitchen sink of nighttime extravaganzas, this nightcap is quite a spectacle. As you sit in an outdoor amphitheater, your eyes are bombarded with dancing fountains, burning waves, water screens, a huge dragon and before you can say "Great balls of fire!" one of those, too. It takes place in a lagoon dominated by an island with a 60-foot mountain.

The plot: Mickey has a nightmare.

Dressed as the Sorcerer's Apprentice, the dreaming mouse conducts fountains in the lagoon like instruments in an orchestra, creating water screens that then play scenes from 1940's "Fantasia." As his powers increase, Mickey shoots fireworks out of his fingers. Then he imagines dancers who form a giant flower, as well as a wildly colorful elephant, giraffe and rhinoceros who lead a jungle full of animals in a surreal version of "I Just Can't Wait to be King."

Selling souvenirs before the show

As images from many classic Disney films appear on large water bubbles, Monstro the whale (from 1940's "Pinocchio") chases Jiminy Cricket, and suddenly lunges right at the audience, splashing guests in the front rows. The theater gets pitch black. "Hey!" Mickey yells. "What's going on?"

Bang! The thunder of a cannon transforms the set into the 17th-century Virginia of Disney's 1995 "Pocahontas." As peaceful Native Americans paddle by in torch-lit canoes, prissy Gov. Ratcliffe claims the island for his king. English settlers sing "Mine Mine Mine" as they burn down trees, dig up land and shoot Indians. Soon, Pocahontas arrives to stop the madness.

After Mickey's dream turns romantic (a boat parade of Ariel, Belle and Snow White) his nightmare returns at full tilt.

The Evil Queen arrives and morphs into the Wicked Witch. "Now I'll turn that little mouse's dream into a nightmare Fantasmic!" she cackles, summoning up water apparitions of nearly every Disney villain. Jafar pops onto the land and becomes a live-action snake, then Maleficent becomes a 40-foot dragon and ignites the waterway with her fiery breath.

But Mickey fights back. "You may think you're so powerful," he tells the dragon, "well, this is MY dream!" Regaining his powers, he lifts the water up to smother the flames and, finding an oh-so-convenient sword in a stone, slays the dragon.

For the finale out comes a showboat filled with characters, piloted by the black-and-white Mickey from the 1928 cartoon, "Steamboat Willie." Then to end the show there's a burst of fireworks and a delightful now-you-see-him, now-you-don't magical Mickey.

The show has 50 performers.

25 min. Capacity: 9,900 (6,900 seats, standing room for 3,000). Arrive 90 min. early to get seats in the center of the theater (a large snack bar helps you kill time). Guests may remain in wheelchairs, ECVs. Assistive listening; reflective captioning. Fear factor: The loud noises, bright flashes and villains frighten some children. Debuted: 1998 (Disneyland 1992).

▶ Often a few seats are available in the front center until 30 minutes before showtime.

disney's
Animal

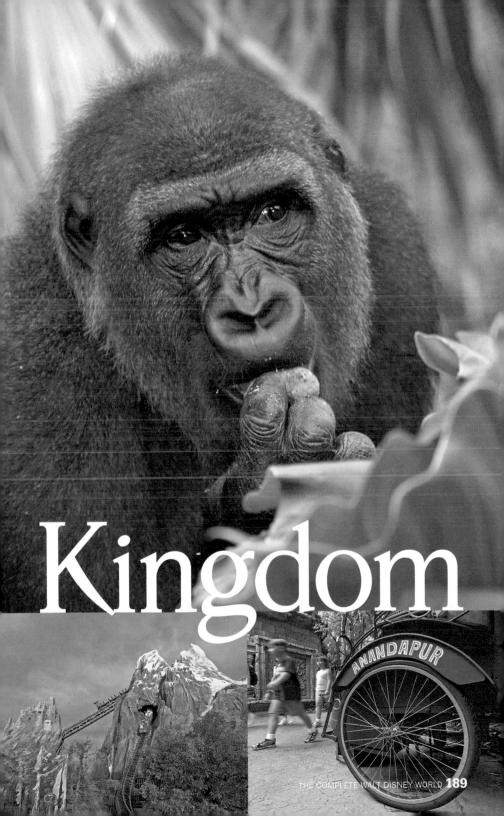

Kingdom

Top left: Festival of the Lion King dancers. **Above:** A Harambe School instructor. **Left:** Chip, safari ready.

though it's not as famous as the Magic Kingdom, in many ways Disney's Animal Kingdom is much more magical. Set in 500 acres of botanical wonder, Disney's largest theme park features a real safari through a 110-acre African wilderness, two Broadway-style shows, a thrilling roller coaster, and up-close encounters with what seems like every strange creature on the planet. The park's mission: to make it easy, and fun, to appreciate the beauty, magnificence and importance of the animal world.

TO ZOO, OR NOT TO ZOO The park's zoo-logical operations are respected world-wide... but are fully hidden, tucked behind, or in, man-made hills, rivers, rocks and streams. Scientists are breeding endangered species, and researchers are studying behaviors such as the low-frequency vocalizations of elephants... but you barely hear about it. The park is a member of the acclaimed Association of Zoos and Aquariums... but the AZA logo appears only on a flag out front.

Why? Because Disney wants you to see the real world of animals, not the artificial world of zoos. "Disney is all about storytelling, and here real live animals help tell the story as their families play out real-life experiences," says the park's executive designer Joe Rohde. "We want people to get a little tug on their heartstrings," adds park vice president Dr. Beth Stevens, "and get people to care about animals."

Laid out in a classic hub-and-spoke style, the park welcomes you with an entranceway free from even a single gift

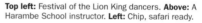

▶ Raining? Try the safari. You'll stay dry, and the animals are often more lively.

shop. Instead, you meander into this celebration of nature through the aptly named Oasis, a re-created tropical jungle filled with fascinating creatures. Your path leads to the centrally located Discovery Island, the lush home of the Tree of Life and Its Tough To Be a Bug attraction as well as the best-looking food stands, restaurants and shops you'll find anywhere. From there five lands radiate outward:

CAMP MINNIE-MICKEY Meant to evoke an Adirondack summer camp where Mickey Mouse and his friends have gone on vacation, this T-shaped walkway is lined with birch and cedar trees and hand-hewn benches. It's home to two theatrical shows — the Festival of the Lion King and Pocahontas and Her Forest Friends — as well as character meet-and-greet pavilions.

AFRICA The largest section of the park presents African animal attractions within the context of the mythical East African port town of Harambe, based on the real Kenyan island town of Lamu. Appearing worn and weathered by decades of sand and rain storms, the detailed village represents a former gold and ivory trading post that now is trying to build an economy based on eco-tourism.

The Swahili architecture features hand-plastered buildings with an often-exposed coral-rock substructure. Roofs are corrugated metal and reed thatch.

Foundations of "old" buildings sit along the main streets, and lampposts bear the phrase "Harambe 1961," the year the village gained independence from Great Britain. Other details include vintage tin signs (mostly authen-

Monkey business. A young girl waits for the parade.

tic) and Kenyan-English advertising posters (mostly fake). Interiors are decorated with East African canned goods, cots and camping paraphernalia. The animal research camp and conservation school (the Pangani Forest Ex-

▶ Hot? Big cups of ice water are free at all counter-service restaurants.

A Magical Day

Can you *absolutely, positively* get to Disney's Animal Kingdom by 8:30 a.m? If so, here's a great plan. The key: getting Expedition Everest Fastpasses as soon as the park opens, then immediately touring the animal exhibits.

8:30 Arrive at the park
As you wait for the gates to open (typically at 8:50), pick up a Times Guide from the Guest Relations window at your left.

9:00 Get Fastpasses for Everest.

9:10 Maharajah Jungle Trek
Go to Asia's Maharajah Jungle Trek. The giant fruit bats will be at their most lively.

9:45 Kilimanjaro Safaris
You'll see plenty of animals, as it's early in the day.

10:30 Pangani Forest Trail
The meerkats and gorillas should be active.

11:30 Expedition Everest
Ask for the front row for the best views, the back seat for the biggest thrill.

12:30 Lunch
Africa's Tusker House has the best food, Discovery Island's Pizzafari the best decor, its Flame Tree BBQ (closest to Everest) the best views. They're all good choices. While you eat, check your Times Guide to confirm your afternoon's show and parade times.

1:20 Festival of the Lion King
Get in line to see the 2 p.m. Festival of the Lion King show. You'll get a great seat.

3:00 Get Fastpasses
for Kali River Rapids. (Don't want to get wet? Check out a performance by Inkas Wasi across from Flame Tree Barbecue.)

3:30 See the parade
It typically starts at 4 p.m.

4:30 Kali River Rapids
Who cares if you get soaked — you're done! (Don't want to get wet? Check out the character greeting trails at Camp Minnie-Mickey. The waiting lines will be short, or nonexistent.)

Assumes operating hours of 9 a.m. to 5 p.m.

Sign of a Yeti? Riders meet the end of the line high in the mountains of the Expedition Everest attraction.

ploration Trail) is scattered with the letters, notes and journals of its head researcher and field workers.

RAFIKI'S PLANET WATCH A short train ride away from Africa is this conservation-themed area, home to a real animal research center and a petting zoo.

ASIA Disney's mythical kingdom of Anandapur is a collage of architectural and landscaping themes that portrays another community trying to save its environment. Locals have turned an ancient royal forest and crumbling hunting lodge into a wildlife preserve (the Maharajah Jungle Trek). Other ruins serve as a bird sanctuary (Flights of Wonder). Nearby, a river-rafting business fights with loggers for control of a turbulent river (Kali River Rapids). Meanwhile, two entrepreneurs are offering mountain climbers a shortcut train ride to Mount Everest, ignoring warnings from concerned villagers about a Yeti (Expedition Everest).

Two monument areas, one Thai and one Nepalese, provide homes for hooting gibbons. Supposedly built in 637

A.D., the temples are covered in bamboo scaffolding as cash-starved villagers try to restore them. Nearby, a crumbling Indian tiger shrine is complete with scarf and garland offerings and bells that represent answered prayers.

Among Asia's best details are its many rusted signs and aged murals. They're not authentic, but sure look to be.

DINOLAND U.S.A. With the most peculiar theming of any Disney land, DinoLand U.S.A. embraces America's fascination with all things dinosaur while simultaneously parodying the stuffiness of scientists and the tackiness of roadside tourist traps and traveling carnivals.

The story begins in 1947, when an amateur fossil-hunter named Chester discovered some dinosaur bones outside his Diggs County gas station. Realizing the importance of the find, the bone-hunter contacted some scientist friends. They banded together to purchase the site, and in 1949 transformed an old fishing lodge on the property into the Dino Institute, a non-profit organization dedicated to the Exploration, Excavation and Exultation of dinosaur fossils.

For nearly six decades, the site has been inhabited by scientists and graduate-student pranksters.

During the 1970s the Institute received a large grant from McDonald's (yep, product placement even in a fictitious story), which allowed it to build a formal museum and state-of-the-art research center, and explore a new archeological technique: time travel.

The old building's museum room became the student cafeteria; its adjacent buildings a dorm and vehicle-maintenance hut. Soon the entire area was opened to the public as DinoLand U.S.A., a "dinosaur discovery park." Tourists poured in.

But the saga doesn't end there.

When the crowds arrived, so did Chester's newfound interest: money. Teaming up with his wife, Hester, he turned his gas station into a souvenir stand — the gaudy Chester & Hester's

Another Magical Day

Get to the park again by 8:30 a.m. and you'll have another great day.

8:30 Arrive at the park
As you wait for the gates to open (typically at 8:50), pick up a Times Guide from the Guest Relations window at your left. Watch for Wes Palm, the talking palm tree.

9:00 The Oasis
Find the anteater, babirusa and wallaby.

9:30 Kilimanjaro Safaris
You'll see animals and behaviors you didn't before.

10:00 Hang out in Harambe
See the entertainers. Check out the school.

11:30 Get Fastpasses for It's
Tough To Be a Bug. The machines are next to the attraction entrance, in front of Disney Outfitters.

11:35 Discovery Island
Wander through the paths of Discovery Island. Find the kangaroos — and the lemurs.

12:15 Lunch
While you eat, check your Times Guide to confirm your afternoon's show times.

1:15 It's Tough To Be a Bug

2:15 Finding Nemo
Get in line to see the 3 p.m. show of Finding Nemo — The Musical. You'll get a great seat.

3:45 Flights of Wonder
It typically starts at 4 p.m.

4:15 Conservation Station
See the indoor exhibits and petting zoo.

5:30 Dinner at Rainforest Cafe.

7:00 DinoLand
Come on a late-night Extra Magic Hours day and see this section of the park after dark. Don't forget Dinosaur, the indoor ride at the back right corner.

Assumes operating hours of 9 a.m. to 9 p.m.

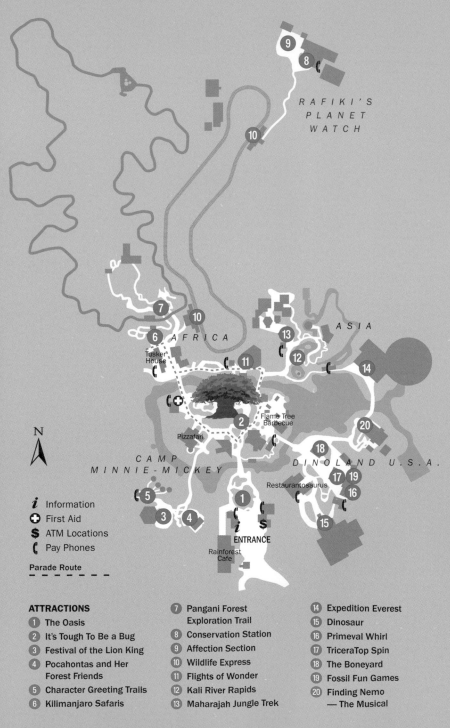

RAFIKI'S PLANET WATCH

AFRICA

ASIA

Tusker House

Flame Tree Barbecue

Pizzafari

CAMP MINNIE-MICKEY

DINOLAND U.S.A.

Restaurantosaurus

N

i Information
✚ First Aid
$ ATM Locations
☎ Pay Phones

Parade Route - - - - - -

ENTRANCE

Rainforest Cafe

ATTRACTIONS

1. The Oasis
2. It's Tough To Be a Bug
3. Festival of the Lion King
4. Pocahontas and Her Forest Friends
5. Character Greeting Trails
6. Kilimanjaro Safaris
7. Pangani Forest Exploration Trail
8. Conservation Station
9. Affection Section
10. Wildlife Express
11. Flights of Wonder
12. Kali River Rapids
13. Maharajah Jungle Trek
14. Expedition Everest
15. Dinosaur
16. Primeval Whirl
17. TriceraTop Spin
18. The Boneyard
19. Fossil Fun Games
20. Finding Nemo — The Musical

A **nutritionist** prepares some of the four tons of food that the park feeds to its animals each day, which includes 5,000 worms and 2,500 crickets. Disney also distributes 2,000 pounds of vegetation and browse (clippings of grasses) daily.

Dinosaur Treasures (an "Emporium of Extinction") that sold trinkets and toys of little value, but high profit margin.

As the couple's fortunes grew, the embarrassed Dino Institute wanted Chester and Hester out, and pressured them to sell. Chester and Hester refused, however, and retaliated by turning their parking lot into a cheap carnival — "Dino-Rama," a play on the word "diorama" — that openly mocks the scientists. The couple's cousins run the attractions, while two moonlighting Institute interns walk around in a couple of Hester's homemade dinosaur outfits. An additional story about the three grad students is told by a paper trail of notes and scribbles throughout and around the Boneyard and Restaurantosaurus.

It's not all a joke. Disney says that, in a subtle way, DinoLand U.S.A. represents the conflict between order and chaos, authority and disobedience.

Attractions include the Dinosaur thrill ride, the carnival rides Primeval Whirl and TriceraTop Spin and the elaborate Boneyard playground.

Park resources

The park's **ATM** (Entrance Plaza) accepts most bank cards. All restaurants, stands and stores accept credit cards and traveler's checks... A hidden oasis, the **Baby Care Center** (behind Creature Comforts, Discovery Island) has changing rooms, nursing areas, a microwave, even a playroom; and sells diapers, formula, pacifiers and over-the-counter medications... Garden Gate Gifts (Entrance Plaza) sells **cameras and accessories** and burns photo CDs... Adjacent to the Baby Care Center, the **First Aid Center** (behind Creature Comforts, Discovery Island) handles minor emergencies and has registered nurses on hand... The park's **Guest Relations** center (Entrance Plaza; walk-up window outside the gate, walk-in office inside) is staffed with cast members ready to answer any question or help with any problem. It has maps and Times Guides for all Walt Disney World theme parks, exchanges some foreign currency and stores items found in the park that day... **Lockers** large enough to store a couple of large bags can be rented just inside the park entrance ($5 per day plus a $2 deposit)... Report **lost children** to Guest Relations or any Disney cast member. Children who lose their parents should tell a Disney cast member... Anything you buy at a park gift shop can be sent to **Package Pick-Up** (Garden Gate Gifts, Entrance Plaza) for you to pick up as you leave. Purchases can also be delivered to your Walt Disney World hotel or shipped to your home.... For day guests **parking** is $10 a day. Those staying at a Walt Disney World resort (and annual passholders) get free parking. A complimentary tram takes you to the park entrance... The **Pet Care Kennel** (Entrance Plaza, 407-938-2100) has clean cages in air-conditioned rooms (see the chapter "Practical Information" for details)... **Security guards** inspect all bags and purses at stations outside the park entrance... Garden Gate Gifts (Entrance Plaza) rents single **strollers and wheelchairs** ($10 per day), double-passenger strollers ($18) and Electric Convenience Vehicles ($35). The ECVs are booked quickly; many are used by overweight guests... The park **tip board** (Discovery Island) displays current waiting times for popular attractions... As for **transportation,** Disney buses run to the park from all Walt Disney World resorts, Disney-MGM Studios, Epcot and the Transportation and Ticket Center. Service from Downtown Disney connects through the TTC. Magic Kingdom guests take a monorail to the TTC, then a bus to Disney's Animal Kingdom.

overview

HOW MANY DAYS? Some say the park is just a half-day experience, but that's only if you have no interest in wildlife (or, for that matter, art, architecture or landscaping). Actually, it can take up to four days to see everything here.

Why? The animals. To stop and enjoy each of the park's five habitats can take up to an hour, but each area is far more rewarding early in the morning, before 11 a.m. In addition, Conservation Station's public animal-care procedures take place only in the morning, and require a separate train trip to get to.

The park has just nine non-animal rides and shows, but they're all worthwhile and, counting waiting times, can take up to an hour each. The parade is one of Disney's most creative proces-

sions. Only the Dino-Rama attractions are traditional short rides.

And the atmosphere itself — the stunning landscaping, the detailed shops and restaurants, the first-class street performers, the museum-like theming — makes you want to slow down and take it all in. Note, however, that the park has 9 miles of walking trails.

Though the animal attractions always close at dusk, the park is sometimes open until 9 or 10 p.m. When it is, it's one of Disney's prettiest night spots. Lit from within the trunk, the upper branches and leaves of the Tree of Life appear to glow. Strings of light bulbs line the paths of Asia, while flashing bulbs add a dose of cheesy charm to the Dino-Rama carnival at DinoLand U.S.A.

Animal Kingdom is home to 1,500 animals representing 250 species.

FUN FACTS 》 150 different animal species have been bred by the park. 》 2.6 million gallons of water cycles through the park's treated-water system five times a day. It's used in the streams, waterfalls and other water features that come in contact with the live animals. 》 Originally the Camp Minnie-Mickey pathway was to connect Discovery Island with the Beastly Kingdom, a never-built area of the park themed to mythical creatures. 》 The word "Harambe" means "coming together" in Swahili. Tamu Tamu means "sweet sweet," Dawa means "strong medicine," Rafiki means "friend." 》 Kilimanjaro is the most famous mountain in Kenya. 》 Africa's seven thatch huts were built on-site by 13 Zulu craftsmen visiting from Kwazulu-Natal, South Africa, using 15 semi-truck loads of Berg grass harvested by relatives back home. 》 Harambe's coral rock is actually volcanic rock from California. 》 Sanskrit for "place of delight," Anandapur is also the name of an actual East Indian town of 35,000. 》 Chakranadi translates to "river that runs in circles." 》 The rusty Asian bicycles were purchased at garage sales. 》 The apatosaurus skeleton that straddles the entrance to DinoLand U.S.A. is a cast of a real 52-foot fossil found in Colorado in 1900. The original is in Chicago's Field Museum. 》 Located between Dinosaur and Dinosaur Treasures, the Cretaceous Trail is the third largest cycad collection in North America. 》 The name of the DinoLand highway — U.S. 498 — refers to the month the Animal Kingdom opened: April, 1998. 》 The Restaurantosaurus Airstream trailer originally belonged to an Imagineer's grandmother.

FUN FINDS Africa: ❶ Sounds of chatting voices, clanking dishes and a radio often come from behind the back door of Africa's Dawa Bar. The sounds represent the residents of the hotel above. Occasionally there's a knocking on a door — a landlady trying to collect back rent. **Asia:** ❷ The "dried mud" pathways include bicycle tracks and footprints made by barefoot Disney cast members and their children. ❸ Each Anandapur business displays a tax license featuring the kingdom's king and queen. The bigger the license, the more taxes that business pays. ❹ Just right of the tiger shrine, visible seams in an authentic Indian marble pavilion reveal where Disney cut the structure apart to ship it to the United States. ❺ Walls and drain covers shoot water at a small play area between Kali River Rapids and the Maharajah Jungle Trek. ❻ Inside one of the siamang temples is an air-conditioned kitchen. Its door is protected by an electrified vine that emits a noticeable slow clicking. **DinoLand U.S.A.:** The Restaurantosaurus abounds in dinosaur and archeological references. Among the best: ❼ the shapes

▶ Behind Africa's Tamu Tamu ice cream, a shady fort offers a hidden resting spot.

formed by greasy hand prints on the walls of the quonset hut garage; **8** the cans of Sinclair Litholine Multi-Purpose Grease and Dynoil ("keep your old dinosaur running") on the shelves of that room; **9** the reproductions of four sketches for the "The Rite of Spring" sequence in Disney's 1930s film project "Concert Feature" that became the 1940 film "Fantasia;" **10** the titles in the juke box in the Hip Joint rec room (e.g., "Dust in the Wind"); **11** the posters in that room for rock bands Dinosaur Jr. and T Rex; and **12** the ambient music, which includes the 1988 Was Not Was hit "Walk the Dinosaur" as well as obscure ditties such as proto-punk icon Jonathan Richman's "I'm a Little Dinosaur" and "Ugga Bugga," a Bruce Springsteen-like tune by one-time child star Bill Mumy. **13** The letters A-I-R-S-T-R-E-A-M on the front of the restaurant's travel trailer have been rearranged to spell I ARE SMART. **14** Four hanging signs above the entrance to the Dinosaur Treasures gift shop read "Rough scaly skin... Making you groan?... Don't despair... Use Fossil Foam" from one direction, "When in Florida... Be sure to... Visit... Epcot" from the other. **15** Tiny plastic dinos ride trains, snow ski and flee lava flows above the gift shop's main room. **16** Boxes stored above Chester's garage floors include "Chester's dig '47," "Chester's pet rocks 1966" and "Train Parts." **17** An oil funnel and gas-pump nozzle are among the items that have been turned into dinosaurs on the shop's walls. **18** The price of gas is 29.9 cents a gallon on Chester's rusty old gas pump alongside the building, as well as on a painted-over sign on the rear roof. **19** "I Like Bananas Because They Have No Bones," a popular 1935 ditty by the Hoosier Hot Shots, is among the bone-themed country songs played on the radio station ("W-BONE") heard in the adjacent restrooms. **20** Two baby dinosaurs hide underneath the adjacent "concretosaurus" folk-art sculpture. One is hatching. **21** Though it appears

Need more cow bell? Not this street performer, who taps out a tune in a Discovery Island band.

to be a stegosaurus shoulder bone, the Boneyard marquee is actually in the shape of Animal Kingdom at the time the park opened, before the addition of Asia. An "N" points to north. **22** "Lost — My Tail" reads one of the notes on the bulletin board across from the Boneyard entrance. It's from the nearby aptosaurus cast, which has a disconnected tailbone. **23** DinoLand's original layout, which included a real fossil preparation area and cast display room on the site of today's Dino-Rama, is shown on a map pinned to the board. **24** Chester and Hester appear in a photo in a corner of the shop's main room and on a poster in the main Restaurantosaurus dining hall.

THE PARK TOOK 2.5 YEARS to build. Starting with a 500-acre flat tract of land, Disney re-landscaped the area with 4.4 million cubic yards of dirt (60 dump trucks a day), a hidden water-treatment system and 4 million plants, adding in a million square feet of rockwork, a full theme-park infrastructure, a variety of attractions and 1,500 animals along the way. The park broke ground in August, 1995, and opened on Earth Day, 1998. It employs more than 4,500 people.

▶ An Extra Magic Hours night? Visit Dino-Rama. The lights make it much more fun.

Clockwise from top left: The idyllic Oasis sets the stage for your day. College interns display spiders and other tiny creatures until 11 a.m. An African spoonbill honks at the photographer.

natural haven of flowering jacaranda trees, lianas, orchids and vines, as well as pools, streams and waterfalls.

The Oasis

Ever seen a babirusa? Swamp wallaby? Black swan? Hyacinth macaw? You will, if you look closely, as you wander this tropical "A"-shaped entranceway that funnels toward Discovery Island. Tucked under a canopy of bamboo, eucalyptus and palms, the area is filled with nearly two dozen exotic species, roaming a

FUN FINDS ❶ The park's dedication plaque sits near a lamppost in front of the black swans. ❷ The Pategonian cavy, the first animal on the right trail, looks like a cross between a kangaroo and a rat. ❸ You can see, and touch, the back of the waterfall, from within the small cave at the end of the Oasis area. ❹ A swaying rope bridge leads out of the cave. It's short, but catches your stomach. Water bubbles up from the rocks underneath it.

▶ Park animals are most active first thing in the morning and late in the day.

Adventureland 2

ARCHITECTURE AND DESIGN

For decades critics have praised Walt Disney World as an example of how functional urban design can entertain with its form. Only Disney, it seems, can create an area for thousands of pedestrians that is simultaneously its own immersive, entertaining environment.

Animal Kingdom takes the idea to a new level. Other Disney parks use Western icons (i.e., a castle) as visual cues, but here Disney uses nonspecific buildings from developing countries, with looks that are virtually unknown in the West.

Nothing looks new. Signs are dented and rusty, paint is cracked, copper green. Even the **Dino Institute**, Disney's spot-on take on the Smithsonian National Museum of Natural History, reflects its inspiration's dusty datedness. The point? To underscore the park's subtle theme of nature's power over man. (Building heights stay below 30 feet, so trees shadow them.)

DISCOVERY ISLAND is Disney's own vision. Six colorful shops, restaurants and snack stands are its best ever. The exteriors are No Worries Caribbean with a hint of Mexican Wedding Dress — bright, happy, patterned and soulful. Each is covered in whimsical animal wood carvings hand crafted on the Indonesian island of Bali, some 1,500 in all. Interiors are just as good, with fanciful animals adorning the ceilings, columns, shelves, walls, even the floors — themselves a mix of colorful textured concrete and inlaid stone and broken-tile mosaics.

In addition, each store has its own theme. Migrating and working animals highlight the main gift shop, **Island Mercantile.** The main rooms of the **Disney Outfitters** clothing store are embellished with animals from the four compass directions of North, South, East and West. The right room has animals of the ground, the left has those of the air (a mural has animal constellations). The **Beastly Bazaar** housewares shop is decorated with crabs, fish and other water creatures, as well as the animals that catch them. The **Creature Comforts** children's store features striped and spotted animals, with ladybug lamps outside.

Bright murals cover the walls of the **Pizzafari** restaurant. Each of the four rooms portrays a different type of animal — those that carry their homes, camouflage themselves, hang upside down or are nocturnal. Bugs rule the porch in back. Hanging from the walls and ceiling are 570 carved animals from Oaxaca, Mexico.

Predators and their prey is the theme of **Flame Tree Barbecue.** The backrest of each chair has four molded predators, each of which corresponds to prey on the tables. Each building has its own motif: mongoose eat geckos in the order area, the seven patio huts have alligators eating fish, anteaters ants, eagles snakes, eels crabs, owls rabbits, snakes mice, spiders butterflies. Lit by lanterns, the area is stunning at night.

Each of the Discovery Island snack stands is subtly themed to its product. **Safari Coffee** is adorned with wide-eyed hyperactive critters such as kangaroo rats. **Safari Popcorn** is trimmed with frogs, snakes and fish snacking on clusters of flies, mice and minnows. **Safari Pretzel** is decorated with eels, octopus, ostriches and other animals that can contort themselves into strange shapes. **Safari Nacho** (today, a sandwich stand) is covered with antelope, baboons and vultures — animals that stick together just like the stand's original offering.

ANIMAL AREAS Within guest view, feeding stations look like trees, stumps, reeds or rocky pools, preserving the look of the wild. Animals are mingled where feasible, separated by natural-looking or invisible barriers where needed.

LANDSCAPING The park has plants from every continent except Antarctica. There are 40 types of palms, 260 grasses and 2,000 kinds of shrubs. DinoLand U.S.A. has many ancient species, including 20 types of magnolia and more than 3,000 palm-like (but cone-bearing) cycads.

A painted sign promotes Asia's Kali River Rapids

discovery island

Animal Kingdom Executive Designer Joe Rohde calls the 145-foot baobab-like Tree of Life "the most impressive artistic feat that we have achieved since the original Sleeping Beauty castle at Disneyland"

rica and snakes over to the back of the Fastpass machines of It's Tough To Be a Bug. There's a Galapagos tortoise along a back trail, which runs between the Africa and Asia gates and wanders under a waterfall. Quiet and tropical, these **Discovery Island Trails** are not marked (Disney wants you to "discover" them) but well worth searching out. In front of the tree are cotton-top tamarins, flamingos, lemurs and an underwater area to view otters.

FUN FACTS ›› The Tree of Life is 145 feet tall, with a 160-foot canopy. ›› Its concrete trunk is 50 feet wide at its middle, 170 feet at its base. It has 8,000 fiberglass branches and 103,000 leaves. ›› The tree took 18 months to build. An oil-rig-style interior frame provides strength and allows for a free-span theater inside that hosts It's Tough To Be a Bug. A giant expansion joint encircles each of the 12 main branches, which lets them sway in the wind. Disney created the trunk outside the park, then cut it into a dozen segments and flew it to a nearby construction site. A crane was used to put the pieces together.

Animals "carved" into the Tree of Life trunk include a tiger and, above it, a porcupine

Tree of Life

✓ Symbolizing the interconnected nature of plants and animals, this massive man-made centerpiece begs a closer look. Pathways take you around and up under it, letting you take in the amazing tapestry of 325 animals that has been sculpted into the gnarled roots, gigantic trunk and thick branches. "We want our visitors to wander up to the tree, to recognize animals and seek out others," says chief sculptor Zsolt Hormay.

Real animals surround the tree. Kangaroos often hop alongside a hidden trail that starts from in front of the Pizzafari restrooms on the walkway to Af-

▶ A main branch is the upturned trunk of an elephant. It's to the left of a bald eagle.

It's Tough To Be a Bug

Elementary-school kids — and their parents — scream with delight at this cartoonish 3-D movie, which stars characters from the 1998 film "A Bug's Life." Located within the Tree of Life, it combines a cute charm, wicked sense of humor and some startling in-theater effects.

As the film begins, mild-mannered ant Flik and his friends demonstrate the survival techniques of some unusual insects. A tarantula shoots poison quills. A soldier termite sprays acid. A stink bug, well, stinks.

Then Hopper crashes the show. What bugs him? People.

"You guys only see us as monsters!" he roars. "Maybe it's time you got a taste of your own medicine!" In comes a giant flyswatter, a can of bug spray, angry spiders and hornets. "Bug bombs, zappers, sticky little motels, nothing can stop us!" Except, that is, a long-tongued chameleon.

"We're pollinators!" shout twirling bees and butterflies in the song-and dance finale, while dancing dung beetles proclaim "If we didn't like the taste, you'd be in shoulder-high waste!"

The best time to go is the last half-hour of the day: there won't be a line and you'll get your choice of seats. For the best focus sit in the middle, toward the back.

8 min. Capacity: 430. Avg. wait: 30 min. morning and afternoon, 10 min. end of day. Fastpass available. Guests may remain in wheelchairs, ECVs. Assistive listening, reflective captioning. Fear factor: Too intense for most toddlers and some preschoolers. Best ages: 6 and up. Debuted: 1999.

FUN FINDS ❶ Just outside the theater, a wall plaque honors Dr. Jane Goodall's commitment to chimpanzees. It's next to

An Audio Animatronic Hopper confronts the audience during It's Tough To Be a Bug

a carving of David Graybeard, one of her most famous subjects. ❷ A giant dung ball is displayed in the lobby. ❸ Lobby posters promote "past" theater shows such as "Beauty and the Bees" and "Little Shop of Hoppers." ❹ The background music features songs from those shows. ❺ The auditorium is the inside of an anthill. ❻ The projection booth is a wasp nest. ❼ The pre-show announcer says "the stinkbug will be played by Claire DeRoom." ❽ After she performs, Flik tells the stinkbug "Hey, lay off the churros!" ❾ As the show ends, fireflies swarm to the exit signs.

FUN FACTS 》》 The show won the 1999 Outstanding Attraction award from the Themed Entertainment Association. 》》 Cheech Marin voices Chili the tarantula. 》》 Kevin Spacey is the voice of Hopper. 》》 When he hears a baby cry, the soldier termite directs his acid at the audience. The baby always cries: it's prerecorded.

Dad: "You're going to love It's Tough To Be a Bug!" Daughter, 4: "No! I don't want to get stinged!"

▶ To feel all the effects, lean back in your seat and keep your feet on the floor.

DISNEY'S ANIMAL KINGDOM

Sitting in a backstage dressing room, singer Nicola Lambo adds the final touches to her Princess Kibibi makeup for a performance of the Festival of the Lion King. At right, a dancer is dressed as an abstract elephant.

12-foot Simba sits atop Pride Rock. Other floats hold a giraffe, elephant and Pumbaa the warthog. Meerkat Timon strolls alongside.

Costumed as African tribal royalty, a quartet of singers offers an chorus of "I Just Can't Wait to be King" before their stage becomes a trampoline for the Tumble Monkeys — acrobats who flip, flop and fly through "Hakuna Matata." "Be Prepared" sets the scene for a mock battle of stilt walkers and a dramatic fire-baton twirler.

Dressed as birds, two ballet dancers embrace and pirouette to "Can You Feel the Love Tonight?" The girl soars high in the air.

The finale is a circle of life, as 50 performers whirl around the stage in a kaleidoscope of color.

28 min. Capacity: 1,375. Avg. wait: 40 min. to get a great seat. ECV, wheelchair accessible. Assistive listening, handheld captioning. Debuted: 1998.

Festival of the Lion King

✓ Dressed as animals, a spirited troupe of dancers and circus acts team up with top-notch singers in this rousing musical spectacle. Capturing the essence of the 1994 film "The Lion King," the in-the-round performance combines the pageantry of a parade, the energy of a tribal celebration and the clap-along fun of songs you know by heart.

The show begins as four floats roll out to the center of the theater. An animated

---

LION CUB SIMBA finds his place in nature's circle of life in Disney's 1994 film "The Lion King." After his father is killed by his uncle Scar, Simba thinks he caused it and flees into exile. Befriended by the warmhearted (and oft-pungent) warthog Pumbaa and freewheeling meerkat Timon, Simba adopts the duo's "hakuna matata" (no worries) attitude. When childhood sweetheart Nala comes back in his life, Simba takes his place as king.

FUN FINDS ❶ The monkeys pick bugs off of audience members. ❷ Their music includes a Tarzan yell, a cow moo, a gargled version of Duke Ellington's 1937 "Caravan" and a snippet of 1923's "Yes, We Have No Bananas." ❸ Timon cracks up watching the monkeys, trembles during "Be Prepared" and swoons throughout "Can You Feel the Love Tonight?" ❹ The giraffe often mouths the words to the songs. ❺ As you exit, Timon says "Could somebody hose down those Tumble Monkeys? They're starting to smell a little gamey."

FUN FACTS ❯❯ The floats originally appeared in a parade at California's Disneyland. ❯❯ Puppeteers inside them control the movements of the elephant, giraffe, Pumbaa and Simba.

▶ Get to the theater 40 minutes early to get one of the best seats.

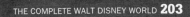

camp minnie-mickey

Pocahontas sings "Colors of the Wind" during Pocahontas and Her Forest Friends

The animals change day to day, but there's usually at least one hawk, porcupine, raccoon or turkey. There's even a large snake. Also on stage are two Audio Animatronic trees: Grandmother Willow and Twig.

In the end, you learn that the only animals that can save the forests are the same ones that can destroy it: humans.

As Pocahontas sings, "You can own the earth and still all you own is earth... until you can paint with all the colors of the wind."

Kids should sit down front, but the best place for you is at the left (otherwise you won't see the face of Grandmother Willow). Presented a few times daily, the show is held in a small tree-shaded theater that replicates a forest glen.

You'll see how Disney trains its animals at one show each day, a "behind-the-scenes" training session. A handler teaches future critter celebrities how to walk or fly to a mark without getting stage fright. Pocahontas is on hand to help with the training.

15 min. Capacity: 350. Avg. wait: 15 min. for a good seat. ECV and wheelchair accessible. Assistive listening. Debuted: 1998.

Pocahontas and Her Forest Friends

Is there really an animal that can save America's forests? Native American legend says there is. But which one?

That's the question posed by this intimate outdoor stage show that — with its first rows reserved exclusively for young children — is a good choice for preschoolers. Sitting a few feet away from the star of Disney's 1995 film, they also get close-up views of a handful of forest animals.

BASED ON THE TRUE STORY of a teenage Native American girl, Disney's 1995 "Pocahontas" dramatizes the meeting of English settlers in Jamestown with a tribe of Powhatan Indians. With help from her Grandmother Willow — a tree spirit — the young nature lover teaches Captain John Smith to respect the world around him.

Character Greeting Trails

You'll meet and greet some of Disney's most popular stars at the ends of these short, shaded walkways across from the Festival of the Lion King Theater. Waiting for you under the small gazebos should be one or two of the Fab Five (Mickey, Minnie, Donald, Goofy and Pluto) as well as characters from films such as 1967's "The Jungle Book," 1994's "The Lion King," 2003's "Brother Bear" or the "Winnie the Pooh" series.

► Late in the day the character greeting trails often have no lines at all.

A painted wall mural at the Pizzafari restaurant

Restaurant guide

TABLE SERVICE **Rainforest Cafe $$** ✔ Beef, chicken, pork and seafood dishes, pasta, pizza, salads, sandwiches and hamburgers. Imaginative breakfast menu. Animated wildlife, lush faux foliage and realistic thunderstorm effects re-create jungle sensations. Mushroom-shaped bar. Huge animal-themed clothing and toy store. Accessible from inside and outside the park. *1,057 seats. Entrance Plaza.*

COUNTER SERVICE **Pizzafari $** ✔ Individual cheese, pepperoni pizzas; quality Italian sandwiches; nice Caesar salad. Cool and comfortable, especially in the large back room. Beautiful murals, floor mosaics and ceiling decor. *680 seats. Discovery Island.* **Restaurantosaurus $** A lavishly wacko dino theme makes up for McDonald's-quality burgers, chicken nuggets, hot dogs. Tucked into the right corner, the Hip Joint room stays peaceful, cool. Breakfastosaurus character buffet with Donald Duck and friends (reservations 407-939-3463) has hot, fresh food, including made-to-order omelets. *750 seats. DinoLand U.S.A.* **Tusker House $** ✔ Healthy choices include black-pepper rotisserie chicken or grilled salmon (with mashed potatoes) and a roasted-vegetable sandwich. First-rate fried chicken sandwich, good chicken salad. Nice breakfast. Disney's best counter-service restaurant. *1,216 seats. Africa.*

OUTDOOR COUNTER CAFE **Flame Tree BBQ $** ✔ BBQ ribs, pork, chicken with baked beans, corn on the cob. Smoked chicken salad. Shady gardens, riverside pavilions. Disney's best outdoor cafe. *500 seats. Discovery Island.*

SNACK STANDS ENTRANCE **Joffrey's Coffee** Pastries, coffee, tea, smoothies. AFRICA **Kusafiri Coffee Shop and Bakery** ✔ Shade-grown, specialty coffee; tea; pastries; fruit; yogurt. **Harambe Fruit Market** ✔ Whole fruit, soft pretzels. *8 seats.* **Harambe Popcorn** Popcorn, churros. **Tamu Tamu** Soft-serve ice cream, yogurt. ASIA **Anandapur Ice Cream Truck** Soft serve. **Asia Slush** Frozen lemonade, pretzels. *16 seats.* **Caramel Corn*** Hot dogs. **Drinkwalla** Frozen drinks, whole fruit. **Mr. Kamal's** Ham, turkey sandwiches; chicken strips. **Royal Anandapur Tea Co.** ✔ Specialty teas, pastries. *12 seats.* CAMP MINNIE-MICKEY **Cookie Cabin*** Hot dogs. **Funnel Cake*** Soft-serve ice cream. DINOLAND U.S.A. **Dino Diner** Hot dogs, popcorn, slushies. *30 seats.* **Dino-Bite** Churros, pastries, hand-dipped ice cream, yogurt. *46 seats, picnic table.* **PetriFries** Fries, cookies. DISCOVERY ISLAND **Safari Coffee** Shade-grown, specialty coffee; pastries; fruit; yogurt. **Safari Nacho*** Turkey, ham sandwiches. **Safari Popcorn** Popcorn, lemonade, punch. **Safari Pretzel** Soft pretzels. **Safari Turkey** Turkey legs, chicken wings.

BARS **Dawa Bar $** African beer, liquor, specialty drinks. *256 seats. Africa.* **Tuki's Tiki Bar $** Specialty drinks, draft beer, smoothies. In the rear outdoor garden of Rainforest Cafe. *30 seats. Entrance Plaza.*

*Some names are holdovers from previous menus

Avg./adult: **$** <$10. **$$** <$20. **$$$** <$30. **$$$$** <$40. Reservations: 407-WDW-DINE

A Kilimanjaro Safari truck roams through the 110-acre African jungle and savannah habitat

Kilimanjaro Safaris

✓ A baby rhino rolling in the mud. A giraffe stretching up to eat leaves. A pair of oryx ramming horns. You never know what you'll see at this terrific attraction, as you take a jerking, jolting open-air truck through 110 acres of perfectly re-created African forest and savannah, all of it teeming with exotic wildlife.

Cheetahs, crocodiles, elephants, hippos, lions, mandrills, ostrich, rhinos, warthogs, wildebeest... they're all here, feeding, fighting, nursing, running and roaming freely in what appear to be wide-open grasslands and forests. There are no visible walls or fences, but plenty of fields, hills and streams.

It can't be *completely* real — if it was the animals would be eating each other — but it so clearly seems to be.

Your adventure begins as you climb in the truck, a specially-made GM vehicle with canvas awnings and high bench seats meant to resemble a converted logging truck. Up front is your guide, the driver. Once everyone's in, off you go into an African forest. Lush grasses shelter the animals, but you may spot a small group of bongos or, if you're really lucky, the shy okapi.

Mouths often wide open, crocodiles bask in the sun. It seems you get too close, as you cross right over the crocs on a low, and bumpy, wooden bridge.

Next you're in the savannah — a grassland range where impala, gazelles and wildebeest forage for food. You might come within a few feet of giraffes, and probably see baboons.

Around a bend, you plunge through a pond as elephants move among the trees. Turning another corner, cheetahs and lions stare down at ostriches, rhinos, warthogs and zebras.

'THEY'VE SHOT BIG RED!' Like nearly all Disney attractions, Kilimanjaro Safaris has a storyline. Your trip starts off as a two-week safari through the 800-acre Harambe Wildlife Preserve, a village's effort to replace its timbering economy with eco-tourism efforts.

As you travel, your guide establishes radio contact with a bush pilot, named

▶ The best trips are early in the day. The animals are energetic, feeding and close.

Wilson, and a wildlife researcher. They're flying ahead of you in their spotter plane.

Just before entering some clay pits, you're told of the reserve's most popular elephants, the matriarch Big Red and her baby, Little Red.

Then there's trouble: poachers! A warden radios your driver with news that Big Red has been wounded and Little Red is missing. Wilson asks your driver to help. He wants your truck to trap the ivory hunters by chasing them out of the preserve and into an eroded gorge. Cutting short your safari, you go on a hot pursuit, hightailing it through gulleys and splashing through geysers. You pass the poachers' tent, where a fire is still smoldering and tusks are scattered about.

Moments later it pays off. As you come to a small clearing, you see the poachers being held at gunpoint, still inside their muddy Land Rover. A baby elephant stands in the back of a second truck. Little Red is safe!

You rejoin the main road and head to the warden's office.

The story makes the trips more consistent, but in this case, fantasy just can't compete with the real thing.

FUN FACTS 》 Disney created the rutted road by coloring concrete to look like soil, then rolling tires through it and tossing in dirt, stones and twigs. 》 The acacias are really Southern live oaks with close-cropped crew cuts. 》 Not everything is real. There's a reason your driver says the termite mounds are 'as hard as concrete.' Those ostrich eggs are also tough to crack. 》 Why does the savannah appear to go on forever? Because the horizon is actually Walt Disney World's 300-acre tree farm, an area not accessible to guests. 》 Animal boundaries include hidden fences, moats and trenches. 》 The safari has the largest collection of Nile hippos, and African elephants, in North America. 》 The animals respond to sound cues to come in at night. Elephants hear (and feel) beating drums. 》 The entire area used to be a flat cow pasture. Disney brought in 10,000 truck loads of dirt and 4 million plants and trees. 》 Kilimanjaro Safaris is the largest attraction at any Disney park. 》 The trucks run on propane.

22 min. Capacity: 1,344. Avg. wait: 20 min. early morning, 45 min. peak afternoon. Fastpass available. ECV users must transfer to a wheelchair. Assistive listening; handheld and activated captioning. Debuted: 1998.

FUN FINDS ❶ A grouping of black-faced royal ibis and East African crowned cranes wander a small habitat behind the attraction's Fastpass machines and to the right of the standby queue. ❷ When the phone rings in the safari office (just inside the standby queue), a machine answers it with the message "Harambe Wildlife Preserve... When it comes to safaris, we go wild!" ❸ The deflated hot-air balloon of the Kinga balloon-safari business (advertised on Harambe posters) is stored in the rafters above the queue. ❹ "Prehistoric" tribal drawings are visible on the gate just past the flamingos and on rocks to your right as you pass the lions.

Riding in one of the attraction's open-sided trucks, a Kilimanjaro Safaris guest videos an elephant dusting itself just a few yards away

▶ Photos are tough. The bouncy ride makes it hard to keep your camera still.

Pangani Forest Exploration Trail

✔ Streams and waterfalls weave through the lush grounds of this self-guided tour of fascinating African animals. It's divided into eight areas.

You'll get a good view of black-and-white colobus monkeys and a yellow-backed duiker at an outdoor hut called the **Endangered Animal Rehabilitation Centre.** Few Americans have ever seen an okapi, but you will at an **observation blind** that also has Stanley cranes. Two colonies of naked mole rats crawl from room to room in "study burrows" in a huge wall display inside a replica **research station.** Other animals include cute spiny mice, a pancake tortoise and a fire skink. You can open some drawers of the research cabinets to find collections of preserved butterflies, feathers, shells, small skulls (including those of bush pigs and dwarf crocodiles), even giant beetles, scorpions and tarantulas.

You never notice that you enter an **aviary,** a rainforest-like screened-in area with a waterfall and pond. Two dozen species of exotic birds fly above you, rest in the trees and scurry on the ground. Don't miss the gigantic nest of the hammercop stork or the hanging homes of taveta golden weavers. A fish-viewing area features a 4-foot-long lungfish.

A 40-foot glass wall makes for a great underwater **hippo viewing area** — especially early when the 100,000-gallon tank is clear. Sometimes, if you're quiet, the hippos come right to the window.

Meerkats stand guard and dig burrows at the **savannah overlook,** which you view from a thatch hut. Gerenuk roam nearby; meerkat and warthog skulls are on display. Next is a **gorilla blind,** then a suspension bridge leads to two **outdoor gorilla habitats.** One side has a family (a silverback, two moms and three kids); the other a bachelor troupe. The gorillas are most active early, when they eat, drink, slap heads and chase each other.

The word "pangani" is Swahili for "place of enchantment."

Meerkats stand guard along the Pangani Forest Trail

▶ The fish on display often suck up small pebbles and spit them out. Kids break up.

Animal Kingdom shopping guide

APPAREL Character Costumes: Creature Comforts *(Discovery Island)* has the best selection of children's pirate and Minnie costumes, as well as a create-your-own-crown station. Island Mercantile *(Discovery Island)* stocks pirate costumes. **Children's Wear:** The park's children's wear store, Creature Comforts *(Discovery Island)* has collections for kids and infants. Mombasa Marketplace *(Africa)* and Island Mercantile *(Discovery Island)* have some shirts. **Fashion:** Disney Outfitters *(Discovery Island)* is Animal Kingdom's adult clothing store, a fashion shop with stylish men's and women's apparel. The womenswear selection often has many cute and stylish items. Don't miss the earrings; some are from Kenya. **Footwear:** Island Mercantile *(Discovery Island)* has adult and children's shoes. Creature Comforts *(Discovery Island)* has children's shoes. The Kali Cart *(Asia)* has sandals. **Sports Apparel:** Disney Outfitters *(Discovery Island)* has jerseys with Disney characters. **T-shirts and headwear:** Island Mercantile *(Discovery Island)* has the most T-shirts and lots of hats. For attraction-specific items check the Dino Institute gift shop *(DinoLand U.S.A., at Dinosaur)*, Kali Cart *(Asia, at Kali River Rapids)* and Serka Zong Bazaar *(Asia, at Expedition Everest)*.

ART The Art of Disney boutique at Disney Outfitters *(Discovery Island)* stocks Disney posters, fine-quality lithographs and "big figs," two foot-high figurines of Mickey, Donald and other classic characters. It also has beautiful painted ostrich eggs, Lenox porcelain figurines and oil paintings. Mombasa Marketplace *(Africa)* features authentic items from Kenya and Zimbabwe, such as hand-painted gift boxes, painted gourds and soapstone carvings.

BOOKS Island Mercantile *(Discovery Island)* has a small selection of bestselling paperbacks, hardcovers and Disney titles. General books about animals are at Out of the Wild *(Conservation Station)* and at the Rainforest Cafe gift shop. Creature Comforts *(Discovery Island)* has some general Disney books for children. Mombasa Marketplace *(Africa)* has books about Africa. The Dino Institute gift shop *(DinoLand U.S.A., at Dinosaur)* has —can you guess? — dinosaur titles. Serka Zong Bazaar *(Asia, at Expedition Everest)* has Mt. Everest books.

CANDY Beastly Bazaar *(Discovery Island)* has chocolates, cookies, gummies, lollipops, jellybeans, chocolate-covered pretzels, sugar sticks and taffy.

CHRISTMAS Disney Outfitters *(Discovery Island)* has a year round Christmas corner with ornaments, stockings and other items.

HOUSEWARES The park's housewares shop is Beastly Bazaar *(Discovery Island)*. It has some great kitchenware and home accessories and nice frames. Island Mercantile *(Discovery Island)* sells frames, photo albums, mugs and snowglobes. Mombasa Marketplace *(Africa)* and the Outpost shop *(Entrance Plaza)* have a few items. Garden Gate Gifts *(The Oasis)* has picture frames.

JEWELRY AND WATCHES Disney Outfitters *(Discovery Island)* sells fine jewelry and watches. The open-air Mandala Gifts stand *(Asia)* has a nice collection of casual jewelry.

PET PRODUCTS Beastly Bazaar *(Discovery Island)* has Disney-themed pet bowls and dishes, clothes, collars, leashes, toys and treats. Island Mercantile *(Discovery Island)* has a smaller collection.

PINS The park's best selection is on the cart in front of Island Mercantile *(Discovery Island)*.

TOYS The park has several good toy spots. Island Mercantile *(Discovery Island)* has a large selection of Disney playthings, including animal plushies, Disney character plushies outfitted in safari garb, video games, DVDs and art supplies. Chester and Hester's Dinosaur Treasures *(DinoLand U.S.A.)* has a surprising toy selection, including a create-your-own Mr. Potato Head station as well as many dinosaur-themed toys. The Dino Institute gift shop *(DinoLand U.S.A., at Dinosaur)* has toy Time Rovers from the attraction and hand-held snapping dino heads. Mombasa Marketplace *(Africa)* has some great non-Disney animal plushies that include cheetahs, elephants, flamingos, giraffes, hippos, parrots and tigers. Cute-as-a-button Yeti plushies are at Serka Zong Bazaar *(Asia, at Expedition Everest)*. The Rainforest Cafe gift shop *(Entrance Plaza)* sells a wide variety of animal-themed plushies and toys. The most unique toy in the park: the awesome Indonesian dragon kites at the Mandala Gifts stand *(Asia)*.

Pleased to meet you. A goat nuzzles the authors' daughter at the Affection Section petting zoo.

Rafiki's Planet Watch

✔ Visiting this animal-care section of the park can be exhausting. To see it means walking to a train station, waiting for a train, taking it to another station and then trekking down a long path. Once you reach the main building, you stay on your feet. To leave, you hike back.

In other words, Rafiki's a beast.

Still, for animal lovers it's terrific. Rafiki's Planet Watch is one of the few places on Disney property where you enter a world that's totally real.

Named after the wise shaman mandrill in the 1994 film "The Lion King," the area features **Conservation Station**, a serious science center with a lot to see. In the mornings, observation windows let you look in on medical procedures on animals up to 500 pounds — expect to see anything from a bandage change on a goat to a root canal on a gorilla. Vets and cast members explain what's going on. Usually about three animals are brought in each morning.

Other windows peer in on researchers studying elephant vocalizations and tracking a sea turtle off the Florida coast.

Adjacent exhibits include a butterfly room, a food preparation area and arachnid, insect and reptile displays. All are typically staffed by friendly, informative cast members.

WITH WHISTLES THAT SOUND like wounded piccolos, the stubby locomotives are replicas of an actual 19th-century engine from the Indian Peninsula Railroad. Built by England's Horwich Locomotive Works, the original featured an Aspinwall side-tank 2-4-2 design. Authentically rusty, with bicycles, fuel, luggage and other supplies lashed on top, Disney's three "Eastern Star Railway" trains were built in 1997 by Severn Lamb Ltd., in Alchester, England.

▶ Take the first train of the day and you'll probably see an exam-room procedure.

You can zoom in on the park's primates, elephants, giraffes and other animals with remote-control Animal Cams. You'll hear rain, booming thunder and buzzing insects in the Song of the Rainforest exhibit, a group of cool, dark, family-sized audio booths.

Eco Hero kiosks let you "speak" with Dr. Jane Goodall or George Schaller of the Tibet Wildlife Reserve. A Caring for the Wild exhibit includes Dr. Goodall's telescope and notebooks of Dian Fossey. A short film narrated by Rafiki offers a look at endangered creatures.

Cast members often play games with kids (including the ever-popular "Poopology") and bring out animals such as lizards, owls, parrots and snakes.

Meet-and-greet characters include Pocahontas, Rafiki and Stanley.

An adjacent petting zoo, **Affection Section** features domestic animals. Roaming free are African pygmy, San Clemente and Nigerian dwarf goats and Gulf Coast native and Tunis sheep. Behind a fence is a Dexter cow, a llama, two rare Guinea hogs and two Sicilian miniature donkeys. The largest goat, a brownish-gray fella named Luke, will steal stuff right out of your pockets.

To get to the area, you take a train from the Harambe Village station in the park's Africa section. Called the **Wildlife Express**, it runs past Disney's "Jurassic Park"-style animal-care facilities.

The long walkway is **Habitat Habit,** a series of signs and displays that offers ways to help foster conservation and attract animals to your backyard. The highlight is a display of cotton-top tamarins. There's also a Kid's Discovery Club spot, a scavenger hunt designed for children ages 3 to 8.

FUN FINDS ❶ Plastered with posters, the walls of the Harambe station are stenciled "Affixing of Advertisements is Forbidden." ❷ Ankole cattle skulls are strapped on the front of the locomotives. ❸ Impressions of a bird, fish, insect, man, shell, snail, reptile, "Lion King" main character Simba and the Tree of Life in the walkway under the Habitat Habit pavilions come together in a Circle of Life as you reach Conservation Station. ❹ In the restrooms, signs on the back of the stall doors give you The Scoop on Poop. In the men's room, placards above the urinals offer the Whiz Quiz. (Did you know elephants pee 20 gallons a day?)

FUN FACTS 》 Complete with a corrugated-metal water tank, the train's African depot is patterned after British structures built in East Africa during the early 1900s. Next to the formal station is a local plaster-and-thatch addition. 》 Why such a fancy train? Because its track was originally designed to be a safari of its own, before the care facilities grew larger than anticipated. 》 The animals shown in the mural above the Conservation Station entrance represent some of the species helped by Disney's Wildlife Conservation Fund. 》 Luke the goat once ate a guest's $5 bill. 》 The thatched-roof huts that sit along the return-train track are authentic. They were made by hand in Indonesia.

Reach out and touch. Conservation Station cast members often bring out snakes and other critters.

▶ Have questions? Cast members cheerfully discuss animal nutrition and health care.

An owl stars in a Flights of Wonder preshow

Kali River Rapids

✓ Ready to get soaked? You should be if you board this rafting ride, which simulates a trip down a threatened rainforest river. Water slops and sprays into your boat as you bob over rapids and through geysers. Soon there's trouble — illegal loggers are destroying the landscape and filling the river with debris. Then you go over a waterfall and splash down the river. *6 min. Capacity: 240. Avg. wait: 15 min. early morning; 45 min. peak afternoon. Fastpass available. ECV users must transfer. Height restriction: 38 in. Debuted: 1999.*

FUN FINDS ❶ The third queue room (Mr. Panika's Shop) offers "Antiks Made to Order." ❷ Pop music star Michael Jackson and the Nike swoosh logo appear on the murals in the last queue room. Jacko rides a raft named the Sherpa Surfer; the Nike icon is painted on a girl's white shirt on the raft Khatmandoozy. The murals were created in Nepal by a fan of Jackson and the shoe company.

Flights of Wonder

Huge birds fly within inches of the audience during this shaded outdoor show, which demonstrates the natural behaviors of cranes, hawks, vultures and other species. The presentation focuses on endangered and threatened birds but has many fun moments. After the host throws a grape in the air for a hornbill to catch, he asks for a child to come down and try it. "I'll toss the grape," he says, "you fly up and get it." Sit in the front center or near an aisle and a bird may fly right over you. *25 min. Capacity: 1,150. Avg. wait: 15 min. ECV and wheelchair accessible. Assistive listening. Debuted: 1998.*

Baloo Me Away, Papa-Do-Ron-Rani and So Sari are among the names of Kali River Rapids rafts

▶ Take your river trip at the end of the day. If you get soaked, it won't matter.

Maharajah Jungle Trek

✓ A re-creation of a decaying hunting lodge turned conservation station, this series of Asian animal exhibits combines exotic wildlife with the architecture of India and Nepal. The trail takes you past a Komodo dragon; into a megabat pavilion; alongside tapir, antelope and tiger habitats; and through a lush garden aviary.

You can skip the bats if you wish, but there's nothing to be afraid of. These are fruit bats, not vampires. They have no interest in people and can't fit through the bars of the viewing area.

Don't miss the tigers — they're often climbing hills, ducking under bushes or scanning the landscape for prey, behaviors you don't see in a regular zoo.

One of Disney's best facades, the buildings and surroundings tell a story of a king and his three sons. As shown in paintings at the second tiger area, one was an architect and built the structures, the second a nature lover who planted the gardens, the third a tiger hunter. The lodge and its forest were later given to locals, who use it today as a wildlife refuge.

FUN FINDS ❶ Just past the footbridge, an environmental history of man is shown in a sequence of stone carvings on a wall to your right. Man emerges out of the water; comes to a paradise rich with wildlife; chops down its tree; experiences floods, death and chaos; and finally gains happiness when he learns

An Asian tiger roams the ruins of an ancient royal hunting lodge at the Maharajah Jungle Trek

to respect nature. ❷ Immediately afterward you enter the tomb of Anantah, the first ruler of the mythical Anandapur kingdom. His ashes are said to be in the large fertility urn in the middle of the room.

FUN FACTS ❯❯ The tiger pool is kept at 70 degrees, and includes fish for the tigers to catch. ❯❯ The bridge over the tiger habitat is actually a wall that separates the carnivores from an area of barred geese. ❯❯ The aviary "weeds" are frayed by hand for a consistent look.

▶ Bats feed first thing in the morning; tigers often play in the water at closing time.

asia

An 80-foot drop highlights your trip aboard the Expedition Everest tea train

The train is rusty. The mountain looks thousands of feet tall. And you can't see the Yeti until the very last second.

As one 8-year-old girl put it, "That monster was like 100 feet tall!" Actually, he's only 18.

What begins as a peaceful trip through a forest turns into a tense chase through a mountain. It doesn't go upside-down, but your 4,000-foot journey climbs nearly 200 feet in the air, stops twice, switches direction, takes an 80-foot drop and hits a top speed of 50 mph. "It's a ride for the entire family," says executive designer Joe Rhode. "It's just a *fast* ride for the entire family."

If you can, ride it at night. The mountain is lit in eery orange and purple, but the track stays dark. You never know where you're at, or where you're going.

Expedition Everest

✓ "I don't know, Charlie. This looks overwhelming to me." Grabbing her husband's arm, the thirtyish blonde stood under waving prayer flags as she looked up at the mountain. She couldn't see what was inside it, but she could hear screams and a distant roar. Every minute or so, out flew a runaway train.

A modern Disney megaride, Expedition Everest combines some mischievous Disney mind games with coaster-like thrills and the excitement of a close encounter of the hairy kind. Aboard an out-of-control railcar that races forward and backward, you swoop into the unknown world of the Yeti — the mythical Himalayan creature also known as the Abominable Snowman.

But it's the mental tricks that psych you out. The exotic village looks real.

A MONSTER MYTH To deepen your experience Disney has built a full back story — a tale of a mythical creature, weird accidents, wise villagers and clueless entrepreneurs.

The story — what Disney calls The Legend of the Forbidden Mountain, and has hidden details of throughout the standby queue* — begins in the 1920s, a time when tea plantations flourished in the mountains of the mythical Asian kingdom of Anandapur. Private rail lines carried the tea to villages, where it was shipped to distant markets. The Royal Anandapur Tea Co. used one such route extensively through the early 1930s, sending "steam-donkey" trains through the mysterious mountains to the village of Serka Zong.

*If you use a Fastpass you miss much of the back story. You skip the temple, store and museum because, as the story goes, you have already booked your trip and gotten your provisions.

▶ Get your Fastpasses early. A day's entire supply of passes is often gone by noon.

Starting in 1933, however, the railroad was plagued with accidents. Some residents drew a connection between the mishaps and increasing British expeditionary attempts to reach the summit of nearby Mt. Everest, invoking the spirit of the Yeti, the mythical, monstrous creature that guards the sacred area. By 1934, equipment breakdowns and strange track snaps caused the tea company to pull up stakes.

The legend of a guardian beast continued to loom among locals, coming to a head in 1982 with the tragic disappearance of the Forbidden Mountain Expedition.

Cut to today. Bob, a Bohemian American who has wandered into Serka Zong, has decided to set up shop. A hippie who came to Asia many years ago, Bob loves the village's Hare Krishna vibe but doesn't believe in the Yeti.

To earn a living, he has teamed up with a local entrepreneur, Norbu. Together they have restored the old railroad to create Himalayan Escapes Tours and Expeditions, a business marketed as a way to help trekkers get to Everest in a new way. Instead of hiking for two weeks through the foothills and over the smaller ranges, now climbers can get to the foot of Everest in just a few hours, riding safely and quickly on Bob and Norbu's quaint old steam train through the scenic Forbidden Mountain.

The enthusiastic duo have just put on a loud and colorful show for their grand opening. Government officials trumpeted the venture as "a landmark enterprise sparking a new era of prosperity and opportunity for Serka Zong."

Now you enter in the story. You've decided to take a trekking

Fair warning. Advisories from frightened locals try to convince you to cancel your trip.

trip up to Mt. Everest. Being a weekend warrior, you've heard about Himalayan Escapes and its short-cut train, and have made your way to Serka Zong. As you enter the village, however, locals have fervently posted warnings on the rocks and buildings.

Undeterred, you walk into Bob's office, the converted first floor of his two-story apartment. Crammed with mountaineering gear, this is where you book your trip, get your permit and meet your guide. Unfortunately, Bob has stepped out for a moment — a sign on his chair reads "Be right back" — so you move on, deciding to head out on your own.

You work your way through the village and to the train station. It's easy to find your way, thanks to the many handy little signs Bob has taped up.

First you come upon a temple. Carved with images of the Yeti in its columns and eaves, it's been erected by villagers out of respect to the creature.

Next you enter Tashi's General Store and Bar, a chance to get provisions for your trek as well as relax for a moment with a pot of tongba, an alcoholic, tea-like brew that could make you see things that aren't actually there.

Then you pass through the village's Yeti museum, an old tea warehouse that's filled with artifacts so realistic you may forget they're all fake. Included are the mangled climbing equipment, shredded tent and fang-punctured canteens that are the only remains of a 1982 expedition, as well as a cast of the creature's footprint. It's run by Professor Pumba Dorjay, a conservation biologist who believes the creature could indeed be real.

Finally you're at the train station, where Norbu and Bob's refurbished Anandapur Rail Service is destined for the foothills of Mount Everest. The hissing transport train has just pulled in and there's an open seat reserved for you. So you board, ready for your calm journey through the mountains.

And that's just what you get. At first.

TRANQUILITY, THEN TERROR Your journey begins as a calm ride. The train rolls over a little hill and around some gentle corners as it passes through bamboo forests and fern groves.

Heading up through an old stone monastery, you do hear some ominous music and maybe a glimpse of a weird totem or mural, but everything is still just hunky dory as you continue into the high, cold (really!) air.

Yeti? Yeah, right.

Then it happens.

Just as you reach the top of the mountain, your train stops. It has to — the rails in front of it have been ripped into a gnarled mass of twisted metal. In a fit of rage, the Yeti has torn apart the track!

As you notice huge footprints in the snow, and a vulture eyeing you from above, your train sits there. Silently.

Suddenly, it loses its grip. You slide backward, careening into a black hole in the mountain's center. But that track leads nowhere, too: you see the skulking shadow of the Yeti smashing it.

Fortunately, your train again breaks loose, sliding forward on still a different track. You drop out of the mountain to safety, only to circle right back in.

Now you meet the Yeti face-to-muzzle. No longer a hypothetical hair man, the massive, mean, monster machine is right in front of you, staring you down. He's ripped up this track too, but just as he takes a swipe at you... you miraculously drop down to another track and hightail it back to the village.

THREE MOUNTAINS IN ONE In reality, the mountain is three free-standing structures. One is the ride, a dynamic system with internal framing that comes all the way down to the foundation. The second is the building, with its beams and columns. The third is the Yeti, with its own independent supports. Though intertwined like spaghetti, the three structures don't touch. If they did, the mountain's plaster and stucco would

▶ Sit in the back for the wildest ride. You'll get whipped harder and fall faster.

flake off. "In some cases we ran building beams down the middle of A-frame columns that support the ride," says project manager Mike Lentz.

Engineering the ride took 15 track designs and more than a year to figure out completely. "I've been here 15 years," says technical supervisor Mark Mesko, "and I've never been through a design collaboration like that."

3 min. Capacity: 170. Avg. wait: 30 min. early morning; 90 min. peak afternoon. Fastpass available, often sold out by noon. Access: ECV and wheelchair users must transfer. Height restriction: 44 in. Fear factor: High. The lift rises high over the ground, you travel backwards in total darkness for 10 sec.; the ride includes one steep, turning drop. Best ages: 8 and up. Debuted: 2006.

FUN FINDS ❶ Plaster on the Fastpass building and gift shop simulates the Himalayan building material of dried yak dung. **❷** A bulletin board note on the wall of Gupta's Gear (left of the main village) reads "Billy — It's a small world after all! Met your brother on the trail... Mikey." **❸** Steam escapes from the train's boiler after it pulls into the boarding area. **❹** It pulls out with a "toot-toot!" **❺** The Yeti's claw marks and footprints appear in the snow to your right at your first stop. **❻** When you stop in the cave, watch the track in front of you. You'll see it flip over.

FUN FACTS 》》 The mountain has 1,800 tons of steel, 18.7 million pounds of concrete, 2,000 gallons of stain and paint and 200,000 square feet of rock work. **》》** The Yeti has a potential thrust of 260,000 pounds of force — more than a 747 airliner. It's Disney's most advanced Audio Animatronics creature. **》》** Much of the queue-line woodwork, including the entire Yeti temple, was handcrafted by Himalayan artists. **》》** The Buddha statues, Nepalese Coke bottles, desk phone and pot-bellied stoves are among 8,000 authentic items Disney imported from Asia. **》》** The 6-acre area has 900 bamboo plants and 100 types of bushes. **》》** The buildings were aged with blowtorches, chainsaws and hammers. **》》** "Serka Zong" is Tibetan for "fortress of the chasm."

YETIS ARE NOT REAL. Scientists worldwide agree there is no credible evidence of an animal roaming the Himalayas that is not an already identified mammal. Some scholars say a Yeti is probably a golden monkey, a Himalayan primate that shares the mythical creature's face, hairy body, blue skin and ability to live in cold climates. The Yeti legend, however, is quite real. For hundreds of years, Himalayan natives have told stories about a humanoid monster that fiercely guards the area around Mt. Everest. The reports increased in the early 20th century, when Westerners began to climb the mountains and reported seeing an "Abominable Snowman."

One of the most famous Western reports appeared in 1925. Traveling with a British geological expedition at about 15,000 feet, Greek photographer N.A. Tombazi saw a large creature moving in some lower slopes. Though it was perhaps a thousand feet away, Tombazi reported its movement was "exactly like a human being, walking upright and stopping occasionally to uproot or pull at some dwarf rhododendron bushes." Tombazi couldn't take its picture, but two hours later he reached the area and found 15 large footprints. Tombazi described them as "similar in shape to those of a man, but only six to seven inches long by four inches wide. The marks of five distinct toes and the instep were perfectly clear... undoubtedly those of a biped."

Western interest in the Yeti peaked decades later. Sir Edmund Hillary, who climbed Everest in 1953, led a 1960 trip attempting to prove, or disprove, the Yeti's existence. Sponsored by the World Book Encyclopedia, the expedition was outfitted with infrared film and trip-wire and time-lapse cameras. It found nothing.

But the myth lived on. The villain-turned-good-guy of 1964's stop-motion "Rudolph the Red-Nosed Reindeer" is a Yeti named Bumbles. Disney added Yetis to Disneyland's Matterhorn bobsled ride in 1978, and the 2001 Disney/Pixar film "Monsters Inc." includes a disgruntled one voiced by John Ratzenberger. "'Abominable!'" he complains. "Why can't they call me the 'Adorable Snowman,' or the 'Agreeable Snowman,' for crying out loud? I'm a nice guy!" Today the legend still lives in Nepal, where the Yeti has a religious meaning to some and is a tourist money maker.

The term "Abominable Snowman" was coined by mistake. While exploring the Himalayas in 1921, British Lt. Col. C.K. Howard-Bury spotted what he thought were gray wolves. When his Sherpa guides told him their prints were those of a "met-teh," or "man-sized wild creature," he misheard them to say "metoh-kangmi," or "snow creature." Reporting this incident, British newspaper editor Henry Newman quoted the words as "metch kangmi," which he said meant "abominable or filthy man of the snow."

▶ Size a concern? Test out a dummy train car to the left of the gift shop.

© DISNEY

Too close for comfort. An angry carnotaurus threatens guests riding a Dinosaur Time Rover.

Dinosaur

✓ You'll remember the last second for days — a ferocious dinosaur gets right in your face and lets loose with an unearthly roar. The rest of this dark indoor ride is almost as tense.

You start off in the rotunda of the Dino Institute Discovery Center, a parody of the Smithsonian's National Museum of Natural History. As you pass earnest murals and displays, a multimedia show explains how an asteroid wiped out the dinosaurs long ago.

In the Orientation Room you meet Director Helen Marsh ("Cosby" mom Phylicia Rashad) via a video hookup. She shows you the Time Rover, a vehicle that will take you back on a peaceful visit to the Age of the Dinosaurs.

But her assistant has a different plan. Once Marsh leaves the room, Dr. Grant Seeker (Wallace Langham, of television's "CSI") secretly reprograms her computer to send you back to a time just before the asteroid strikes, to bring an iguanodon to the present.

Boarding your vehicle, your first stop is a flashing, smoky time tunnel. You emerge 65 million years earlier in a dark prehistoric forest. As you careen forward you see many dinosaurs, including an alioramus swallowing its dinner.

A McDonald's poster outside the Dino Institute shows a scene from the indoor ride

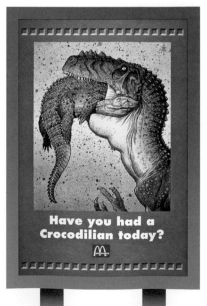

Have you had a
Crocodilian today?

THEORIES OF EXTINCTION

ASTEROID IMPACT

CLIMATE CHANGES

EGG-EATING MAM

THE DINO INSTITUTE

DISEASE

A queue-line mural parodies a stuffy museum

Suddenly a huge carnotaurus starts chasing you. Then it gets worse — your power starts to fail. As a massive meteor destroys your trail, it appears that you, too, are about to become extinct.

In a final burst of speed, you find your iguanodon, narrowly miss the last lunge of the carnotaurus and crash back to the present. Security monitors show you did indeed pick up the iguanodon.

3 min. 30 sec. Capacity: 144. Avg. wait: none early morning, 30 min. peak afternoon. Fastpass available. ECV and wheelchair users must transfer. Assisted listening, video captioning. Height restriction: 40 in. Fear factor: Intense. Debuted: 1998 (as Countdown to Extinction).

FUN FINDS ❶ Just outside the building, a dedication plaque is dated April 22, 1978 — exactly 20 years before the attraction opened. ❷ The Smithsonian parody includes a diorama with an obvious plastic rat glued to an obvious plastic tree, beneath which swim plastic fish in a plastic pond. ❸ Dr. Seeker claims flash photography "interferes with the homing signal." ❹ Actually an above-ground warehouse, the "underground research facility" is cooler than the earlier rooms, and has flickering lights. ❺ Monitors in the gift shop show the iguanodon continuing to wander the building. ❻ A cast of an ancient sea turtle hangs over the gift shop.

FUN FACTS ❯❯ An "enhanced motion vehicle," your Time Rover gets its lurching movements from 3,000 PSI of hydraulic pressure. On-board tanks hold 100 gallons of fluid. ❯❯ An iguanodon named Aladar starred in Disney's 2000 film, "Dinosaur."

Dino-Sue

A cast of the largest, most complete tyrannosaurus rex fossil ever found (Sue, uncovered in South Dakota in 1990) stands in front of the Dinosaur attraction. Named after paleontologist Sue Hendrickson, the 67-million-year-old creature is estimated to have been 45 feet long and 14 feet tall. Much of the real fossil's bonework (now at Chicago's Field Museum) was done in the late 1990s in front of Disney guests, where today's Dino-Rama carnival sits.

morning; 20 min. peak afternoon. Fastpass available. ECV and wheelchair users must transfer. Height restriction: 48 in. Fear factor: There's one steep drop. The spinning can affect those with inner-ear problems. Debuted: 2002.

FUN FINDS ❶ The time portal in the queue is decorated with egg beaters and hubcaps. ❷ As you return to the boarding area Hester says "Please stand up before exiting."

TriceraTop Spin

Toddlers love these friendly dinos, who climb, dive and tilt as they fly around a huge toy top. The colors are vivid — the top alone is orange, blue and red. Extra eye candy includes flying comets and some surprising pop-ups (watch the top). After dark the spokes are outlined with white light bulbs. Add in some manic banjo music and, in the morning or after dark, a nice breeze, and even dad will crack a smile. Each dino seats four, so small families can ride together.

1 min. 30 sec. Capacity: 64. Avg. wait: 15 min. early morning; 30 min. peak afternoon. ECV users must transfer to a wheelchair. Debuted: 2001.

Dumbo XL. Unlike its famous cousin, TriceraTop Spin has room for four... as well as short lines.

Out for a spin. Primeval Whirl guests prepare to start spinning as they head down a drop.

Primeval Whirl

✓ A spoof of the Dinosaur attraction, this spinning roller coaster also takes you back to the age of hitchhiking dinosaurs, but this time in a Time Machine: a 1950s-styled candy-colored car "equipped" with a kitchen timer, clock radio and alarm clock. The scenery combines cheesy cartoon clocks and vortexes with comic dinosaurs and meteors.

It's a wild trip. The ride whips you into your fellow time travelers as it twists along a switchback track. After a big drop (i.e., once the meteors hit) your car starts to spin.

2 min. 30 sec. Capacity: 52 on each of two tracks. Avg. wait: 5 min. early

FUN FACT ❱❱ "Primeval Whirl" is a takeoff of "Primeval World," a straight-faced diorama that appeared in California's Disneyland.

▶ To avoid getting dizzy on Primeval Whirl, stare at the orange radio in front of you.

A dino double! A Fossil Fun Games prize winner.

The Boneyard

Disney's best playground, this faux dig site combines a towering maze of nets, slides and tunnels for elementary-age kids with a sandy pit for preschoolers. "Fossils" include a triceratops, T-rex and wooly mammoth. You may lose sight of your kids, but there's only one exit.

FUN FINDS ❶ The ambient music (pirate radio station W-DINO) includes the Move's 1970 "Brontosaurus" and the 1977 Blue Oyster Cult classic "Godzilla." ❷ Notes sound when you knock on the "xylobone" behind the Jeep. ❸ Dino tracks in the right corner trigger roars when you step on them. ❹ Debates about dinos appear on signs throughout the area.

Fossil Fun Games

It's not that hard to win $15 plushies at three of these silly carnival games. Use your free hand to cradle the front of your gun at the $2 Fossil Fueler water-squirt game. Don't anticipate the popping heads at the $2 Whac-A-Packycephalosaur. Roll the balls softly at the $2 Mammoth Marathon racing derby.

The easiest way to win: Play these three when there is only one other player. You'll have a 50 percent chance of winning a $10 toy. If you have two kids and no one plays against them, your $4 bet has to pay off.

Other games require more luck, such as the extra-bouncy $3 Bronto Score basketball toss or the $3 Comet Crasher ball toss. Smaller prizes can be traded in for larger ones, and everything can be sent to package pickup.

Dark slides are among the finds at the Boneyard

▶ Wacky Packy is the easiest Fossil Fun Game for children.

Finding Nemo — The Musical

✓ "Wow," said the 40-year-old man under his breath, watching the show with his wife. "WOW!!!" said the 3-year-old girl nearby, standing in her seat as she beamed at her older brother.

Singers who somersault as they "swim" high above the stage... giant jellyfish that billow through the theater... a trike-pedaling sting-ray... a chorus line of shimmying sharks... the innovative creativity seems to never end in this Broadway-quality retelling of the 2003 smash-hit movie, "Finding Nemo." With an appeal every bit as awe-inspiring and broad-based as the film, this beautiful spectacle of color, movement and imagination redefines the meaning of the term "puppet show."

The main characters are costumed live singers who act out their roles as they simultaneously operate larger-than-life animated puppets. Peripheral characters are brought to life by other puppetry styles, including Japanese bunraku (one puppet is operated by multiple puppeteers), shadow and rod. Many of the puppets are huge — sea turtle Crush is the size of a Volkswagen, and Nigel the pelican stands 22 feet tall.

The dazzling production also includes acrobats, dancers, animated backdrops and terrifically abstract props, like a fish net comprised simply of six bowed ladders in a circle.

Ah, but what about the music? You've never heard it before. Is that a problem? No. The songs are easily accessible, and presented as fun musical numbers that fit seamlessly into the story, almost as if they were always part of it. Besides, how can you not like a dancing shark?

The production has a big-time pedigree. The puppetry comes from Michael Curry, who did the park's parade floats as well as the puppets in the Broadway version of Disney's "The Lion King." Its songs were written by Robert Lopez, the Tony Award-winning co-composer of the Broadway musical "Avenue Q," and his wife Kristen Anderson-Lopez, co-creator of Broadway's "Along the Way." The show's director is Peter Brosius, the Tony-winning artistic director of The Children's Theatre Company of Minneapolis. Another sign of quality — all 18 actors are singing live. Unlike Walt Disney World's other stage shows, no one here is lip-synching.

The production takes place in the now-enclosed Theater in the Wild, located along the walkway that runs between DinoLand U.S.A. and Asia.

35 min. Capacity: 1,700. Avg. wait: 30 min. to get a great seat. Fastpass available. ECV, wheelchair accessible. Reflective captioning. No photography. Debuted: 2007.

FUN FINDS ❶ As Nemo longs to explore "the big blue world," Marlin warns "Sharks are not our friends, Nemo. Haven't you seen 'Jaws'?" ❷ Later, unsure of his aquarium surroundings, Nemo bangs into the glass. ❸ After the other pet fish welcome Nemo with their "Wannahockaloogie" chant, Peach remarks "I don't know why we can't just say 'Hello.'" ❹ Knocked out after a mine explosion, Dory mumbles "The sea monkey has my money... I'm a natural blue..." ❺ After Crush and the sea turtles perform an elaborate production number, Dory exclaims "Hey look! Turtles!" ❻ She once calls Nemo "TiVo." ❼ As you leave, the movie's "Mine! Mine!" gulls appear to bid you "Bye! Bye!"

IN THE 2003 FILM "Finding Nemo," curious clownfish Nemo defies his overprotective father, Marlin, and swims out to a boat, only to be captured by a diver hunting for aquarium fish. Determined to find his son, Marlin encounters Dory, an absentminded blue tang, as well as sharks, jellyfish and sea turtles. Meanwhile, Nemo, relocated to a fish tank in Sydney, makes new friends who teach him that he's stronger than he thinks, and help him reunite with his dad.

▶ Sit in the middle to see the full spectacle, along the catwalk to be immersed in it.

park puzzler

How much do you really know about Disney's Animal Kingdom?

1) During the Festival of the Lion King, Timon doesn't want the Tumble Monkeys to pack up because it's time for...
a. "The Circle of Life."
b. "Hakuna Matata."
c. "Our snappy South Seas Medley."

2) What song plays in the lobby of the Tree of Life Theater?
a. "Beauty and the Bees."
b. "Herbie and the Fleas."
c. "The Flowers and the Trees."

3) The Dino-Rama character shown at right is named...
a. Carnysaurus.
b. Conniesaurus.
c. Cheesysaurus.

4) The name of the scientist who sends you back in time at the Dinosaur attraction is...
a. Bunsen Honeydew.
b. Tom Morrow.
c. Grant Seeker.

5) Which animal appears in the logo for Disney's Animal Kingdom but not at the park?
a. A dragon.
b. A mouse.
c. A unicorn.

6) According to your driver, how long is your trip supposed to take on Kilimanjaro Safaris?
a. Two weeks.
b. Two months.
c. Two years.

7) What activity is specifically not allowed on the Wildlife Express Train?
a. Cooking.
b. Camping.
c. Fishing.

8) What infamous celebrity is shown riding a raft in the Kali River Rapids queue line?
a. Paris Hilton.
b. Michael Jackson.
c. Mick Jagger.
d. Courtney Love.

9) In Finding Nemo — The Musical, Nemo sings that he wants to explore:
a. A whole new world.
b. The big blue world.
c. Part of your world.

Answers, page 319

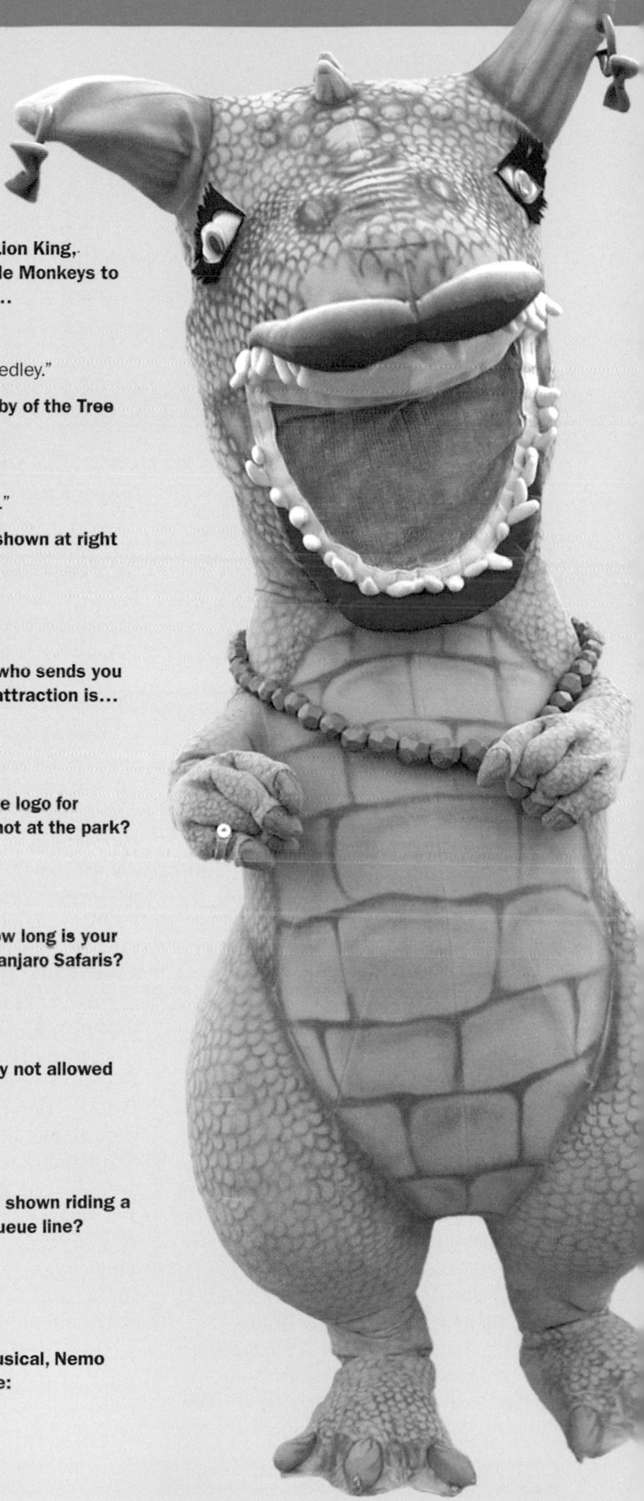

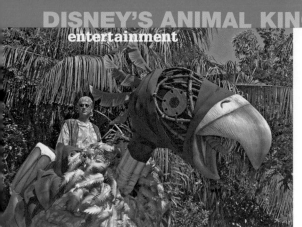

A drummer stands atop a macaw in Mickey's Jammin' Jungle Parade

Mickey's Jammin' Jungle Parade

✔ Towering puppets, whimsical stilt-walkers, colorful Jeeps and Land Rovers, dozens of dancers and infectious music combine to celebrate the harmony between man and animals in this lively procession.

There are 17 floats and vehicles and plenty of Disney characters. It's all up close and personal, on shady, winding pathways that are often just 12 feet wide.

Handcrafted in a leafy motif from what appears to be natural materials, the mechanical puppets include an antelope, chameleon, crane, frog, giraffe, monkey, peacock and wildebeest. The abstract animals move like real creatures: the chameleon sticks out its tongue; the frog jumps. Four drummers ride atop a camel, elephant, kangaroo and macaw.

Dancing down the street are 10 "party animals" (creature-costumed stilt-walkers), 10 "party patrol" safari guides as well as Pluto, Chip 'n' Dale, Timon from Disney's 1994 film, "The Lion King," Terk from 1999's "Tarzan," Baloo and King Louie from 1967's "The Jungle Book," even Brer Bear and Brer Rabbit from the 1946 "Song of the South."

A fun back story ties it all together. With each character riding in his or her own safari truck, Mickey and Rafiki (the mandrill from "The Lion King") are try-ing to take Minnie, Donald and Goofy camping. Trouble is, none of the three know how to pack. Donald totes a leaky boat. Minnie brings steamer trunks of clothes, a dresser, lamp and bathtub. Goofy's the worst: he's packed everything from his bowling trophy to, literally, his kitchen sink.

The catchy "Rhythm of One" soundtrack features Disney versions of the 1954 New Orleans standard "Iko Iko," South African legend Miriam Makeba's 1960s dance classic "Pata Pata" and "Mas Que Nada," the 1966 signature tune of Brazil's Sergio Mendes. "I am you. And you are me," the anchor song goes. "We're just one great big family."

Selected at random each morning, up to 25 park guests also ride in the parade.

Travels in a circle around Discovery Island. It starts, and exits, in Africa, at the gate between the Tusker House restaurant and Kilimanjaro Safaris. 15 min. Choose a viewing spot 30 min. early to get a shady, curbside seat. Special viewing locations available for those in wheelchairs and ECVs. Assistive listening. Debuted: 2001.

FUN FINDS ❶ Minnie's bathtub blows bubbles. ❷ It has a rubber ducky: Donald. ❸ Goofy's hood ornament is his bowling trophy. It topples over as his engine overheats. ❹ Strapped onto Goofy's hood is Aladdin's magic lamp and carpet. ❺ Goofy has a Donald Duck life preserver. ❻ Timon's backpack is full of bugs. ❼ The driver of the hippo rickshaw is the animal's pic-pic bird. ❽ The kangaroo has a spring for a tail. Its drummer sits in its pouch. ❾ The mane and tail of the zebra-costumed stilt-walker are brooms.

FUN FACT ≫ The party animals and safari guides also appear as dancers, stilt-walkers and (hidden) puppeteers at the Festival of the Lion King.

▶ The parade passes through Africa twice — on its way out and back.

Street performers

✓ **The Adventure Begins** is the park's opening ceremony *(Entrance Plaza)*. Rafiki appears at the gate 15 minutes early, then Goofy, Minnie and Pluto lead you from Discovery Island to Kilimanjaro Safaris... **The Adventure Continues** *(Asia and DinoLand U.S.A.)* is a character boat that travels past Flame Tree Barbecue and the DinoLand gate... **Wes Palm** *(Entrance Plaza)* is a roving potted palm that talks (and listens)... Covered in a 10-foot foliage costume, stilt-walking performance artist **DiVine** *(Asia, along the walkway to Africa)* blends into the landscape... Double backflips and mid-air voguing highlight the choreography of the **G-Force** trampoline troupe *(DinoLand U.S.A., at Dinosaur Treasures)*... Kids guess the animal when funnyman **Gitar Dan** *(Rafiki's Planet Watch, at Conservation Station)* sings about it... Botswanans, Namibians and South Africans talk about their homelands at the three-bench **Harambe School** *(Africa, behind the fruit market)*. The 1 p.m. lesson is Harambe history... Vibrant costumes and ritualistic dances make Andes acoustic group **Inkas Wasi** *(Discovery Island, across from Flame Tree Barbecue)* fun to watch as well as listen to... The best limbo dancers and jump-ropers you'll ever see, the **Karuka Acrobats** *(Africa)* also fly through hoops... So unaffected you'd never guess he's a legendary percussionist who once played with B.B. King, **Mor Thiam** ("Chahm") *(Africa)* often invites children to play with him. A master of the goblet-shaped Djembe drum, he's the father of R&B artist Akon... **Pipa the Talking Recycling Can** *(Rafiki's Planet Watch)* chats with guests as he wanders around Conservation Station... Disguised as

Tam Tams of Congo (top), **Inkas Wasi** (above)

three dippy painters, **Smear, Splat & Dip** *(DinoLand U.S.A., at Dinosaur Treasures)* is really a balance and juggling troupe... Turn the beat around: you'll love to feel the percussion of the **Tam Tams of Congo** *(Africa, at Dawa Bar)*, a rousing native quintet who call, dance, shout and whistle... Strolling steel-drum band the **Tropicals** *(Discovery Island)* sometimes plays Disney tunes... Five drum sets, lots of cow bells and a zendrum create the syncopated rhythms of world-music percussionists **The Village Beatniks** *(Discovery Island, across from Flame Tree Barbecue)*.

▶ Guest Relations has the showtimes for all Animal Kingdom performers.

Western lowland gorilla

ANTEATER

A walking vacuum cleaner, the Latin American **giant anteater** (*The Oasis*) sucks up ants and termites with its toothless snout. It can flick its 2-foot tongue 150 times a minute, eat 30,000 insects a day, yet sleep 15 hours a day. Growing up to 9 feet long, an anteater has the largest claws of any mammal and the longest tongue of any mammal for its size. *To protect its claws, an anteater walks on its front knuckles. It uses its tail as a blanket when it sleeps. Though fed a prescribed diet, Disney's anteater still digs for insects.*

Giant anteater

ANTELOPE

The beautiful **bongo** *(Kilimanjaro Safaris)* has white stripes on its chestnut coat. This shy, rarely seen creature is known as the Ghost of the Forest. The largest of all forest antelopes, it can weigh up to 600 pounds. The delicate **gerenuk** *(Pangani Forest Exploration Trail)* stands up to feed on the high leaves of trees. Its hip joints swivel to let its backbone line up with its hind legs. The most agile antelope, the **impala** *(Kilimanjaro Safaris)* can leap up to 10 feet in the air and turn in mid-flight. It can run up to 40 mph and take bounds of almost 40 feet. A male attracts females (and scares off other males) by repeatedly sticking his tongue out, a display known as tongue flashing. The **Patterson's eland** *(Kilimanjaro Safaris)* is the world's largest antelope. It can stand 6 feet tall and weigh 1,500 pounds. The aggressive **sable antelope** *(Kilimanjaro Safaris)* drops to its knees to engage foes with its sizable horns. When at rest, a group of the animals will lie in a circle with its heads facing out, protecting young that lie in the middle. The tiny **Thomson's gazelle** *(Kilimanjaro Safaris)* commonly known as the Tommy, stands only 2 or 3 feet tall, but can run at speeds up to 50 mph. Still, it is the favorite prey of the cheetah. The **white-bearded wildebeest** *(Kilimanjaro Safaris)* is also known as the gnu, the sound of its call. The gregarious animal sleeps in rows, gives birth in large groups and migrates annually in a herd of up to 1.5 million — the world's single largest movement of wildlife. Named for its habit of diving into underbrush when frightened, the chunky **yellow-backed**

duiker ("diver" in Afrikaans) *(Kilimanjaro Safaris)* is the largest duiker, growing up to 3 feet. *Permanently attached, antelope horns are not shed.*

APES

The largest and loudest gibbon, the 3-foot-tall **siamang** *(Asia, at the monument towers between Flights of Wonder and Kali River Rapids)* inflates a sac at its throat to produce a hoot that can reach 113 decibels, nearly as noisy as a jet aircraft at 100 yards. Early most mornings a family's adult female will start a group call that can last 30 minutes. The monogamous mates sometimes sing duets to express affection. Family members often groom each other and usually don't venture more than 30 feet apart. The father shares in raising a baby and takes over child care after an infant's first year. A siamang's arms are longer than its legs, a feature which lets the ape swing through tree branches that can be 30 feet apart.

A crescendo of eerie siren-like whoops is the territorial call of the smaller **white-cheeked gibbon** *(Asia, near the exit to Kali River Rapids)*. It travels up to a mile each day, farther than any other forest ape or monkey. The animal's agility makes it virtually invulnerable to predators, but human activities (rain forest farming, logging and military activities) have destroyed most of its habitat. It lives in southern China, Laos and North Vietnam. Males and juveniles are black with white cheeks. Females and newborns are blond.

The **western lowland gorilla** *(Pangani Forest Exploration Trail)* is the most populous gorilla subspecies, with about 94,000 animals living in the wild. The world's largest and most powerful primate, a gorilla is also the least aggressive, as it is generally shy and peaceful. The iconic chest-beating is just a display. The ape lives in a group of five to 30 animals, of which the most mature male serves as the benevolent dictator. Identified by the silver hair on his back, this "silverback" will even baby sit an infant while mom looks for food.

Like humans, gorillas have fingerprints, 32 teeth, can stand upright, have the same sexual cycle (females menstruate about every 28 days, births happen after 9 months, juveniles mature at around 11 or 12 years), use tools and can learn sign language.

Disney has a family of six gorillas (one silverback, two adult females, three juveniles) plus three bachelors.

BABIRUSA

With a face only a mother could love, the freakish **babirusa** *(The Oasis)* looks like a giant pig with a dental problem. In males, huge upper tusks extend through the snout. Like a macaw, a babirusa eats clay to cleanse its system. Though its name means "pig-deer," a babirusa is more closely related to a hippo. It lives in Indonesia.

BATS

The largest bat in the world, the **Malayan flying fox** *(Maharajah Jungle Trek)* has a wingspan of up to 6 feet, so massive it can't take off from the ground. The **Rodrigues fruit bat** *(Maharajah Jungle Trek)* has a 3-foot span. Bats are the only flying mammals.

Gerenuk

These two species are vegetarians. *The Disney bats cling to their hanging food with their claws and eat it upside down. They groom and lick each other to express affection, often nuzzling snouts. They turn rightside-up to relieve themselves. The bats can sense rain coming. Just before it starts to sprinkle, the bats fold up, just as when it's too hot or sunny*

CAVY

The world's second largest rodent, the **Patagonian cavy** *(The Oasis)* can weigh 25 pounds. Related to a guinea pig, it uses its long legs to run up to 28 mph and leap up to 6 feet. It lives around the Andes mountains of South America.

CHEETAH

Using its long tail for balance, a **cheetah** *(Kilimanjaro Safaris)* can accelerate from 0 to 70 mph in three seconds. The fastest land animal, it can easily outrun any creature, but only over a short distance. Adapted for traction, its claws are only slightly curved and only partially retract. *As*

Rodrigues fruit bat

can go up to two years between meals, using its tail fat for nourishment. Only about 500 are left in the United States, all in southern Florida. *Disney's creature often lies with its mouth wide open to keep cool. A croc has no sweat glands.* Growing even bigger, the **Nile crocodile** *(Kilimanjaro Safaris)* can reach 20 feet long. The aggressive animal will run onto land to snatch prey. Life starts off sweet: hatchlings call to their mother from inside their eggs when ready to hatch, then both parents roll the eggs in their mouths to crack the shells. The mom carries her foot-long newborns in her jaws to water, then guards them for up to six months. *Disney's Nile crocs are trained to come in at night. Keepers ring a bell and dangle food in front of an enclosure.*

DEER

Axis deer *(Discovery Island)* are sure strange. Living in herds of both sexes, the almost-constantly rutting males make loud bugle-like bellows. Meanwhile, the females fight. Like boxing kangaroos, they paw at one another while standing on their hind legs. The world's most endangered deer, the **Elds deer** *(Maharajah Jungle Trek)* lives only in a 15-square-mile marsh around Loktak Lake in Eastern India. Its unusual antlers curve outward then upward and sport at least six points. The **Reeves muntjac** *(The Oasis)* is known as the barking deer, due to the sound it can make when alarmed. The male grows large canine teeth that curl from its lips, like tusks.

DUCKS

One of the smallest diving ducks in the world, the **bufflehead** *(The Oasis)* is less than a foot long. To

the cats naturally hunt in daylight, safari guests see them eyeing intended prey.

CRANES

The **East African crowned crane** *(Discovery Island)* has

East African crowned crane

the perfect camouflage for the tall grass of its wetland habitat: a brush-like crest of golden feathers. It's the only crane that roosts in trees. Listen for its loud, honking trumpets. Standing 6 feet tall, the **sarus crane** *(Maharajah Jungle Trek)* is the world's tallest flying bird. Its wingspan is 8 feet. *The courtship ritual of cranes is one of the animal kingdom's strangest behaviors. A pair will bow toward each other and each will hop, jump, strut and flap its wings as it circles the other. The duo also performs a unison call: a lengthy series of coordinated honks and squawks.*

CROCODILES

Much larger than its alligator cousin, the brawny **American crocodile** *(DinoLand U.S.A.)* can grow up to 15 feet long and weigh 2,000 pounds. It

attract females, a male will puff up its crest, bob its head and show off its diving skills. The duck was originally called the Buffalo Head, a reference to the male's large noggin. The **white-backed duck** *(Pangani Forest Exploration Trail)* can stay under the water for up to 30 seconds. It's an endangered species. With a high-pitched three-note whistle, the **white-faced whistling duck** *(Discovery Island)* sounds like a squeak toy. When it's afraid, it sounds a single note. The bird lives in Africa, the Caribbean and Latin America. Nearly extinct, the **white-winged wood duck** *(Maharajah Jungle Trek)* once thrived in the rainforests of Southeast Asia. Today most of its habitat is gone.

ELEPHANT

The largest land mammal, the **African elephant** *(Kilimanjaro Safaris)* can weigh 11,000 pounds. It has few natural enemies but has been relentlessly hunted for its tusks, a prize that is actually made of the same ingredient as human teeth: ivory dentine.

An elephant's trunk combines a long nose with an upper lip. It can hold up

to 3 gallons of water. Two finger-like projections at the tip can pluck grasses and manipulate small objects. The trunk has 40,000 muscles, more than in a human body.

An African elephant can make a variety of vocal sounds, including low frequency rumbles that are below the human range of hearing, but can be heard by other elephants up to 5 miles away.

An elephant's skin is so sensitive it can feel a fly landing on it.

Females can breed for three to six days every four years. Bulls find mates by listening for female tummy rumbles that can be heard for miles. When mating takes place, the entire herd often takes part in a noisy melee known as the mating pandemonium. Females and calves mill, circle, wave their trunks and trumpet loudly for up to an hour. The gestation period is 21 months.

Three baby elephants have been born at Disney, through both artificial insemination and natural breeding. The first, a male, arrived in 2003.

Reeves muntjac

A female was born in 2004; another female in 2005.

When the breeding program began, Disney baby-proofed its elephant habitat by increasing its shade, closing gaps between boulders and installing a shallow backstage pool that allows the calves to safely explore water and learn to swim. "We're the only zoo in North America that has three African elephant calves on display," reports John Lehnhardt, the park's director of animal operations.

FLAMINGOS

These beautiful birds get their pink color from carotene-rich spirulina, an algae common in brackish lakes in Africa. The paler **greater flamingo** *(Kilimanjaro Safaris)* gets the algae indirectly by eating insects, shrimp and other small creatures that themselves have consumed the algae; the brilliantly colored **lesser flamingo** *(Discovery Island)* eats it directly. Spending much of their day with their heads upside down, flamingos stir

Baby Nadirah nuzzles her mom Donna in 2006

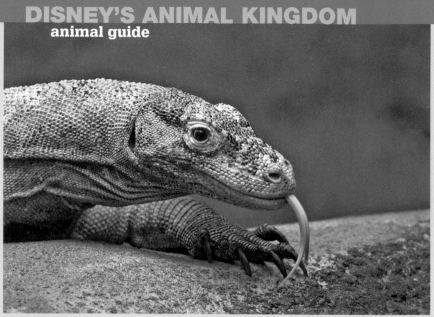

Komodo dragon

up the mud with their webbed feet, then suck and filter the murky water through their bills. *Like most wading birds, a flamingo is most comfortable while standing on one leg, and what appears to be its knee is actually its ankle.*

Gray kangaroo

GIRAFFE

The world's tallest animal, the **reticulated giraffe** *(Kilimanjaro Safaris)* can stand up to 19 feet tall. Its 6-foot legs support a 6-foot torso that's topped by a 6-foot neck and, finally, a foot-high head. It balances with help from an 8-foot tail (the longest of any land mammal) and rests on feet the size of dinner plates: each one is up to a foot wide. It's an interesting creature — a giraffe has a stride of 15 feet and can run up to 45 mph; its tongue can be up to 20 inches long; its heart 2 feet wide; its lungs can hold 12 gallons of air; and its neck has only seven vertebrae, the same number as man. Females give birth standing up. Newborns drop head-first to the ground. Babies average 6 feet tall and grow an inch a day. Although generally quiet, giraffes are not mute. Calves bleat; adults can grunt, hiss, moo and snort. Unlike most grazing animals, a giraffe can't lower its head to the ground without splaying its legs.

GOAT

It's the devil! Well, really it's an **African pygmy goat** *(Rafiki's Planet Watch),* but people have associated it and its relatives with Beelzebub since the animal was domesticated 10,000 years ago. For centuries Satan was thought to be able to transform himself into a goat at will, and is still often portrayed with the creature's hooves and horns. Some farmers once believed that owning a goat would protect them from the devil, or that when a goat could not be found it was meeting with him. Sailors once thought a goat on board would ensure a calm sea, which helped the 18-inch-tall African pygmy goat become common in North America. Its natural barrel shape makes it appear to always be pregnant.

GUINEA FOWL

The **Kenya crested guinea fowl** *(Discovery Island)* is a black bird covered in tiny white polka dots. It's a rare breed of the creature that Egyptians domesticated in 2400 B.C. Renaissance traders often confused it with a turkey. It's known to take an occasional dust bath.

HIPPOPOTAMUS

A cross between a pig and a whale, the chubby **Nile hippopotamus** *(Kilimanjaro Safaris, Pangani Forest Exploration Trail)* spends its day in the water. With its ears, eyes and nose on top of its head, the hippo can keep track of its surroundings while hiding its bulk under the surface. It has webbed feet, and can hold its breath for 12 minutes.

The animal feeds after dark, eating land grasses, leaves and bark. With the largest mouth of any land mammal, it can eat up to 150 pounds of food a night.

An aggressive, territorial animal, the hippo kills more humans than any other creature in Africa. Over a short distance the 6,000-pound animal can outrun a man.

Hippos were once thought to sweat blood. They ooze a pinkish oil that moisturizes and protects their skin from sunburn. Disney's herd is the largest in the country.

White ibis

Ring-tailed lemur

IBIS

Easily identified by its large spoon-shaped bill, the **African spoonbill** *(The Oasis)* fishes for its food by swinging its open bill in the water. The birds have an odd mating ritual. Males will offer a female sticks for her nest. When she accepts one (which isn't often) she has chosen her mate. The behavior is often on display with Disney's birds. The most common bird at Animal Kingdom, the **white ibis** is not one of Disney's creatures. Abundant in Florida, thousands of ibis have flown into the park and stayed for its lush habitat and plentiful food. Hundreds roost each evening in the trees along the Discovery River. The bird is easy to identify by its orange downcurved bill that's as long as its legs. It's the mascot of the University of Miami.

KANGAROOS

The only large mammal that hops, a kangaroo can jump 9 feet in the air, leap 40 feet and reach speeds of 30 mph. Tendons in the back legs act like giant springs. At full speed it can outpace a racehorse. At rest, a kangaroo's weight is supported by the tripod of its hind legs and tail.

A newborn resembles a jelly bean. Only an inch long, the hairless, still-developing baby has no back legs. Called a joey, it climbs into its mother's pouch, where it stays put for nine months. A mother produces different milk for different-aged joeys. In some species, a female can control the progress of her pregnancy so that each newborn has an open teat in her pouch. Gestation typically takes 35 days, but can be delayed for nearly a year. The world's largest marsupial, the **red kangaroo** *(Discovery Island)* can stand 6 and a half feet tall and weigh 200 pounds. It's colored to match the red

Cotton-top tamarin

soil of the Australian desert outback. The red kangaroo can go without drinking as long as green grass is available. The **swamp wallaby** *(The Oasis)* is a small kangaroo, standing no more than 33 inches tall. The **western gray kangaroo** *(Discovery Island)* is the least common large kangaroo in American zoos. *Kangaroos cannot walk backwards. Males box each other to establish dominance. When it's hot, Disney's kangaroos lick their forearms to stay cool.*

KOMODO DRAGON

The world's largest lizard, the **Komodo dragon** *(Maharajah Jungle Trek)* can grow up to 10 feet long and weigh 250 pounds. Using its long, forked tongue as a nose, it picks up scents of animals up to 2 miles away. With a burst of speed that can reach 15 mph,

the dragon can kill its prey by simply biting it… then leisurely following it until it dies. The dragon's saliva contains so much lethal bacteria that death is inevitable. Living in the wild only on a few Indonesian islands, a wild Komodo eats deer, goats, pigs (and other

Komodos) and can go six months without a meal. Because adult dragons cannibalize young ones, juveniles often roll in feces as a deterrent. Young dragons also conduct appeasement rituals, pacing around a feeding circle and lurching from side to side in a "circle of death." *To flee an attacker, a Komodo can vomit the contents of its stomach — which can hold 200 pounds of food — to increase its speed.*

LEMURS

The **collared lemur** *(Discovery Island)* sports reddish-blond muttonchops. Living in a group of up to 30 animals, the **ring-tailed lemur** *(Discovery Island)* uses its long tail as a flag — to tell others where it is or warn them of danger. *Unlike most mammal groups, a lemur family is led by a female. Males compete for her with a stink fight: Each rubs its tail with a smelly odor from its wrist glands, arches its tail over its back and shakes it at another male while baring its teeth. The competition can last an hour. Found only on the island of Madagascar, the primitive primate is named for its big eyes and haunting howl; the word lemur is Latin for ghost.*

African lion

Okapi

LION

Known as the king of beasts, the **African lion** (*Kilimanjaro Safaris*) is the largest African carnivore. Its roar can be heard 5 miles away. Living in a pride of about 15 members, females do the hunting, slowly stalking their prey as a team before sprinting forward in a surprise attack. They can run up to 37 mph and leap up to 40 feet. Males defend the pride; their manes protect their necks in a battle. Lions sleep up to 20 hours a day.

LLAMA

Related to a camel, the **llama** (*Rafiki's Planet Watch*) is a domesticated pack animal. Tamed in the 16th century in the Andes mountains of South America, the sure-footed creature can carry up to 100 pounds. In the 2000 Disney film "The Emperor's New Groove," Emperor Kuzco (David Spade) was turned into a llama by his power-hungry advisor, Yzma (Eartha Kitt).

LUNGFISH

The **African lungfish** (*Pangani Forest Exploration Trail*) can breathe air and crawl. It has two swim bladders that take oxygen from the air when the animal surfaces. It lives in small pools of water that often evaporate, at which time it uses its long, fleshy fins to plod along in the mud. Its ancestors developed true limbs and evolved into early four-legged land animals.

MEERKAT

It takes a village — at least when it comes to meerkats. A type of mongoose, the **slender-tailed meerkat** (*Pangani Forest Exploration Trail*) works with others in organized, multifamily communities of up to 30 individuals. The burrowing animals divide up jobs such as babysitting, searching for food or sentry duty — a chore shared by rotating guards throughout the day.

MONKEYS

One of the smallest monkeys, the **cotton-top tamarin** (*Discovery Island*) is about the size of a squirrel, but can still leap 10 feet. It's named for the puffy crest of white fur on top of its head. Living in Colombia, the creatures mate for life and live as a family. Older siblings help care for the infants. Active most of the day, Disney's tamarins usually take a nap about 4:30 p.m. The world's most colorful mammal and largest monkey, the **mandrill** (*Kilimanjaro Safaris*) is the inspiration for the character Rafiki in Disney's 1994 film "The Lion King." The non-aggressive, social creature bares its teeth as a greeting, not a threat. It makes a huge smile, with the corners of its mouth wide open, exposing its huge canines. The most colorful mandrills are males who have mated with many females. If a mandrill is upset, it may energetically beat the ground.

NAKED MOLE RAT

The giant queen keeps a male harem and rules with brute force, shoving her soldiers and workers around to prod them into action. Everyone's naked, and blind, but all individuals have their own identity — a custom odor achieved by carefully rolling around in the community toilet. Such is the underground world of the **naked mole rat** (*Pangani Forest Exploration Trail*), the only mammal that organizes itself into ant-like colonies. The animal digs with its four buck teeth but doesn't swallow dirt — the teeth are outside of its mouth in front of hairy lips and side skin folds that close completely. Neither a mole nor rat, but plenty naked, the pink, virtually hairless creature is related to a guinea pig.

OKAPI

The only mammal that can lick its own ears and eyelids, the **okapi** (*Kilimanjaro Safaris, Pangani Forest Exploration Trail*) uses its 14-inch tongue for grooming as well as eating. Its odd appearance combines the body and face of a stubby giraffe with the black-and-white legs and rump of a zebra. Related to a giraffe, its head is topped with the same skin-covered knobs and it walks in the same unique way: simultaneously stepping with the front and hind leg on the same side of its body. It sleeps only five minutes a day. The solitary creature lives only in the dense Ituri Forest of the Democratic Republic of Congo, an area so remote the species wasn't discovered until 1900.

White rhinoceros

OSTRICH

The world's largest bird, the **ostrich** *(Kilimanjaro Safaris)* has 2-inch-wide eyes, the largest of any land creature. Its eggs, the largest of any living animal, can weigh nearly 2.5 pounds each. An ostrich doesn't fly but can run up to 45 mph — faster than any other two-legged animal. To stay cool the ostrich fans itself with its wings. *An ostrich doesn't really stick its head in the sand. To hide, it lays its head on the ground.*

Asian tiger

OTTER

It's hard to leave the **Asian small-clawed otter** habitat *(Discovery Island)* when the animals play or feed. The world's smallest otters, they chase each other on the ground at speeds up to 18 mph and swim after each other in the water. They are especially cute when they wash up after a meal: their unique (for otters) non-webbed paws look like hands.

RHINOCEROS

It's been on earth for 60 million years, but today only 10,000 are left — less than 15 percent of the number that roamed Africa as late as 1970. Why? Because poachers continually kill it for its horn — an alleged aphrodisiac in Chinese folk medicine despite the fact that it's really just a big toenail. Growing from the rhino's skin, it's made of the same material (keratin) as a human nail and grows back when you cut it. The nearly extinct **black rhino** *(Kilimanjaro Safaris)* is a solitary herbivore that uses its hooked lip like a finger to select leaves and twigs. It can live 40 years. The larger **white rhino** *(Kilimanjaro Safaris)* is a brownish-gray creature that gets its name from its wide upper lip — "white" is a mistranslation of "wijt," the Afrikaans word for "wide." *Rhinos wallow in mud to protect their skin, which is sensitive to insects and sunburn. They can charge at 40 miles per hour.*

STORKS

The world's largest stork, the 5-foot **marabou stork** *(Pangani Forest Exploration Trail)* has a 14-inch bill and an 8.5-foot wingspan. Known as the world's ugliest bird, it has a pickax bill, two unsightly pouches and a naked cranium studded with scab-like spots. The carrion-eating critter communicates by clattering its bill; it has no voice box. The **painted stork** *(Discovery Island)* gets a bright pink patch on its back during breeding season. The male **saddle-billed stork** *(Discovery Island, Kilimanjaro Safaris)* has a yellow wattle; the female yellow eyes. The best-known stork species, the **white stork** *(Discovery Island)* lives in African grasslands. The German legend about the bird bringing babies exists because for centuries it has migrated from Africa to nest on northern German chimneys and roofs in the spring, a time of many human births. Lifelong mates take turns incubating and feeding their young.

TAPIR

The world's largest tapir, the **Malayan tapir** *(Maharajah Jungle Trek)* can weigh up to 700 pounds. Looking like a fat black pig with a white saddle, it's actually related to both a horse and a rhino. Its front feet have four toes, but its back feet only have three.

TIGER

One of the world's most beautiful creatures, each **Asian (or Bengal) tiger** *(Maharajah Jungle Trek)* has its own stripe pattern, as well as large false eyes and white spots on the backs of its ears. The patterns are on both its fur and skin. Noted for its sheer power, an Asian tiger can drag up to 3,000 pounds, five times its own weight. The 8- to 10-foot animal can leap 30 feet and, thanks to its large webbed paws, swim easily. Its ears turn individually and can rotate 180 degrees. *Disney's tigers typically sleep on their backs by the second viewing window, and often play in their fountain area after 4 p.m., especially during hot weather.*

TORTOISE

The world's most primitive tortoise, the **Asian brown tortoise** *(DinoLand U.S.A.)* has heavy overlapping scales. The largest living tortoise, the 5 foot-long, 500-pound **Galapagos tortoise** *(Discovery Island)* lives only in the Galapagos archipelago, 600 miles west of Ecuador. It can live at least 150 years, but it's a slow life. The reptile's top speed is only 0.16 mph.

WARTHOG

No other face looks like that of a male **common warthog** *(Kilimanjaro Safaris)*. Covered in wart-like growths of skin, it has two sharp 6-inch lower tusks and two curved upper tusks that can grow as long as 2 feet. Perhaps realizing he's no Prince Charming, he relies on his singing skills to attract women — at breeding time a male performs a courtship chant of rhythmic grunts. The creature eats roots and, like other pigs, keeps cool by taking mud baths. *The most famous warthog? Pumbaa, from Disney's "The Lion King."*

ZEBRA

The unique stripes on every **Grant's zebra** *(Kilimanjaro Safaris)* serve as camouflage — the pattern blends right into tall grasses. Even in an open field, a single zebra's stripes break up its silhouette, making it less recognizable to predators, and a herd of complex stripes makes it tough to track any one animal.

Tunis sheep, Rafiki's Planet Watch

Because black absorbs heat more than white, the animal's black areas have an extra layer of protective fat. Zebras themselves are attracted to the pattern. Studies have shown that when stripes are painted on a wall, a zebra will walk over to it. Related more to an ass than a horse, a zebra has the same long ears, short mane, tufted tail and front-leg only "chestnuts."

Animal guide field and library research by Micaela Neal.

Creatures great and small

Animal Kingdom has 1,500 animals, representing 250 different species. Besides those listed in this guide, fascinating animals in The Oasis include the yellow-bellied slider turtle and rhinoceros iguana and many beautiful birds. Discovery Island has the toothy tambaqui fish. Other animals on Kilimanjaro Safaris include ankole cattle, greater kudu and scimitar-horned oryx. Interesting birds in Africa include the ground hornbill and pink-backed pelican, and, at the Pangani aviary, one of the largest flocks of carmine bee-eaters in North America. The Asian aviary (at Maharajah Jungle Trek) has the most birds of all, including the New Guinea masked plover (shown at right) and the world's largest pigeon. Finally, a huge variety of bugs, butterflies, scorpions, snakes, tarantulas and other small critters live at Rafiki's Planet Watch, including the world's most colorful amphibian, the Latin American poison dart frog. The petting zoo includes the rare Sicilian miniature donkey.

Water Parks

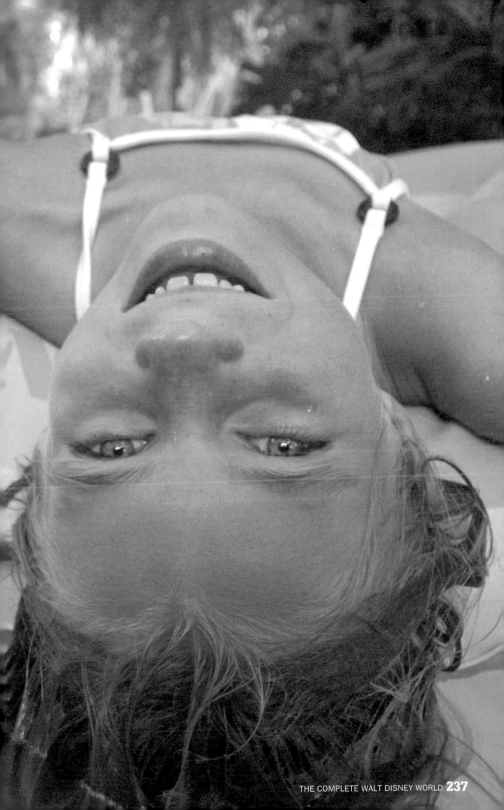

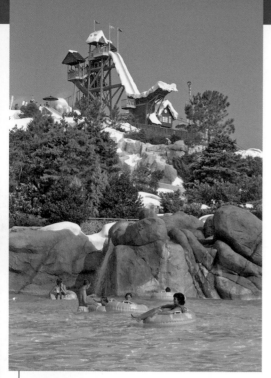

The United States has more than a thousand water parks, but no others offer the immersive theming of these Disney gems. Instead of plastic culverts and poles you see mountain streams and trees. And since it's Disney, everything is spic-and-span.

Typhoon Lagoon offers more shade, unique snorkeling and face-first rides, bigger waves and more for preschoolers. Blizzard Beach has more sun; longer, faster slides; and the most for preteens and teens.

Each park has a swimwear and sundries shop. Apparel brands include Billabong, Fresh Produce, Quicksilver and Roxy (Blizzard Beach has an especially great selection). Other items include beach towels, bug spray, camera supplies, magazines, paperbacks, even waterproof diapers.

giggles, squeals and laughs fill the air. Close your eyes at Blizzard Beach and Typhoon Lagoon and you'll hear more happy people than anywhere else at Disney. Why? Because it's just so much fun to ride a water slide, float down a lazy river or splash in a pool — especially when you're in such a fully realized fantasy atmosphere.

The parks also share a number of policies. Swimwear can't have rivets, buckles, or exposed metal. Strollers and wheelchairs are welcome, but not available for rent. Tubes, boogie boards and other water toys are not allowed to be brought in (small sand toys are OK), but all tube rides have complimentary tubes.

Picnic coolers and food are allowed, though glass containers and alcohol are not (the parks do sell beer, even alcohol). You can bring your own towels. Unfortunately, though the parks close during inclement weather, admission is nonrefundable.

On busy days the water parks fill to capacity and close, sometimes by 11 a.m.

▶ If bought separately, water park tickets are $39 for adults, $33 for children 3–9.

Blizzard Beach

It's a zany combination: a water park that looks like a ski resort. Disguised as ski slopes, water slides extend down the sides of Mt. Gushmore, a 90-foot snow-capped peak. Around it is a beach, wave pool, lazy river and children's areas. You enter the park through an alpine village, buildings that include changing rooms, lockers, food stands and shops. The 66-acre park sits east of Animal Kingdom.

You can get a **locker, towels** and **lifejackets** from the Beach Haus shop just inside the gate and at Snowless Joe's, which is next to the lockers, **dressing rooms** and **showers**. Lockers and towels rent for a small fee; lifejacket use is complimentary. The lockers themselves are located at Snowless Joe's, near the Ski Patrol Training Camp and at Downhill Double Dipper. **Sunscreen** is sold at the Beach Haus and at the Sled Cart across from Lottawatta Lodge. There's an **ATM** at the front of the park, near the ticket and **Guest Relations** windows. A **First Aid** station is to the right of the Beach Haus. Cast members take **lost children** to Snowless Joe's. **Lost and Found** is at Guest Relations. The park has no package pick-up service or baby care center, but restrooms have baby changing stations. Blizzard Beach **parking** is free. The park's phone number is **407-560-3400**.

A GOOFY IDEA As Disney tells it, in early 1995 Central Florida experienced a freak winter storm, which blanketed the area with snow. Watching the flakes fall outside of their Walt Disney World offices, the company's Imagineers had a brainstorm: "Let's build a ski resort!"

Immediately they went to work, rushed to create a huge mountain, a ski jump, slalom courses, a chairlift, a lodge and more. But just as the resort was finished, the warm weather returned and the snow turned to slush.

Reluctantly, the Imagineers began to board things up. But then they spotted a lone alligator, blue from the cold but full of energy. Strapping on skis, he careened down the jump, flew through the air, landed on the women's restrooms, crashed into the gift shop... and emerged with a smile.

Watching this happy "Ice Gator," the Imagineers realized that their failed ski resort would make a terrific water park! The ski jump could be a body slide. The slalom, bobsled and sledding runs could be mat and tube rides. The slushy creek would make a perfect lazy river.

Basking in their genius, the Disney Imagineers named their creation Blizzard Beach, and proudly opened it to the public... on April Fools Day, 1995.

A Magical Day

Can you *absolutely, positively* get to the park 30 minutes before it opens? If so, here's a great schedule for Blizzard Beach. The key: getting done with the slides by 11:30 a.m.

8:30 **Arrive at the park**
The gate usually opens early. When it does, get a locker key and head to the rope line at the bridge over Cross Country Creek.

9:00 **Do the slides**
Work your way around the park in a counter-clockwise pattern. Save the kids' areas, the river and the pool until later.

11:30 **Eat lunch**
There are shady tables at Lottawatta Lodge.

12:30 **Play in the pool**
Often you can cool off under a waterfall.

1:30 **Do the kids' spots**
Tikes Peak and the Ski Patrol Training Camp.

3:00 **Ride the river**
Want a treat? Try a kiwi snow cone at Snow Balls.

4:00 **Re-ride your faves**
The lines disappear during the park's last hour.

Assumes operating hours of 9 a.m. to 5 p.m.

▶ Bring hotel soap bars and shampoo. After your shower you'll walk out refreshed.

Clockwise from left: The Thin Ice Training Course, Cross Country Creek, Tikes Peak. **Right:** The boy in front of her chickened out, but that didn't stop this teen from going down Summit Plummet.

Children's area

TIKES PEAK Rideable baby alligators, gentle slides and an ankle-deep squirting "ice" pond highlight this watery playground for preschoolers. There's also a fountain play area, a little waterfall, many small sand boxes and lots of lawn chairs, chaise lounges and picnic tables for parents. Kids may want to wear water shoes: the pavement can get hot. *Height restriction: Must be under 48 in.*

Preteen area

SKI PATROL TRAINING CAMP This inventive spot features **Fahrenheit Drop,** cabled T-bars that drop kids into an 8-foot pool; and the **Thin Ice Training Course,** slippery walks on floating "icebergs" with overhead rope grids for support. Also here: wide **Snow Falls** slides designed for a parent and child to ride together; **Cool Runners,** two short, bumpy tube slides; and **Frozen Pipe Springs,** a short, steep and covered body slide.

Lazy river

CROSS COUNTRY CREEK Circling the park, this 3,000-foot stream flows under bridges, over springs and through a cave with ice-cold dripping water. Most of the 25-minute journey is lined with palms and evergreens. The river has seven entry points. The water is 2.5 feet deep.

▶ Hit the creek after lunch, when your body needs a break from the water slides.

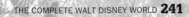

Body slides

SLUSH GUSHER This one fools you. Ninety feet above the beach, you start off slow and stay in control over the first drop. But then... off you go into the wild blue yonder! You definitely get some airtime here, thanks to some playful Disney designers who followed the second lip with a super-steep drop-off. The whole trip takes about 10 seconds; top speeds can reach 50 mph. The 250-foot flume has the look of a melting snow-banked gully. *Height restriction: 48 in.*

SUMMIT PLUMMET The tallest, fastest water slide in the country, this 66-degree, 350-foot chute includes a 120-foot free fall. Looming 30 feet above Mount Gushmore, the launch platform is a mock ski jump that, if real, would send you flying over the parking lot.

Lying down at the top of the ramp, you cross your arms over your chest, cross your feet at the ankles and — in the most unnerving moment of all — push yourself off the edge of this real

Topped by umbrellas, the seats of a chair lift take you to the top of Mt. Gushmore for easy access to Slush Gusher, Summit Plummet, Teamboat Springs and, on less crowded days, Snow Stormers and Toboggan Racers. Skis stretch out beneath your feet. If there's a crowd to board, take the single-rider line for a much shorter wait.

A rider gets airborne on Slush Gusher

Tower of Terror. There's a blur of sky and scenery as you fall straight through the lift ramp (which triggers a blast of water) then a roar of water as you splash into the run-out lane. The impact can send much of your swimsuit where the sun has never shone. Speeds can reach 60 mph. Unless you wear a T-shirt, the trip can sting your skin.

The fall is so scary even some of its designers don't care for it. "I made the mistake when we were building it of going up the stairs and looking down," says Disney Imagineer Kathy Rogers. "I thought, 'There's no way I'd put my body in there!' I did it once and said, 'Done!'"

There are no exit stairs, so if you chicken out you have to squeeze your way back down the crowded entrance steps, doing what cast members call "the walk of shame."

Don't want to go? There's an observation deck in front of the small chalet, and a shaded viewing area at the end of the ride complete with a real-time display of each rider's speed. *Best ages: 10 and up. Height restriction: 48 in.*

▶ Blizzard Beach is typically closed for maintenance in November and December.

Wave pool

MELT-AWAY BAY Nestled against the base of Mt. Gushmore, this one-acre pool appears to be created by melting-snow streams that feed into it. Bobbing waves wash through the water for 45 minutes of every hour. Perfect for sunbathing, a sandy beach lines the shore. The pool is a great spot for Monkey in the Middle.

Mat slides

SNOW STORMERS When you were a kid, did you have a sled? If so, these three racing slides will bring back those memories. Lying face-first on a mat, you weave down a hill of S-curves dug into the ground like high-banked gullies. The 350-foot track is plenty fast, even a little scary — as you careen up the corners the splashing water makes it tough to see. A horizontal line on the wall gives you a point of reference. Want to win the race? Keep your elbows on the mat and your feet up. *Best ages: 8 and up.* **TOBOGGAN RACERS** Based on an amusement park gunnysack slide, this 8-lane, 250-foot mat slide builds speed as you race down a series of dips — face first. Great for families, it's more fun than scary. To go fast, push off quickly and lift up the front of your mat slightly so it doesn't dig in the water. Regardless of technique, heavier riders usually win.

Above: Mell-Away Bay. **Below:** Toboggan Racers.

▶ Buses run to Blizzard Beach from all Disney resorts and parks but Magic Kingdom.

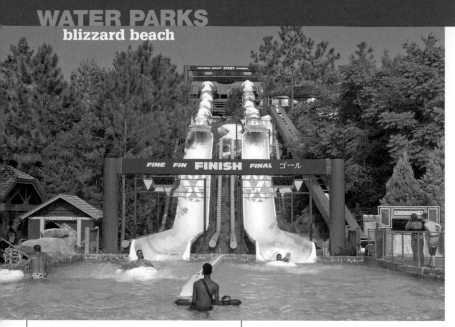

Tube slides

DOWNHILL DOUBLE DIPPER Disney's scariest tube rides, these side-by-side racing runs take you through a tunnel with two drops (steep enough to catch

Teamboat Springs is a 1,200-foot-long family ride

Downhill Double Dipper is Disney's scariest tube ride

some air) before shooting you through a curtain of water and into a catch pool. You compete with the rider next to you, and your elapsed time is shown at the finish line down below. The 230-foot ride stands 50 feet high. Speeds reach 25 mph but seem much faster. *Height restriction: 48 in. Best ages: 10 and up.*

RUNOFF RAPIDS You trek up 127 steps to ride these three flumes, but they're worth every huff and puff. Two of them allow double tubes, letting friends or family members ride together. A third is like a watery Space Mountain, enclosed in darkness except for some starry pinlights. All three 600-foot slides make you feel like a bobsledder, sliding you up on their banked curves before shooting you out into a catch pool. *Best ages: 7 and up.*

TEAMBOAT SPRINGS Grumpy papa, moody teenager, creaky grandma — it

EACH MORNING Disney opens Blizzard Beach by having the waiting crowd count down a guest who's already perched on Summit Plummet. Want it to be you? Get to the park early, be among the first to the rope line and strike up an energetic, funny conversation with the waiting cast member.

▶ Pull up on your Double Dipper handles just before the pool to fly across the water.

doesn't matter. Everyone in your family will smile on this, the world's longest family raft ride. Riding in a raft the size of a kiddie pool, you slide down a twisting, splashy, 1,200-foot course. You spin around on the tight curves, which may toss you up high on their banked walls. One thing's for sure: your rear end will get soaked — 30 holes line each raft's bottom edge. A 200-foot ride-out area takes you under a collapsing roof that's dripping with cool water. For the wildest ride put the big bodies on one side of your raft, the lightweights on the other.

FUN FINDS AT BLIZZARD BEACH
❶ The eclectic soundtrack mixes summertime classics with Christmas songs. Tunes include Jimmy Buffett's 1985 "Jolly Mon" and a Baha Men version of "Hakuna Matata." ❷ Equipment from the Sunshine State Snow Making Co. sits along the queue of Toboggan Racers and on the banks of Cross Country Creek past Reindeer Landing. ❸ Barrels of equipment and "Instant Snow" from the Joe Blow Snow Co. sit along the walkways to Slush Gusher, Summit Plummet and Teamboat Springs. ❹ Snow is melting off a roof of a small building across from the Downhill Double Dipper entrance marked "Safe to Approach Unless Melting." ❺ Across from the Beach Haus gift shop, a sign reading "Caution — Low Flying Gator" has a drawing of Ice Gator jumping from Summit Plummet. His ski tracks are visible on the roof of the women's dressing room behind it. In front of the sign is an Ice Gator-shaped hole in the side of the shop. ❻ "Ancient" drawings on the walls of the Cross Country Creek cave include a beach chair with umbrella, Ice Gator, a Yeti, people in

Runoff Rapids allows friends to ride together

tubes, people on skis and a skier with a leg cast. ❼ The Northern Lights shine through the cave's ceiling. ❽ B-r-r-r-occoli and Sleet Corn are planted in Ice Gator's garden alongside the creek just past Manatee Landing. ❾ As you float by Ice Gator's house he often sneezes and says "Anybody got a hanky?"

▶ For the fastest Rapids ride go tandem — the more weight, the wilder the trip.

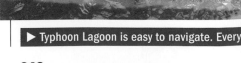

STRONG WAVES OCCUR AT ANY TIME PLEASE HOLD SMALL CHILDRE BY THE HAND

Not always heeded, a surf-pool sign warns parents

Typhoon Lagoon

With an atmosphere that's one part Hawaii, two parts Gilligan's Island, this tropical water park is an unsung Disney masterpiece. Like the Magic Kingdom, its perfect theme, passionate design and variety of attractions make it easy to have a great time.

Across the street from Downtown Disney, the lushly landscaped 61 acres include a surf pool, a water roller coaster, a saltwater snorkeling pool and much

more. There are many sunbathing spots and lots of pavilions with picnic tables.

Lockers, towels and adult, child and infant **lifejackets** are available at High 'N Dry Towels next to the **dressing rooms** and **showers** just past Singapore Sal's beach shop. Lockers and towels rent for a small fee; lifejacket use is free. Some lockers are at Shark Reef. **Sunscreen** is sold at the entranceway gift stand and Singapore Sal's, which also has an **ATM.** A **First Aid** station sits behind the Leaning Palms restaurant. **Lost children** are taken to High 'N Dry Towels. **Lost and Found** is at the **Guest Relations** windows at the entrance. The park has no package pick-up service or baby care center, but restrooms have baby changing stations. **Parking** is free. The Typhoon Lagoon phone number is **407-560-7223.**

Masks on, Shark Reef guests get tips from a lifeguard before launching into deep water

▶ Typhoon Lagoon is easy to navigate. Everything circles the central surf pool.

Every half hour Mount Mayday tries to dislodge Miss Tilly with a 50-foot gush of water. A lush trail leads close enough to see the ship's barnacles.

A FOOTLOOSE FAIRY TALE Once upon a time there was a bayside village called the Placid Palms Resort, which was tucked into the valley of a great volcanic mountain. Over the years it had been subject to earthquakes and geothermal rumblings, but life remained tranquil. Even when cruise ships arrived, the Placid Palms stayed a quiet, thatch-roofed little haven.

Then came Hurricane Connie, in 1955. For one hour furious winds pounded the area. A boat blew through a building. A surfboard sliced through a tree. Crates of fireworks blew in from Mr. Pleasure's nearby island warehouses. A next-door fruit processing plant lost its walls but gained a tractor, which teetered on the roof. A small harbor had been cut off from the sea, trapping an overturned boat, thousands of

FUN FACTS ❯❯ With 10 miles of plumbing, the park circulates 35 million gallons of water daily. **❯❯** The 95-foot Mount Mayday pumps 40,000 gallons of water a minute to its nine water slides. **❯❯** Miss Tilly is actually 17 tons of molded and painted concrete. **❯❯** There are 30 acres of water. **❯❯** The park has a rarely seen mascot, Lagoona Gator. **❯❯** Early concepts for the park included a beached cruise ship and a swamped logging camp.

A Magical Day

Can you *absolutely, positively* get to the park 30 minutes before it opens? If so, here's a great plan for Typhoon Lagoon. The key: doing the slides, tubes, reef and creek before noon.

8:30 Arrive at the park
Once you park your car or get off the bus, it will take nearly 30 minutes to put on sunscreen, get in the park, rent a locker and get in line at the Castaway Creek bridge.

9:00 Slides, tubes, reef
Starting with Crush 'n' Gusher, circle the park counterclockwise and do the slides, tubes and Shark Reef. The lines will be short until you're almost done.

11:00 Cruise the creek
Castaway Creek won't be too crowded yet.

12:00 Eat lunch
The Leaning Palms restaurant, a walk-up counter with outdoor tables, has the largest menu: burgers, sandwiches, hot dogs, pizza.

12:30 Play in the pool
Check the surf sign for the wave schedule.

2:00 Relax
Build a sandcastle, read a book, take a nap. Have kids? Sack out at Ketchakiddee Creek.

4:00 Re-ride your faves
The lines disappear during the park's last hour.

Assumes operating hours of 9 a.m. to 5 p.m.

fish and even a few sharks. Suffering the worst fate was a shrimp boat named Miss Tilly. Blown in from Safen Sound, Florida, it became impaled on the peak of Mount Mayday.

"No worries!" said the laid-back villagers. Sign paint in hand, they renamed the Placid Palms the Leaning Palms, the center of a new topsy-turvy tropical playground of pools, rapids, rivers and streams. They christened the spot Typhoon Lagoon.

And they lived happily ever after.

▶ Typhoon Lagoon offers surfing lessons before park hours. Details: 407-939-7873.

Lazy river

Family float. Orlando's Rathbun family relaxes under the lush landscaping on Castaway Creek.

CASTAWAY CREEK This shady, palm-lined stream takes you on a tropical journey around the park. Along the way you'll be sprayed by misters along the shore, drizzled on by the tank and pipes of a broken-down waterworks, and, as you're forced through a waterfall at a cave entrance, completely soaked. There's a lot to look at. You pass three crashed boats, travel alongside the Ketchakiddee Creek playground and go under a suspension bridge. Once the river splits in two. The 2,100-foot waterway is 15 feet wide and 3 feet deep. It moseys along at 2 feet per second; a round trip takes about 25 minutes. There's never a wait, though the river can get crowded in the afternoon.

Children's area

KETCHAKIDDEE CREEK What was once, according to Disney, a no-man's land of volcanoes and geysers has become an elaborate tyke-sized water park with 18 activity spots. Your toddler will likely break into a huge grin as he or she splashes through the tube slide's three little dips toward the end of this palm-lined, 100-foot course. The surrounding area is filled with ankle-deep pools and creeks and low bubbly fountains. A 12-foot Blow Me Down boiler is topped with

Dads join in the fun at Ketchakiddee's S.S. Squirt

▶ Hook your ankles over each other's Castaway Creek tubes to make a family flotilla.

Braced for impact, a summertime crowd at the Typhoon Lagoon surf pool awaits a breaking wave

hoses that shake, shimmy and squirt. More adventurous kids will hurl themselves down the two slip 'n' slides — cushy 20-foot mats with 20-degree drops. Everyone has a blast at the S.S. Squirt. Using swiveling water cannons, you'll squirt each other with multiple streams of water as you take sides in a battle of oversized sand sculptures. To keep you soaked, a whistle shoots a continuous spray in the air. Many families build sandcastles. When you run out of energy there are many shady chairs and picnic tables. *Height restriction: must be under 48 in. for slides.*

Surf pool

It's not everyone's cup of chowder, but this giant wave pool is a perfect playground to many kids and adults. The surf's up all day, and the waves vary between bobbing swells about 2 feet high and body-surfable breakers up to 6 feet. Emerging with a "whoomph!" from two underwater doors, 80,000 gallons of water sweep across the pool every 90 seconds. Each wave is met with hundreds of people who swim into it, swim with it, jump over it or get knocked on their keisters by it. A small sign in front of the pool — the Surf Report — shows the wave schedule.

Twice the size of a football field, the 2.5-acre mushroom-shaped lagoon includes two wading pools with kid-sized slides and two infant-friendly tide pools with bubbling water and climb-on boats. It's bordered by a white sandy beach.

FUN FACTS ❯❯ The pool is 500 feet long and up to 8 feet deep. **❯❯** It can hold 1,200 swimmers. **❯❯** Its walls are 126 feet apart and rise 7 feet above the static water level. **❯❯** The system uses 2.75 million gallons of water. **❯❯** The waters are maintained at 75 to 80° F.

▶ **The wave can't be ignored. Even in the shallows its impact can knock you over.**

At left, New Jersey's Amanda Mathus, 14, braces for the splash on the Stern Burner Storm Slide, which goes through a tunnel. **Below,** green means go at Humunga Kowabunga, a 214-foot enclosed tube that drops at a 45-degree angle.

The aquatic world of the Caribbean comes alive in Shark Reef, a large saltwater pool where snorkelers swim fin-to-fin with small sharks and tropical fish. Family members can watch through the underwater portholes of a wrecked ship.

Humunga Kowabunga

Body slides

HUMUNGA KOWABUNGA Like Splash Mountain without the boat, these zippity speed slides drop you and (usually) your swimsuit 51 feet in just a couple of seconds. The three identical dark tubes sit at 60-degree angles and extend 214 feet. Speeds can reach 30 mph. Arch your back to avoid scraping it. Even better, wear a T-shirt. Don't want to go? A waiting bench overlooks the catch pool. *Height restriction: 48 in.*

STORM SLIDES You'll slide up on high banked corners on these swooping body flumes, which take you through rocky gulches on the shady side of Mount Mayday. Each slide is different: Rudder Buster (on the left, as you stand at the boarding area) has a small tunnel; Stern Burner (in the middle) has a longer dark tunnel; Jib Jammer (on the right) has no tunnel. Top speed is 20 mph. The slides' average length is 300 feet.

BAY SLIDES Located in the calm left corner of the surf pool ("Blustery Bay"), these two 35-foot slides are for children too old for Ketchakiddee Creek but too young for the Storm Slides or Humunga Kowabunga. One is uncovered, with a few gentle bumps; the other has a 4-foot tunnel. The climb is just 10 steps and it only leads to the slides. Most moms and dads catch their kids at the bottom. *Height restriction: must be under 60 in.*

Saltwater snorkeling

SHARK REEF Darth Vader lives! You hear nothing but your own breathing as you snorkel past "smiling" rainbow parrotfish and other tropical beauties — as well as passive rays and leopard and bonnethead sharks — in the crystal-clear water of this simulated reef. It's the only wild-animal encounter at any Disney park that comes free with park admission. The fish usually swim away from you, but if you're very still one may come close. You're not rushed, and you can stretch out your time by taking a break on the small center island.

A nearby shop provides complimentary use of masks, snorkels and vests. You rinse off in an outdoor shower before entering. Changing areas, lockers, showers and a picnic area are nearby. Don't want to go? Portholes in an overturned, walk-through sunken tanker let you view your family as they swim by.

For a greater experience, an optional **Supplied Air Snorkeling** adventure introduces you to the basics of scuba diving. Run by the National Association of Underwater Instructors (NAUI), the 30-minute session ($20) includes use of a pony tank, mouthpiece (regulator), flippers and instruction. You can't dive deep, but you get plenty of time in the pool. *Age restriction: 5 and older.*

FUN FACTS » Shark Reef holds over 2,000 fish and 362,000 gallons of saltwater. **»** The water temperature is 68° F. **»** The coral, sponges and stationary invertebrates are fiberglass. **»** The fish are fed like those in a home aquarium. Members of Epcot's Seas with Nemo & Friends Animal Care Team toss in food pellets and Romaine lettuce.

▶ Take your time floating at Shark Reef. You're not allowed to swim backward.

Above: A Toronto 7-year-old splashes into the Keelhaul Falls catch pool as her dad looks on. **Left:** Mayday Falls. **Below:** Gangplank Falls.

Tube slides

KEELHAUL FALLS This gentle, 400-foot course is essentially one big "C" curve. It gets off to a nonthreatening start and slowly builds up speed. It's never scary: the ride ends just as you slide up on a bank. For a more intense time go down backward. Every turn will be a surprise.

MAYDAY FALLS This swervy, rippled flume simulates white-water rafting. It's a relatively long, fast course (460 feet at about 15 feet per second) and a triple vortex may turn you around. There's one small waterfall. Lean back to go faster.

GANGPLANK FALLS The three- to five-passenger rafts on this short family adventure are plenty of fun. You brave waterfalls, dripping caves and squirting pipes as you twist your way past crates of fireworks on the banks. The course is 300 feet long, so it's over in about 30 seconds. As

▶ Each tube slide lasts less than 30 seconds. Ride them early when lines are short.

© DISNEY

you ride, try to position your raft so everyone but you gets soaked. **CRUSH 'N' GUSHER** Wheee! With both lifts and dips, this water-jet-powered tube ride gives you the experience of a roller coaster. Riding in either a two- or three-person tube, you're dropped by a conveyor belt into a flume, then thrust forward with a burst of speed. If you lean back, a lip before each drop may get you airborne. (Push down with your feet to stay in control.) The three slides offer different experiences. Pineapple Plunger has two peaks and three medium-length tunnels. Coconut Crusher has one peak and a long, short, then medium-length tunnel. Banana Blaster is the longest ride by a few seconds, but it doesn't take three-person rafts. It has one peak, with one long tunnel and two medium tunnels. Each ride lasts about 30 seconds. The slides average about 420 feet. A bonus: the waiting line is out of the sun, under a roof.

The attraction is themed to be the towering remains of a fruit-packing plant. The flumes, as the story goes, were once wash spillways that cleaned fruit before it was shipped. Hidden behind the dressing rooms, the remote 5-acre area (jokingly named Out of the Way Cay) also includes a small gradual-entry pool and lots of beach chairs and chaise lounges. *Height requirement for slides: 48 in.*

FUN FINDS AT TYPHOON LAGOON ❶ The message spelled out by the nautical flags hanging just to the right of the entrance turnstiles reads "Piranha in pool." ❷ The surf pool wall appears to be a levee ready to burst. Wooden planks

Water jets propel Crush 'n' Gusher riders uphill

spit water between the seams. ❸ Under the clock tower, the decor around Lagoona Gator's shack includes an alligator totem pole. ❹ Inside the window are posters and flyers for The Beach Gators ("So cold blooded, they're hot!") and the film "Bikini Beach Blanket Muscle Party Bingo." A copy of Surfin' Reptile magazine includes the article "How to Get a Golden Tan Without Being Turned into a Suitcase." ❺ At the Happy Landings snack bar, a rack of outboard motors lets you squirt water through their props at Castaway Creek floaters. ❻ The name of the defunct Crush 'n' Gusher fruit company is Tropical Amity (say it slowly). ❼ Ripped open by a long-gone Great White, a "shark-proof" cage sits along the Shark Reef walkway, past the showers. ❽ A sign on a Ketchakiddee Creek slide promotes a boat-washing business: "Keels hauled, decks swabbed. Sorry no sailors washed."

▶ Typhoon Lagoon is typically closed for maintenance in January and February.

Downtown Disney

The five-story **DisneyQuest** building is one of the anchors of Downtown Disney West Side

1 ocated near the eastern edge of the Disney property, 120-acre Downtown Disney is a mini metropolis of nightclubs, restaurants, shops and theaters. It's divided into three sections. The largest area, the 66-acre **West Side,** is an entertainment, restaurant and shopping district. It includes a Cirque du Soleil theater, DisneyQuest and a House of Blues restaurant and concert hall. Slyly sharing the name of the land where young men turn into jackasses in the 1940 film "Pinocchio," **Pleasure Island** is 72,000 square feet of adult-oriented comedy and dance clubs. Origi-

nally known as the Walt Disney World Shopping Village, the **Marketplace** is a 1970s open-air mall. The 25 waterside shops and restaurants wrap around outdoor stands and kiddie rides.

RESOURCES Rental **lockers** are located at the Marketplace marina near Cap'n Jack's Restaurant and across from the Motion dance club at Pleasure Island.* **ATMs** are at the House of Blues and Wetzel's Pretzels on the West Side, the Rock 'n' Roll Beach Club at Pleasure Island, near Summer Sands and inside the World of Disney store at the Marketplace. **Strollers and wheelchairs** are available at the West Side and Marketplace Guest Relations offices. Downtown Disney has no package pick-up service, first aid station or baby care center, but most restrooms have baby changing stations. Downtown Disney **parking** is free.

* There are also lockers at the spiral staircase landing of 8TRAX and on the second floor of Mannequins

ACCORDING TO DISNEY LORE the Pleasure Island clubs were once shipping warehouses of adventurous businessman Merriweather Pleasure. One spot, today's Adventurers Club, was his library. Mr. Pleasure disappeared when the fictional Hurricane Connie destroyed the area (and created the nearby Typhoon Lagoon) and the buildings were converted into nightclubs. Recent renovations have added boat docks that let water taxis shuttle guests between the two ends of the area, the West Side and Marketplace.

▶ The parking lot behind Cirque always has plenty of spaces. Others are often full.

AMC Theater

There are 24 auditoriums at this 110,000-square-foot movie complex. Eighteen have stadium seating for unobstructed viewing; two have balconies and screens that reach three stories tall. *5,390 seats.*

A 3-D pirate adventure at DisneyQuest

DisneyQuest

Virtual reality experiences highlight the attractions at this five-story collection of video and electronic games, which is presented as a one-price indoor theme park. The best games are **Pirates of the Caribbean: Battle for Buccaneer Gold,** which takes a crew of four into an interactive 3-D world for five minutes; **Aladdin's Magic Carpet Ride,** a virtual-reality hunt for the magic lamp; and **Buzz Lightyear's AstroBlaster,** where you battle other guests in cannon-firing bumper cars. Creative types will also love the **Animation Academy,** where 30-minute classes teach you how to draw a Disney character. The 100,000-square-foot building also includes unlimited play on classic arcade games such as Pac-Man. Evening crowds can create 30-minute waits for the most popular games. *Admission: $36 adults, $30 children ages 3-9. Height restrictions: 51 in. for CyberSpace Mountain virtual roller coaster and Buzz Lightyear's AstroBlaster, 48 in. for the Mighty Ducks Pinball Slam lifesize pinball game, 35 in. for Pirates of the Caribbean. Open daily from 11:30 a.m. to 11 p.m. Sun.–Thur., midnight Fri. and Sat. Children 9 and under must be accompanied by an adult. Retail shop; two counterservice restaurants. 407-828-4600.*

House of Blues

One of a handful of restaurant and music halls created by Hard Rock Cafe founder Isaac Tigrett and entertainer Dan Aykroyd, this two-story performance venue features lots of original folk art, hardwood floors and quality sound and lighting. A wide range of acts play here; there are shows almost every night. The adjacent restaurant has free entertainment late. *All ages. General admission. Info and tickets: 407-934-BLUE (2583) or www.hob.com. Restaurant diners get priority admission into the concert hall.*

The House of Blues concert hall

▶ **DisneyQuest is least crowded on fair-weather weekdays between 4 and 6:30 p.m.**

The elegant Cirque du Soleil theater is reminiscent of a circus big top

La Nouba

Created specifically for Disney, this wondrous Cirque du Soleil spectacle fills you with delight

✓ With costumes, choreography, music and stagecraft that rival the best Broadway extravaganza, this invigorating Cirque du Soleil production blends the ancient traditions of the European circus with modern acrobatics, dance and street entertainment, captivating you like no American circus can. There are no animals, just humans — acrobats, dancers, clowns, gymnasts and others — putting on a show that's filled with action, color, whimsy and a quirky sense of humor. Designed uniquely for the family audience of Walt Disney World, it's performed on a custom-built Elizabethan-style stage.

The acrobats alone are impressive enough. Up high are tightrope walkers, trapeze artists and, in the show's most beautiful moment, hanging aerialists wrapped in huge red-silk ribbons. Onstage, performers cavort and somer-

sault inside a pair of giant open wheels and jump, spin and twist on two BMX bikes. Four ever-smiling Asian girls dance, flip and climb on each other as they play Diabolo. A finale gymnastic ballet features power-track and trampoline performers. Their surreal diving in and out of windows looks exactly like a film running backwards.

But there's so much more.

Always on stage, sideshow characters participate sometimes as performers, sometimes as spectators. Les Cons ("the nuts"), a quartet of all-white simpletons, automatically dance whenever they hear music. A flightless Green Bird has escaped from her cage. Meanwhile, clowns Balto and Serguei act as children, moving boxes, playing Cowboy and Indian or scaling the moon.

Each scene is presented as a figment of the imagination of a cleaning woman, another stage character who eventually becomes a princess (after all, this *is* Disney) though not quite in the same way as Cinderella.

There's no master of ceremonies; instead the whole show is scored live by a vibrant band. Hidden in towers alongside the stage, guitar, horn, keyboard and violin players perform in perfect sync with the action. Their zesty mix of classical, jazz, hip hop, klezmer, techno and even bluegrass adds an emotional accent to every performer. Some songs have vocalists — an androgynous male who performs at high alto registers and a spirited female who adds some Gospel soul. Both sing exclusively in French. The acoustics are crystal clear.

Though it doesn't tell a tale, La Nouba does have story elements. The opening is a meeting of two worlds, a modern ur-

FUN FACTS 》 The name "La Nouba" comes from the French phrase "faire la nouba," which means to party. 》 With an average age of 30, the 72-person cast comes from 14 countries. Many are from Russia. 》 There are over 300 costumes and headpieces. Most performers wear three different outfits. 》 The materials include real and synthetic hair, horsehair and feathers. 》 Plaster head molds are made for each performer to ensure that headpieces, masks and wigs fit perfectly.

▶ Get to your seats early. The clowns come out 10 minutes before showtime.

Above: Dressed in pinstripes and a tiny bowler, the Walker roams the stage like Charlie Chaplin. Always optimistic, he feels whatever he sees. **Below:** Based on a Chinese yo-yo game, the Diabolos act features young Asian girls who dance, flip and climb on each other as they toss a wooden spool back and forth. It often steals the show.

Above, Elena Day dresses for her role as the Green Bird, a depressed, awkward creature who has escaped her cage but can't fly. Watching every act from the side of the stage, the audience favorite remains trapped like a marionette with tangled strings. **At left,** the lonely Titan confronts the other characters throughout the show. He marches assertively through the world of La Nouba, like a nightmare waiting to take over a dream. **Below,** the show begins with an invasion by the lock-step Urbanites.

Shoe technican Catherine Delgado stretches new shoes for the Walker. Every day about 250 pairs of shoes are checked and touched up for the show.

ban society and an early 20th-century circus. The Urbans — determined, depersonal, de-saturated — march in lock step as they toe society's line. By contrast, the circus folk think for themselves. Costumed in neon colors, they each march to their own beat.

Movie buffs will find references to 1997's "The Fifth Element" (the odd music and warbling diva) and 1998's "Dark City" (the looming cityscapes and unexpectedly moving floors). Art lovers will sense Calder and Matisse.

What's it all mean? The show's purpose, its producers say, is to "wake up the innocence in your heart." You'll be surprised how much it succeeds.

$63–$112 adults, $50–$90 for children 3-9. 90 min. show, no intermission. 1,671 seats. Best ages: 4 and up. No photography. Showtimes 6 p.m. and 9 p.m. Tues.–Sat. Tickets can be purchased six months in advance. Info and tickets: 407-939-7600, www.cirquedusoleil.com or at the Cirque box office at Downtown Disney.

WHERE TO SIT Every seat's good, but spending the money to sit down front does pay off — you'll see every costume and makeup detail, every smile and grimace, every tensed muscle. You'll hear the clowns squeak and grunt, and the acrobats shout verbal cues. Catch the eye of a performer and he or she might wink back.

FUN FINDS ❶ A rooster crows at the end of the opening parade. ❷ The eyes of the German Wheel performers glow in the dark. ❸ The Flying Trapeze performers are androgynous. The males wear tutus. ❹ The musicians often dance as they perform in the tower. ❺ During the chair act the cleaning woman hangs her laundry. ❻ The Diabolo girls return later to watch part of the show from a floating bench.

LE BACKSTAGE BIZARRE
As part of the research for this article, the author spent an afternoon with the La Nouba performers as they prepared for a show. His notes:

4:15 I start off in the fitness center. As I chat with a muscleman, three little Asian girls wander in. Dropping their school books and circling around me, they pull out this giant spool thing and FLING IT RIGHT AT MY HEAD! (Well almost! I swear it brushed back my hair.) Then they do it again. And again! They giggle. I leave.

4:30 Hangin' out in the Green Room, I sit down by a nice gray-haired man who, I later learn, is one of the clowns. Watching CNN, we laugh together at the stupid politicians. Then he tells me a long, passionate story. In French. I don't speak French.

5:00 Outside on a patio, a bunch of shirtless guys play backgammon, foosball and ping pong. They look like frat brothers. Except for the eyeliner.

5:15 Makeup and shower time. Wearing only towels, perfect slabs of men half my age file past me in the narrow halls. But I can't feel too inadequate — they're each wearing more makeup than Gwen Stefani.

5:30 Twenty minutes until show time. Back in the gym, a pair of acrobats stretch their legs while a blue-lipsticked bike dude checks his sprockets. In the hall, a trumpeter runs the scales while a white-faced guy greets me with a burst of, I think, opera.

5:45 Yikes! Time to go! I race out to grab my daughter, who's next door at DisneyQuest.

5:50 We race up the steps and into the theater — just two footsteps ahead of the clowns.

▶ **Front-row center is Row 1, Section 103. Tickets go on sale six months in advance.**

Pleasure Island clubs

8TRAX You'll boogie down to '70s rock and disco at this traditional dance club. *Lounge seats 96.*

✔ **ADVENTURERS CLUB** Convinced they are terribly British world travelers from the 1930s, improvisational actors wander the floor to chat with guests, tell stories and burst into song. Meanwhile, trophy heads speak, masks move their eyes, a be-headed adventurer refuses to shut up. The most unique Pleasure Island nightspot, the club was designed by Joe Rohde, who later created Animal Kingdom. Plan to stay at least 90 minutes.

BET SOUNDSTAGE Run by the Black Entertainment Television company, this hip-hop and R&B club serves appetizers.

✔ **COMEDY WAREHOUSE** The Who, What & Warehouse Improv. Co. makes fun of everything in sight as they interact with guests. Fine for preteens and older, every show is different. *290 seats.*

MANNEQUINS DANCE PALACE A dance floor rotates as the gyrating Island Explosion dancers add atmosphere at this award-winning club. You enter from a third floor elevator that opens to catwalks, stage rigging and enough mannequins to give the illusion of a theatrical warehouse. *178 seats in the lounge.*

MOTION Backed by a huge video screen, a disc jockey spins the latest dance tunes at this two-story temple of groove. A younger, grinding crowd.

ROCK 'N' ROLL BEACH CLUB Live bands cover songs from the 1950s to the 1990s at this three-story rock 'n' roll mecca, which features a large dance floor.

$9.95 for one club; $20.95 for all clubs. Adventurers Club and Comedy Warehouse require the multiclub ticket and admit guests under 18 if they are with an adult.

Top: Rock 'n' Roll Beach Club. **Above:** 8TRAX.

The dance clubs require guests to be 21 or older. Open nightly 7 p.m. to 1 or 2 a.m. Info: 407-WDW-2NITE (939-2648).

▶ **The best Pleasure Island family spot: The Adventurers Club.**

The sushi bar at the Wolfgang Puck Grand Cafe

West Side

✔ **BONGOS CUBAN CAFE $$–$$$** This Cuban restaurant is housed in a unique triangular building that's dominated by a two-story adobe pineapple. The interior features mosaics and murals that recall the B.C. (Before Castro) Cuba of the 1940s and 1950s, as well as conga-drum bar stools. The food reflects the culture of Miami's Little Havana district. It combines humble-but-mouth-watering Cuban sandwiches (hot roast pork, ham, Swiss cheese, dill pickles and mustard on toasted, pressed bread), black bean soup and plantains (sweet pan-fried bananas) with upscale choices such as Zarzuela de Mariscos — sauteed lobster, shrimp and scallops in a homemade creole sauce. There's dancing and live entertainment Fri. and Sat. starting at 9 p.m. The restaurant was created by pop-music star Gloria Estefan and her husband/producer, Emilio. Better than most Epcot restaurants. *Serves lunch, dinner. 550 seats, including 50 outside (some on an upstairs balcony) and 87 at the bar. Direct line for information: 407-828-0999.*

✔ **HOUSE OF BLUES $$** Traditional southern food such as jambalaya, ribs, shrimp and home-made cornbread is served in a folk-art decor. A Gospel Brunch, held at 10:30 a.m. and 1 p.m. Sundays in the music hall, features made-to-order omelettes, cheese grits, BBQ chicken, jambalaya, catfish and red beans and rice. Live entertainment Thr.–Sat. at 11 p.m. in the restaurant, Tue.–Sun. 6–11 p.m. at the outdoor, full-service Front Porch Bar. *Serves lunch, dinner. 578 seats, including 158 outside at the restaurant and 36 at the bar. Direct line for information: 407-934-BLUE (2583).*

PLANET HOLLYWOOD $$$ Shaped like a planet, this three-story restaurant is filled with movie memorabilia, including the blue gingham dress Judy Garland wore in 1939's "The Wizard of Oz," the ax used by Jack Nicholson in 1980's "The Shining," the prop heads of Adam and Barbara from 1988's "Beetlejuice" and a handbag and gloves from the wardrobe of Marilyn Monroe. The menu has everything from hamburgers, chicken, fajitas, pasta, ribs, steaks, as well as a variety of entree salads. *Serves lunch, dinner. 800 seats. Direct line for information: 407-827-7827.*

✔ **WETZEL'S PRETZELS $** This indoor counter stand serves yummy hot hand-rolled soft pretzels with a variety of coatings. There's also fresh-squeezed lemonade, as well as Haagen-Dazs ice cream, milkshakes, sundaes, sorbets and waffle cones. *36 outdoor seats.*

✔ **WOLFGANG PUCK GRAND CAFE $–$$$$** This collection of four restaurants includes a takeout counter, a casual cafe, a sushi bar and an upscale dining room. The noisy but spacious cafe features California-style entrees such as smoked salmon pizza and a mild pumpkin ravioli, as well as steak and an especially good chicken, both served with deliciously creamy garlic mashed potatoes. The upstairs, black-linen dining room offers a more refined menu and a great view. B's Lounge and Sushi Bar is noteworthy. The boldly colored restaurant was designed by Puck's partner and wife, Barbara Lazaroff. There's often no wait before 7:40 p.m., when the first Cirque show ends. *Serves lunch, dinner. 736 seats, including 150 in the dining room and 30 at the sushi bar. Direct line for reservations: 407-938-WOLF (9653).*

Pleasure Island

✔ **RAGLAN ROAD IRISH PUB & RESTAURANT $$$** Run by Irish proprietors and an Irish chef, this pretension-free Irish restaurant and bar is the real thing. The authentic decor is filled with antiques, including two 130-year-old bars that feature large dividers with leaded glass. The bar has a full selection of Irish ales, stouts, lagers and whiskies. The food is a step beyond tradition — a menu of pub classics that have

Avg./adult: $ <$10. $$ <$20. $$$ <$30. $$$$ <$40. Reservations: 407-WDW-DINE

gone to cooking class. The tender meats are topped with subtle glazes; the smooth mashed potatoes with crispy braised cabbage. Desserts include a rich bread pudding served with creamers of warm butterscotch and creme anglaise. The best dish is the creamy, subtle Rustic Chicken soup. It will warm your soul. The tab here can approach $40 per person with a couple of ales, but with the live band and table step-dancer (after 8 p.m. every night but Sunday) it's still a great value. Ask to sit at the center table (an old parson's pulpit) for an unforgettably close performance. The restaurant is named after a street on the south side of Dublin that was immortalized in a 1960s folk song. The adjacent Cooke's of Dublin offers counter-service fish and chips, with fried candy bars for dessert. *Lunch, dinner starting at 3 p.m. 600 seats, including 300 outside. Merchandise shop; two outdoor bars. Pleasure Island admission not required. Direct line for reservations: 407-938-0300.*

The unique shepherd's pie at Raglan Road

Marketplace

PORTOBELLO YACHT CLUB $$-$$$ This upscale Italian restaurant features imaginative pasta, pizza, seafood and steak. The kid's menu has grilled chicken and fish. *Serves lunch, dinner. Seats 326. Direct line for reservations: 407-934-8888.*

FULTON'S CRAB HOUSE $$$-$$$$ It looks like a steamwheeler, but inside is a white-tablecloth, traditional seafood restaurant that has crab, fish, lobster, oysters, scallops, shrimp, steak; also specialty cocktails and martinis. The lakeside of the Constellation Room has the best view. The best outdoor seats are on the lower-level dock. The kid's menu has filet mignon. *Serves lunch, dinner. 660 seats. Direct line for reservations: 407-934-BOAT (2628).*

MCDONALD'S $ The well-known fast food restaurant. The quietest tables are in back. *254 seats, including 114 outside.*

GHIRARDELLI SODA FOUNTAIN $ You can eat at a booth, table or bar at this busy ice-cream parlor, which features cones, waffle cones, banana splits, chocolate drinks, floats, milkshakes and specialty sundaes. The hot fudge sauce is made fresh daily. A small chocolate shop is adjacent. *Seats 88, including 22 outside. Direct line for info: 407-934-8855.*

✔ **EARL OF SANDWICH $** Owned by the ancestors of the fourth Earl of Sandwich, this counter-service restaurant serves quality sandwiches. Tasty hot choices include the Beef 'n'

Bleu (roast beef and bleu cheese), the Hawaiian BBQ (ham, Swiss cheese, pineapple and barbecue sauce) and the Ultimate Grilled Cheese (bleu, brie and Swiss, with bacon and tomato). The crusty bread is baked all day; the beef is roasted every morning. A good side dish: the chunky cole slaw with touches of garlic and sour cream. The best deal: the $1.25 cup of steaming hot, creamy-orange tomato soup. Also fresh-baked brownies, cookies. Crowded, but well worth it. *190 seats, including 65 outside. 407-938-1762. To the left of Once Upon a Toy.*

WOLFGANG PUCK EXPRESS $ Hidden behind Disney's Days of Christmas, this small indoor counter serves individual pizzas, omelettes, waffles and a Crispy Cornflake French Toast for breakfast; pizzas, quesadillas and sandwiches for lunch and dinner. *133 seats, including 109 outside. 407-828-0107.*

RAINFOREST CAFE $$$ A robotic rain forest comes to life every few minutes as you choose from beef, chicken, pork and seafood dishes, pasta, pizza, salads, sandwiches or hamburgers. *Serves lunch, dinner. 575 seats. No sameday reservations. 407-827-8500.*

CAP'N JACK'S RESTAURANT $$-$$$ Every table has a view of the water at this 1970s throwback, which sits over Village Lake. Shrimp cocktail, lobster tails, clam chowder, crab cakes and a strawberry margarita are among the features. *Serves lunch, dinner. 113 seats, including 15 at the bar. Direct line for reservations: 407-828-3971.*

Crowds wander the West Side walkway

© DISNEY

West Side

CANDY CAULDRON This dungeon-style candy shop has lots of jellybeans and an open kitchen that makes candied apples, chocolate-covered strawberries and other treats.

CIRQUE DU SOLEIL STORE Stunning Cirque-branded scarves, purses and fashion apparel (mixing Italian prints and hand beading) make this store more than a souvenir shop. Also here: great masks and circus caps, figurines inspired by the show, even Diabolo games. Located beneath the auditorium, next to the box office.

HOUSE OF BLUES COMPANY STORE Hot sauce, incense, even cornbread mix is tucked into this unique shop. There's some interesting folk art and blues CDs, and lots of funky House of Blues apparel, even for infants.

HOYPOLOI This collection of uncommon art offers often-soulful home-accent pieces made of ceramic, glass, metal, stone and wood.

MAGIC MASTERS You pick a trick from the menu board, then a magician performs it. Want to buy? See the man at the register. The family-friendly shop is a replica of Harry Houdini's private library. Can you find the secret door?

MAGNETRON A tiny shop filled with thousands of fun, unusual, silly refrigerator magnets.

MICKEY'S GROOVE This general assortment of Disney character and other merchandise includes clothing, pins, souvenirs and toys.

PLANET HOLLYWOOD ON LOCATION Attitude and fashion T-shirts and other apparel.

POP GALLERY This bright collection of pop art includes paintings, three-dimensional wall hangings and some wild glass sculptures.

SOSA FAMILY CIGARS This premium cigar shop often has hand-rolling demonstrations.

STARABILIAS This collection of nostalgic memorabilia includes music, movie, political and historical items.

SUNGLASS ICON This sunglasses shop sells Ray-Ban and other brands.

VIRGIN MEGASTORE You'll find a good-sized fashion store (with kooky shirts, caps, purses and figurines) inside this hip 49,000-square-foot shop, as well as a wide-ranging collection of DVDs and CDs and an eclectic selection of books, magazines and video games. The second-story Coco Moka Cafe has sweets, coffees and deli and panini sandwiches that rival those of pricey places nearby. Some of its 50 seats are on an outdoor balcony.

Pleasure Island

ORLANDO HARLEY-DAVIDSON It's everything Harley but the hogs — apparel for men, women and kids, collectibles, even pet products.

SHOP FOR IRELAND Irish merchandise includes apparel, infantwear and leprechaun hats. Also Guinness apparel; cookbook from chef Kevin Dundon. At Raglan Road.

Marketplace

ARRIBAS BROTHERS This dimly lit, carpeted shop has hand-cut crystal and hand-blown glass items. Glassblowers work before your eyes.

ART OF DISNEY Oil paintings, lithographs, theme-park attraction posters, Lenox china figurines, plates, vases and other quality art pieces.

BASIN The aroma of this all-natural skin-care store will intoxicate you as you walk in. Massage and shampoo bars, bath bombs, body butters, lotions and salt and sea scrubs. Also a make-your-own candle station.

DISNEY'S DAYS OF CHRISTMAS Filled with ornaments, this year-round Christmas shop also sells collectibles and figurines. An embroidery and engraving area can personalize your find.

DISNEY'S PIN TRADERS This open-air shop has a lot of pins, but many facings of the same one. A good spot to find limited-edition pins, albums, display sheets and carrying cases.

DISNEY TAILS Set in a corner of the Pooh Corner store, this pet-care and pampering nook has bandanas, clothes, toys, treats and collar-ID tags.

DISNEY'S WONDERFUL WORLD OF MEMORIES Half of this nice shop is a scrapbooking center, half a photo-album and picture-frame boutique. It's also one of Disney's best bookstores.

GHIRARDELLI CHOCOLATE SHOP. A great aroma envelops this collection of chocolate candy, fudge sauce, baking cocoa and hot-chocolate mix.

The princess room at World of Disney

GOOFY'S CANDY CO. Clerks will top an apple, cookie or marshmallow with your choice of crushed candy, nuts and chocolate drizzle. The jellybean and lollipop collection is huge; a coffee counter has lattes and cappucinos.

LEGO IMAGINATION CENTER This crowded store offers dozens of LEGO boxed sets as well as the world's largest Pick-A-Brick wall, where 320 bins let you buy individual pieces. Don't miss the giant display creations, including Brickley the sea serpent outside in Village Lake.

MICKEY'S MART Dozens of small toys and souvenirs, all priced under $10.

MICKEY'S PANTRY This surprisingly complete housewares shop stocks lots of Mickey-styled appliances and kitchen items, as well as non-Disney cooking supplies, tableware, even wine.

ONCE UPON A TOY This 16,000-square-foot toy store has Hasbro classics like Lincoln Logs and Tinkertoys, as well as many fun items based on Disney theme parks. The playful decor includes a huge Game of Life spinner rotating upside down on the ceiling.

POOH CORNER Winnie-the-Pooh-themed apparel, backpacks, pillows, plushies, sleepwear, toys. Adorable infant onesies and dresses.

RAINFOREST CAFE STORE Adjacent to the cafe, this shop sells restaurant- and animal-themed apparel, plushies and toys. Kids love the animated creatures along the walls, as well as Tracy the talking tree.

SUMMER SANDS Geared primarily to young women, this swimwear shop features Roxy suits, board shorts and lightweight fashionwear. For the older set — men and women — there's upscale Tommy Bahama apparel.

TEAM MICKEY'S ATHLETIC CLUB Disney character T-shirts, caps, sports jerseys and golf attire. Also Billabong, similar brands. Stocks nice coats and sweatshirts during the winter. Some ESPN items.

WORLD OF DISNEY The world's largest Disney emporium, this 51,000-square-foot department store stocks the most popular Disney items. Designed for crowds, wide hallways consume much of the space and the displays typically have multiple facings of the same item. It is organized well. There are separate rooms for girls (here all known as Princesses), Ladies and Juniors, Boys, Men, Infants, Hats and T-shirts, Housewares, Home Accessories, Jewelry and Pins, Candy and Snacks, and Souvenirs. The store's not spot is the **Bibbidi Bobbidi Boutique,** a styling salon for young girls where Fairy Godmothers apply cosmetics and style hair. Its ten chairs book far in advance. *(Info and reservations: 407-WDW-STYLE (939-7895).)*

The Disney-Hasbro toy store, Once Upon a Toy

Diversions

DODGE

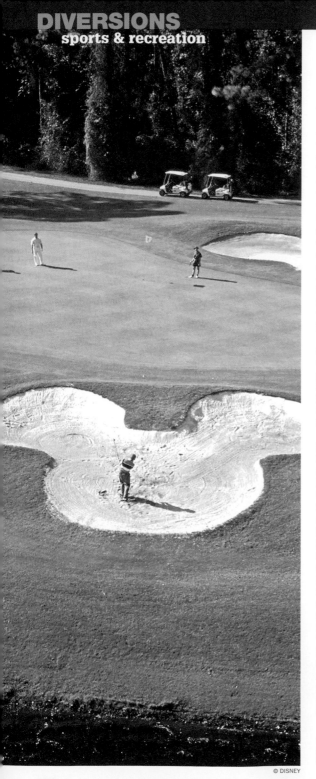

Golf

Grouped into three distinct facilities, each of the six Disney golf courses offers a different experience. There's the long course and the short course. The flat course and the hilly course. The water course. And the great-for-kids 9-hole. Home to incredible numbers of deer, egrets, herons, otters, even alligators and an occasional bald eagle, each course is designated as a wildlife sanctuary by the Audubon Cooperative Sanctuary System. All but the Lake Buena Vista course roam far from civilization — from most holes you view no buildings, only nature.

The best months to play are September, April and May, when the weather's nice and good tee times are easier to book. Build in some extra time into your round, as the pace may be slower than you expect – it's humid down here!

MAGNOLIA COURSE

How's that shoulder turn? It needs to be efficient on this long-game course, a beautiful rolling terrain that sits in a forest of more than 1,500 magnolia trees. The Magnolia features elevated tees and greens and 97 bunkers, the most of any Disney course. And the greens are quick. Host to the final round of Disney's PGA Tour tournament since 1971, the course has tested pros from Jack Nicklaus to Tiger Woods. *Yardage: 5,232–7,516. Par: 72. Course rating: 69.4–76.5. Slope rating: 125–140. Designer: Joe Lee. Year open: 1971. Location: Shades of Green, across from Disney's Polynesian Resort.*

The mouse trap. Magnolia's No. 6 green is fronted by a bunker in the shape of Mickey Mouse.

© DISNEY

PALM COURSE

Pretty water fountains. Ugly water hazards. This palm-lined beauty has them both. Water hazards line seven holes and cross six. Shorter and tighter than the Magnolia, the Palm is home to most of the play during Disney's PGA Tour event. It has a few long par 4s and a couple of par 5s that can be reached in two using a fairway wood. The large, elevated greens can be maneuvered with good lag putting. Hole No. 18, a long par 4, has been ranked the fourth toughest on the PGA Tour. *Yardage: 5,311–6,957. Par: 72. Course rating: 69.5–73.9. Slope rating: 126–138. Designer: Joe Lee. Year open: 1971. Location: Shades of Green, across the street from Disney's Polynesian Resort.*

OAK TRAIL COURSE

This 9-hole walking course lets the developing golfer learn the game. With small greens and two good par 5s, the course requires you to be accurate with your short irons. The longest hole, the 517-yard No. 5, features a double dogleg. Water hazards cross three fairways. Most greens and tees are elevated. The score card lists separate pars for children 11 and under and 12 and over. *Yardage: 2,532–2,913. Par: 36. Course rating: 64.6–68.2. Slope rating: 107–123. Designer: Ron Garl. Year open: 1980. Location: Shades of Green, across from Disney's Polynesian Resort.*

EAGLE PINES COURSE

Old enough to remember what a phonograph record looked like after you left it out in the sun? These wavy, undulating greens will bring back that warped memory. The course is relatively short; on a couple of holes you can drive the green. Visually intimidating, Eagle Pines combines a flat terrain with an unforgiving rough of grass, sand and pine straw. *Yardage: 4,838–6,772. Par: 72. Course rating: 66.6–72.5. Slope rating: 119–135. Designer: Pete Dye. Year open: 1992. Location: Disney's Eagle Pines & Osprey Ridge Golf Club, just east of the Fort Wilderness Resort & Campground.*

OSPREY RIDGE COURSE

This one is flat out beautiful. Set within uncharacteristically rolling Florida terrain, this course winds through challenging dense vegetation, oak forests and moss hammocks. More than 70 bunkers, mounds and a meandering ridge provide obstacles, banking and elevation changes. Some tees and greens are more than 20 feet above their fairways. The course often has swirling winds. One bit of relief: waste bunkers along the fairways play differently than regular bunkers. Their sand is fairly hard, so you can play a shot out of one with a more-normal swing. *Yardage: 5,402–7,101. Par: 72. Course rating: 69.5–74.4. Slope rating: 123–131. Designer: Tom Fazio. Year open: 1992. Location: Disney's Eagle Pines & Osprey Ridge Golf Club, just east of the Fort Wilderness Resort & Campground.*

LAKE BUENA VISTA COURSE

The least forgiving Disney course, LBV features narrow, tree-lined fairways and small greens, and 10 holes have water hazards. Though you tee off at Disney's Saratoga Springs Resort, much of the course weaves through the Old Key West Resort, so it demands accuracy on the tee shot as well as the approach (errant tee shots fly into the woods, between condos or out on a street). Hole No. 7 has an island green; No. 18 is a 438-yard dogleg. *Yardage: 5,194–6,819. Par: 72. Course rating: 68.6–73.0. Slope rating: 123–133. Designer: Joe Lee. Year open: 1972. Location: Disney's Saratoga Springs Resort.*

LESSONS

PGA pros offer year-round instructional programs for all golfers, regardless of age or skill level at all three golf centers — Shades of Green, Eagle Pines & Osprey Ridge Golf Club and Lake Buena Vista. Choose from one-on-one instruction focused on a specific skill, video analysis of your swing or on-course playing lessons that include course management and strategy, club selection and short-game skills ($50–$150). *Individual lessons and clinics: 407-WDW-GOLF (4653). Group lessons: 407-938-3870.*

Greens fees: $50–$190 for 18-hole courses (required electric cart rental included); $38 for the 9-hole Oak Trail ($20 for those under 18). Club and shoe rental available. Proper golf attire required. 18-hole courses have putting greens and driving ranges. Transportation provided from Disney-owned resorts. Reservations accepted 90 days in advance for Disney resort guests, 30 days for other players. Cancellations require 48 hours notice. For more information call 407-WDW-GOLF (4653) or visit www.disneyworldgolf.com.

All Disney greens are being converted from TifDwarf to ultra-dwarf TifEagle turf, a shorter type of Bermuda grass that provides a truer, faster roll. Going course by course, the project will be finished in 2009.

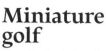

Miniature golf

Dramatic classical music from Disney's 1940 film "Fantasia" plays in the background as you putt alongside dancing-ostrich topiaries and sneaky magical brooms on the Gardens course at **Disney's Fantasia Gardens** (407-560-4870). A second set of links, Fantasia Fairways is a miniature version of a real golf course, with bunkers, roughs and undulating hills. Its challenging holes are up to 103 feet long. Adjacent to the Walt Disney World Swan and Dolphin Resort, the complex is busy at night, when tee-time waits can be an hour.

Serious golfers are nowhere to be found at **Winter Summerland** (407-560-3000). Squirty the Snowman sprays you on the Winter course; fish get you as you cross a bridge on the Summer links. Elves' vacation trailers dot the landscape.* Getting a hole in one is pretty easy; the greens often funnel into the cups. Located next to daytime-only Blizzard Beach, this complex is often deserted at night.

Both complexes: $10.75 ($8.50 ages 3–9). Open 10 a.m.–11 p.m. (last tee time 10:30 p.m.). All courses have 18 holes. Same-day reservations accepted (in-person only). General info: 407-WDW-PLAY (939-7529).

* The story? Late one Christmas Eve, as Santa was flying over Florida, he glanced down and saw — incredibly — snow! Landing his sleigh, he purchased the spot and turned it into a vacation retreat for his elves: a Winter Summerland. Later, the elves added two golf courses. Dividing into two camps, they built one course for elves who enjoyed the snow, another for those who loved the sun.

Her eye on the ball, Micaela Neal prepares to putt into a Cinderella snow castle at Winter Summerland

"Mom, that music is freaking me out!" — Girl, 6, as she and her family play the Fantasia Gardens course.

Surfing lessons

Know how to swim? In decent shape? If so, then you are almost guaranteed to learn how to ride the crest of a wave at the **Craig Carroll Surfing School,** held before park hours (often just after dawn) at Disney's Typhoon Lagoon surf pool. Conducted on dry land, a step-by-step introductory lesson is easy to follow, then instructors plop in the water to demonstrate the technique. Once you're in the pool you get plenty of personal attention. After each attempt Carroll critiques you from the lifeguard stand, then an instructor in the water adds more tips. Waves average about 5 feet for adults; half that for kids. Though about 70 percent of students succeed, females tend to do better. "Girls don't think as hard about it, and try to do exactly what you say," Carroll says. "Boys tend to think it's a macho thing." A pro surfer since the 1970s, Carroll coached world-champion Kelly Slater and runs the Ron Jon Surf School in Cocoa Beach. *$140. Must be 8 yrs. or older and a strong swimmer. Most students have never surfed. Days and hours vary with season. 2.5-hour lesson has 30 min. on land, 2 hrs. in water. Surfboards provided. Spectators welcome. Max. 12 students a day; classes usually sell out early.*

Instructor at his side, a student practices his stand-up technique before getting into the water

Danielle Finke, 20, gets off her knees on her second attempt

Reservations accepted 90 days early at 407-WDW-SURF (939-7873).

Stock car driving

The engine rumbles. You tremble. And then you're doing it! Tearing down a real race track driving a 630-horsepower stock car — and you're the only one in it. (Now *this* is no Mickey Mouse ride.) Held at the Walt Disney World Speedway, the **Richard Petty Driving Experience** starts off with a training session, including some time out on the track. Then, wearing a fire cap, driving suit and helmet, you climb through the window,

FUN FACTS)) Once worn down, the foot-wide tires are sold for $5.)) Nicknamed the "Mickyard," the one-mile tri-oval was built in 1995 by the Indy Racing League. Many pro races were held here, including five Indy 200s and some Craftsman Truck Series events. A large grandstand held over 51,000 fans. Racing stopped in 2000.

pop on the steering wheel and strap in. Before you know it you're on the track. Almost always in a turn, you tail your instructor in a car of his own. He watches you in a mirror, and drives as fast as you can handle. (I got up to 122 mph — fastest in my class! — and even passed a guy on Lap 7.) Built by Petty's company, your NASCAR-style vehicle features a tube frame, huge V-8 and 4-speed clutch. The doors don't open, and the bodies are covered with logos. Most drivers are men, but women often go faster. "Guys sometimes just want to hear the roar of the engine," my instructor said. *(Rides $99. Drives $399–$1249 (8–30*

laps). Drives require reservations (call 2 wks. early) and include training. Adj. to the Magic Kingdom parking lot. Must be 16 to ride, 18 to drive. Spectators welcome. Information: 1-800-BE-PETTY or at www.1800bepetty.com.)

RICHARD PETTY DRIVING EXPERIENCE

The author at the wheel

Water sports

Working out of two locations, Sammy Duvall's Water Sports Centre *(info and reservations: 407-939-0754)* will take you parasailing, water-skiing or tube riding. **Parasailing** on the 450-acre Bay Lake will give you a birds-eye view of Walt Disney World. Hundreds of feet above the ground, you glide through the air attached to an open parachute while being pulled by a powerboat. You take off and land on the back of the boat, so you never get wet. *(Single riders $95 for 8–10 min. at 450 ft. or $120 for 10–12 min. at 600 ft. Tandem riders $160 for 8–10 min. at 450 ft. or $185 for 10–12 min. at 600 ft. Min. weight per flight 130 lbs. Max weight 330 lbs.)* You can **water-ski** (combo or slalom) or **tube** behind a MasterCraft 197 inboard, or **wakeboard or kneeboard** from a MasterCraft X 2 on either Bay Lake or the 45-acre Barefoot Bay at Disney's Caribbean Beach Resort. The instructors are friendly and patient, especially with children. *($155 first hr., $125 per addl. hr. per boat. Up to 5 skiers. Includes equipment, driver, instruction. Extra charge if picked up from Disney's Fort Wilderness, Grand Floridian, Polynesian or Wilderness Lodge. Caribbean Beach location open seasonally.)* The business also rents personal watercraft (see next page). A world-renowned skier, Duvall has won more than 80 pro championships. He was ranked No. 1 in the world for either ski jumping or overall for 17 straight seasons.

A mom and her daughter take off on a parasailing flight behind Disney's Contemporary Resort

Bike and surrey rentals

Ten Walt Disney World resorts rent bicycles as well as multi-seat surreys. You'll find them at Disney's BoardWalk, Caribbean Beach, Coronado Springs, Fort Wilderness, Old Key West, Polynesian (surreys only), Port Orleans, Saratoga Springs, Wilderness Lodge and Yacht and Beach Club (bikes only) resorts. *Bicycles $8 an hr., $22 per day. Surreys $18–22 per 30 min.*

Boat rentals

With the largest rental boat fleet in the world and a variety of lakes, lagoons and canals, Walt Disney World has nearly every way imaginable to get you out on the water. Your options include power boats, sailboats, pedal boats, kayaks and canoes. Outboard options include two-seat **Sea Raycer runabouts,** built exclusively for Walt Disney World by Sea Ray *($24 per 30 min., $38 per hr. Ages 12 and up may drive if accompanied by a licensed driver. Min. height 60 in. Max. weight 320 pounds per boat),* 17-foot

A Sea-Doo personal watercraft skims along Bay Lake

Boston Whaler Montauks *($33 per 30 min.)* and 21-foot **SunTracker pontoon boats** *($42 per 30 min.).* Sailboats include 12-foot **Sunfish** *($20 per hr.),* and 13-foot **Hobie Cats** *($25 per hr.).* Other choices include **canoes** *($6.50 per 30 min.)* and **pedal boats** *($6.50 per 30 min.).* For marina locations on each boat call 407-WDW-PLAY (939-7529). The Walt Disney World Swan and Dolphin Resort rents **swan pedal boats** *($12–$14 per 30 min.).* Three-seat Sea-Doo **personal watercraft** are available at Sammy Duvall's Water Sports Centre at Disney's Contemporary Resort, for either non-guided rides on Bay Lake or morning group excursions around Bay Lake and the adjacent Seven Seas Lagoon. *(Non-guided rides $75 per 30 min., $125 per hr. Excursions $125 per hr. Max. 3 riders per vehicle, combined weight under 400 lbs. Operator must be 16 with a valid driver's license; renter must be 18. 407-939-0754.)*

Fishing

Catching a largemouth bass is almost guaranteed when you take one of Disney's **pontoon-boat fishing trips.** More than 70,000 bass

The authors' daughter holds one of the many largemouth bass she caught during a morning trip

fingerlings were released into the 450-acre Bay Lake and 172-acre Seven Seas Lagoon during the initial construction of Walt Disney World in the late 1960s. Organized fishing tours didn't begin until 1977 (leaving bass to grow and breed undisturbed for years), all fishing is catch-and-release, and only a handful of anglers — those who take these tours — are on the water at any time. Fishing with knowledgable guides, guests routinely catch bass weighing from 2 to 8 pounds. Most trips catch five to 10 fish; guests average 2.5 per hour. Trips go out on Bay Lake, the Seven Seas Lagoon, the 25-acre Crescent Lake between Epcot and Disney-MGM Studios, the 15-acre Lago Dorado at Disney's Coronado Resort and the 43-acre Village Lake behind Downtown Disney. Bay Lake and the Seven Seas Lagoon are teeming with fish, but the largest (up to 14 pounds) are in Crescent and Village lakes. All programs are run by BASS — the Bass Anglers Sportsman Society. *Cost: $200–$235 for 2 hrs. for up to 5 guests, $405 for 4 hrs., each add'l hr. $100. Children's hour $28 (ages 6–12). Includes bait* (shiners addl.), guide, equipment, refreshments and digital camera. No license required. Tours available early morning, mid-morning, early afternoon. More Info: 407-WDW-BASS (939-2277). Reservations up to two weeks in advance. You can fish from the shore with a **cane pole or casting rod** at Disney's Fort Wilderness Resort & Campground (407-824-2900) and Disney's Port Orleans Resort — Riverside (407-934-6000). Cost: Poles $3.75 for 30 min., $8.50 all day. Rods $5.25 for 30 min., $9.25 all day. Bait addl. Catch-and-release only. No license required. No reservations.

Horseback riding

Guided 45-minute **horseback rides** along shady pine and palmetto trails inside Disney's Fort Wilderness Resort & Campground are available daily from the Tri-Circle D Livery, beginning at 8:30 a.m. Go early and you'll likely see wild animals, including snakes and deer. $42. Ages 9 and up. Min. height 48 in. Max. weight 250 lbs. No trotting. Reservations (required) can be made up to 30 days in advance at 407-WDW-PLAY (939-7529). Smaller kids can take a short **pony ride** at the resort's petting farm. The parent walks the pony. $4, cash only. Ages 2–8. Max. weight 80 lbs. 10 a.m.–5 p.m. daily. Info: 407-824-2788.

Jogging

Walt Disney World has many jogging trails. A wooded 1.5-mile trail threads through Disney's Fort Wilderness Resort & Campground. There's a bike path to the Fort Wilderness trail from Disney's

Wilderness Lodge. Guests can take a leisurely mile stroll on the promenade that surrounds Crescent Lake and connects the Epcot resorts or the 1.4-mile promenade around the lake at Disney's Caribbean Beach Resort. There are two trails at Disney's Port Orleans Resort (one-mile and .7-mile) and a mile trek around Lago Dorado at Disney's Coronado Springs Resort. Shorter trails are at Disney's Contemporary Resort, Disney's Polynesian Resort and Disney's Grand Floridian Resort & Spa.

Tennis

Walt Disney World has 34 lighted courts and tennis programs for guests of all ages and abilities. **Organized programs** are available at Disney's Grand Floridian Resort. These include private lessons ($75 per hr.), group clinics ($15), seasonal camps ($150 per week) and convention-style tournaments for groups ($25 per person). Experienced players can play a match against a Disney pro that includes analysis and critique ($75 per hour). A pro shop rents rackets and ball machines and re-strings and re-grips guest rackets. Other tennis courts are located at resorts throughout the Disney

Jogging along the promenade that connects the Epcot resorts

property. Though some resorts reserve their courts exclusively for their own guests, those at Disney's BoardWalk, Contemporary, Fort Wilderness and Yacht Club resorts are open to guests staying at any Disney resort. The courts at Fort Wilderness are open to all Disney guests. All **regular court use** is complimentary except use of the courts at the Grand Floridian, which go for $8 por hour. For more information call 407-WDW-PLAY (939-7529).

Horseback riding at Disney's Fort Wilderness Resort & Campground

Campfire

It's free! Held at a small outdoor amphitheater, **Chip 'n' Dale's Campfire Sing-a-Long** lets you bond with your kids without draining your bank account. You'll roast marshmallows in your choice of two fire pits, join in a 30-minute sing-a-long with the chipmunks, then watch a Disney movie on a large (if somewhat dim) screen. There's a different movie every night. Choose a bench seat to interact with the characters. A snack bar sells s'mores kits, packs of marshmallows and even sticks, as well as hot dogs and beer. *(No charge. Nightly. Behind the Meadow Trading Post at Disney's Fort Wilderness Resort & Campground. Times and schedules: 407-824-2727.)*

Carriage and wagon rides

Horse-drawn **carriage rides** are available at Disney's Fort Wilderness Resort & Campground, Disney's Port Orleans Riverside Resort and Disney's Saratoga Springs Resort. The buggies hold up to four adults or a small family. The Fort Wilderness

Guests aboard the Breathless take a trip around Crescent Lake

trips travel through natural areas. Night trips are romantic. *($35. 25 min. 6–9:30 p.m. Those under 18 must ride with an adult. Reservations accepted 90 days in advance at 407-939-PLAY (7529). Same-day availability info at 407-824-2832). Fort Wilderness also offers* **wagon rides** *through its trails. You ride with up to 32 other guests. ($8 adults. $5 children 3–9. 45 min. 7 p.m. and 9:30 p.m. Fireworks-viewing rides often available. Departs from Pioneer Hall. Children under 11 must ride with an adult. No reservations. Group rides available with 24 hrs. notice at 407-824-2734.)*

Charters

You can charter the **Grand 1 luxury yacht** (a 45-foot Sea Ray) for a cruise on either the Seven Seas Lagoon or Bay Lake for up to 13 people. A captain and deckhand are included. *($400 per hr. Food, butler optional. Leaves from Disney's Grand Floridian Resort. 407-824-2682).* Want a private viewing of Wishes? A

Kids roast marshmallows at Chip 'n' Dale's Campfire Sing-a-Long

pontoon boat will take you and nine friends out on the Seven Seas Lagoon to watch it. The trip takes about an hour. *($200–$250. Snacks provided. Leaves from Disney's Contemporary, Grand Floridian and Wilderness Lodge resorts.)* A second pontoon boat can take your group to Epcot's World Showcase Lagoon to watch Illuminations. *($250. Snacks provided. Leaves from Disney's Yacht and Beach Club Resort.)* You'll cruise in style aboard the **Breathless,** a 24-foot mahogany replica of a 1930s Chris-Craft. *(Ages 3 and up. 10-min. ride: $30. 30-min. ride: $85. Illuminations cruise: $250. Leaves from Disney's Yacht and Beach Club Resort.)* For details on charters call 407-WDW-PLAY (939-7529).

Disney Cruise Line

The two ships of the Disney Cruise Line, the Disney Magic and Disney Wonder, sail to the Bahamas and the Caribbean from nearby Port Canaveral. Each has lots of entertainment, including a dance club, piano

© DISNEY

© DISNEY

The Disney Wonder

Dolphin encounter

You'll learn about the anatomy and behavior of bottlenose dolphins, and spend 30 minutes in knee-deep water with them, on the 3-hour **Dolphins in Depth** program. No interaction is guaranteed, but you may even get to feel a heartbeat against your hand. Trainers work with you individually. You'll watch biologists doing actual dolphin research. Proceeds go to the Disney Wildlife Conservation Fund. *Cost: $150. Includes T-shirt, photo of you and a dolphin, refreshments. Wet suits provided. Epcot admission not required. Ages: 13 and up. Those under 18 must be with an adult. No swimming required. 3 hrs. Mon.–Fri. More information: 407-WDW-TOUR (939-8687).*

bar, a pirate-themed deck party with fireworks, character greetings and Broadway-style musicals. There are gobs of child and teen activities, while adults-only areas include a pool, coffee shop and sports bar. A fitness center has pre-loaded iPod Shuffles; a spa offers private suites with hot-tub verandahs. The dining plan gives you meals in three themed restaurants always with the same tablemates and wait staff; after a few nights you'll have a tableful of friends and servers who know your tastes. Every trip stops at Disney's private 1,000-acre island, Castaway Cay, where activities beyond the beach include guided walking tours, lagoon snorkeling, parasailing, personal-watercraft ecotours and swimming with stingrays. A mile-long tram ride takes those over 18 to an adult beach that has its own open-air bar and barbeque, couples' hammocks and massage cabanas. *All-inclusive rates start at $429 per person for 3-night cruises, $849 for 7-night excursions, based on double occupancy. Discounts for children and addl. room guests. Some packages include a Walt Disney World stay. Each ship has 877 staterooms, most with a bath-and-a-half. Two larger ships will be added in 2011 and 2012. Info: 888-325-2500 or at disneycruise.com.*

Diving and snorkeling

Certified divers can spend 40 minutes inside a 5.7-million-gallon saltwater aquarium at **Epcot DiveQuest**, a guided trip held at The Seas with Nemo & Friends pavilion at Epcot. You'll swim with more than 65 marine species, including non-aggressive sharks, rays, tropical fish and a 400-pound sea turtle. You suit up in waist-deep water and explore with up to 12 others. The program includes a presentation on marine life research and conservation and an overview of the pavilion. All gear is provided, as are lockers and showers. *Cost: $140. No theme park admission required. Ages: 10 and up. 3 hrs. Open-water scuba certification required; ages 10-11 must be diving with an adult. More info: 407-WDW-TOUR (939-8687).*

The **Epcot Seas Aqua Tour** lets you snorkel in the tank for 30 minutes with scuba-assisted snorkel (SAS) equipment. You also tour the aquarium, learn about the marine life you'll see, and are shown how to use the equipment. *Cost: $100. No theme park admission required. Ages: 8 and up. Those under 18 must be with an adult. 2.5 hrs. More info: 407-WDW-TOUR (939-8687).* Proceeds from the experiences go to the Disney Wildlife Conservation Fund.

Spas

Elaborate massages are among the offerings at the spas at Disney's Grand Floridian Resort, Disney's Saratoga Springs Resort and the Walt Disney World Dolphin. Treatments at the **Grand Floridian Spa** *(407-824-2332)* use the oils of Florida citrus fruit, as well as algae and sea salt. Couples can get massages together in a candlelit room. The **Saratoga Springs Spa** *(407-827-4455)* offers stone therapy and hydro massages and a rosemary-spring bath. The Grand Floridian and Saratoga Springs have treatments for children ages 4 through 12. All locker areas include a steam room, sauna and indoor whirlpool. The Dolphin's **Mandara Spa** *(407-934-4772)* is an Asian-inspired retreat with couples suites, a steam room and two indoor gardens. It features Balinese, Hawaiian Lomi Lomi, Japanese shiatsu and Thai massages; Chinese Tui Na; tooth whitening; and elaborate teen programs.

Specialty tours

The **Around the World at Epcot** tour lets you test-drive a Segway Human Transporter *($80. Ages 16 and up. Max. weight 250 lbs. 2 hrs.).* The longest and most elaborate Walt Disney World tour, **Backstage Magic** takes you behind the scenes at the Magic Kingdom, Epcot and Disney-MGM Studios. *($199, lunch included, no theme park admission required. Ages 16 and up. Mon.-Fri. 7 hrs.)* You tour the vet hospital, elephant barn and other animal facilities of Disney's Animal Kingdom (and may get up-close and personal with a giraffe or rhino) on the **Backstage Safari.** *($65. Ages 16 and up. Mon., Wed., Thr., Fri. 3 hrs.)* The **Behind the Seeds** tour gives you a closer look at the four greenhouses and the fish farm that are part of Epcot's Living with the Land attraction. *($12,*

The Grand Floridian Spa offers superb manicures and pedicures

$10 ages 3–9. All ages. 45 min.) You skip — literally — through the Magic Kingdom as part of **Disney's Family Magic Tour,** a primer for first-time visitors with children. *($27. All ages. 2.5 hrs.)* Learn the mysteries behind the creation, development and operation of the Magic Kingdom — and go backstage and down into the Utilidor — on **Disney's Keys to the Kingdom** tour. *($60, lunch included. Ages 16 and up. 4.5 hrs.)* **Mickey's Magical Milestones** tour reviews the development and success of Mickey Mouse as you travel the Magic Kingdom, again with stops backstage. *($25, lunch included. Ages 10 and up. Mon., Wed., Fri. 2 hrs.)* Get an inside look at the operations of Magic Kingdom's Walt Disney World Railroad on **The Magic Behind Our Steam Trains** tour. *($40. Ages 10 and up. Mon., Tue., Thr., Sat. 3 hrs.)* Epcot's **Undiscovered Future World** tour lets you hear stories about Walt Disney's

Wearing a jockey-style costume that hasn't changed since 1971, a Magic Kingdom guide leads guests on the park's popular Keys to the Kingdom tour

ultimate dream, visit all the Future World pavilions and glimpse backstage areas. *($49. Ages 16 and up. Mon., Wed., Fri. 4 hrs.)* The **Wild by Design** tour reviews the art, architecture and storytelling of Disney's Animal Kingdom. *($58, continental breakfast included. Ages 14 and up. Thr. and Fri. 3 hrs.)* The **Yuletide Fantasy** tour reviews the holiday decorations of the Magic Kingdom, Epcot and a few resorts. *($69, no theme park admission required. Ages 16 and up. Seasonal. 3.5 hrs.)* **Disney's Wide World of Sports Guided Tour** gives you an inside look at the complex on selected days when sporting events are scheduled. *(Complimentary. All ages. 1 hr.)* **Custom VIP Guided Tours** are arranged based on your custom itinerary. *($125 per hour, minimum 6 hours. All ages. Information: 407-560-4033.)* Details for each standard tour are available by calling 407-WDW-TOUR (939-8687).

© DISNEY

Disney's Wide World of Sports

Buzzing with activity, this 220-acre complex resembles a modern-day Olympic Village. On a typical summer day, 15-year-olds from Argentina compete in an international cricket exhibition. Inside an indoor fieldhouse, 100 girls basketball teams battle for the Amateur Athletic Union (AAU) National Championship. Next door youth baseball teams slug it out on the same ball field used by the Atlanta Braves during Spring Training, while softball squads from across the country compete on multiple fields for a national fast-pitch title. Meanwhile, on still more fields, the Tampa Bay Buccaneers are holding their annual training camp.

The Florida Picturesque-style compound includes a 7,500-seat baseball stadium, 5,500-seat old-style indoor fieldhouse, baseball quadraplex, six softball fields, nine multi-sport fields, a 400-meter track and field center and 10 tennis courts.

Over 11,000 events are held here each year, an average of more than 30 per day. Participating groups include the AAU, Pop Warner, the United States Specialty Sports Association and U.S. Youth Soccer.

California's Lauren Matheson breaks past a defender in a U14 Girls U.S. Youth Soccer match

Spectators can attend amateur events for a nominal fee. Special-event tickets (i.e., Spring Training) are available through Ticketmaster outlets or at the complex box office. For more information call 407-828-FANS (3267).

Eighty percent of the baseball stadium's seats are between first and third base

© DISNEY

SPECIAL EVENTS

DISNEY'S PIRATE & PRINCESS PARTY

Like Mickey's Not-So-Scary Halloween party, this Magic Kingdom evening event features its own parade and fireworks show, and encourages kids and their parents to dress up in costumes. Extras include dance parties, a

Above: The Magic Kingdom Easter parade features the Azalea Trail Maids of Mobile, Ala. **Below:** Atlanta Braves Spring Training at Disney's Wide World of Sports

haunted riverboat ride and a quest for beads and chocolate treasures. Most rides are open, too. *$37 adults; $30 children 3-9. Apx. a dozen evenings during Jan., Feb, Mar. Information and tickets: 407-W-DISNEY (934-7639).*

MARATHON WEEKEND

A pair of running events — a 26.2-mile full marathon and a 13.1-mile half marathon — highlight this early-January weekend. Typically more than 30,000 athletes compete; participants travel through the theme parks. There's also a 5K run for families and children. The weekend includes a health and fitness expo at the Wide World of Sports Complex. *Entry fees: $75 (26.2), $45 (13.1), $25–30 (5K). Disabled runners welcome. Advance registration is required; the entry deadline is typically early Nov. Details at 407-939-7810 or disneysports.com.*

SPRING TRAINING

The Atlanta Braves hold their Spring Training at Disney's Wide World of Sports Com-

plex. Workouts begin in February. In March the team plays more than a dozen exhibition games against other Grapefruit League teams. *Training sessions $11, games $14–$22. Tickets go on sale in January. Information and tickets: 407-939-1500, 407-839-3900 (Ticketmaster) or on the web at disneysports.com.*

ESPN: THE WEEKEND

Legendary athletes join popular ESPN broadcasters during this no-extra-charge fan-fest at Disney-MGM Studios. Events include question-and-answer sessions, star motorcades, interactive sports activities and live telecasts. *Early March.*

ST. PATRICK'S DAY

Two locations mark the Irish holiday with special events: The Raglan Road restaurant at Downtown Disney's Pleasure Island, and the U.K. pavilion at Epcot's World Showcase.

INTERNATIONAL FLOWER AND GARDEN FESTIVAL

This two-month Epcot garden party decorates the park with about 70 character topiaries, 80 floating water gardens, 300,000 bedding plants and 30 million blooms. Disney's most elaborate one-park promotion, the festival includes dozens of daily hands-on seminars and planting demonstrations and celebrity guest speakers. Kids love the walk-through butterfly garden, which often includes a live exhibit showing how a caterpillar forms a chrysalis and emerges as a butterfly. Themed weekends celebrate art, bugs and Mother's Day. Nightly Flower Power concerts feature acts from the 1960s and 1970s, often including Monkees singer Davy Jones. Vendor booths line some of the walkways. *No extra charge. April–May. Info: 407-W-DISNEY (934-7639).*

EASTER
The Magic Kingdom Easter Day parade includes the Easter Bunny and the colorful Azalea Trail Maids from Mobile, Ala. (who make their own dresses).

STAR WARS WEEKENDS
This fan-fest includes autograph booths featuring Star Wars characters and others involved in the creation of the classic motion pictures. Other highlights: roving characters, special motorcades, question-and-answer sessions, trivia games and children's activities. Merchandise includes an incredibly popular Darth Mickey plushie and a Darth Tater version of Mr. Potato Head. Many guests dress up. Get there when the park opens to get the full effect. *No extra charge. May–June. Info: 407-W-DISNEY (934-7639).*

GAY DAYS
Tens of thousands of gay men and women come to Walt Disney World (especially the Magic Kingdom) during the first weekend in June, most wearing red shirts in a sign of solidarity. Straight parents with children may be uncomfortable, though showing kids that even some old folks and yes, parents, are gay can be an enlightening message. Few guests are flamboyant. There is, naturally, less demand for strollers as well as shorter lines at Fantasyland attractions. Disney does not sponsor the event but doesn't interfere with it. *Info: 407-896-8431 or at gaydays.com.*

4TH OF JULY
Usually the most crowded day of the year, Independence Day features a Magic Kingdom fireworks show that surrounds guests on Main Street U.S.A.

MAGICAL BEGINNINGS
Geared to families with kids too young for elementary school, this promotion opens the Magic Kingdom's Fantasyland an hour early a few days a week for Disney World resort guests. It also features a series of very popular concerts at Disney-MGM Studios that star Disney Channel performers such as The Wiggles and Doodlebops. *No extra charge. Six weeks from mid-Aug. to the end of Sept. Info at 407-W-DISNEY (934-7639).*

NIGHT OF JOY
Live concerts by at least a dozen Contemporary Christian artists highlight this two-night event at the Magic Kingdom. Most

Cheerleaders lead a celebrity motorcade at ESPN: The Weekend

attractions are open, too. *Adv. tickets $40 adults; $68 for two nights. Day of event $5 more. Often sells out. Early Sept. Info and tickets: 407 W-DISNEY (934-7639).*

Arlo Guthrie does a different show for each set at Epcot's Flower and Garden Festival

TOM JOYNER FAMILY REUNION

Urban radio's No. 1 morning man hosts this Labor Day weekend celebration. Events include concerts by top-shelf African-American musicians and comedians as well as family activities. *Info: 888-TJ-FAMILY (888-853-2645) or at blackamericaweb.com.*

July 4th Magic Kingdom fireworks

MICKEY'S NOT-SO-SCARY HALLOWEEN PARTY

There's nothing but fun at this charming event, held at the Magic Kingdom on many nights from mid-September through October. Despite the silly name, the Boo-To-You parade is terrific; it starts with a galloping headless horseman. The Happy HalloWishes fireworks show is just as inspired *as the regular Wishes. There are lots of free-candy stations; most attractions are open and uncrowded. Families often dress up together in homemade costumes; we once saw a walking, talking Fastpass machine. $43 adults; $36 children 3-9. Many dates offer $6 savings if bought in advance. Friday-night events near Halloween, and the holiday itself, often sell out. Info and tickets: 407-W-DISNEY (934-7639).*

INTERNATIONAL FOOD AND WINE FESTIVAL

Booths around Epcot's World Showcase feature food and wine samples from Spain, India, Italy, Turkey, Ireland, Poland and other countries during this six-week festival. Other events include cooking demonstrations, gourmet dinners and wine seminars. Nightly Eat to the Beat concerts feature classic pop acts such as Little Richard and Three Dog Night. The demonstrations, seminars and entertainment are included in the regular Epcot ticket price. *Oct.–Nov. Info: 407-WDW-FEST (939-3378).*

FUNAI GOLF CLASSIC

You'll be just a few feet away from the top names in golf with a pass to this October PGA golf tournament. Tiger Woods usually plays. The purse tops $4 million. *$10 for practice-round days, $30 championship-round days, $50 for all rounds. Held at Disney's Magnolia and Palm courses at the Shades of Green resort, across the street from the Polynesian. Food packages available. Info and tickets: 407-835-2525 (the Greater Orlando Chamber of Commerce).*

© DISNEY

FESTIVAL OF THE MASTERS

One of the top art festivals in the country, this Downtown Disney event features 200 artists, each of whom has won a primary award at a juried art show within the past three years. Works include paintings, photographs, sculptures and jewelry. Even more interesting are the pieces at the adjacent House of Blues folk-art festival, which features self-taught creators, many of whom are fascinating. Cirque du Soleil artists perform in front of their theater each afternoon. Chalk artists cover 6,000 square feet at the Marketplace. Held annually since 1975. *No charge. Info: 407-824-4321.*

ABC SUPER SOAP WEEKEND

Dozens of hot hunks and daytime divas from the ABC-TV programs "All My Children," "General Hospital" and "One Life to Live" are on hand to greet guests, sign autographs and participate in question-and-answer sessions during this two-day fan-fest at Disney-MGM Studios. Other festivities include motorcades and a nighttime Street Jam that features many of the stars rockin' out on a Hollywood Boulevard stage. You know if you're in this cult; if not it's still tons of guilty-pleasure fun. Get here when the park opens; the crowds are thick. *No extra charge. Typically mid-Nov. Info: 407 397-6808.*

Crowds get close to the action at the Funai Golf Classic

Dopey and other Disney characters dance down Main Street during the parade at Mickey's Not-So-Scary Halloween Party

Christmas

There's no snow (no *real* snow) but the days between Thanksgiving and New Year's are Disney's most magical time of year, filled with enough spirit to warm the heart of any Scrooge. The mood is most contagious at the Magic Kingdom, with four special shows, a great parade and an amazing fireworks display. Epcot has holiday storytellers and a Candlelight Pro-

Rudolph is a rock star at Mickey's 'Twas the Night Before Christmas

cessional, while Disney-MGM Studios features holiday street theater, a revised parade and the Osborne Family Spectacle of Dancing Lights. Disney's Animal Kingdom reworks its parade and adds some kitschy decorations. *See the regular attractions early, saving your time after lunch for Christmas fun.*

MAGIC KINGDOM

Disney's main park salutes the fun and community spirit of the American secular Christmas. Remember when you and your neighbors got together for holiday sing-a-longs? When carolers came to your door? When your town held its big Santa Claus parade?* No? Well Disney does, and brings it back

* Once held in many U.S. cities, Santa Claus parades marked the start of the Christmas season. Weaving through a downtown, each ended with reindeer pulling Santa's sleigh. One remaining version is the Macy's Thanksgiving Day Parade in Manhattan.

with **Celebrate the Season** ✔, a campy musical revue on the castle forecourt stage that parents enjoy as much as their kids do. The 20-minute show kicks off with "Let's Have a Joyous Celebration," as a dozen gliding ice skaters remember "the shopping and the traffic and the holiday sights!" The dancing continues as Pluto leads the "Santa Claus Parade." Using his bone as a baton, Mickey's pet whistles in a kitschy klatch of dancing reindeer, hoofing horses and way-too-happy elves. After high-kicking Santa Goofy arrives to "Must Be Santa," a quartet of bake-shop coquettes sweet-talk him with "Mr. Santa." But when Mickey gives Minnie her gift (a live performance of "The Nutcracker Suite"), Donald Duck will have none of it. Angry that there was no present for him, the duck knocks the jester aside and attempts the dance himself. Chip 'n' Dale do the same to an Asian dancer, then Country Bears Wendell, Shaker and Liver Lips mimic the leaps of a Russian Cossack duo. Everyone is back onstage for the finale, a medley of holiday classics. Watch the reindeer act out "Rudolph the Red-Nosed Reindeer": at first they don't let poor Rudolph (Pluto) join in their reindeer games. *At night spotlights and dark surroundings add a theatrical flair.*

Mickey's 'Twas the Night Before Christmas ✔ is an 11-song, tongue-in-cheek take on the classic poem.* *"While visions of sugar plums danced in their heads"* brings out the Sugar Plum Fairy, a serious dancer who performs to "The Nutcracker Suite" until a pair of tutu-trimmed hippos (from the "Dance of the Sugar Plum Fairy" segment of the 1940 film, "Fantasia") steal the show. *"When what to his wondering eyes should appear but a miniature sleigh and some tiny reindeer"* delivers an antler-wearing Pluto and a guitar-playing Rudolph, who performs "Run, Run, Rudolph." *"When down the chimney Saint Nicholas came with a bound"* cues Santa Goofy to roll out of the fireplace. One of the show's best moments takes place out of the spotlight. Aghast as Minnie recites her Christmas list during "Santa Baby" (she wants a convertible, a ring…) Mickey nearly faints when she sings "Think of all the fellas that I haven't kissed." (Adults will notice that the unmarried Mickey and Minnie are, *ahem,* sharing a bed.) The music comes from a live orchestra. Sit up close to see the sax player quickly grab a flute to add embellishments to the Toyland "Christmas Medley." The 20-minute show is held at Tomorrowland's Galaxy Palace Theater.

At **Belle's Enchanted Christmas,** the friendly Disney hero-ine uses audience volunteers to share the story of her first Christmas in the Beast's castle, the tale told in Disney's 1997 video "Beauty and the Beast: The Enchanted Christmas." Six kids go on stage; a dad plays the Beast. The 16-minute Fairytale Garden show is usually packed. Get there 30 minutes early to get a good seat, 15 minutes early for any seat at all. *Sit by the stage steps and your child may be picked for the show.*

The **Country Bears Christmas Special** is an 18-minute Audio Animatronic concert featuring hillybilly bears and some funny lyrics. During "Tracks in the Snow," host Henry warbles *"When the snow begins a'fallin' and your blood begins to freeze, it's time to stomp and holler and slap your hairy knees."* Later the Five Bear Rugs sing *"This Christmas, dear ol' Santa won't show up I bet. If he comes down our chimney, he might just get et."* On the theater's side wall, talking trophy head Melvin the moose sports outdoor Christmas lights in his antlers; his deer buddy Max has a Rudolph-like red light bulb on his nose.

Choreographed to a medley of songs, **Mickey's Very Merry Christmas Parade** ✔ is the most elaborate Walt Disney World procession of the year. It includes 230 smiling, dancing, sometimes skating cast members among its five live bands and 15 floats and carriages. You'll swear it's twice as long as its 16 minutes. The

Dressed for cold weather on an 80-degree Florida day, castle dancers Celebrate the Season

first half is filled with a dozen Disney characters in holiday garb, Mickey and Minnie Mouse lead the way, followed by the pink hippos from 1942's "Fantasia," here on roller skates. Horses escort a succession of princesses, including Ariel, Aurora ("Sleeping Beauty"), Belle and, riding in her glass carriage pulled by six prancing white ponies, Cinderella. The second half is a Santa Claus parade. Santa's Workshop stars dancing toys such as Raggedy Ann and Andy, a human police car and Woody, Buzz Lightyear, Jessie and Bullseye from 1995's "Toy Story." In Toyland, Santa's kitchen elves teach their life-size gingerbread men how to march, while Chef Goofy bakes some more. Finally, nine campy dancing reindeer (led by Rudolph, who often high-fives the crowd) clear the way for Santa, speaking live from his rooftop sleigh. One of the bands is the marching toy soldiers from Disney's 1961 film, "Babes in Toyland;"

* Clement Clarke Moore's 1822 poem "'Twas the Night Before Christmas" introduced the idea that St. Nick has a sleigh and reindeer.

Clockwise from above: Tamborine dancers escort a Dixieland paddlewheeler; toy soldiers come to life as a real marching band; a roller-skating snowflake dancer twirls down Main Street; Winnie the Pooh escorts his pals from the Hundred Acre Wood; pink hippos skate alongside the crowd.

another is composed of the green army men from "Toy Story." Dad will love all the dancing girls — whirling skaters, twirling maidens, dance-hall dames shaking their tamborines, sashaying Peppermint Patties and hip-thrusting xylophone players. Other extra touches: the "Toy Story" characters become lifeless between songs and you can smell the aromas of Mickey's tree, Goofy's gingerbread men and Mrs. Claus' candy. *See the parade from a front row. Most performers are on the street, not on floats.*

Explosions form Christmas images in the sky during **Holiday Wishes** ✔, a six-act pyro-technic show that's synchronized to "Rudolph the Red-Nosed Reindeer" and other songs. During "O Christmas Tree" the castle turns green, a star explodes at its top and boxed presents float around it. Smiley-face fireworks introduce the "Nutcracker Suite;" later sparklers twirl on the castle. The castle lighting is filled with detail. During the opening number snowflakes fall on Cinderella's home, then lights on its forecourt stage flash along to the beat. During the "March of the Wooden Soldiers," projected images portray cranking toy gears and marching toy soldiers. The best viewing spots are on the north end of Main Street, between the Casey's Corner hot dog stand and the Walt and Mickey statue.

Taking place on the balcony of the Main Street train station, the 10-minute **Tree Lighting Ceremony** features the Main Street Philharmonic, carolers cutting the rug to "It's the Most Wonderful Time of the Year" and an audience

Regis Philbin and Kelly Ripa host the television parade

countdown to light the tree. It takes place just before sundown, about 5:15 p.m. Through Christmas Eve **Santa Claus meets children** just off Main Street, to the left of City Hall. **Lumberjack Donald Duck** meets and greets as he sells trees next to the Mad Tea Party. On some evenings it **snows on Main Street.** There's a 100-percent chance of the (artificial) white stuff at every Mickey's Very Merry Christmas Party (see next page) and occasional flurries other evenings.

The oddest Magic Kingdom event is the filming of its annual **television parade** that airs each Christmas Day on ABC. Usually taped the first weekend in December, the production fills Main Street and the Cinderella Castle stage with cameras, crews and celebrities, as well as recurring hosts Regis Philbin and Kelly Ripa. The work

moves at a snail's pace. Hang out for awhile and you'll see celebrities painstakingly perform take after take of the same few-second sequence and hear lots of backstage chatter. Confused stars complain "I haven't rehearsed this!;" impatient directors bark "Will the elves *please* return to their boxes!!!" *Want to be on camera? Be happy and wear bright, festive clothes.*

Decorations. Two areas of the park are nicely decorated. Main Street U.S.A. is elaborate. Trimmed with candles,

candy canes, popcorn and gingerbread men, a 65-foot spruce re-creates the traditional American tree. Underneath sits a real toy train and other classic toys. Hanging over the street, thick garlands are adorned with plaid bows, poinsettias, pine cones, fruit, sometimes even candles and bells. Poinsettias hang from the lampposts; the trolley has bows along its roof and one on its horse's bridle. Some second-story windows have

---

HOLIDAY HITS. The Magic Kingdom's holiday celebration is filled with music — the vintage pop songs that were once the universal soundtrack of the American Christmas experience. **"The Christmas Waltz"** was a Top 40 hit for The Carpenters in 1978. Written in 1954 for Frank Sinatra, the song's music is simply a finger-exercising routine that was a favorite of composer Jule Styne... **"Deck the Halls"** combines a 17th-century Welsh tune (often played by Mozart) with lyrics from an anonymous 19th-century American... Cowboy star Gene Autry got the idea for 1947's **"Here Comes Santa Claus"** as he rode his horse in the 1946 Hollywood Christmas parade. Though he was supposed to be the procession's major draw, Autry noticed children were far more interested in the guy behind him, yelling "Here comes Santa Claus! Here comes Santa Claus!"... 1963's **"It's the Most Wonderful Time of the Year"** was penned for television crooner Andy

Williams by George Wyle, who later wrote the theme to the 1960s TV show "Gilligan's Island"... First published in 1840 as "One Horse Open Sleigh," **"Jingle Bells"** is a tribute to sleigh races that took place down snow-filled Salem Street in Medford, Mass. Writer James Pierpont added the catchy chorus and retitled the song in 1857... **"Mr. Santa"** is a 1955 novelty version of the No. 1 1954 Chordettes hit, "Mr. Sandman"... **"Must Be Santa"** debuted on the "Sing Along with Mitch [Miller]" TV show in 1961, a program that featured an on-screen bouncing ball that highlighted each song's lyrics... Tchaikovsky's **"The Nutcracker Suite"** is a medley of tunes the famed Russian composer created from his own Nutcracker ballet. First performed in 1892, it includes the tale of a family whose Christmas presents include two life-sized dolls, which each take a turn to dance... **"O Christmas Tree"** is an English version of the 16th-century German Christmas

carol, "Oh Tannenbaum" ("Oh fir tree")... In 1949, Gene Autry recorded **"Rudolph the Red-Nosed Reindeer"** at the urging of his wife, Ina, who felt kids could relate to its ugly-duckling theme. Based on a 1939 newspaper ad for the Montgomery Ward department store, the song became the best-selling single in the history of Columbia Records... In 1958 **"Run, Run, Rudolph"** peaked at No. 69 for rock and roll pioneer Chuck Berry... **"There's No Place Like Home for the Holidays"** was a No. 8 hit for TV singer Perry Como in 1954... **"Santa Baby"** was a No. 4 hit in 1953 for Eartha Kitt, who 47 years later lent her voice to the role of Yzma in Disney's animated film, "The Emperor's New Groove"... **"We Wish You A Merry Christmas"** is a 16th-century English Christmas carol... Published in 1934, **"Winter Wonderland"** wasn't popular until after World War II. Both Perry Como and the Andrews Sisters scored million-seller hits with the song in 1946.

Menorahs. Inside the stores, garland embellishments often match the nearby merchandise. For example, there are tiny toys in the Emporium greenery. At Mickey's Toontown Fair, Mickey and Minnie have decked their roofs with giant light strands; each bulb is about 18 inches long.

The Goofy convention. The week between Christmas and New Year's is the Magic Kingdom's most crowded of the year, and not the time to be here. Not only does the park often close (reach its 80,000-person capacity) around lunchtime, the throng is largely made up of people who appear to have IQs somewhere south of Goofy's, crowding the rides and restaurants as they wander the park aimlessly. If you must come this week, arrive at the park by 7:30 a.m. Use the morning for attractions, see the noon parade, then leave. Return after dark for the castle show, Holiday Wishes and, after the crowd is gone, more attractions. The week *before* Christmas is much better. All the holiday events are happening but the monster crowd isn't here yet.

An easy way to enjoy the holiday fun is **Mickey's Very Merry Christmas Party** ✔. Held every few nights from Thanksgiving through a few days before Christmas, these 7–to-midnight events have crowds of only 10,000 to 25,000 but give you all the holiday events, cookies and hot chocolate. All major rides are open, too. Advance tickets are $40 for adults, $30 for kids 3–9 (regular admission not required). For the best time get to the park by 6:30 p.m. and see the second parade, which is far less crowded. The least crowded party is the Sunday after Thanksgiving; those on December Fridays and Saturdays sell out early.

EPCOT
Most holiday festivities at Epcot are cultural performances in the World Showcase. Sharing legends and traditions from all over the globe, the **Holidays Around the World Storytellers** ✔ perform to small crowds outside of each pavilion. In **Canada**, comic lumberjack Nowell describes Boxing Day, the Inuit's impish Nalyuks and the legend of "people who come to homes dressed in strange outfits. We call them... relatives!" At the **U.K.**, Father Christmas tells how holiday cards and decorating with holly and mistletoe began in his countries. In **France**, Père Noël comically explains how children leave shoes on their doorsteps for him to put presents in. In **Morocco**, a drummer describes the Festival of Ashura, which gives presents to kids who behave well. In **Japan** a vendor explains Daruma dolls, pupil-free good-luck charms that children paint eyes on as they make wishes. At the **American Adventure** one storyteller explains Hanukkah, another describes the principles of Kwanzaa. In **Italy**, good witch La Befana, who slides down chimneys to leave treats for kids, explains why she travels on the day the Three Kings came to Bethlehem. **Germany's** St. Nicholas fills you in about the first Christmas tree and Nutcracker as well as the Christmas pickle, a hidden tree ornament that rewards its finder with an extra present. At the **China** pavilion, the Monkey King spins a tale of how he defeated a

Epcot's **Lights of Winter** syncs its lights to holiday music

monster and found a magic stick. In **Norway**, Epcot's strangest storytelling skit has farm girl Sigrid sure that Christmas Gnome Julenissen doesn't really exist, though you can see him easily. At **Mexico**, the Three Kings explain the customs of Posada, a six-week celebration that starts just before Christmas. Each storyteller performs every hour or so from noon until dusk. Some appear after dark.

An inspirational religious pageant, the **Candlelight Processional** ✔ recounts the birth of Jesus Christ with more than 400 singers and a 50-piece orchestra. Narrated by a different celebrity every few evenings, the one-hour show often includes "O Come All Ye Faithful," "O Holy Night" and "The Hallelujah Chorus." It takes place three times a night at the 1,950-

China's Monkey King

The Disney-MGM Studios parade has a Genie bearing gifts and a vile message from Cruella de Vil

seat America Gardens amphitheater. Though free with park admission, it's so popular that on peak days the only way to see it is to buy a Candlelight Processional Dinner Package (407-939-3463), which includes dinner at an Epcot table restaurant and guaranteed seating. The packages are priced so the show is still, in essence, free if you order the priciest menu items. Otherwise you wait up to three hours in the standby line and are not guaranteed a seat.

At Showcase Plaza, the 15-minute **Mickey's Tree Lighting Treat** features Mickey Mouse and Santa Goofy each night at dusk. Afterward, an archway over the adjacent main walkway becomes the flashing **Lights of Winter,** which is synchronized to holiday music as well as the nearby Innoventions fountain (don't miss the oboe accents of "The Dance of the Sugar Plum Fairy"). **Illuminations** features a 4-minute holiday finale narrated by Walter Cronkite. Prior to Christmas **Santa and Mrs. Claus** sit at the American Adventure to hear wishes and pose for photos. An

oom-pah band plays carols at Germany's Biergarten restaurant. **Guests drum holiday songs** in African rhythms with the Outpost's OrisiRisi. China's **Dragon Legend Acrobats** bring a New Year's Lion to life.

Decorations. Epcot's holiday entrance display changes yearly. Lovely at night, Germany's courtyard is decked out with twinkling trees, wreaths and garlands. Its miniature-train village has its own tiny decorations and tree lot. Inside the American Adventure's Liberty Inn a cast member sells apple cider, hot chocolate and cookies from within a small gingerbread house.

DISNEY-MGM STUDIOS
The Studios embraces the bright lights and big-city charm

of an urban holiday. Portraying fictitious old movie stars, hangers-on and has boons, the **Citizens of Hollywood** ✔ performs holiday skits on Hollywood and Sunset boulevards. In its best routine ("the Hollywood Glee Club"), the characters sing "O Christmas Tree" using only those three words and "Jingle Bells" to the tune of "Joy to the World." The finale is "The Twelve Days of Christmas," with guests joining in to say what they *really* want as gifts: "Eight pink cell phones… seven Malibu beach houses… six pair of clean socks… " Show times are often available at the Guest Relations office. The **Hollywood Holly-Day Parade** ✔ is a tribute to the song "Winter Wonderland." Led by Santa Goofy and Rudolph Pluto, doz-

The **Osborne Family** Spectacle of Dancing Lights on New York Street

ens of characters skip and shimmy past Echo Lake and down Hollywood Blvd. while others ride in a motorcade. One of Miss Piggy's presents is tagged "To Moi, From Moi."

Decorations. Silver strands hang from the 65-foot tree out front and form the garlands above Hollywood Boulevard. Sunset Boulevard lampposts have glittery red and silver stars straight out of a 1940s holiday musical. At the Streets of America each shop window, balcony and brownstone is decorated differently, reflecting its tenant. One dweller is celebrating Hanukkah. Around the cor-

A FAMILY FUSE
The Spectacle of Lights began at the Arkansas home of business tycoon Jennings Osborne in the 1980s, when he strung 1,000 red lights as a Christmas gift to his daughter, Breezy. Soon his 22,000-square-foot home was covered in huge displays and millions of lights, a visual overload some neighbors didn't appreciate. Since moving the display to Disney in 1995 the family has created over 30 other exhibits, including one at the Graceland mansion in Memphis, Tenn. On New York Street, look for the family's giant stockings hanging above a fireplace.

ner, Pizza Planet has huge strands of lights while a giant Santa climbs up the fire escape of Engine Co. No. 1. At night the **Osborne Family Spectacle of Dancing Lights** ✔ covers two dozen facades along the two boulevards as well as the side streets by the Stage 1 gift shop and Mama Melrose's Ristorante Italiano. Hundreds of strands of lights dance in time to Christmas songs as they hang from the rooftops to form huge twinkling nets, while a spinning carousel, giant rotating globe and other animated displays tower above. Dozens of rope-light angels fly over the square at the end of New York Street; others pray to a nativity creche. The five million lights use 12 miles of extension cords and 800,000 watts of power. Disney adds to the fun by spraying "snow" (soap bubbles) from overhead spouts and serving hot chocolate, pretzels and beer.

DISNEY'S ANIMAL KINGDOM
The Animal Kingdom festivities consist of a parade, a singing troupe and some decorations. A reworking of the park's regular parade, the 12-minute **Mickey's Jingle Jungle Parade** adds a holiday touch to its characters, animal floats and safari trucks. Her Jeep topped with a tub of marshmallows, Minnie is

baking treats — you can smell the chocolate — and has set out some for Santa. Donald is making it snow (check the back of his truck for his cache of Mickey-eared ice cream bars). Santa Goofy's vehicle is hung with stockings, each for a different character (one's for Goofy!), while his naughty and nice lists both include Donald. Mickey's Jeep has a train hood ornament with Stitch as its engineer. As for the parade animals, the giant parrot has become a partridge in a pear tree. The soundtrack is spiced with holiday lyrics. Its shout of animal movements ("and stomp and jump and leap and soar!") is tagged with "and thumpity-thump-thump!" At Camp Minnie-Mickey the a capella **Campfire Carolers** do some unusual tunes, and aren't above a few jokes. When one singer says she wants an "opotamus" for Christmas, the others correct her. "You must mean a hippopotamus!" "No, he doesn't have to be very cool."

Decorations. Most of the park's holiday decor takes a natural approach. The 65-foot entrance tree is adorned with metal and wood animals, while its ambient music features flute-and-drum renditions of classics such as "Silent Night." Garlands at the Discovery Island shops are filled with straw, grain stalks, flowers and berries. Each of the dozen trees at Camp Minnie-Mickey belong, on close inspection, to a particular Disney character. Lilo's tree has Elvis records and her handmade doll. At DinoLand U.S.A., tacky proprietors Chester and Hester have decked out Dino-Rama with shredded-plastic trees, candy canes and a giant gleeful snowman. At the Dinosaur Treasures gift shop the couple's personal tree is trimmed with pink flamingos and Styrofoam snowmen; the store itself is lined with hollow-plastic Santas and Santa heads. Dino-Rama music includes obscure novelties such as the 1956 Spike Jones tune "My Birthday Comes on Christmas" and Augie Rios' 1958 "Donde Esta Santa Claus?"

MORE CHRISTMAS FUN

At **Downtown Disney** holiday events typically include carolers, a tree lighting, concerts by visiting Magic Music Days musicians, a strolling brass quintet, toy-soldier stilt walkers and photos with Santa Claus. Each **Disney resort** is trimmed for

Cheerleading camp counselors at the Animal Kingdom parade

the season. The largest tree, a 75-foot display in front of the Contemporary Resort, features 77,000 lights. The 45-foot tree at the Grand Floridian sits inside the lobby, with 45,000 lights sparkling within a Victorian theme. Many resorts spice up the season with confectionery displays. A 16-foot-tall gingerbread house sits in the Grand Floridian lobby. A concoction of honey, sugar, egg whites and apricot glaze covers its wood frame. Similar creations include miniature villages at the Animal Kingdom Lodge and the Contemporary Resort; Santa's workshop at the Board-Walk; a carousel at the Beach Club; and a sugary mountain at the Yacht Club. Not edible, the displays are treated with preservatives so they will last 45 days in open air.

NEW YEAR'S EVE

Disney rings in the New Year with events at the Magic Kingdom, Epcot, Disney-MGM Studios and Downtown Disney.

The Magic Kingdom typically stays open until 1 a.m. There's a fireworks show at midnight, a glimpse of which is shown on ABC-TV as part of the broadcast from New York City's Times Square. At Epcot, World Showcase events can include a big band orchestra, Latin dancing and disc jockeys spinning Euro and techno rock. A late performance of Illuminations adds a New Year's countdown and a coda of "Auld Lang Syne." Disney-MGM Studios often hosts a street party, with a band and disc jockey at the Sorcerer's Hat,

free hats and horns and a midnight fireworks show at the Chinese Theater.

All the theme-park events are included with any park ticket. That's not the case, however, at Disney's biggest bash, held at Downtown Disney's Pleasure Island. A special-ticket party at about $90 per person, it's restricted to those 21 or older.

A BACKSTAGE HOLIDAY.
Decking the halls of Walt Disney World is a full-time job for 26 employees, who toil backstage at a 70,000-square-foot Holiday Services warehouse 12 months of the year. When I stop by one early November afternoon, each cast member is hard at work. Some scurry past me pushing shrink-wrapped wardrobe carts, each tagged with its ID number ("MK 035"), contents ("Checked and Fluffed Garland") and destination ("Main Street Train Station 2nd Floor"). Others drive forklifts loaded with crates of ornaments, or use long poles to remove giant 3-D stars from the rafters. Outside, electricians test out what appears to be some sort of complex utility pole. "This is the guts of the Main Street unit," one says, showing me that the inside of the Magic Kingdom's 65-foot signature tree is nothing but a huge electrical transformer. Nearby, the tree's greenery sits in six circular sections, some more than 10 feet tall. In a few days it will all be trucked over to Main Street, then a crane will stack it together like a giant ring-toss game. The six-hour job will be done overnight, so guests never see the construction. There are similar trees at Epcot, Disney-MGM Studios and Disney's Animal Kingdom. Each tree is used up to five years. And yes, it is a 12-month job. In the spring the staff cleans and repairs the decorations. In the summer it designs new ones. In the fall the group gets ready to install the decorations; after Christmas it puts everything away.

ALL-STAR RESORTS

$–$$ This big complex consists of three nearly identical 10-building resorts, each with a strong theme. All-Star Music has 40-foot guitars, trombones and other instruments. All-Star Movies is dominated by towering film stars including a 35-foot Buzz Lightyear and a 21-foot Herbie the Love Bug. All-Star Sports is defined by giant basketballs, football gear and surfboards. One difference between the resorts is how long you wait for the bus: the pick-up/drop-off order is Sports, Music, Movies. *Near Disney's Animal Kingdom. Disney Value Resorts.* **Movies:** *1900 rooms, 1991 W. Buena Vista Dr. 407-939-7000.* **Music:** *1492 rooms, 214 suites, 1801 W. Buena Vista Dr. 407-939-6000.* **Sports:** *1920 rooms, 1701 W. Buena Vista Dr. 407-939-5000. Typ. room: 260 sq. ft. Disney transportation: Bus. Each property has 3 pools. 246 acres.*

WHERE TO STAY

Disney resorts

Disney runs 19 resorts on its Florida property, which it divides into five categories. Motel-style **Value Resorts** have food courts, pizza delivery, pools, playgrounds and hourly luggage service. Most rooms sleep four. Large complexes, the **Moderate Resorts** add restaurants, limited room service, pools with slides, bellhops and some on-site recreation. Most rooms sleep four. **Deluxe Resorts** add full room service, club levels, fitness centers, kids activities, child care and valet parking. Most rooms sleep five. Often available for

nightly rentals, **Disney Vacation Club** (DVC) time-share units have kitchens and sleep up to 12. A category of its own, the **Fort Wilderness Resort & Campground** is a wooded area with campsites, cabins and RV hookups, as well as a lakeside village that includes a restaurant, general store and unique activities. All resorts have shops, arcades, laundry services and free transportation to Disney theme and water parks and Downtown Disney. For reservations call 407-WDW-MAGIC (939-6244).

All addresses are in the city of Lake Buena Vista, ZIP code 32830. All phone numbers go to a central information center.

ANIMAL KINGDOM LODGE

$$$$ Are you decent? A giraffe may be watching you dress at this African-style wildlife resort, where 200 species of exotic animals come within 30 feet of hotel balconies. Unlike any other resort in Florida, the lodge showcases the beauty and wonder of African culture. The six-story building features thatched roofs and rich woods. An impressive collection of African art and cultural pieces includes a 16-foot mask created by the Igbo people of Nigeria. Rooms have handcrafted furniture and art, much of it from Zimbabwe. Meandering paths extend into the savannah, which is filled with antelope, wildebeest, zebras and other creatures 24 hours a day. Native African docents answer

Standard room, high season ¢ <$80. $ <$110. $$ <$160. $$$ <$220. $$$$ >$220.

questions. Near Disney's Animal Kingdom. A Disney Deluxe Resort. 1,278 rooms, 15 suites. Typ. room: 344 sq. ft. 2 restaurants. 33-acre live-animal savannah, wildlife activities, night-vision goggles. Massage and fitness center. Disney transportation: Bus. On 74 acres. 2901 Osceola Pkwy. 407-938-3000.

BEACH CLUB
$$$–$$$$ This pale-blue-and-white "stick-style" resort reflects the look of 19th-century seaside cottages. Rooms feature cool colors, French doors and porches. Adjacent to Epcot's International Gateway entrance. A Disney Deluxe Resort/DVC. 583 rooms, 205 villas. Typ. room: 381 sq. ft. 3 restaurants, character breakfast. Elaborate swimming area with three pools and a lazy river, beach (no swimming). Hair salon, health club. Meeting space. Disney transportation: Boat (Epcot, Studios), bus. On 25-acre Crescent Lake. 1800 Epcot Resorts Blvd. 407-934-8000.

BOARDWALK INN & VILLAS
$$$$ A re-creation of a grand New Jersey oceanside village, this stylish resort features a wide waterside promenade lined with quaint shops, interesting restaurants, even a dance hall. The exterior appears to be a trio of unrelated complexes, each with its own period architecture. Hidden from the water, the Inn's two-, three- and four-story buildings surround private courtyards and manicured gardens.

Rooms have cozy floral fabrics. Adjacent is the Atlantic Dance hall and Jellyrolls dueling-piano bar. Near Epcot and Disney-MGM Studios. A Disney Deluxe Resort/DVC. 372 rooms, 6 suites, 14 two-story cottages, 533 villas. Typ. room: 385 sq. ft. 4 restaurants, bakery, ice cream shop, pizza window, grocery. 3 pools, 2 tennis courts, small book and extensive video library, bicycle and surrey rentals, carnival games, pole fishing.

Disney's BoardWalk Resort

Health club. Business center; conference center adjacent. Disney transportation: Boat (Epcot, Studios), bus. On 25-acre Crescent Lake. 2101 N. Epcot Resorts Blvd. 407-939-5100.

CARIBBEAN BEACH
$$–$$$ Colorful metal-roofed buildings and hundreds of palms give this resort a re-

Disney's Animal Kingdom Lodge, Disney's Beach Club Resort

© DISNEY

beam. *Within walking distance of the Magic Kingdom. A Disney Deluxe Resort. 1,013 rooms, 25 suites. Typ. room: 394 sq. ft. 3 restaurants, character meals. 2 pools, tennis center, volleyball courts, boat and personal-watercraft rentals, fishing, water sports. Hair salon, health club. 90,000-sq.-ft. convention center. Disney transportation: Boat (MK), monorail (MK, Epcot), bus. 55 acres, on 450-acre Bay Lake. 4600 N. World Dr. 407-824-1000.*

CORONADO SPRINGS

$$–$$$ With tile roofs, mosaics and arched windows and doorways, this spawling resort recalls 16th-century Mexico and the American Southwest. Landscaping features streams, cactus and sagebrush. A central recreation area includes a dig-site themed pool. *Near Disney's Animal Kingdom. A Disney Moderate Resort. 1,877 rooms, 44 suites. Typ. room: 314 sq. ft. 4 pools, bike and boat rentals, volleyball court. Hair salon, health club. 95,000-sq.-ft. convention center. Disney transportation: Bus. 125 acres on 15-acre lake. 1000 Buena Vista Dr. 407-939-1000.*

FORT WILDERNESS

Campsites ¢, Cabins $$$$ Secluded from adjoining sites by trees and other natural surroundings, each campsite has a level, paved pad with a coquina rock bed, a charcoal grill, picnic table and hook-ups for water, electric, sewer and cable. All are located near air-conditioned comfort stations. Air-conditioned cabins sleep six; each has an equipped kitchen, deck, grill and picnic table. Daily housekeeping provided. *784 campsites, 409 cabins. Restaurant, dinner shows, BBQ and picnic areas, grocery.*

laxed feel. Spread around a one-acre island play area, five clusters of two-story buildings each has its own pool and laundry facilities. Indoor food and shopping area. A 1.4-mile promenade around a central lake serves joggers and bicyclists. *A Disney Moderate Resort. 2,112 rooms. Typ. room: 314 sq. ft. 6 pools; bike, surrey and boat rentals. Disney transportation: Bus. 200 acres on 42-acre lake. 900 Cayman Way. 407-934-3400.*

CONTEMPORARY

$$$–$$$$ The monorail comes through the middle of this 15-story A-frame landmark, which also spreads out over two large three-story wings. The black-and-white room decor has muted accents of reds, greens and yellows. The atrium features a 90-foot mural of the American Southwest, created in 1971 by It's a Small World artist Mary Blair. Look for the three-legged blue goat alongside the monorail

© DISNEY

Disney's Fort Wilderness Resort & Campground, Grand Floridian and Old Key West resorts

2 pools, 2 tennis courts, basketball courts, boat rentals, fishing excursions, cane pole and casting rod rentals. Carriage and wagon rides, horse and pony rides, nature trails, small petting zoo. Kid's activities. Nightly campfire with outdoor movie. Electric cart rentals. Pets allowed with a fee. Disney transportation: Boat (MK), bus. 740 acres, on 450-acre Bay Lake. 3520 N. Ft. Wilderness Trail. 407-824-2900.

GRAND FLORIDIAN

$$$$ Reminiscent of a 19th-century Florida resort, this genteel hotel is surrounded by canary palms, southern magnolias and gardens. The white Victorian buildings have gabled red-shingle roofs and 120 miles of scrolls, turnposts and curved moldings. Interior features include armoires and marble-top sinks with old-fashioned fittings. Most rooms include two queen-size beds plus a day bed. The five-story lobby is topped with three illuminated stained-glass domes. The exterior is based on California's Hotel Del Coronado, the setting for the 1959 film, "Some Like it Hot." Near Magic Kingdom. A Disney Deluxe Resort. 842 rooms, 25 suites. 5 restaurants. Typ. room: 440 sq. ft. Afternoon tea. Character meals and teas. 3 pools (1 zero-entry); basketball, 2 tennis courts, volleyball courts; fishing excursions; hair salon, health club, spa. Disney transportation: Boat (MK), monorail (MK, Epcot), bus. 40 acres, on 172-acre Seven Seas Lagoon. 4401 Grand Floridian Way. 407-824-3000.

OLD KEY WEST

$$$$ This resort's lush palms and pastel, tin-roofed build-ings will give you a craving for key-lime pie. Every villa has a view of the woods, a waterway or the Lake Buena Vista golf course. Near Downtown Disney. A DVC property. 531 units, ranging from 376 to 2,202 sq. ft. Grocery. 2 tennis courts; basketball, shuffleboard and volleyball courts; fishing excursions. Health club. Disney transportation: Boat (Downtown Disney), bus. 50 buildings on 74 acres. 1510 N. Cove Rd. 407-827-7700.

POLYNESIAN

$$$-$$$$ With spacious rooms, a good pool and monorail service to the Magic Kingdom, this vintage 12-building complex is themed to the South Seas, with many palms, waterfalls, torch-lit walkways and other exotica. The rooms have hand-carved furnishings and flat-screen TVs. Near Magic Kingdom. A Disney Deluxe Resort. 853 rooms, 5 suites. Typ. room: 391 sq. ft. 2 restaurants. Character meals. Dinner

show. 2 pools (zero-entry); basketball and volleyball courts; beach (no swimming); surrey and boat rentals; fishing excursions; jogging trail. Meeting space. Disney transportation: Boat (MK), monorail (MK, Epcot), bus. 39 acres on 172-acre Seven Seas Lagoon. 600 Seven Seas Dr. 407-824-2000.

POP CENTURY
$–$$ This 11-building homage to 20th-century pop culture is covered in color, with giant props such as 41-foot Rubik's Cubes and 65-foot bowling pins. Everything is themed: the laundry at the 1950s pool looks like a bowling-shoe storage bin. The 1960s buildings are the closest to the bus stand, food court and lobby. A Disney Value Resort. 2,880 rooms. Typ. room: 260 sq. ft. 3 pools, jogging trail. Disney transportation: Bus. 177 acres,

Disney's Pop Century and Port Orleans Riverside Resorts

on 33-acre lake. 1050 Century Dr. 407-938-4000.

PORT ORLEANS FRENCH QUARTER
$$–$$$ Narrow tree-lined avenue-like walkways connect seven ornate rowhouses at this New Orleans-style resort. Along the way are secluded fountains and ivy-covered arches. The Doubloon Lagoon pool has colorful alligator fountains and a slide in the shape of a dragon. Near Downtown Disney. A Disney Moderate Resort. 1,008 rooms. Typ. room: 314 sq. ft. No table-service restaurant. Fishing excursions, jogging trail. Disney transportation: Boat (Downtown Disney), bus. 2201 Orleans Dr. 407-934-5000.

Disney's Polynesian Resort

PORT ORLEANS RIVERSIDE
$$–$$$ The grounds steal the show at this sprawling Natchez-themed complex. Spacious lawns, gardens, tree-shaded walkways and a peaceful river make it a surprisingly relaxing retreat. The 3.5-acre Ol' Man Island recreation center resembles an old-time water hole. Inside the restaurant are the working gears of a 32-foot cotton press. Near Downtown Disney. A Disney Moderate Resort. 2,048 rooms. Typ. room: 314 sq. ft. 6 pools; bike, surrey and boat rentals; cane pole rentals; jogging trail. Carriage rides. Kid's river adventure cruise. Fall and winter campfires. Disney transportation: Boat (Downtown Disney), bus. 1251 Riverside Dr. 407-934-6000.

SARATOGA SPRINGS
$$$$ The only Disney resort with a golf course, this peaceful grouping of luxury condos features spacious grounds, colorful architecture and an equestrian theme that alludes to the late-1800s heyday of its namesake New York town. A

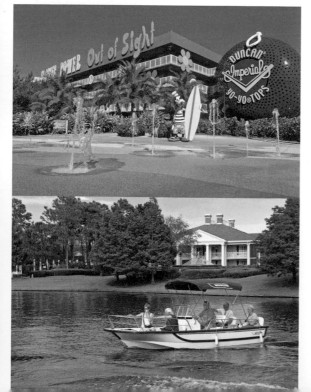

Disney's Saratoga Springs and Yacht Club resorts

DVC property. 828 units, ranging from 355 to 2,113 sq. ft. Grocery. Zero-entry pool; 2 tennis courts, golf course, arts and crafts, basketball half-court and shuffleboard courts, bike and surrey rentals, board games, pool table, table tennis. Jogging trail. Carriage rides. Spa. Disney transportation: Boat (Downtown Disney), bus. 65 acres on 43-acre Village Lake. 1960 Broadway. 407-827-1100.

WILDERNESS LODGE
$$$$ Yellowstone's Old Faithful Inn was the inspiration for this impressive resort. A soaring lobby features 60-foot columns of bundled logs and an 82-foot three-sided stone fireplace (which, if you look closely, contains fossilized remains that re-create the geological record of the earth). A bubbling indoor hot spring expands into a geothermal area which eventually becomes the outdoor swimming pool, or at least appears to. Surrounded by towering pines, cypress and oaks, the lobby building and its two wings are secluded. Grounds feature a volcanic meadow with color pools, brooks and geysers spewing streams up to 100 feet into the air. Guestrooms have patchwork quilts, etched armoires and Old West artwork. *Near Magic Kingdom. A Disney Deluxe Resort/DVC. 701 rooms, 27 suites, 136 villas. Typ. room: 344 sq. ft. 2 restaurants. 2 pools, bike and surrey rentals, bike and jogging path to Fort Wilderness, fishing excursions, health club, nature trails. Architecture tour held every Wed.–Sat. at 9 a.m. Disney transportation: Boat (MK), bus. 150 acres on 450-acre Bay Lake. 901 Timberland Dr. 407-824-3200.*

YACHT CLUB
$$$$ Oak floors, antique chandeliers and rich millwork and brass evoke the 1870s summer homes of Martha's Vineyard and Nantucket at this silvery-gray clapboard hotel. Decorated in blues and whites, all rooms have French doors that open onto porches or balconies. A croquet lawn leads to a lighthouse marina. *Near Epcot and Disney-MGM Studios. A Disney Deluxe Resort. 606 rooms, 24 suites. Typ. room: 381 sq. ft. 2 restaurants. Elaborate swim area features three pools and a lazy river, 2 tennis courts, volleyball court, beach (no swimming), bike and surrey rentals, boat rentals, boating and fishing excursions. Jogging trail. Hair salon, health club. 73,000-sq.-ft. convention center. Disney transportation: Boat (Epcot, Studios), bus. On 25-acre Crescent Lake. 1700 Epcot Resorts Blvd. 407-934-7000.*

Disney's Wilderness Lodge

The Disney difference

Some benefits of a Disney resort are obvious. The themed architecture and decor, landscaping and quality restaurants immerses you in a vacation experience. Disney's reputation as a clean, family environment is well deserved: grounds crews, maintenance workers and security guards seem to be everywhere. The convenient location makes it easy to take a midday break from theme-park or other adventures.

But there's more.

Each day one of the four theme parks opens one hour early, or stays open up to three hours late for Disney resort guests. Water parks also participate. These **Extra Magic Hours** offer you uncrowded time in the parks and make it easier to plan out your vacation. (You still need a park ticket, of course.) **Complimentary transportation** (boats, buses and monorails) takes you to all theme and water parks, golf courses and Downtown Disney. A Disney resort I.D. — your **"Key to the World"** — lets you charge park food, merchandise and other services to your room. Disney's free **package pickup and delivery** service will take

anything you buy from Disney and deliver it to your room.

Resort guests also get **preferred tee times** at Disney's six golf courses.

Disney's innovative **Magical Express** service offers complimentary shuttle and luggage delivery from the Orlando International Airport (OIA) to your Disney resort. In other words, you don't have to rent a car and you completely bypass baggage claim and your bags are automatically placed in your room. When it's time to return home, you check your luggage at your hotel (domestic flights only) and then hop on a bus back to the airport. If your flight departs late in the day, you can check out of the hotel, check your luggage at the desk nearby, then go off and still fully enjoy your last day at Disney.

The best part? There's no real catch. You have to book the service at least 10 days in advance. Participating airlines for return luggage check-in include American, Continental, Delta, JetBlue, Northwest, Ted and United. The service is extraordinarily popular. On some days more than 10,000 people use it, and that's just on the *incoming* buses.

Cleaning the theming. A Disney maintenance worker washes a prop at the Pop Century Resort.

For details call Magical Express Guest Services at 866-599-0951. *The Walt Disney World Swan and Dolphin, Shades of Green and the Downtown Disney resorts are not included in the program.*

Monorails take guests of the Contemporary, Polynesian and Grand Floridian resorts directly to the Magic Kingdom

Also at Walt Disney World

SHADES OF GREEN

¢–$$$$ The only Armed Forces Recreation Center (AFRC) in the continental United States, this quality full-service resort is for the exclusive use of U.S. military members and their families. *Near Magic Kingdom. 575 rooms, 5 suites, 5 jr. suites, 1 disabled-access suite with roll-in shower. Rooms are at least 400 sq. ft. 3 restaurants, lounge, snack bar, ice cream shop, pool grill, room service. 2 pools, 2 tennis courts, 3 golf courses adjacent, arcade, playground, remote-controlled boats. AAFES general store, gift shop. Washer/dryers. Laundry service. Fitness center. Meeting facilities. Multi level parking garage. Guests can get discounted Disney tickets and greens fees, as well as Extra Magic Hours. Bus service to various Disney locations. 1950 W. Magnolia Palm Dr. (across from Disney's Polynesian Resort). Information at 407-824-3400 or shadesofgreen.org.*

WALT DISNEY WORLD SWAN AND DOLPHIN

$$$$ The Dolphin and Swan share similar elements of postmodern "entertainment" architecture, but each has a distinctive appearance. The tallest structure at Walt Disney World, the Dolphin's 27-story triangular tower has two 12-story arching wings topped with 56-foot statues of "mahi-mahi" dolphin fish. A 9-story clamshell fountain cascades down the rear. The Swan, a 12-story arching rectangle with two 7-story wings, is crowned with 47-foot swan statues. The wings of the Dolphin are topped with 20-foot tulip fountains; the wings of the Swan with 20-foot clam shell spouts.

The buildings are joined by a palm-lined promenade that splits a lagoon. Seen together, they tell a story. The Dolphin is a tropical mountain. Surrounded by huge banana palms, it has a waterfall flowing from within it. As the water reaches a coastline, it splashes onto a huge sand dune — the Swan. Riding the surge are the swans. The rooms feature luxurious Heavenly Beds. Lobbies boast colorful chandeliers and woven metal and rosewood paneling. Kids love the fiberoptic shooting star in the Dolphin foyer. The complex was designed by Michael Graves, known for his distinctive line of housewares sold at Target stores. *Near Epcot and Disney-MGM Studios. 5-acre recreation complex includes 3-acre grotto pool area with tropical waterfall and slide, 4 tennis courts, basketball and volleyball court, table tennis, Swan pedal boats for rent. Jogging trail. Free art and architecture tour. Guests receive on-site Disney ticketing, Extra Magic Hours and Disney-guest preferred tee times, but not Magical Express service or Disney room-charging privileges. Disney transportation: Boat (Epcot, Studios); bus. On 25-acre Crescent Lake. Typ. room: 360 sq. ft. Special rates for nurses, teachers and members of the U.S. military. Many convention guests.* **Dolphin:** *1,377 rooms, 132 suites. 4 restaurants. 24-hour convenience*

Walt Disney World Swan (top) and **Dolphin** (above) resorts

store. Arcade. Health club. Spa. Launderette. Business center. 202,000-sq.-ft. convention center. A Starwood Sheraton property, not owned by Disney. 1500 Epcot Resorts Blvd. 407-934-4000. **Swan:** *687 rooms, 69 suites. 2 restaurants, sushi bar, character meals. Arcade. Health club. Business center. 52,000-sq.-ft. convention center. A Starwood Westin property, not owned by Disney. 1200 Epcot Resorts Blvd. 407-934-3000.*

WALT DISNEY WORLD SWAN AND DOLPHIN RESORT

Disney resort restaurants

1900 PARK FARE $$$ American. Character breakfast buffet with Mary Poppins and friends. Afternoon tea with Alice, the Mad Hatter. Dinner buffet with Cinderella and friends has prime rib, seafood, pasta. Carousel animals, antique "Big Bertha" organ. Book dinner weeks early; Cindy's a popular gal. *Grand Floridian. 267 seats.* Nearby ✔ **Garden View Lounge** holds a midday tea with Aurora ("Sleeping Beauty") and a character-free afternoon tea.

✔ **ARTIST POINT $$$$** A creative menu features cedar-roasted salmon, elk tenderloin, grilled buffalo top sirloin. Oregon, Washington State wines. Light woods, cathedral ceiling, American Northwest landscape art. Elegant. Dinner. *Wilderness Lodge. 225 seats.*

✔ **BEACHES & CREAM $** Bustling 50s-style soda shop. Hamburgers, turkey burgers, milkshakes, giant sundaes. *Beach Club. 58 seats.*

✔ **BIG RIVER GRILLE & BREWING WORKS $$** American. Microbrewery. Veal, chicken dishes use beer sauces. Good pasta, sandwiches, cheese soup. *BoardWalk. 190 seats, including 50 outside.*

BOATWRIGHT'S $$–$$$ Menu is American with Cajun flavors. Looks like a shipbuilding yard. Breakfast, dinner. *Port Orleans Riverside. 206 seats.*

✔ **BOMA $$** Outstanding mix of interesting food, surroundings and value. African-inspired menu with fish, meat and vegetable dishes, many similar to those of rural America. Great soups. Served all-you-can-eat from buffet-like stations in an exhibit kitchen. Many American options. Breakfast, dinner. *Animal Kingdom Lodge. 400 seats.*

✔ **CALIFORNIA GRILL $$$** Creative American. Top picks: mussels, grilled pork, sushi, desserts. 100-item wine list. Romantic. Great view. Dinner. *Atop the Contemporary. 363 seats.*

CAPE MAY CAFE $$$ Character breakfast with Chip 'n' Dale, Goofy, Minnie Mouse offers eggs, bacon, sausage, etc. Dinner "clambake" buffet. *Beach Club. 234 seats.*

✔ **CHEF MICKEY'S $$–$$$** Energetic napkin-waving character buffet with Mickey and Minnie Mouse, Chip 'n' Dale, Pluto, sometimes Goofy and Donald Duck. American cuisine. Reserve your table a month early. Breakfast, dinner. *Contemporary. 405 seats.*

CÍTRICOS $$$ Mediterranean. Creative appetizers accent light herb-based menu. Single-table, glass-walled room available. Nice wines. Show kitchen. Dinner. *Grand Floridian. 190 seats.*

CONCOURSE STEAKHOUSE $$–$$$ American. Good breakfast cinnamon buns and quesadillas, steak-like burgers for lunch, yellow-fin tuna for dinner. Wave to the passing monorail passengers; many wave back. *Contemporary. 220 seats.*

ESPN CLUB $$ Sports bar with 100 televisions. Lunch, dinner. *BoardWalk. 450 seats.*

FLYING FISH CAFE $$$ Grilled seafood, steaks. Nightly specials. Named for a 1934 Coney Island coaster, the Flying Turns. Dinner. *BoardWalk. 193 seats.*

FRESH MEDITERRANEAN MARKET $$ American breakfast buffet with juice bar. Market-style lunch menu features salads and sandwiches with

Above: Todd English's bluezoo, Walt Disney World Dolphin

Avg./adult: $ <$10. $$ <$20. $$$ <$30. $$$$ <$40. Reservations: 407-WDW-DINE

Mediterranean flavors. Request the Verandah for a quiet spot. *Dolphin. 264 seats.*

GARDEN GROVE CAFE $$ American breakfast and lunch buffet. Japanese breakfast available. Weekend character breakfast with Goofy, Pluto Sat.; also Chip 'n' Dale Sun. *Swan. 150 seats.*

GRAND FLORIDIAN CAFE $$-$$$ American. Good Eggs Benedict for breakfast. Lunch has tasty sandwiches and French onion soup. Dinner offers everything from cheeseburgers to surf and turf. *Grand Floridian. 326 seats.*

GULLIVER'S $$$ Character dinner meal with Rafiki, Timon (Mon., Fri.); Goofy, Pluto other nights. Cuisine: Italian (Tue., Thr., Sun.), Southern (Mon., Wed., Sat.), Seafood (Fri.) buffets. The decor recalls the cage in which Queen Caribbean kept her swan in Jonathan Swift's 1726 novel, "Gulliver's Travels." *Swan. 150 seats.*

✔ **IL MULINO $$$** It's the seafood that makes this elegant Italian eatery special. Best bets: shrimp, snapper. A calm, airy version of the NYC legend. Dinner. *Swan. 224 seats.*

✔ **JIKO $$$** Disney's top gourmet dinner choice. African-influenced meat, seafood; creative salads, appetizers. Largest S. African wine collection in U.S. Stylized "Lion King" decor. *Animal Kingdom Lodge. 300 seats.*

✔ **KIMONOS $$** Sushi, sashimi. Specialties include gyoza, duck satay. Extensive sake menu. Karaoke at 9:30 p.m. Kids can order non-sushi items. Dinner. *Swan. 105 seats.*

✔ **KONA CAFE $$** American with Asian flavors. Kona coffee. Breakfast (Tonga Toast!), lunch, dinner. *Polynesian. 163 seats.*

MAYA GRILL $$-$$$ Mexican-Caribbean meat, fish, poultry dishes; several with native Mayan seasonings. Run by the son of the proprietor of the San Angel Inn in Mexico City. Breakfast, lunch, dinner. *Coronado Springs. 220 seats.*

NARCOOSSEE'S $$$$ Seafood, steak. Over water. Dinner. *Grand Floridian. 150 seats.*

✔ **'OHANA $$$** American with Asian flavors. Family style. Character breakfast (Mickey Mouse, Pluto, Lilo and Stitch). Dinner grills meats, seafood on open pit. *Polynesian. 300 seats.*

OLIVIA'S CAFE $$ American via Key West: pork chops, pasta, conch chowder, key lime pie. Breakfast, lunch, dinner. *Old Key West. 122 seats.*

✔ **SHULA'S STEAK HOUSE $$$$** American. Many steak choices, huge lobster. Est. by Miami Dolphins coach Don Shula; clubby decor themed to his undefeated 1972 season. Menus painted on footballs. Dinner. *Dolphin. 215 seats.*

SHUTTERS $$ American with Caribbean flavors. *Caribbean Beach. Dinner. 132 seats.*

✔ **SPOODLES $$$** American breakfast with egg dishes; Mediterranean dinner with tapas. Open kitchen. Takeout pizza. *BoardWalk. 206 seats.*

✔ **TODD ENGLISH'S BLUEZOO $$$** International, New American seafood. Interesting flavors. Signature "dancing fish;" Cantonese lobster. Soft techno music. Younger crowd. Dinner. *Dolphin. 400 seats.*

TRAIL'S END $$ American buffet. *Fort Wilderness. 212 seats.*

TURF CLUB BAR & GRILL $$ Equestrian-style casual. Sandwiches, pork ribs. Patio tables overlook golf course. Lunch, dinner. *Saratoga Springs. 150 seats, inc. 50 outside.*

✔ **VICTORIA & ALBERT'S $$$$** The most formal Disney dining. Seven-course prix-fixe menu includes a choice of four European entrees, customized daily. Excellent wine list. Romantic atmosphere, with a live harpist. Strict dress code. Chef's table. AAA Five Diamond winner. Dinner. *Grand Floridian. 80 seats.*

✔ **WHISPERING CANYON CAFE $$-$$$** Family-style skillet meals offer smoked, grilled, barbecued meats. Good sandwiches, salads. Rowdy kids games and races. Be prepared if you ask for ketchup. *Wilderness Lodge. 281 seats.*

YACHT CLUB GALLEY $$ American. Breakfast buffet. Good sandwiches; varied dinner. Calm. Fun Kids Puzzle dessert. *Yacht Club. 280 seats.*

YACHTSMAN STEAKHOUSE $$$$ An open-air kitchen prepares filet mignon and other steaks on hardwood-fired grills. Some seafood. A good bet: the slow-roasted prime rib. Dinner. *Yacht Club. 286 seats.*

Dinner shows

✔ **DISNEY'S SPIRIT OF ALOHA DINNER SHOW** Dancing, drumming and music from Hawaii, New Zealand, Samoa, Tahiti, Tonga. Native cast. Family-style American with Asian flavors. Book early. *$50.22 inc. tax and gratuity for ages 10 and over, $25.43 for ages 3 to 9. 5:15, 8 p.m. Tues.-Sat. Polynesian*

✔ **HOOP-DEE-DOO REVUE** This rootin, tootin' troupe of six Wild West performers has just ridden into town for some downhome dancin,' singin' and carryin' on. The all-you-can-eat meal features barbecue ribs, fried chicken, corn on the cob, strawberry shortcake and yes, beer. Is it knee-slappin'? Boy howdy — especially after a few beers. Book well in advance. *$50.22 inc. tax and gratuity for ages 10 and over, $25.43 for ages 3 to 9. 5:15, 7:15, 9:30 p.m. nightly. Fort Wilderness.*

MICKEY'S BACKYARD BBQ Dance with characters as you feast on barbecue chicken, pork ribs, burgers and hot dogs. Lemonade, beer. *$39.01 inc. tax and gratuity for ages 10 and over, $25 for ages 3 to 9. 5:15, 7:15, 9:30 p.m. Thr.-Sat. March-Dec. Fort Wilderness.*

A kid's guide to Disney pools

By Micaela Neal, age 12

A Disney pool and your average pool are very different. Since just being wet is fun, any pool with people has a happy atmosphere. But in Disney it's even happier, because there are more happy people and usually more things to do.

A normal pool is nothing but a pool: a big, water-filled rectangle. But a normal Disney pool has at least a fun shape and probably a swervy slide. Almost all Disney pools also have a sauna, kiddie pool (sometimes with a little slide of its own) and nice snack area where you may be able to buy an ice cream sundae. A normal pool sometimes makes you leave just to get a soda!

At my neighborhood pool, there are often old women lying around on their backs. Many times there are no kids around except little tiny ones with their moms. I swim laps, but if I want to play there's really not much to do. But when I go to a Disney pool it's different. I see eager kids playing with each other, even if they don't know each other, and parents playing with their kids. I'm around laughing teenagers. I

watch happy moms who catch their happy little toddlers coming down the kiddie slides.

If you're staying at Disney, knowing about the pools is important, because you can only swim at those at your own resort. Here's a list of the pools, in order of how fun they are:

The best Disney pool is really a miniature water park at the **Yacht and Beach Club.** Called Stormalong Bay, it has a small lazy river that tired parents can float down on a rented tube and a big kiddie pool that has a real sand bar. In fact, all the pools here have actual sand on the bottom. The best part is the slide, Disney's longest. It's supposed to be a broken mast of an old ship. As you go down through it, you get showered by two waterfalls. A second kiddie pool has a tiny slide of its own. If you get hungry go right next door to Beaches and Cream, which has huge ice cream sundaes. *Open 10 a.m. to 8 p.m.*

Another great pool is Nanea at the **Polynesian Resort**. It has the most exciting and unpredictable slide — a dark, slippery tunnel with eerie colored lights. It goes through a

"volcano" that spurts water. The pool has underwater Hawaiian music, though it's usually hard to hear. If you're in a wheelchair, there's a zero-entry side so you can get in easily. This is a great pool to float around in after a morning at the Magic Kingdom. *Open 7 a.m. to 10 p.m.*

A third great pool choice is Ol' Man Island at **Port Orleans Riverside.** The pool has the most waterfalls to soak your head under. The slide swerves and turns while dribbling water on you. This pool is surrounded by trees, giving it great shade. It's a nice place to relax. *Open 7 a.m. to midnight.*

At **Port Orleans French Quarter** you slide down the tongue of a giant serpent, which if you look closely is swimming through the nearby cement. This Doubloon Lagoon pool is themed to Mardi Gras, as the resort is meant to look like pre-Katrina New Orleans. Stationed all around is a band of big fiberglass alligators playing all kinds of instruments. Some stand in front of a huge water-drizzling clam. One gator's um-

The author jumps backward into a Contemporary Resort pool

A sand bar at Stormalong Bay, at Disney's Yacht and Beach Club

brella has become a shower, dripping water on whoever wants to be rinsed off. Another alligator plays a water-gushing clarinet. A third plays a squirting saxophone just for tots in the kiddie pool. *Open 7 a.m. to midnight.*

The next best pool is the Grotto in between the **Swan and Dolphin.** There is a huge waterfall to get soaked under and a volleyball net at one end, where you can play with a free ball you get from the pool deck. A row of tiny waterfalls are near the volleyball net. Two lap pools are nearby. The best time to come here is in the summer. Every Saturday night they show a Disney movie at the pool, and give out tubes to float in while you watch it. *Open 9 a.m. to 9 p.m.*

Another resort worth staying at just for the pool is **Wilderness Lodge.** This pool, Silver Creek Springs, gets its water from a man-made creek. It has a zero-entry entrance, too. A geyser outside the pool spurts a giant column into the sky for about five minutes every hour on the :05 (example: 6:05). A great slide sprays you with mist as you ride down. *Open 7 a.m. to midnight.*

At the **Contemporary,** the pool closest to the lake is round. It gets deeper as you head to the middle. The main pool has a large fountain, a big column of water in the center and a row of smaller fountains.

The slide just swerves until it reaches the bottom. *Open 7 a.m. to midnight.*

The eighth best Disney pool is the Dig Site at **Coronado Springs.** A replica version of an ancient Mexican building overlooks the pool. The best part here is the Jaguar Slide. As you twist down it, a fiberglass jaguar spits water at you. *Open 10 a.m. to 8 p.m.*

The next best is the Luna Pool at the **BoardWalk.** The theme here is a combination circus and carnival. Fiberglass elephants are all around. One trumpets water from its trunk. Another sprays water into the pool. One stands lonely by the lifeguard stand. The last sprays water into the kiddie pool. The border tiles around the pool have Dumbo silhouettes on them. The 200-foot-long Keister Coaster water slide slips you in a circle twice, then tosses you out of a huge clown's gaping mouth. *Open 10 a.m. to 8 p.m.*

The most relaxing Disney pool is the Uzima Pool at **Animal Kingdom Lodge.** It has a fine slide that turns a lot in the sun. Outside the pool there's a flamingo viewing area where you can watch some of these beautiful birds enjoy the nice Florida weather. It's the only Disney pool that is open all night. *Open 24 hours.*

At the **Caribbean Beach Resort,** the Old Port Royale pool has a pirates theme. The

"buildings" and bridges that surround it look like an old Caribbean fort. Cannons spray mist at you. A waterfall is here too, between two decorative spitting lion faces. The slide is short, though still fun. *Open 7 a.m. to midnight.*

Next is the Beachside Pool at the **Grand Floridian.** This also has a pounding waterfall to soak yourself in, and a zero-entry area. The slide swerves like the Contemporary one, only this one's longer. Just outside the pool is a fountain and a lap pool. *Open 10 a.m. to 8 p.m.*

As far as Vacation Club pools go, the main one at **Saratoga Springs** *(open 7 a.m to midnight)* has a short slide in the dark, and the main pool at **Old Key West** *(open 7 a.m. to midnight)* goes under a footbridge, with a slide that goes through a two-story dark sandcastle. There's a quiet kiddie pool.

The pools at **Pop Century** *(open 7 a.m to midnight)* and the **All-Star Resorts** *(open 8 a.m. to midnight)* don't have slides, but do have strange shapes and fun fountains.

The best at Pop Century is the Hippy Dippy Pool in the 1960s area, where flowers on the outside of the pool spray you. The kiddie pool has a flower shower. At the All-Star Resorts, the Sports pool has Goofy squirting you with a baseball pitching machine. The Three Caballeros shoot you with water in the Music pool. A pool in All-Star Movies has Fantasia Mickey spraying water from his fingers.

The pool at the **Fort Wilderness Resort & Campground** is just a plain old rectangle. Still, everyone is in a good mood and having fun. *Open 10 a.m. to midnight.*

Any of these pools can be fun. Even at one of the duller ones, you can take up a whole afternoon playing Monkey in the Middle with your dad's hat.

Downtown Disney resorts

Located at the east end of the Disney property, this collection of hotels and resorts is run by outside companies but offers many Disney amenities, including free theme-park shuttles and discounts at Disney golf courses. All the resorts have swimming pools, game rooms, play areas and wireless and high-speed Internet access. Originally referred to as Disney's Hotel Plaza, the area was first developed in the early 1970s. *All addresses are in the city of Lake Buena Vista; ZIP code 32830.*

BEST WESTERN LAKE BUENA VISTA $–$$ Three restaurants, children's play area, fitness center, game room. *325 rooms. 18-story tower. 2000 Hotel Plaza Blvd. 407-828-2424.*

BUENA VISTA PALACE $$$ Eight restaurants inc. Australian-themed Outback, Disney character breakfast. Salon, fitness center, tennis and volleyball courts. Large spa (407-827-3200). Top-floor lounge. Largest, tallest Downtown Disney resort. *1,012 rooms. 27-story tower. On 27 acres. 1900 Buena Vista Dr. 407-827-2727.*

DOUBLETREE GUEST SUITES $$–$$$ Restaurant, fitness center, playground, tennis court. Children's check-in and theater. Sweet Dreams bedding program. Aviary in lobby. The only all-suite hotel on Disney property. *229 suites. 7 stories. 2305 Hotel Plaza Blvd. 407-934-1000.*

GROSVENOR $–$$ Restaurant, English pub, Sat. murder-mystery dinner show, Disney character breakfast Tue., Thur., Sat. Sherlock Holmes museum. Health club. Basketball, shuffleboard, tennis, volleyball courts. Pronounced "GROVE-nor." *626 rooms. 19-story tower, two wings. On 13 acres. 1850 Hotel Plaza Blvd. 407-828-4444.*

HILTON $$$ Six restaurants inc. Benihana, Disney character breakfast Sun. Hair salon, cyber cafe, health club, golf pro shop. Three pools. The only Downtown Disney hotel with Disney's Extra Magic Hours benefit. *814 rooms. 1751 Hotel Plaza Blvd. 407-827-4000.*

HOLIDAY INN $ Restaurant, health club, playground. Kids eat free with a paying adult. *14 stories. 323 rooms. 1805 Hotel Plaza Blvd. 407-828-8888. **Closed at press time.***

ROYAL PLAZA $$ Spacious rooms with separate sitting areas. Some have kitchenettes, wet bars or whirlpool tubs. Restaurants, fitness center, tennis courts. Renovated in 2006. *394 rooms. 17 stories. 1905 Hotel Plaza Blvd. 407-828-2828.*

From top: Buena Vista Palace, Best Western, DoubleTree, Grosvenor, Hilton, Royal Plaza.
PHOTOS: DOWNTOWN DISNEY HOTEL ASSN.

Outside Disney

Quoted distances are to the closest Walt Disney World entrance gate. Particular Disney theme parks may be up to 7 miles farther.

BARCELÓ ORLANDO $–$$ Restaurants, pool. Free access to adjacent YMCA Aquatic Center. *7 mi. to WDW. 8444 International Dr., Orlando, 32819. 407-345-0505.*

BEST WESTERN LAKESIDE $–$$ Breakfast restaurant, heated pools, sand playgrounds. *2 mi. to WDW. 7769 W. U.S. 192, Kissimmee, 34747. 407-396-2222.*

BUENA VISTA SUITES $$ Restaurant, heated pool. Pets allowed for fee. Free breakfast buffet. *Free WDW (2 mi.), mall shuttle. 8203 World Center Dr., Orlando, 32821. 800-537-7737.*

CARIBE ROYALE ORLANDO $$–$$$ Restaurants; pool with water slide, waterfall. By outlet malls. *Free WDW shuttle (2 mi.). 8101 World Center Dr., Orlando, 32821. 800-823-8300.*

CELEBRATION HOTEL $$–$$$ Restaurant, pool. *Free WDW shuttle (4 mi.). 700 Bloom St., Celebration, 34747. 888-499-3800.*

CELEBRITY RESORTS ORLANDO ¢–$ Restaurant, indoor and outdoor pools. *5 mi. to WDW. 2800 N. Poinciana Blvd., Kissimmee, 34746. 800-423-8604.*

COUNTRY INN & SUITES LBV $–$$ Heated pool, some kitchens. Free continental breakfast. *Free WDW shuttle (1 mi.). 12191 S. Apopka Vineland Rd., Lake Buena Vista, 32830. 407-239-1115.*

COUNTRY INN & SUITES MAINGATE $–$$ Pools, kitchens. Pets allowed for a fee. *Free WDW shuttle (5 mi.). 5001 Calypso Cay Way, Kissimmee, 34746. 407-997-1400.*

COUNTRY INN & SUITES INT'L DR. $–$$ Pool. Free continental breakfast. *Free WDW shuttle (8 mi.). 7701 Universal Blvd., Orlando, 32819. 407-313-4200.*

Gaylord Palms Resort & Spa

Embassy Suites International Drive South

COURTYARD AT MARRIOTT VILLAGE $–$$ Breakfast restaurant, indoor/outdoor pool. *Shuttle to WDW (1 mi.). 8623 Vineland Ave., Orlando, 32821. 877-682-8552.*

COURTYARD BY MARRIOTT LBV $–$$ Breakfast restaurant, heated pools. *Free shuttle to outlet mall and WDW (1 mi.). 8501 Palm Pkwy., Orlando, 32836. 407-239-6900.*

CROWNE PLAZA $–$$ Restaurant, pools. Near outlet mall. *4 mi. from WDW. 12000 International Dr., Orlando, 32821. 407-239-1222.*

EMBASSY SUITES INT'L DR. JAMAICAN CT. $$$ Sauna, indoor/outdoor pool. Free made-to-order breakfast. *8 mi. to WDW. 8250 Jamaican Ct., Orlando, 32819. 800-327-9797.*

EMBASSY SUITES INT'L DR. SOUTH $$$ Restaurant, sauna, pools. Free cooked-to-order breakfast. *Free WDW shuttle (6 mi.). 8978 Intl. Dr., Orlando, 32819. 800-433-7275.*

EMBASSY SUITES LBV $$ Restaurant, indoor/outdoor pool, sauna, kitchenettes. Free cooked-to-order breakfast. *Free WDW shuttle (1 mi.). 8100 Lake Ave., Orlando, 32836. 800-257-8483.*

EMBASSY SUITES ORLANDO AIRPORT $–$$ Restaurant, pool. Free cooked-to-order breakfast. Free airport shuttle. *16 mi. to WDW. 5835 TG Lee Blvd., Orlando, 32822. 407-888-9339.*

FAIRFIELD AT CYPRESS PALMS $–$$ Pool, BBQ area. *4 mi. to WDW. 5324 Fairfield Lake Dr., Kissimmee, 34746. 407-397-1600.*

FLORIDAYS ORLANDO $$–$$$ Restaurant, pools, kitchens, balconies. Two-person jetted tubs. *Free WDW shuttle (3 mi.). 12550 Floridays Resort Dr., Orlando, 32821. 866-797-0022.*

GAYLORD PALMS $$$ Restaurants, heated pools, convention space, spa, hair salon. 5-acre tropical atrium with alligators, koi, other live animals. Incredible Christmas display. *Free WDW shuttle (1 mi.). 6000 W. Osceola Pkwy., Kissimmee, 34746. 877-677-9352.*

GRAND BEACH SUNTERRA $$$–$$$$ Pool, kitchens, lakefront, water sports. Condo rentals. *2 mi. to WDW. 8317 Lake Bryan Beach Blvd., Orlando, 32821. 866-396-0883.*

Standard room, high season ¢ <$80. $ <$110. $$ <$160. $$$ <$220. $$$$ >$220.

HILTON GARDEN INN SEAWORLD $–$$ Restaurant, pool. *4 mi. from WDW. 6850 Westwood Blvd., Orlando, 32821. 407-354-1500.*
HILTON GARDEN INN UNIVERSAL $–$$ Restaurant, pool. Rooms have large work desks with lamps. *9 mi. to WDW. 5877 American Way, Orlando, 32819. 407-363-9332.*
HOMESUITEHOME NIKKI BIRD $–$$ Cafe, 3 pools. *1 mi. to WDW. 7300 W. U.S. 192, Kissimmee, 34747. 407-396-7300.*
HYATT REGENCY GRAND CYPRESS $$$$ Restaurants, pools, convention space, private lake, 4 golf courses, spa, equestrian center, nature trails, canoeing, air-boat rentals. *Free WDW shuttle (1 mi.). One Grand Cypress Blvd., Orlando, 32836. 800-233-1234.*
HYATT REGENCY INT'L AIRPORT $$–$$$ Restaurants, heated pool, beauty salon, spa, convention services. Atop airport. *Free WDW shuttle (16 mi.). 9300 Airport Blvd., Orlando, 32827. 800-233-1234.*
INTERNATIONAL PLAZA $$–$$$ Restaurants, heated pools, spa, beauty salon. Miniature golf. *Free WDW shuttle (6 mi.). 10100 Intl. Dr., Orlando, 32821. 800-327-0363.*
JW MARRIOTT GRANDE LAKES $$$–$$$$ Restaurant, pool, spa, sauna, golf course. *Free WDW shuttle (7 mi.). 4040 Central Florida Pkwy., Orlando, 32837. 800-576-5750.*
LAKE BUENA VISTA RESORT VILLAGE $$–$$$ Restaurant, heated pool, kitchens, spa. 2- and 3-bed. condos. *Free WDW shuttle (2 mi.). 8112 Poinciana Blvd., Orlando, 32821. 866-401-2699.*
LAKE SUITES $–$$ Heated pool, kitchens, sandy beach, BBQ area. Pets allowed for a fee. Free breakfast. *Free WDW shuttle (5 mi.). 4786 W. U.S. 192, Kissimmee, 34746. 866-809-3553.*
MARRIOTT CYPRESS HARBOUR VILLA $$–$$$ Pools, sauna, kitchens, washer/dryers, marina, water sports. 2 bed./2 ba. villas. *4 mi. from WDW. 11251 Harbour Villa Rd., Orlando, 32821. 800-845-5279.*
MARRIOTT DOWNTOWN $$$–$$$$ Restaurants, pool, meeting space. Adjoins Amway Arena. *16 mi. to WDW. 400 W. Livingston St., Orlando, 32801. 407-843-6664.*
MARRIOTT ROYAL PALMS $$$$ Restaurants, pool, kitchens, lakefront, washer/dryers. Next to Orlando World Center Marriott Resort, free access to its amenities. *2 mi. from WDW. 8404 Vacation Way, Orlando, 32821. 407-238-6200.*
MARRIOTT'S GRANDE VISTA $$–$$$ Restaurant, pool, kitchens, sauna. Lakefront. *5 mi. from WDW. 5925 Avenida Vista, Orlando, 32821. 407-238-7676.*
NICKELODEON FAMILY SUITES $$ Restaurants, salon. Fun pools, decor, activities, character breakfast. Run by Holiday Inn. *Free WDW*

Hyatt Regency Grand Cypress, JW Marriott

shuttle (1 mi.). 14500 Continental Gateway, Lake Buena Vista, 32821. 877-387-5437.
OMNI CHAMPIONSGATE $$$–$$$$ Restaurants, heated pool with lazy river, water slides. Two golf courses, golf academy, spa, steam room. *7 mi. to WDW. 1500 Masters Blvd., Orlando, 33896. 407-390-6664.*
ORLANDO AIRPORT MARRIOTT $$$$ Restaurants, indoor/outdoor pool, sauna. Free shuttle to airport. *16 mi. from WDW. 7499 Augusta National Dr., Orlando, 32822. 407-851-9000.*
ORLANDO VISTA HOTEL $–$$ Restaurant, pools. *Free WDW shuttle (1 mi.). 12490 S. Apopka Vineland Rd., Orlando, 32836. 407-239-4646.*
ORLANDO WORLD CENTER MARRIOTT $$$$ Restaurants, pools (waterfalls, slides), spa, sauna, golf course and instruction, meeting rooms. *Free WDW shuttle (2 mi.). 8701 World Center Dr., Orlando, 32821. 800-228-9290.*
PEABODY ORLANDO $$$$ Restaurants, pool, beauty salon, spa, convention space. Daily mallard march to and from the hotel fountain every day at 11 a.m. and 5 p.m. *6 mi. to WDW. 9801 Intl. Dr., Orlando, 32819. 800-732-2639.*
RADISSON CELEBRATION $$ Restaurant, pool with slide. *Free WDW shuttle (2 mi.). 2900 Parkway Blvd., Kissimmee, 34747. 800-634-4774.*
RADISSON WORLDGATE $–$$ Restaurants, pools. *Free WDW shuttle (1 mi.). 3011 Maingate Ln., Kissimmee, 34747. 407-396-1400.*
RENAISSANCE ORLANDO AIRPORT $$–$$$ Restaurant, pool, meeting space. 1 mi. from Orlando Intl. Airport. *16 mi. to WDW. 5445 Forbes Pl., Orlando, 32812. 407-240-1000.*

RENAISSANCE ORLANDO SEAWORLD $$ Restaurants, heated pool, convention space, spa. Across the street from Seaworld. *Free WDW shuttle (4 mi.). 6677 Sea Harbor Dr., Orlando, 32821. 800-327-6677.*

RESIDENCE INN BY MARRIOTT CONVENTION CENTER $$ Heated pool, meeting space, kitchen available. Froe breakfast. Pets allowed for a fee. *Free WDW shuttle (7 mi.). 8800 Universal Blvd., Orlando, 32819. 407-226-0288.*

RESIDENCE INN BY MARRIOTT LAKE BUENA VISTA $$$ Restaurant, heated pool. All rooms are suites with kitchens. Free breakfast. *Free WDW shuttle (1 mi.). 11450 Marbella Palm Ct., Orlando, 32836. 407-465-0075.*

RESIDENCE INN BY MARRIOTT SEAWORLD $$ Restaurant, pool, kitchens. Free breakfast. Pots for a fee. *Free WDW shuttle (4 mi.). 11000 Westwood Blvd., Orlando, 32821. 800-889-9728.*

RITZ-CARLTON GRANDE LAKES $$$$ Restaurants, heated pools with lazy river, beauty salon, spa, convention space, Greg Norman-designed golf course, concierge floor. Life-size chess board. *7 mi. to WDW. 4012 Central Florida Pkwy., Orlando, 32837. 800-576-5760.*

ROSEN CENTRE $$$ Restaurants, heated pools, spa, salon, convention space, concierge floors. Free shuttle to Fla. Mall. *6 mi. to WDW. 9840 Intl. Dr., Orlando, 32819. 800-204-7234.*

ROSEN PLAZA $$ Restaurants, pool, meeting space. Froe shuttle to Fla. Mall. *6 mi. to WDW. 9700 Intl. Dr., Orlando, 32819. 800-627-8258.*

ROSEN SHINGLE CREEK $$$ Restaurants, indoor/outdoor pools, spa, sauna, salon, convention space, golf course. *7 mi. to WDW. 9939 Universal Blvd., Orlando, 32819. 866-996-9939.*

SARATOGA VILLAS AT MAINGATE $$ Restaurant, pools. All suites with kitchens. *Free WDW shuttle (4 mi.). 4787 W. U.S. 192, Kissimmee, 34746. 800-936-9417.*

HAWTHORN SUITES LAKE BUENA VISTA $–$$ Pool. All suites with kitchens. Free breakfast. *Free WDW shuttle (1 mi.). 8303 Palm Pkwy., Orlando, 32836. 407-597-5000.*

SERALAGO HOTEL & SUITES $ Restaurants, pools. Pets allowed for a fee. *Free WDW shuttle (4 mi.). 5678 W. U.S. 192 Hwy., Kissimmee, 34746. 877-78-HOTEL (784-6835).*

SHERATON SAFARI LAKE BUENA VISTA $$ Restaurants, pool complex, meeting space. African theme. *Free WDW shuttle (1 mi.). 12205 S. Apopka Vineland Rd., Orlando, 32836. 407-239-0444.*

SHERATON VISTANA LAKE BUENA VISTA $$–$$$ Restaurants, pool. All suites with kitchens. *Free WDW shuttle (1 mi.). 8800 Vistana Centre Dr., Orlando, 32821. 407-239-3100.*

SHERATON VISTANA VILLAGES $$–$$$ Restaurants, pool, sauna. All suites with kitchens,

Hyatt Regency Orlando International Airport

washer/dryers. *Free WDW shuttle (3 mi.). 12401 Intl. Dr., Orlando, 32821. 407-238-5000.*

SPRINGHILL SUITES CONVENTION CENTER $–$$ Heated pool, sauna. Free continental breakfast buffet. *7 mi. to WDW. 8623 Universal Blvd., Orlando, 32819. 407-938-9001.*

STAYBRIDGE SUITES INT'L DRIVE $$ Heated pools, kitchens, meeting space. Free continental breakfast. *7 mi. to WDW. 8480 Intl. Dr., Orlando, 32819. 800-238-8000.*

STAYBRIDGE SUITES LAKE BUENA VISTA $$–$$$$ Heated pools, kitchens. Free continental breakfast. *Free WDW shuttle (1 mi.). 8751 Suiteside Dr., Orlando FL 32836. 800-866-4549.*

VILLAS OF GRAND CYPRESS $$$$ Restaurants, heated pool complex, convention space, 4 golf courses and academy, spa with room services, equestrian center, lake, nature trails. *Free WDW shuttle (4 mi.). 1 N. Jacaranda St., Orlando, 32836. 800-835-7377.*

WESTIN GRAND BOHEMIAN $$$–$$$$ Restaurants, heated pool. *14 mi. to WDW. 325 S. Orange Ave., Orlando, 32801. 866-663-0024.*

WORLDQUEST $$$–$$$$ Restaurant, pool. *2 mi. to WDW. 8849 Worldquest Blvd., Orlando, 32821. 866-663-0024.*

WYNDHAM ORLANDO $$–$$$ Restaurants, heated pools, sauna. Family suites have bunk beds, play areas. Pets allowed for a fee. *8 mi. to WDW. 8001 Intl. Dr., Orlando, 32819. 407-351-2420.*

Jacuzzi suite at the Westin Grand Bohemian

A **mischievous painter** has converted hearts on a pair of boxer shorts on the mural in the Snow White's Scary Adventures loading area to the three-circle shape; the silhouette also appears on the cottage chimney, directly under two flowers.

Hidden Mickeys

The image of Mickey Mouse is hidden everywhere in Walt Disney World. Throughout the resort's history, architects, painters and landscapers have subtly placed the three-circle head-and-ears silhouette of the company's mascot, or occasionally a profile or full-figure shape, into theme-park attractions, building architecture, interior design and even the general landscape. Like hunting for Easter eggs, finding these hidden icons can be a fun way to add variety to your day, or at least kill time in a line. *Note: The following list (all three-circle silhouettes unless noted) does not include instances when the shape is meant to be obvious (i.e., the Mickey ears atop the Disney-MGM Studios water tower).*

Magic Kingdom

ENTRANCE AREA
As wedding-bell clappers on souvenir bricks in the walkway.

ADVENTURELAND
Landscape: As white flowers on the first shield on both sides of the bridge from Main Street.
Jungle Cruise: "You're a Bendel bonnet, a Shakespeare's sonnet, you're Mickey Mouse!" go the lyrics of Cole Porter's 1935 hit "You're the Top," which plays occasionally on the radio in the queue... On the crashed airplane, between and below the windows... As yellow spots on the back of a giant spider on your right in the Cambodian temple, just past the snakes... In the temple's framing directly above each of the statues on your left, nearly impossible to see because of the darkness. Some are Hidden Minnies, as they include a bow (three smaller circles) on top of a central head.
The Enchanted Tiki Room Under New Management: On the doors, as 2-inch berries on a stem underneath a bird's tail (four feet off the ground)... A small carved face is wearing Mickey ears at the bottom of Iago's perch.
Magic Carpets of Aladdin: As a 3-inch impression in the wood grain hub floor (facing the Sunshine Tree Terrace, most visible after a rain)... Set in the pavement behind the camel facing the ride, as a design painted on two yellow stones of a four-piece bracelet.

FRONTIERLAND
Frontierland Shootin' Arcade: Hit the back-wall target and you'll see a ghost rider in the sky wearing Mickey ears and gloves.
Splash Mountain: As stacked barrels on your right as you climb the second lift... As a three-orbed fishing bobber on your left (to the left of a picnic basket, inside the mountain just past Brer Frog fishing with his toe on top of Brer Gator)... Formed out of a hanging rope on your right in the flooded cavern (behind a lantern, just past a turtle on a geyser)... Reclining as a full figure in the sky to the right of the riverboat (after the big drop, as the upper outline of a

cloud with his head to the right).
Big Thunder Mountain Railroad:
As three rusty gears on your right
after you go under the rib cage.

LIBERTY SQUARE

Hall of Presidents: At the tip of
George Washington's sword in a
painting in the lobby, just to the
right of the theater entrance.
Haunted Mansion: The foyer and
two stretching rooms form the
shape... As the left-most place
setting on the near side of the
ballroom banquet table... As a
black silhouette in the final scene
of the graveyard, at the end of the
uplifted arm of the Grim Reaper
(visible on your extreme far right
inside a crypt, just after your
doom buggy turns away from the
tea party)... On the right side of
Madame Leota's souvenir cart, on
the index finger of a painted hand,
beneath the word "Parlour."
Columbia Harbour House: As
circular wall maps in the room
across from the order counter.
Liberty Tree Tavern: As painted
grapes at the top of a spice rack
in the lobby, right of the fireplace.

FANTASYLAND

Mickey's PhilharMagic: As seven
1-inch-wide white paint splotches
in the lobby mural. From the right,
they appear between the third and
fourth bass violin, between the
second and third clarinet, above
the second trumpet, below the
second trumpet, to the left of the
fourth trumpet, and twice to the
left of the sixth clarinet (one's a
stretch)... In the tubing of the
French horn in the theater's right
stage column... As shadows on the
table in the film's "Beauty and the
Beast" scene, visible as Lumiere
sings the word "it's" in the lyric,
"Try the gray stuff, it's delicious!"
(Lumiere's hands cast Mickey's
ears; his base Mickey's face)... As
a hole in a cloud Aladdin's carpet
flies through... As three domes
atop a tower on your left when the
carpets dive toward Agrabah... In
the gift shop, as music stands
along the top of the walls.
Peter Pan's Flight: As scars on
the fourth painted trunk on your
left as you face the turnstile,
about 4 feet off the ground.
It's a Small World: As 6-inch
purple flower petals in the Africa
room, on a vine hanging between
the giraffes on your left.
Pinocchio Village Haus: As a tiny
dark blue sparkle of fairy dust in
the Blue Fairy room, above the
letter "a" in the word "dreams"...
As a cutout on the back of one of
the restaurant's wooden chairs.

**Snow White's Scary
Adventures:** On the
loading-area mural,
on shorts on the
dwarf's clothesline
and among stones
on the cottage
chimney... In the
ride's first dark
scene, on top of the
Queen's magic
mirror... Wearing
dwarf clothes, a full-
figure dwarf-nosed
Mickey appears
with a shovel on the
lower right of the
entrance to the
dwarfs' mine.
**The Many Adventures of Winnie
the Pooh:** On the radish marker
in Rabbit's garden.
Pooh's Playful Spot: On the
front-door transom of the house.

MICKEY'S TOONTOWN FAIR

The Barnstormer: In the queue,
on the seat-back of a helicopter
above Goofy's drafting table.
Minnie's Country House: As a
hanging kitchen skillet and pots.
Mickey's Country House: In the
garage, as hubcaps, paint stains
on an apron and as a Mickey-
eared shaped small bale of hay.

TOMORROWLAND

Landscape: As a softball-sized
impression in the concrete
between the entrances of the
Tomorrowland Transit Authority
(TTA) and Astro Orbiter, about 5
feet from a TTA support column.
**Buzz Lightyear's Space Ranger
Spin:** In the queue room, a profile
of Mickey appears on a poster as
a green land mass on the Earth-
like planet Pollost Prime. The
planet also appears to the left of
the Viewmaster in the queue, on
the right as you battle the video
Zurg and in the final battle scene
(the photo room) on the left... A
Mickey profile appears on your left
as you enter Zurg's spaceship,
behind the battery-delivering
robot and under the words
"Initiate Battery Unload"... As an
image on a painted video monitor
on a mural across from actual
monitors that show ride photos...
In a painted window to the left of
the full-size pink character
Booster, as a cluster of three stars
at the top center of a star field...
As a second star cluster at the
bottom right of that field.
Carousel of Progress: In the
1940s scene, Mickey's sorceror's
hat sits on a stool to the right of
the exercise machine... In the
finale, a nutcracker Mickey sits on

A hanging skillet and two pots
form a Hidden Mickey in the
kitchen of Minnie's Country
House at Magic Kingdom

the mantel, a Mickey plushie rests
under the Christmas tree, a white
Mickey salt shaker sits to the right
of a knifeholder on the bar, and
an abstract painting of Mickey as
the Sorceror's Apprentice hangs
on the wall to the right of the
dining table... The three circles
appear on the television as
engines of a spaceship during the
first moments of a video game.
Tomorrowland Transit Authority:
On a customer's belt buckle in
the beauty salon, on your right
just after you enter the Buzz
Lightyear/Laugh Floor building.
Mickey's Star Traders: In a wall
mural as loops of a highway, the
headlights of a train, a group of
satellite dishes, glass domes of
the building, clear domes
covering a city and as Mickey
Ears on top of two windows.

Epcot

FUTURE WORLD

Spaceship Earth: As blots on the
top right of a piece of parchment,
made by the sleeping monk... As
bottle rings on the table of the
first Renaissance painter... On
the baseball cap hanging above
the American boy's bed and on
the alarm clock on his dresser.
Innoventions West: As a blue
mole on the cheek of a boy in an
IBM ThinkPlace mural. Wearing a
fez, he appears on the wall of the
left Thinking of You video-postcard
station... A girl in the ThinkPlace
video wall is wearing a Mickey hat.
Body Wars: A three-dimensional
Mickey face appears in green
broccoli-like body tissue just
above a blue vein in the mural
above the ride entrance.

Mission Space: As overlapping craters on the moon in the courtyard, above and to the left of the Luna 8 impact site... As tiny round tiles in the courtyard patio, 40 feet from the Fastpass entrance. The ears are blue; the head black... In the queue a notepad on the left desk reads "Mickey and Goofy are scheduled to launch at exactly 3 p.m."... As craters on Mars on the far left and right monitors above the desks... As part of the grid on a circuit board to the upper left and right of the joystick consoles for the post-show video game, Expedition Mars... As black craters in the mural behind the cash registers in the gift shop, under Minnie's foot... A profile of Mickey appears in the reddish dust in the photos of space on the gift shop ceiling. He's in the center of the room, directly above a Space Mickey statue... As three electrical boxes on the gift shop walls (one is a Mickey profile).

Test Track: As washers on the edge of the left side of a desk near queue area 7b... Mickey has signed off on inspection stickers on a test car in the queue. Appearing on a vehicle in area 5b, the signature on the Fastpass and Single Rider side of the car reads "M. Mouse;" on the Standby side "Micky" (yes, misspelled)... As stains on the fender on the left side of the Corrosion Chamber... As similar stains on a car door on the right side of the chamber... As crash-test stickers on a car to your left in the Barrier Test area. They're on an open gas-tank filler door... As a coil of hoses on the left floor, just before the Barrier Test wall.

MouseGear: As wall gauges behind the main cash registers.

Soarin': As a blue balloon at the beginning of the Palm Springs scene, held by a man behind a golf cart at the far lower left... As a small silhouette on the golf ball that flies toward you (flinch and you'll miss it)... In the second burst of Disneyland fireworks, in the center of the screen.

Living with the Land: In the waiting area, a profile of Mickey is formed by bubbles in the mural on the back wall (underneath the word "nature") while one green and two blue circles form an angled Mickey in the mural behind the loading area (about 7 feet from the right wall, a half-foot off the floor)... As trays of red-leaf lettuce surrounded by trays of green... As green test-tube caps

behind the lab windows alongside the final greenhouse.

Sunshine Seasons Food Court: As crystals in snowflakes on the carrying trays.

Journey into Imagination with Figment: A Mickey-eared headphone sits in the Sight Lab, on top of the left wheeled table... As two small circular carpets and a flowered toilet seat in Figment's bathroom... Between the "I" and "M" in the logo for Imageworks... In place of a letter in the eyechart in the Kodak demonstration area at the entrance to ImageWorks.

WORLD SHOWCASE

Canada: On both sides of the left totem pole underneath the top-most set of hands... As wine-rack bottles behind the Le Cellier Steakhouse check-in counter.

U.K.: As a tennis racket, soccer ball and rugby ball on a hanging sign for the Sportsman's Shoppe.

France: The courtyard's metal grates incorporate the three circles into their design... As a bush in the fleur-de-lis hedge garden... In a second-floor window of the house in the background of the "Impressions de France" wedding reception.

Morocco: As brass plates on the left green door of the Souk-Al-Magreb shop... As a window in the dome of a minaret on the photo backdrop in Aladdin's indoor meet-and-greet area. Mickey's in the upper right-hand segment, next to a small ladder.

Japan: In the metal tree grates in the courtyard... As the center of a drain cover in the koi pond across from the department store, near a bamboo fence.

American Adventure: As three rocks at the beginning of the first film in the American Adventure show, behind and to your right of a kneeling pilgrim woman.

Germany: In the center of the crown of the left-most Hapsburg emperor statue on the second story of Das Kaufhaus... Mickey's often in the train village, standing in a window of the hilltop castle.

Norway: Mickey appears three times in the mural behind the Maelstrom loading area: As Mickey Ears on a Viking in the middle of a ship toward the left, as shadows on the blouse of a cruise-line worker (her right pocket is Mickey's head, her clipboard ring is his nose) and at the far right on the watch of a bearded construction worker wearing a hard hat... As black circles on King Olaf II's tunic

embroidery in the Stave Church.

Mexico: As three clay pots at the end of the second marketplace scene in El Rio del Tiempo.

Disney-MGM Studios

HOLLYWOOD BOULEVARD

Cover Story: The shape of Mickey's ears appears in the black decorative molding below the second-floor windows.

Great Movie Ride: As a silhouetted profile in the second-story windows of the Western Chemical Co. building, on your left side as you enter Gangster Alley... Mickey's tail and one of his shoes are visible on a poster underneath the one for "The Public Enemy" on the alley's left wall... As a profile on a piece of broken stone below the Ark of the Covenant in the Well of Souls. Facing left, the light-gray Mickey hides in plain sight on a dark-gray rock... A full-figure Mickey pharoah appears on the Well's left wall, just past the second statue of Anubis. An Egyptian Donald Duck is serving him some cheese.

ECHO LAKE

Tune-In Lounge: As washers used to secure the top of coffee tables.

Prime Time Cafe: As dining-table red napkin and utensil holders.

BACKLOT

Star Tours: An Ewok child holds a Mickey Mouse doll in the pre-boarding video.

Toy Story Pizza Planet: As clusters of stars in a mural above the cash registers near the pizza-slice constellation and to the left of the spaceship... A three-quarter profile of Mickey appears as craters in the moon in a wall mural above the arcade.

Jim Henson's MuppetVision 3-D: On Gonzo's inflatable ring float in the courtyard fountain... In small sketch of a DNA model in the "5 Reasons" poster in the outdoor queue area... As a test pattern in the early moments of the preshow video... In the film's final scene, park guests behind the fire truck hold Mickey balloons.

Stage 1 Company Store: Outside, as purple paint drips on a recessed light under a bronze lion head... As green drips on a shelf of a wood bureau along a side wall... Mickey's red shorts hang above the hotel desk.

Mama Melrose's Ristorante Italiano: As a spot on the right shoulder of a dalmation in a lobby statue... As a leaf on a vine to the right of the check-in podium, at the bottom right of a lattice fence. **The Writer's Stop:** As yellow stickers on ceiling stage lights. **Streets of America:** As Steamboat Willie articles in newspapers on the San Francisco backdrop. **Lights Motors Action Extreme Stunt Show:** A vintage full-figure Mickey appears in the Antiquites Brocante ("Secondhand Antiques") window... As a gear and two circular belts in the top right corner of the motorcycle shop window. **Disney-MGM Backlot Tour:** As a blue-sky cutout in the white clouds of the "Harbor Attack" backdrop... In the prop room on the door of the yellow "Marvin's Room" refrigerator and as cannon balls hanging from the ceiling... At Catastrophe Canyon, as gauges to your right on top of the third barrel from the exit... A full-figure Mickey hides in a mural to your right just as you enter the AFI exhibit. He stands on top of a gravestone about halfway up the right third of the scene. **SUNSET BOULEVARD** **Landscape:** Impressions along the curbs read "Mortimer & Co. Contractors 1928," a reference to Walt's original name for his mouse when he created him in 1928. **Rosie's All-American Cafe:** As three gauges on a welding torch behind the order counter. **Rock 'n' Roller Coaster Starring Aerosmith:** Twice on the building's sign: Steven Tyler's shirt has Mickey silhouettes and the boy is wearing mouse ears... As three pieces in a beige section of the foyer's floor mosaic, just before you leave the room... As a distorted carpet pattern in the first display room of G-Force Records... As cables on the floor of the recording studio... On the registration sticker on each of the limo's rear license plates... As the "O" in the phrase "Box #15" on a trunk along the ride exit walkway. **The Twilight Zone Tower of Terror:** As a pair of folded wire-rim glasses on the lobby's concierge desk (the temples form Mickey's face, the eye rims make his ears)... 1932's "What! No Mickey Mouse?" is the song featured on some sheet music in the left library, on the bookcase directly in front of the entrance door... The little girl in the TV video is holding a 1930s Mickey doll... As large, round ash doors beneath the fire box on a brick furnace in the boiler room (on your right just after you've

entered the boiler area)... As water stains just left of a fuse box on the boiler room's left wall, just past where the queue divides... On the 13th floor, in the center of the stars as they come together to form a single beam of light. **Fantasmic:** As bubbles when Pinocchio arrives in the water screens. The puppet's bubble forms Mickey's head; two adjacent ones his ears.

Animal Kingdom

DISCOVERY ISLAND
Tree of Life: As moss on the trunk, to the left of a buffalo, near a tiger, facing the park entrance... Upside down, just above a hippo's eye on the side of the trunk that faces the walkway from Asia to Africa. **It's Tough to be a Bug:** As spots on a root in the lobby, left of the theater's handicapped entrance. **Pizzafari:** As the nocturnal room, to the left of a large tiger, behind a frog. **CAMP MINNIE-MICKEY** **Landscape:** A profile of Mickey appears as the opening of a wooden birdhouse that often hangs in the courtyard. **Pocahontas and Her Forest Friends:** As a shadow in the grass between two trees and as another shadow (a profile) above a fallen tree on the left of a stage backdrop, and as rocks on a dirt path on the backdrop's right. **Funnel Cake:** As sideways accents in the carved woodwork of this ice-cream stand. **AFRICA** **Harambe:** As a large shape of gray pavement on the walkway in front of Harambe School, behind the Fruit Market. A school bench may be sitting on it... As a drain cover with the letter "D" on it and two round pebble groupings, just left of the main entrance to Mombasa Marketplace, across from Tusker House... As another drain cover (this time with the letter "S") and two round pebble groupings in front of Tamu Tamu Refreshments, facing Discovery Island. **Kilimanjaro Safaris:** As the flamingo island.

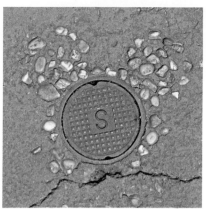

A walkway drain cover and two pebble groupings form a Hidden Mickey near Animal Kingdom's Tamu Tamu Refreshments

Pangani Forest Exploration Trail: In the research station, as a small shape on a backpack to the left of the naked mole rat exhibit. **RAFIKI'S PLANET WATCH** **Planet Watch train station:** As blue circles in the cross beams in the rafters. **Landscape:** As overlapping circles in the grates of the trees in Affection Section and in the lobby of Conservation Station. **Conservation Station:** The entrance mural includes many Hidden Mickeys. On the left wall, left to right: As a pupil of a squirrel... As wrinkles on a hippo's chin (a Mickey profile)... As a scale behind the eye of a crocodile... As a shadow on a walrus's neck to the right of his tusks... As an owl's pupils... As a spot on a yellow fish (partially obscured by an octopus)... as black spots on a butterfly's left wing (above a bat). **On the right wall, right to left:** As a pink spot on the abdomen of a spider (above a white owl chick)... In the pupil of an opossum... As black spots on the yellow wings of a butterfly (above an arm of a praying mantis). **On the middle wall, right to left:** As a ostrich's pupil... As scales on the back of a green snake... And as a sucker on the bottom of a starfish (a Mickey profile)... On the top of a butterfly body (a smiling, detailed Mickey face)... as spots on the wings of a butterfly (under a monkey) and as a silver frog's left pupil (a Mickey profile). Many Hidden Mickeys also hide in the **"Song of the Rainforest"** area. Left to right: As the petals of a yellow flower... As a white spot on a fly above a flower... As a shadow on a tree in front of the rainforest doors (a Mickey profile)... As a white spot on a tree to the left of "The Accidental Florist" sign... As a spot on the tree bark, across from the fly, about 4 feet off the ground... As an impression in a tree's bark in the "Song of the Rainforest" sign to the lower right of Grandmother Willow's face (a Mickey profile)... As a nearby painted hole in a leaf... As spots on a wooden cockroach inside a tree in the front of the rainforest area... As three dark green spots on the side of a chameleon above the "Giant Cockroach" sign at the right of the rainforest area... And finally, as three round petri dishes in the far left window of the reptile display room.

Affection Section: As a pattern on a sheared sheep... As three orange spots on the stage wall, to the right of the lizard door.

ASIA

Maharajah Jungle Trek: At the second tiger viewing area, as swirls of water under a tiger in the first mural to your right... As a golden earring — and as three small bushes — in the first mural to your left... As rocks in a mountain range above a flying dove in the second mural to your left... As swirls in a cloud formation in the second painting to your right... Past the tigers, as a leaf in a mural to your left, about 9 feet off the ground... In the top right of a mural left of the Elds Deer habitat, an orange flower and two leaves creates a detailed Mickey face and waving arm... As beads on a necklace in the middle stone carving, just before the aviary entrance.

Expedition Everest: In the queue, as a tiny Mickey hat worn by a Yeti doll in Tashi's Trek and Tongba Shop, on the top shelf of a cupboard to the right... As black water bottle caps in a display of patches in the same shop... As a dent and two holes in a tea kettle that's part of the wreckage of a camp in the Yeti museum... On the left wall after the museum, a Mickey with eyes, a nose, and a Sorcerer's hat appears as wood stains in a photograph that shows a woman with a walkie-talkie.

DINOLAND U.S.A.

Landscape: As cracks in the asphalt in the parking area next to the Cementosaurus, to the left of Dinosaur Treasures... On a Steamboat Willie cast member pin on the right of the fourth hump on the back of the Cementosaurus...

As three small, black scales on the back of the red and green hadrosaurus at the beginning of the Cretaceous Trail.

Boneyard: As a large water stain under the drinking fountain near the entrance... As a quarter and two pennies laying on a table behind a fence-in area, on the second level by the slides in the back... As a fan and two hard hats in a fenced-off area at the back of the wooly mammoth excavation.

Primeval Whirl: As three craters on meteors throughout the ride.

Dinosaur: Along the indoor queue, as lily pads in the second diorama on your right... In the same diorama, as green spots on the largest tree trunk to the left of its lower right branch... As gray clouds above a carnotaurus tail (below the meteor) on a poster advertising souvenir ride photos ("We took your photo 65 million years ago!"), just before you enter the gift shop... As three scales on the neck of a carnotaurus on a mural behind the photo counter.

Finding Nemo — The Musical: As three decorative blue bubbles, two lit and one drawn, at the bottom left of the stage wall.

Water parks

BLIZZARD BEACH

Beach Haus: As three rocks in a painted scene, on a wall light fixture near the changing rooms.

Cross Country Creek: As four stones on a bridge over the creek at the back of the park. The top stone is Mickey's Sorcerer's hat.

Chairlift: As three rocks on a ledge on Mt. Gushmore, visible under the chairlift track.

TYPHOON LAGOON

Crush 'n' Gusher: On the second floor of the launch tower, as paint circles on the floor in front of the handicapped elevator.

Storm Slides: As an extension on a wooden step halfway up the walkway, across from a lantern, just before an anchor on the right.

Castaway Creek: On the bottom of a railing strut on the bridge past Shark Landing.

Ketchakiddie Creek: As a hole in the wall of the cave, about a foot off the ground, left of a drain.

Diversions

GOLF COURSES

Magnolia: As a sand trap near the 6th green.

Osprey Ridge and Eagle Pines: As a practice green (a profile).

MINIATURE GOLF

Fantasia Gardens: As the 12th green of the Gardens course.

Winter Summerland: On the 16th hole of the Winter Course, as a gingerbread cookie that pokes out of a stocking on a mantelpiece (a full-body Mickey)... Another Mickey sits in a sleigh (with Minnie and Pluto) on a mantelpiece on the 16th hole of the Summer Course.

WALT DISNEY WORLD SPEEDWAY

Landscape: As the infield pond (a photo hangs in the lobby of the Richard Petty Driving Experience).

Downtown Disney

MARKETPLACE

Landscape: As a giant 20x20 foot arrangement of fountain squirters in the pavement at the Marketplace entrance nearest Hotel Plaza Boulevard, to the right of Earl of Sandwich. The squirters themselves are small Mickeys.

Once Upon a Toy: As robotic claws that hold toys, suspended from a track hung from the ceiling... As blue support bars under stands that hold plushies.

World of Disney: In a mural in the Women and Juniors room, as a red and white design on a blue flag to the left of the Queen of Hearts and as a golden design on Tweedledee's red sumo cloth... In a mural in the facing room, as a design above the doors to the Chinese Theater behind the floating Three Little Pigs.

WEST SIDE

DisneyQuest: As repeating ancient symbols in the carpet of Adventureport and the cafe on the 5th floor.

Cirque du Soleil: As three black tiles just inside the doors of both the women's and the men's restrooms outside the box office.

Resorts

ALL-STAR MUSIC

Around the Jazz Inn buildings, as a screw top on top of a cymbal... As beige designs on the front and back of the giant boots around the County Fair buildings.

ALL-STAR SPORTS

Between the buildings, as a large round platform and two gray pavement ovals... As a repeating pattern of a baseball and two white circles in the carpet in the gift shop.

ANIMAL KINGDOM LODGE
As a design inside the mouth of the second tall figure to the left of the entrance, above the lower roof... On the right spotted creature just inside the main entrance, as a yellow spot on the middle of its back... As a design on the right middle chandelier in the main lobby, facing the registration counter... As a leaf about two-thirds of the way up the left outdoor vine staircase at the rear of the building, visible from the Overlook (a Mickey profile)... In the Overlook, as spots on the tallest giraffe in the stone carving to the left of the pelican viewing area... As dents in rock on the Overlook's planted walkway, about 4 feet off the ground... As three dents in a brown rock wall behind the main pool slide, about 3 feet off the ground... As a small green shape to the right of a wall above the Mara snack bar... Inside the snack bar, as a hole in a painted leaf on a wall in front and above the wine selection, and in another leaf on the upper left wall, the third leaf from the left tree.

BOARDWALK
In the resort's main entrance foyer, as a brown spot on the neck of a white carrousel horse... As a second brown spot on its rump... As a cloud on the sign for Seashore Sweets to the top right of the left woman... As repeating red berries in the carpet in front of many elevators.

CORONADO SPRINGS
Jutting out from a bolt, a detailed Mickey face is on the top left of the left door of the main entrance... As impressions in the sidewalk near the lamppost closest to the resort's boat and bike rental.

GRAND FLORIDIAN
As repeating tan designs on the border of the carpet on the lobby staircase... As a repeating white pattern on the tan wallpaper.

OLD KEY WEST
As three seashell imprints in the walkway that leads from Building 36 to parking spaces.

PORT ORLEANS RIVERSIDE
As a design on an Indian's sandal in the food court.

SARATOGA SPRINGS
As a white design at the bottom of the spa signs outside of the spa.

WILDERNESS LODGE
As three stones above and to the right of the lobby fireplace... As lumps of earth about a third of the way up a stream that flows from the geyser by the pool... As three nuts in a small bulletin board at

the entrance to Roaring Fork Snacks... As leaves in the wallpaper in the guest room hallways... As dents in the wood on a beam to the right of the exit to the Boat and Bike Rental... As dents in the wood on the second closest post to room 4035 and on the post closest to room 5066.

YACHT AND BEACH CLUB
On the wallpaper in the guest room hallways, as repeating white designs on a tan background... In the entrance hall to the Solarium, as wheels of spare, trunk-mounted tires of the far left yellow car and far right blue car in the first painting to the left (Mickey faces)... In that same painting, as the hood ornament on the right red car and right blue car... As a cloud in the second painting to the left (a detailed Mickey face)... as a red balloon held by a girl at the right of the third painting on the left wall... As a yellow balloon held by the girl next to her.

Christmas

MAGIC KINGDOM
Mickey's 'Twas the Night Before Christmas: As a snowman standing on the left side of the opening backdrop... As the top of a hatrack on the right of the stage.
Mickey's Very Merry Christmas Parade: As a snowman on the back of Santa's sleigh... As the handles of the parade banners.
Holiday Wishes: As crystals along the edge of each snowflake projected on the castle.

DISNEY-MGM STUDIOS
The Osborne Family Spectacle of Dancing Lights: Twenty-two Hidden Mickeys can shift locations from year to year. One is formed by a hat and "ears" of a lifesize toy solder, another is created by the face and ears of a snowman. The best one is in the smoke of a large toy train. (Kermit the Frog and other Muppets hide in the giant Christmas bulbs on the apartments left of Al's Toy Barn.)

ANIMAL KINGDOM
Entrance area: As ornaments on the Christmas tree.

Other hidden characters

MAGIC KINGDOM
Stitch hides in the exit area of Buzz Lightyear's Space Ranger Spin. He's riding in a tiny red spaceship behind the photo counter (to left of the words "8 x

10") and across the hall in a star field in the Captain Nebula mural... The abstract face and hat of **Donald Duck** appears on an upholstered chair's backrest in the Haunted Mansion, just left of the endless hallway.

EPCOT
In Cranium Command, Bobby's sister carries a **Minnie Mouse** purse to school... **Donald Duck** and **Pluto** appear as abstract images in the ceiling of the Mission Space gift shop. Donald's head and neck are visible to the Hidden Mickey's right. Closest to the ride exit, Pluto's face points toward the cash registers.

DISNEY-MGM STUDIOS
Minnie Mouse hides in the center of the Great Movie Ride boarding-area mural. Facing left, her profile is just above and to the right of a tile roof, tucked under some palm fronds... "Star Wars" characters appear on the left wall in the ride's Well of Souls. A center carving two blocks up from the floor shows a pharaoh holding **R2-D2** while **C-3PO** repairs him with a screwdriver. (The same carving appears on the same wall in the "Raiders of the Lost Ark" movie). Some say **Goofy** appears on the outside wall of the Star Tours gift shop along the walkway that leads to MuppetVision 3-D. One of the fake light fixtures has a center box that looks similar to Goofy's face and light covers that resemble his ears... **Gonzo** appears as a chalk drawing wearing 3-D glasses on the right wall of the MuppetVision 3-D building... The hidden name of **Walt Disney** appears in the Tower of Terror lobby. Often covered in dust, a Photoplay magazine on the concierge desk features "Four Pages of Hilarious Star Caricatures by Walt Disney."

ANIMAL KINGDOM
Baloo's head and neck appear as peeling, cream-colored paint on a wall in the Harambe fort, behind Tamu Tamu Refreshments, next to the area where Baloo appears.

BLIZZARD BEACH
A hidden **alligator** appears at Blizzard Beach, in the hill at the rear of Melt-Away Bay. A high rock is its snout, the rock below is his front left foot.

WINTER SUMMERLAND
Goofy and **Donald Duck** nutcrackers are on the left side of the mantelpiece on the 16th hole of the miniature golf course.

Hidden Mickey field research by Micaela Neal. ("This took forever!")

Randa McNally explores Adventureland

Watching Mickey's Toontown Tuners

Anderson, Philip Longfellow. "The Gospel in Disney: Christian Values in the Early Animated Classics." Augsburg Books, 2004.

"The Annotated Classic Fairy Tales" edited by Marie Tatar. W.W. Norton & Company Ltd., 2002.

Appelbaum, Stanley. "The New York World's Fair 1939/1940." Dover Publications, 1977.

Barrie, J. M. "Peter Pan." Charles Scribner's Sons, 1911, 1985.

Borgenicht, David. "The Classic Tales of Brer Rabbit." Running Press, 1995.

Brode, Douglas. "From Walt to Woodstock: How Disney Created the Counterculture." University of Texas Press, 2004.

Canemaker, John. "The Art and Flair of Mary Blair: An Appreciation." Disney Editions, 2003.

Connellan, Tom. "Inside the Magic Kingdom." Bard Press, 1997.

Corey, Melinda and Ochoa, George. "The American Film Institute Desk Reference." Stonesong Press, 2002.

Dunlop, Beth. "Building a Dream: The Art of Disney Architecture." Harry N. Abrams, 1996.

"E.Encyclopedia Animal." DK, 2005.

Eisner, Michael and Schwartz, Tony. "Work in Progress." Random House, 1998.

Finch, Christopher. "The Art of Walt Disney." Harry N. Abrams, 2004.

Finch, Christopher. "Jim Henson: The Works: The Art, the Magic, the Imagination." Random House, 1993.

Finch, Christopher. "Walt Disney's America." Abbeville Press, 1978.

Fjellman, Stephen M. "Vinyl Leaves: Walt Disney World and America." Westview Press, 1992.

Flower, Joe. "Prince of the Magic Kingdom: Michael Eisner and the Re-making of Disney." Wiley, 1991.

Gifford, Clive. "Media and Communication." DK, 1999.

Greene, Katherine and Richard. "The Man Behind the Magic: The Story of Walt Disney." Viking, 1991, 1998.

Griswold, Jerry. "The Meanings of 'Beauty and the Beast,' a Handbook." Broadview Press, 2004.

Hahn, Don. "Disney's Animation Magic." Disney Press, 1996.

Harris, Joel Chandler. "The Complete Tales of Uncle Remus." Houghton Mifflin Company, 1955.

Heide, Robert and Gilman, John. "Mickey Mouse: The Evolution, the Legend, the Phenomenon!" Disney Editions, 2001.

Hench, John. "Designing Disney: Imagineering and the Art of the Show." Disney Editions, 2003.

"The Imagineering Field Guide to Epcot at Walt Disney World." Disney Editions, 2005.

"The Imagineering Field Guide to the Magic Kingdom at Walt Disney World." Disney Editions, 2005.

Kinney, Jack. "Walt Disney and Assorted Other Characters." Harmony, 1988.

Kurtti, Jeff. "Since the World Began: Walt Disney World's First 25 Years." Hyperion, 1996.

Lamb, Bob. "Field Guide to Disney's Animal Kingdom Theme Park." Roundtable Press, 2000.

Lambert, Pierre. "Mickey Mouse." Hyperion, 1998.

Malmberg, Melody. "The Making of Disney's Animal Kingdom Theme Park." Hyperion 1998.

Maltin, Leonard. "The Disney Films." Disney Editions, 1995, 2000.

Maltin, Leonard. "Of Mice and Magic: A History of American Animated Cartoons." Penguin Books, 1987.

Mannheim, Steve. "Walt Disney and the Quest for Community." Ashgate Publishing, 2002.

Marling, Karal Ann. "Designing Disney's Theme Parks: The Architecture of Reassurance." Hyperion, 1997.

Milne, A.A. "Winnie the Pooh." Puffin Books, 1926, 1992.

Mosley, Leonard. "Disney's World." Scarborough House, 1990.

Neary, Kevin and Smith, Dave. "The Ultimate Disney Trivia Book Vols. 1–3." Hyperion, 1992, 1994, 1997.

"Official Guide: New York World's Fair 1964/1965." Time Inc., 1964.

Philip, Neil. "The Complete Fairy Tales of Charles Perrault." Albion Press Ltd., 1993.

Philip, Neil. "The Illustrated Book of Myths: Tales and Legends of the World." DK, 1995.

Price, Harrison "Buzz." "Walt's Revolution! By the Numbers." Ripley Entertainment, 2004.

Rafferty, Kevin. "Walt Disney Imagineering." Disney Editions, 1996.

Samuelson, Dale. "The American Amusement Park." MBI, 2001.

Schickel, Richard. "The Disney Version: The Life, Times, Art and Commerce of Walt Disney." Simon & Schuster, 1968, 1985, 1997.

Schroeder, Russell K. "Disney: The Ultimate Visual Guide." Dorling Kindersley Ltd., 2002.

Schroeder, Russell. "Walt Disney: His Life in Pictures." Disney Press, 1996.

Smith, Dave. "Disney A to Z: The Official Encyclopedia." Hyperion, 1998, 2006.

Smith, Dave. "The Quotable Walt Disney." Disney Editions, 2001.

Smith, Dave. "Walt Disney: Famous Quotes." Disney's Kingdom Editions, 1994.

Smith, Dave and Clark, Steven. "Disney: The First 100 Years." Hyperion, 1999.

Surrell, Jason. "The Haunted Mansion: From the Magic Kingdom to the Movies." Disney Editions, 2003.

Surrell, Jason. "Pirates of the Caribbean: From the Magic Kingdom to the Movies." Disney Editions, 2005.

Taylor, John. "Storming the Magic Kingdom." Knopf, 1987.

Thomas, Bob. "Building a Company: Roy O. Disney and the Creation of an Entertainment Empire." Hyperion, 1998.

Thomas, Bob. "Walt Disney: An American Original." Hyperion, 1994.

Thomas, Frank and Johnston, Ollie. "The Illusion of Life: Disney Animation." Disney Editions, 1995.

Tieman, Robert. "The Disney Treasures." Disney Editions, 2003.

Twain, Mark. "The Adventures of Tom Sawyer." Fine Creative Media, 2003.

"25 Years of Walt Disney World." Disney's Kingdom Editions, 1996.

"Walt Disney Imagineering: A Behind the Dreams Look at Making the Magic Real." Hyperion, 1996.

"Walt Disney Resort: A Magical Year-By-Year Journey." Hyperion, 1998.

Watts, Steven. "The Magic Kingdom: Walt Disney and the American Way of Life." Houghton Mifflin, 1997.

Zicree, Mark Scott. "The Twilight Zone Companion." Silman-James Press, 1982, 1989.

Zipes, Jack. "The Complete Fairy Tales of the Brothers Grimm." Bantam, 1992.

VIDEO

Cocteau, Jean. "Beauty and the Beast." Criterion, 2003.

"Frank and Ollie." Walt Disney Pictures, 2003.

"Modern Marvels: Walt Disney World," A&E Home Video, 2006.

"Walt Disney Treasures: Behind the Scenes at the Walt Disney Studio." Walt Disney Video, 2002

"Walt Disney Treasures: The Chronological Donald, Vol. 1 and 2." Walt Disney Video, 2004, 2005.

"Walt Disney Treasures: Disney Rarities." Walt Disney Video, 2005.

"Walt: the Man Behind the Myth." Walt Disney Home Entertainment.

New York Times archive

Orlando Sentinel archive

PARK PUZZLER ANSWERS Magic Kingdom 1b, 2d, 3c, 4d, 5b, 6a, 7b **Epcot** 1b, 2b, 3b, 4b, 5b, 6c, 7a **Disney-MGM Studios** 1c, 2a, 3c, 4c, 5c, 6a, 7a, 8c **Disney's Animal Kingdom** 1c, 2a, 3b, 4c, 5a, 6a, 7a, 8b, 9b

Phone directory

Tweedledum takes a call at Magic Kingdom